Listen to Learn

Using American Music to Teach Language Arts and Social Studies (Grades 5–8)

Teri Tibbett

JOSSEY-BASS
A Wiley Imprint
www.josseybass.com

Published by Jossey-Bass
A Wiley Imprint
989 Market Street, San Francisco, CA 94103-1741   www.josseybass.com

ISBN 0-7879-7254-1

Printed in the United States of America
FIRST EDITION
PB Printing   10 9 8 7 6 5 4 3 2 1

This book is dedicated to my grandfather Lawrence Tibbett, for his devotion to American music, and to my children Alex Nelson and Haley Nelson, for carrying on the tradition.

Acknowledgments

I have many people to thank for their help in compiling this work. Some of those I wish to thank for their editorial support are as follows: Jerome S. Kleinsasser, professor of music, California State University at Bakersfield; Charles-David Lehrer, assistant professor of music, California State University at Northridge; J. B. Dyas, executive director, Brubeck Institute; Linda Rosenthal, professor of music, University of Alaska Southeast; Maria Williams, associate director and assistant research professor, Arts of the Americas Institute, Native American Studies and Music, University of New Mexico; ethnomusicologist Virginia Giglio, Ph.D., president, NativeCulture.com, and author of *Southern Cheyenne Women's Songs* (1994); Tony Isaacs, Indian House Records; Laurel Sercombe, University of Washington, Ethnomusicology; Richard Keeling, former associate professor, Department of Ethnomusicology, UCLA, and author of *Cry for Luck* (1992) and *North American Indian Music* (1995); Rosita Worl, Ph.D., president, Sealaska Heritage Institute; Jason Baird Jackson, assistant curator of ethnology and assistant professor of anthropology, Sam Noble Oklahoma Museum of Natural History, University of Oklahoma; David Katzeek, traditional Tlingit tribal leader; Roby Littlefield; Aaron Bryant; Susan Baxter, Juneau School District; Don Drew, host of "Mule Train" on KTOO Radio; Leo Novoa and Rick Bellagh for translations; Greg Steele; Robert Cohen; Rachel Beck; Sadie Ingalls; Marlon Lumba; Lori Tibbett; and Steve Nelson.

I also offer special thanks to Alex Nelson and Haley Nelson for their patience and feedback; to Jenn Coots for hours compiling the lists; and to Michael, Brandon, Derek, Cody, Akira, and Kevin for being the guinea pigs. My special gratitude goes to Susan Kolwicz and Win Huppuch for their initial support in getting this book written.

About the Author

Teri Tibbett is a musician and teacher living in Alaska. She has taught music to all grades throughout Alaska since 1976, both as an itinerant music teacher and in her own school, the Juneau School of Creative Arts. In 1988, she designed and produced the music curriculum for the Alaska State Department of Education Correspondence Study program, which included audio lessons for children who learn at home. She has published an early childhood music program for parents and teachers called *Making Music with Children,* and has consulted with many Alaska school districts in designing their music curricula.

Teri performs regularly in concerts, at music festivals, and at other public events, and has made recordings of original, Alaskan, and children's music. She has arranged and directed music for theater and created *Living the Alaska Life,* a one-woman show depicting Alaskan lifestyles through songs and images, which she has performed for visitors to Alaska since 1986. She is a freelance features writer for magazines and newspapers, and hosts a weekly music radio show of contemporary and ethnic music on Juneau's public radio station.

Teri is the mother of two children and holds a bachelor's degree in liberal arts, cum laude, from the University of Alaska. She has additional training in music, Spanish, and early childhood education. Her grandfather was New York Metropolitan Opera singer Lawrence Tibbett. Her Web site is *www.tibbett.com.*

Contents

Unit Four: New American Music

Introduction

The lessons in this program provide a way to use the history of American music to engage students in reading, writing, social studies, science, geography, and music activities. The lessons trace the music traditions of Native American, European-American, African-American, and Latin American cultures. There are lessons on blues, jazz, classical, opera, country, Tejano-conjunto, salsa, rock, rap, and more. Language arts activities offer opportunities to learn vocabulary, write about favorite music, and investigate songs as poetry. Social studies activities follow American music history and investigate the lives of great American musicians. Science-related activities look at sound and how instruments make sound. Math and geography activities do calculating and charting with music-related themes. Fine arts activities offer storytelling, learning new songs, and drawing to illustrate music.

The Value of Music Education

Most Americans listen to music daily—awakening to a radio alarm, listening to CDs at home or while driving in a car, on television, at the movies, when shopping, when standing in an elevator, or waiting on hold over the telephone. Many of us would notice if there was suddenly no music anywhere, yet on a day-to-day basis many of us probably don't pay much attention to it.

In determining the value of music education, we should remember that the music we hear every day was performed and composed by trained and practiced musicians, and it is likely that most of them got their start in a school classroom.

Music education is losing importance in American schools, indicated by less and less funding for it. Children are exposed to fewer music traditions, fewer classics, and many are getting their primary music exposure from radio, television, and their own CDs. This is fine, but the scenario has the consequence that students will grow up with a very narrow view of what music is, and what it can be.

Research shows that music education is more important than simply developing an appreciation for music. Music enhances a person's ability to read, speak, analyze, discern patterns, and develop fine motor control, among other things. Music can be a history lesson, a language lesson, a reading lesson, a poetry lesson, a science lesson, a geography lesson, or a lesson in culture and social studies. When we offer music to children, we help them become better readers, speakers, mathematicians, scientists, historians, and comprehenders of all the information we hand them daily—in addition to being better appreciators of music.

Because of reduced funding for the arts, regular classroom teachers are having to pick up the responsibility of exposing students to the arts. Many teachers feel inadequate to teach music and squirm at the idea of having to do so. It is the goal of this curriculum to offer easy-to-follow lessons, with handouts, activities, and audio CD examples, that can be used as a simple step-by-step curriculum or as a resource to supplement an existing program. You do not have to be musical to present the lessons, and your students do not have to be music students. You simply have to know the value of music and commit yourself to offering it. If you go through all the lessons and perform most of the activities you will not only give your students an overview of American music history but will help them to experience the value of music.

Teri Tibbett

How to Use This Book and CD Set

The lessons in this book follow a time line from the earliest American music to the present. You can follow them sequentially and get an approximate history of American music, or you can pick and choose the lessons to match your needs. Each lesson has a lesson plan with activity suggestions, activity sheets, and directions. The materials include student handouts for reading, quizzes, and vocabulary sheets; there are science activities, poetry and geography activities, and bonus challenges. The accompanying CD offers samples from most genres mentioned, and there are listening cues included in the student handouts.

About the Music

America has been called a melting pot of cultures. It is certainly true that American music is a melting pot of musical styles, mixing influences from Europe, Africa, Latin America, Native America, and others. Jazz, the blues, soul, funk, country, bluegrass, Tejano-conjunto, klezmer, rock, and rap are all American music styles that mix the traditions of many cultures. In these lessons, students will be introduced to these musical styles, they'll learn about some of the key players, and they'll listen to authentic music examples. Please note that it is beyond the scope of this curriculum to present a comprehensive or in-depth study of all American music styles. We offer our apologies for those genres omitted.

Set Up a Musical Classroom

Consider setting up your classroom to be music-friendly. Use CDs or tapes, music magazines, pictures of famous musicians, instruments, and other musical props to spark curiosity. Here are some suggestions:

- Play music in the background whenever possible—when students come into class and during quiet times, clean up, art periods, snack, lunch, or transitions. Bring in your own music to share and allow students to bring in theirs. Encourage students to take turns bringing in favorite CDs to play for the rest of the class, at these mentioned times.

- Put a CD or cassette player in a corner of the room with headphones and a music magazine, or book, or music notebook to peruse while listening to music. Consider using this music time as a reward, or prize, for doing the bonus challenges offered in the lesson plans.

- Have instruments available for playing during music time. Shakers, drums, bells, rasps, sticks, gongs, are all fun to play along with live or recorded music. Instruments draw student attention and help maintain focus.

- Hang pictures of famous musicians with their names and accomplishments written below.

- Hang a map of North America where students can add pushpins to places of important musical interest.

- Compile notebooks with reports on famous American musicians.

- Compile songbooks with lyrics to favorite songs or songs in this book.

- Compile an "Encyclopedia of Instruments" containing all the instruments studied in this book.

Materials and Activities

Each lesson in this book includes handouts and other materials for learning about American music. Following is an overview of what this book contains:

The Basics

- *Student handouts:* Student handouts are articles discussing different genres of American music. They can be read silently or aloud or as a group. Play CD selections and encourage discussions about the music. Afterward, students should put their handouts into individual music notebooks. *(Link to language arts, history, geography, science, social studies.)*

- *Activity sheets:* Activity sheets included in each lesson and in the appendix invite students to answer questions, investigate topics, research musicians, and so on. Put finished pages in music notebooks. *(Link to language arts, social studies.)*

- *CD music:* Music selections for each unit are included on the accompanying music CD. Selection cues are written in the student handout and should be played during or after reading the text. *(Link to music appreciation.)*

- *Quizzes:* Quizzes offer a way to assess student understanding of the lesson. *(Link to language arts.)*

- *Music notebooks:* Each student should have a music notebook in which to keep all the student handouts, completed activity sheets, and corrected quizzes for each lesson.

Additional Materials and Activities

- *Music Vocabulary:* This activity sheet invites students to write out musical terms and definitions included in the lesson. See the glossary for definitions. *(Link to language arts.)*

- *Vocabulary Challenge:* Students pick some or all of the words in the lesson's vocabulary list to use in a paragraph, essay, short story, or poem. *(Link to language arts.)*

- *Discussion:* Discussions are encouraged to stimulate interest, deepen knowledge, and assess student understanding. *(Link to language arts, social studies.)*

- *The Science of Music:* These sections in the student handouts examine music as it relates to the science of sound, with explanations and activities for deeper understanding. *(Link to science.)*

- *Bonus Challenges:* Bonus challenges in the student handouts offer additional projects that students can undertake alone or in groups.

- *My Opinion Page:* This activity sheet offers students the opportunity to freely express their opinions about the music presented in a lesson. *(Link to language arts, music appreciation, critical thinking.)*

- *Music on the Map:* Use this activity sheet to create a map and legend showing musically important places, such as musicians' birthplaces, music hot spots, and so on. *(Link to geography.)*

- *Great American Musicians!* Use this activity sheet to introduce American musicians whose talents have made them notable. *(Link to language arts, history.)*

- *My Musical Traditions:* This activity sheet invites students to describe their families' music traditions. *(Link to language arts, social studies.)*

- *Trace an Ancestor:* Students discover and investigate their own and other students' cultural backgrounds. *(Link to language arts, social studies.)*

- *Oral Tradition:* This activity demonstrates the practice of passing words or songs from one person to another by telling or singing, using the game "Telephone." *(Link to social studies.)*

- *Sing a Song:* The goal is to learn a new song from the lesson and sing it. Lyrics can be found in the student handouts; audio music is on the accompanying CD. Use the *How to Teach a Song* teacher's guide in the appendix to help you do it. *(Link to singing, melody, rhythm, language arts.)*

- *Illustrate the Music:* The goal of this activity is for students to illustrate a song or piece of music by drawing, coloring, or painting their ideas of what the music "looks" like on paper. *(Link to language arts, visual arts.)*

- *A Musical Story:* Students produce a musical skit or play inspired by music. It must have a musical plot and include one musical element—such as a song, melody, rhythm, dance, lip-synch, percussion, or other instrument accompaniment. Consider performing this activity after students have completed each unit. *(Link to language arts.)*

- *Invite a Music Expert:* Invite musicians who work in the genre you are studying to visit your class and share their instruments and musical talents. *(Link to social studies.)*
- *Families of Instruments:* Students divide the instruments mentioned in a lesson into instrument families that are grouped according to how they make sound. *(Link to science, language arts, visual arts.)*
- *Instrument Shuffle:* A leader calls out an instrument family group and students hold up a picture of an instrument from that group. *(Link to language arts.)*
- *Research an Instrument:* This activity encourages students to pick an instrument mentioned in the lesson and research its history, what it's made of, how it produces sound, and any interesting facts about it. *(Link to language arts, natural science, history.)*
- *Encyclopedia of Musical Instruments:* Create a picture book of musical instruments mentioned in the lessons with research completed by students. The result is a compilation of all the instruments found in the unit. *(Link to drawing, language arts.)*
- *Call-and-Response Singing:* This activity practices call-and-response, or antiphonal, singing. *(Link to singing.)*

Activities in Specific Units

- *In Which Native American Region Do You Live?* The goal of this activity is to learn about the Native American music region students live in—which tribe or group was or is living nearest them, and that group's musical traditions (Unit One). *(Link to social studies, history, language arts, geography.)*
- *Dogrib Hand Game:* This is a musical guessing game from the Dogrib First Nations tribe in Canada (Unit One). *(Link to rhythm.)*
- *Who Took the Cookie from the Cookie Jar?* This African-American ring game is played in a circle; students chant the song while clapping hands and thighs alternately in a steady rhythm. The goal is to keep the rhythm going while repeating the chant when it's your turn (Unit Three). *(Link to language arts.)*
- *Syncopation:* Students tap rhythm patterns included in the handout on drums, desktops, or knees to learn about syncopation (Unit Three). *(Link to rhythm.)*
- *Metaphors in Spirituals:* Students look at the lyrics in African-American spirituals for their metaphorical content (Unit Three). *(Link to language arts.)*
- *Underground Railroad:* Students research the Underground Railroad and how it helped transport the slaves to freedom; they also do research on the "signal songs" used to communicate escape plans and investigate their meanings (Unit Three). *(Link to history, language arts.)*

- *Playing on the Downbeat:* In this activity students practice playing a rhythm that accents the downbeat (Unit Three). *[Link to rhythm.]*

- *Charting the Charts:* The goal of this activity is to track a song on the *Billboard* charts and analyze its movement over a span of time. This helps students understand one of the ways the music industry observes the public's tastes in music (Unit Four). *[Link to math, economics.]*

- *Music in the Movies:* This activity invites students to listen to the background music in movies to discover the way it creates mood and to understand the idea that mood is created both by what we see on the screen and what we hear in the background (Unit Four). *[Link to language arts, visual arts.]*

- *Pick an Opera:* The goal is to get to know an American opera—its story line, characters, music, the difference between recitatives and arias, and so on, by listening to the opera, reading synopses, and reporting on what they learn. The class compiles an "American Opera Notebook" containing each student's review (Unit Four). *[Link to language arts.]*

- *Visit the Grand Ole Opry:* Students learn about its history, listen to a broadcast, watch a show, and report about what they learned (Unit Four). *[Link to language arts.]*

- *Pick a Music Style:* Students research a branch of music in a genre, such as swing, bebop, or fusion (branches of jazz) or doo-wop, surf music, hard rock, punk, or grunge (branches of rock). Students research the genre's history and find music examples, and the class compiles a music notebook containing each student's review (Unit Four). *[Link to language arts].*

Native American Music

Contents

Unit One: Overview

By the time Christopher Columbus arrived in North America in 1492, there were over six hundred Native American groups living on the continent with their own languages, systems of government, religions, ceremonies, and musical traditions. They sang, danced, and played drums, rattles, and rasps. Their songs were passed through the generations by the oral tradition. Ethnomusicologists have grouped Native American music into regions according to similarity in styles. The regions are Eastern Woodlands, Plains, Southwest, Great Basin and Plateau, California, Northwest Coast, Subarctic, Arctic, and Hawaii.

Singing is considered the most important part of most Native American music. Singing can carry important tribal history and values, or contain the power to heal a sick person or bring good luck in hunting. Sacred songs are highly honored and usually performed only at special occasions. Other songs include social songs, love songs, lullabies, and memorial songs.

Rhythm instruments, when played along with the singing, serve to call forth spirits and bring spiritual power. The most common rhythm instruments in traditional Native American music are drums, rattles, and rasps. Rhythm instruments are generally played as accompaniment to the singing and dancing, and not as featured instruments themselves. Traditionally, they were made from materials that were found nearby—for example, tree trunks and animal skins for drums, turtle shells and animal horns for rattles, sticks for rasps, and so on. Traditional pitched instruments include flutes, whistles, horns, and string bows. Flutes were not usually played in ceremonies or dances, but were played by the men as love calls to the women. Whistles were used for calling long distances or sending warnings, or in special dances. Horns imitated the call of animals and scared away enemies. String bows were plucked.

Contemporary Native American musicians continue to sing and perform the ancient music in special ceremonies and occasions and come together to share traditions at modern intertribal powwow gatherings. Some contemporary Native American musicians are mixing the traditions of their ancestors with rock, jazz, country, folk, and rap and composing lyrics that describe current issues, lifestyles, concerns, and experiences.

This unit provides an overview of Native American music traditions, including songs, dances, instruments, regional styles, and contemporary styles. Native American populations treat music with great respect and reverence. In teaching this music, it is important to consider certain issues that may not be common knowledge. For example, keep the following in mind:

- Many Native American songs are reserved for special occasions only. It would be inappropriate to sing one kind of a song out of context—for example, to sing a healing song on a stage or in a public auditorium. Similarly, it is not always appropriate for the general public to sing certain tribal songs. The songs provided in these lessons are public songs offered with permission.

- Many Native American tribes were given names by foreigners who did not know their real names in the Native American language. Whenever possible try to use the name the tribes call themselves. For example, the Sioux call themselves *Lakota, Dakota,* or *Nakota.* The Nez Percé were named by the French for their pierced noses; they call themselves *Nim-i'ipuu.* The *Ani Yunwiya* were called Cherokee by a neighboring tribe, meaning "the people who speak another language."

♪ Lesson 1. Traditional Native American Singing

Lesson Overview

Native American singing styles vary from tribe to tribe and region to region across America. The songs are influenced by the conditions and traditions of each tribal group and are performed for reasons ranging from healing to love. Sacred songs are highly honored and are usually performed only at special occasions. In most traditions, singing with drums and rattles can be used to call forth spiritual influences to aid in healing and other important outcomes. Social songs are performed in public for thanksgiving, honor, memorials, and social gatherings.

Vocabulary. Singing, traditions, compose, oral tradition, sacred songs, ceremonials, lullaby, rhythm, high pitches, low pitches, call-and-response, chorus, lyrics, vocables, chants.

Purpose. To introduce songs from a variety of traditional Native American cultures; to learn about different singing styles; and to learn where Native American songs come from.

Preparation. Read the **Traditional Native American Singing** student handout to familiarize yourself with the material. Preview the CD samples (see cues in student handout) and have the CD ready for playing for the students. Be prepared to do some or all of the activities included in this unit. Also, make sure that each student has a music notebook for keeping handouts, activity sheets, opinion pages, and so on, when they've completed them. *Suggestion:* Invite students to sit in a talking circle for any discussions about Native American music. (See next section for description of talking circles.)

Materials

- **Traditional Native American Singing** student handout *(following)*
- **Traditional Native American Singing Quiz** *(following)*
- **Traditional Native American Singing Quiz Answer Key** *(following)*
- **Music Vocabulary** activity sheet *(Appendix)*
- **My Opinion Page** activity sheet *(Appendix)*
- **How to Teach a Song** teacher guide *(Appendix)*
- **Music notebooks**
- **CD music** examples on accompanying CD; cues in student handout
- **Additional music selections**

Activities

- Pass out the **Traditional Native American Singing** handout for students to read silently or aloud as a group. Afterwards, have students put the handout in their music notebooks. *[Link to language arts, history, geography, social studies.]*

- Give the **Traditional Native American Singing Quiz** to assess student understanding of the lesson.

- Go over the music vocabulary at the top of the student handout either before or after reading the text. Refer to the glossary for definitions. *Suggestions:* Include these words in a regular class vocabulary lesson, or pass out flashcards with a vocabulary word on one side and the definition on the other and allow students to drill each other. Use the **Music Vocabulary** activity sheet to write out definitions. *[Link to language arts.]*

- Offer the **Vocabulary Challenge.** Students pick some or all of the words in this lesson's vocabulary list to use in a paragraph, essay, short story, or poem. *[Link to language arts.]*

- **Talking Circle.** Discuss the lesson's topic as a group before and after reading the student handout. Consider having the discussion in a "talking circle." *Step 1:* Have everyone sit in a circle. *Step 2:* Explain the rules: you'll use a "talking stick" (or other object, such as a stone, feather, or large bead) to pass from person to person. The person holding the object is the one whose turn it is to speak. Students should listen and respect each other's opinions. Each is allowed to speak honestly, without interruption, and opinions are not criticized, judged, or argued. Students are free to let the object pass without speaking if they choose. *Step 3:* Ask students to say what they already know about Native American music. *Step 4:* Read the student handout aloud or silently, then discuss it again, passing the talking stick or object around the circle, allowing each to add what they've learned. *Suggestion:* Allow extra turns if desired. *[Link to language arts, social studies.]*

- **The Oral Tradition.** The oral tradition is the practice of passing words or songs from one person to another by telling or singing; this practice has kept Native American songs alive for many generations. This activity demonstrates this tradition by playing the game "Telephone." *Step 1:* Sit in a circle and announce that this activity is like the game Telephone. In this version, each student in the circle counts as a "generation." For example, the first student is the "child," the next student is the "parent," the next is the "grandparent," the next is "great-grandparent," and so on, until every student is named (you may have twenty-five "generations" but it will clearly illustrate the concept). *Step 2:* The oldest generation (the last great-grandparent) begins by whispering a short phrase to the person next to him or her. Keep the phrase simple so that it is easy to remember. *Suggested phrases:* "The hunting is good beyond the meadow" or "The blueberries are very sweet this year." Each student passes the phrase by whispering to the student next to him or her until it reaches the last student (that is, the last generation) who says the phrase aloud to everyone. *Step 3:* Discuss what happened to the phrase as it passed from generation to generation. What did it start out being? What did it end up being? How does this process happen in real life? *Step 4:* Do it all again with a different intent. This time stress the importance of memorizing the phrase and getting it right. In this round, make sure each person is clear on what was said, even requiring the person hearing it to repeat it back to be sure. Note that Native Americans take great care to teach the songs and histories of their culture so that they will be remembered accurately from generation to generation. *(Link to social studies.)*

Extension Activities

For step-by-step directions and activity sheets, see the appendix.

- **My Opinion Page.** Give students a chance to express freely their own opinions about the music they hear. *(Link to language arts, critical thinking.)*

- **Sing a Song.** The goal of this activity is to learn a simple song from this lesson. *Suggested songs to sing:* "Gayowajeenayho," "Haagú S'é," "E Komo." *(Link to singing, language arts, rhythm, melody.)*

- **Illustrate the Music.** Students illustrate a song or piece of music by drawing or painting their ideas of what the music "looks" like visually. *Suggested songs to illustrate:* "Song for a Woman Who Was Brave in War," "Coyote Warrior Song," "Arowp—Song of the Mockingbird," "Haagú S'é," "Ockaya—Corn Grinding Song." *(Link to language arts, visual arts.)*

- **Music on the Map.** Create a map and legend showing musically important places, such as musicians' birthplaces and the music hot spots mentioned in the lesson. *(Link to geography.)*

- **Invite a Music Expert.** Invite a Native American musician to visit your class and share his or her instrument and musical talent with the students. *(Link to social studies.)*

- Consider bringing in **additional selections of music** from other sources to expand the music examples for this lesson. Search the Internet, library, or local music store to find them. Try *www.oyate.com*.

Name _____ Date _____

Iroquois singers and dancers

Traditional Native American Singing

Vocabulary: singing, traditions, compose, oral tradition, sacred songs, ceremonials, lullaby, rhythm, high pitches, low pitches, call-and-response, chorus, lyrics, vocables, chants

All Native American cultures have **singing** in their **traditions**—whether singing to a baby or singing to remember a war hero, ask for good weather, or perform a blessing ceremony. Sometimes songs are **composed** by an inspired person. At other times they come to people in dreams, or in visions, offering wisdom and guidance; these are not considered to be made up by the composer, but rather "given" to him or her by a higher power.

Many Native American songs are ancient, passed through the ages by the **oral tradition**. Early Native Americans did not use written language to record their songs, histories, and traditions. Instead, they passed this information from one person to another by telling, or singing. For example, a father might teach his son a healing song. The son then grows up and teaches it to his son, and he to his son, and so on for many generations. In this way, ancient songs and their messages are remembered throughout time. In modern times, traditional songs are also being sung to reinforce cultural identity and learn traditional languages.

Singing can hold special meaning at important occasions and is always respected for its power. Singing, with drums and rattles, is used to call forth spiritual help to aid in healing, success in war or hunting, and other important outcomes. Singing is also performed at social occasions where the people sing welcome songs, dance songs, love songs, memorial songs, and exit songs. "Gayowajeenayho" is a welcome song sung at social gatherings from the Haudenosaunee (Iroquois) tradition in the Eastern Woodlands region.

Gayowajeenayho—Welcome Song

Gayo-wah-jee-nay-hay yah-ah hay-ay-oh
Gayo-wah-jee-nay-ay-ho *(Repeated)*

Michele Stock. Used by permission.

Sacred Songs

Sacred songs are like prayers. They can be requests for guidance or calls for help. They can be used as an expression of worship or a way to show thanks. Native American sacred songs are not usually performed in public or recorded on tapes or CDs. It is their very nature to be reserved for special occasions and treated with respect.

Sacred songs are often performed in ceremonies for special outcomes. Hawaiians perform sacred songs to help the plants grow large and strong. The Diné (Navajo) *Night Chant* ceremony is for healing. The Plains *Sun Dance* is performed for the rebirth of the spirit and to renew the natural relationship between humans and nature.

In many groups, singing songs by one group demands a response from another group to ensure social and spiritual balance.

Because sacred songs are not usually performed in public, it is rare to hear them unless you belong to a Native group or receive a special invitation to hear them. It is important to note that many tribes had property laws that governed the ownership of songs.

Heroes and Heroines

Like other people from all cultures, Native Americans sing about heroes and heroines—describing great acts of courage and important events in their histories. Songs may tell about a famous war hero, or recall someone who was able to fight a bear and win, or a clever tribe member who outsmarted an evil spirit. Through songs, people and events are remembered and their stories are passed down through the generations.

"Song for a Woman Who Was Brave in War" tells the story of *Bicáganab,* an Ojibwa (Chippewa) woman from the Eastern Woodlands region who fought the neighboring Dakota (Sioux) warriors when they raided her camp. She fought them with a club and then jumped into the water. When they followed her, she ripped and tore at their canoe, the canoe fell apart, and the warriors fell into the water where she hit them with her paddle. The people watching said she looked like a ferocious bear.

Song for a Woman Who Was Brave in War

Eh-nee-wek way ween zhah-wah-so
Ween ghi-zhah-wah-so
Min-dee-mo-yahn
Way . . . Zhah-wah-so-nah-dah-go-nahn
Yah, eh, yah, eh, way, ah, hay.

Very much did she defend her children.
She was the old one,
We the children.
She fought for all of us.
Yah, eh, yah, eh, way, ah, hay.

From *A Cry from the Earth.* Copyright © 1979 John Bierhorst.
Ancient City Press, Santa Fe, New Mexico. Used by permission.

Song for a Woman Who Was Brave in War
CHIPPEWA

Sung by Odjibway, about 1908

ĕniwĕk: very much | we: meaningless | win: she [gi-]zhawaso: defending her children | mĭndimoyan: the old one (female) ([gigi-] zhawasonadagonan: fought for us all | ya e we a he: meaningless

Warrior Songs

Warrior songs offered power for fighting and success in war. In many traditions, warrior societies sang and danced in **ceremonials** that called for success and protection in war. The women sang songs of missing the warriors, and sang of their relief when the men returned. The Pawnee "Coyote Warrior Song," from the Plains region, asks for protection.

Coyote Warrior Song

Ah! Tee-rus tah-kah-wah-hah
Tee-raht-pah-ree—ho!
Tah-tah-rah kee-ta-wee-rah
Hah-wah reh-rah-wee-rah—heh-yo!

Oh great expanse of the blue sky,
See me roaming here,
Again on the warpath, lonely.
I trust in you, protect me!

From *The Indians' Book,* by Natalie Curtis.
Dover Publishing, New York, 1907. Used by permission.

Cheyenne warrior, circa 1927. Photograph by Edward S. Curtis.
Courtesy of McCormick Library of Special Collections, Northwestern
University Library, Evanston, Illinois. Used by permission.

The Kiowa *Wind Songs* were sung by both the warriors and those who stayed at home. "Gomda Daagya" is a woman's song.

Gomda Daagya—Wind Song

Pah-ko eh'k'ianda
Pah-ko eh'k'ianda
Pah-ko eh'k'ianda
Ayee apo
Hayee ankom oyom gee-ee-eh

I have one love.
I have one love.
I have one love.
And he is far away,
On the warpath.
Eh-yeh, eh-yeh.
Lonely are the days and weary.

From *The Indians' Book,* by Natalie Curtis.
Dover Publishing, New York, 1907. Used by permission.

Nature and Animal Songs

Many traditional songs are inspired by things in nature: the weather, the animals, or the natural environment. The Yup'ik (Eskimo) in the Arctic hear songs blowing in the coastal winds. In the Ni Míi Puu (Nez Percé) tradition, receiving a song from an eagle brings good luck in hunting. A Cherokee legend tells of parents singing songs to their children that they learned from listening to the wolves singing to their puppies and to the bears singing to their cubs. A Pawnee legend tells of a man who went into the wilderness and met a bear who taught him songs and dances to bring back to his village.

The Inupiat (Eskimo) song "Aa Narvaga—Song of the Loon and the Muskrat" is a song to the loon who is visiting the muskrat's lake.

Aa Narvaga—Song of the Loon and the Muskrat

By Jennie Jackson

Aa narvaga
Aa narvaga
Aa narvaga
U-kiu-mun ag-laan nar-van?

Ah, my lake.
Ah, my lake.
Ah, my lake.
Is it your lake even in winter?

Jennie Jackson. From *Introduction to Alaska Studies: Creative Response.* University of Alaska Rural Education Materials Development Center. Courtesy of Northwest Arctic Borough School District. Used by permission.

AA NARVAGA
Masruan

Aa, narvagaa
Aa, narvagaa
As, narvagaa
Ukiumun aglaan narvan?

Taamnagguuq Malgi akpittuq. Aagauraagaqsiruq uvva narvautaa
ni Kigvaluuram. "Aa, narvaga," itnauraaqhuni. Kigvaluuram sauk
tignigaa, "Ukiumun aglaan narvan?"

chanted by the Loon (3 times)

Aa nar - va - gas   Ae   nar   va

squealed high by the Muskrat

ga a   U -   kiu - mun   ag -laan   nar - van?

THE SONG OF THE LOON AND THE MUSKRAT
Jennie Jackson (Inupiaq)

Ah, my lake
Ah, my lake
Ah, my lake
Is it your lake even in winter?

It is said that Loon was singing, oh so proudly. He raised his head up
so high and sang. Here is was on Muskrat's lake, yet he was singing,
saying the words, "Ah, my lake." Muskrat suddenly scolded him in a
squeaky but harsh little voice. "Is this your lake even in winter?"

Credit: "The Song of the Loon and the Muskrat" by Jennie Jackson.
Ilustration by J. Leslie Boffa. Courtesy of Northwest
Arctic School District. Used by permission.

Songs can be requests for good weather for growing crops. In the Southwest region, good weather songs are performed during elaborate ceremonials with dancers, drummers, and singers. The Hopi *Snake Dance* is sung as part of a nine-day ceremonial performed to bring rain. The ceremonial includes collecting snakes from the desert and dancing with them around the neck, and even in the mouth. A perfectly performed ritual is very important for a good outcome, and so great care is taken in performing these songs and dances correctly.

Lullabies

Parents have always sung to their babies to soothe them and to teach them. In old times, **lullabies** offered "sleep magic" to lull babies to sleep in cradleboards hanging from trees, rocking to the **rhythm** of the song. Lullabies also offered gentle instructions for how to grow up with good values and skills. Mothers sang to their daughters about being good sewers and gatherers. Fathers sang to their sons about being good hunters and warriors.

"Haagú S'é"—A Boy's Lullaby—is a Tlingit lullaby. It encourages little boys to grow up to be good fishermen.

Haagú S'é—A Boy's Lullaby

From Charles Joseph, Kaal.átk'

Haagú s'é, Haagú s'é
K'isáani heeyahaa
téel' aaheix oowax'aká
wa.éich gwaa eeyataká
hee eenaa aa, hee eenaa aa
hee eenaa aa, hee eenaa aa

Come here a moment, little boys.
Dog salmon are resting
By the log jam in the stream.
You can go spear one!

From Charles Joseph, Kaal.átk'. Used by permission.

Comanche mother and child, 1921. Photograph by Edward S. Curtis.
Courtesy of McCormick Library of Special Collections, Northwestern
University Library, Evanston, Illinois. Used by permission.

Unit One: Native American Music

Women's Songs

Historically, Native American women sang songs that reflected the events of their lives. Navajo blanket weavers sang to bring magic to their blankets and to make them more attractive. Mothers sang game songs with their children to keep them entertained. Zuni women sang while grinding the corn, calling for the rain to nourish their crops. "Ockaya" says that the corn is talking, saying that the clouds are coming. The song asks for the clouds to come this way.

Ockaya—Corn Grinding Song

Eh-lu hon-kwah lo-nah, ee-yah-ah-neh
Eh-lu hon-kwa hli-tohn ee-yah-neh
Leh-kwa
Kay-lah ai-yahn toh-wah
Peh-neh ai-yah-yeh
Mah-ai-ho-mah ahn-tu-nah
Ai-yahn-tu-nah
Ho-lon-eh-leh-teh
Lilth-no keh-lah
Kiah-weh kwai-ee-nu-wah-neh

Beautiful, see the cloud, the cloud appear.
Beautiful, see the rain, the rain draw near.
Who spoke?
[It was] the little corn ear,
High on top of the stalk.
Saying while it looked at me,
Talking aloft there.
Ah, perchance the floods
[This way] moving.
Ah, may the floods come this way.

From *The Indians' Book,* by Natalie Curtis.
Dover Publishing, New York, 1907. Used by permission.

The Cheyenne "Rabbit Song" is sung while bouncing babies playfully on laps, like little rabbits. It is also sung for children while they hop around on the ground, making bunny ears with their fingers.

Rabbit Song

By Rhoda Young Bird Braxton

Vo go hii sso
Hos ssta ma hi
A no da va hi
Baby no zi i va hi
Vo go, vo go, vo go!

Lesson 1. Student Handout continued

> Little rabbit, little rabbit,
> Threw me out, kicked me!
> Little rabbit, little rabbit, little rabbit!

"Rabbit Song"
Rhoda Young Bird Braxton, 1/19/91

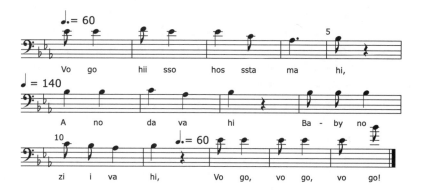

Singing Styles

Native American singing styles vary from region to region. Some sing in the middle pitches with relaxed throats and smooth melodies, while other traditions have developed strong, high-pitched voices with pulsing rhythms.

In Plains singing, both the men and the women sing. Traditionally, the women sat behind the drummers and their voices sang above the men's voices. In many songs, the singers begin singing on **high pitches** and then descend down to **low pitches** in the course of a song. Plains singers are also known for adding shouts, or yips and howls, in the middle of a song.

Native singing sometimes imitates things in nature, like animals and birds. In a Hupa "Brush Dance Light Song" the singers make yipping sounds like coyotes. In a Kwakw'ala (Kwakiutl) "Raven Song" the singer calls "gka, gka" like a raven. In an Unangax̂ (Aleut) dance song, the singers imitate the cries of seagulls.

Inuit (Eskimo) throat singing in the Arctic is a style of singing usually performed by two women. The singers stand close together with their faces almost touching, repeating low sounds in a fast, pulsing rhythm. The singing goes back and forth, and can go on for a while or end abruptly when one of the singers laughs or smiles. Throat singing is said to represent the sounds of animals and birds.

One distinct practice among some tribes is the **call-and-response** style of singing. Call-and-response is when a leader sings out a line and a **chorus** answers back. In the eastern traditions, there were men's choruses and women's choruses who sang back and forth to one another.

> **Call-and-Response Singing.** Call-and-response singing is when a leader "calls" and the others "respond." It is also called *antiphonal* singing. *Anti* has to do with "opposite" and *phonal* has to do with sound. Opposing-sound! With call-and-response, the singing goes back and forth. This can mean two groups taking turns back and forth, or a leader singing first and a chorus responding.

Lyrics and Vocables

Traditional Native American songs are sung with both **lyrics** and **vocables.**

Lyrics are the words of a song. Lyrics have meaning and they tell a story or describe a situation, like the story of General Custer's defeat at Little Bighorn in Wilmer Mesteth's song "I Had No Ears," or the woman fighting enemy warriors in "Song for a Woman Who Was Brave in War." Vocables are syllables without recognizable meaning, but they are just as important as the lyrics because the sounds themselves can have power and influence.

Chants may be made up of both lyrics and vocables. They may be long like a poem, or have no recognizable meaning as with vocables. Chants can last for hours or even days. In both the Diné (Navajo) *Night Chant* curing ceremony and the Zuni *Creation Story,* the singers sit for many hours and chant the sacred texts in ceremonials that last many days and nights.

Singing styles vary from region to region and depend not only on the traditions of the group but on outside influences, including the environment, contact with other groups, revelations from the Creator, and personal experiences.

♫ CD track #1. Listen to "Gayowajeenayho—Welcome Song," performed by Michele Stock. This song is sung at social gatherings in the Haudenosaunee (Iroquois) tradition in the Eastern Woodlands region. Notice the melodious and smooth singing style.

> "Gayowajeenayho—Welcome Song," sung by Michele Stock. Recorded by Milt Lee. ℗ 2000 Oyate Productions. Used by permission.

♫ CD track #2. Listen to "I Had No Ears," performed by Wilmer Mesteth, from the Plains region. This is a historical song describing the Lakota people's victory over General Custer's soldiers in 1876. The song begins with vocables, then follows with lyrics in the Lakota language. Listen to how the pattern of vocables-lyrics repeats several times. Also notice the strong, pulsing rhythm and high-pitched to low-pitched singing.

> "I Had No Ears," sung by Wilmer Mesteth. Recorded by Milt Lee. ℗ 2000 Oyate Productions. Used by permission.

♫ CD track #3. Listen to Sandoval Begay, a Diné (Navajo) from the Southwest region, singing with rattles in "Dance Song of the Night Chant."

Recording: "Dance Song of the Night Chant" (Navajo) by Sandoval Begay from the recording entitled *A Cry from the Earth: Music of the North American Indians,* Folkways 37777, provided courtesy of Smithsonian Folkways Recordings. © 1979. Used by permission.

♫ CD track #4. Listen to "Haagú S'é" (A Boy's Lullaby), from the Northwest Coast region, performed by Roby Littlefield in the Tlingit language.

"Haagú S'é," from Charles Joseph, Kaal.átk'. Recorded and sung by Roby Littlefield at Dog Fish Camp on the *Tlingit Dléigoox' (Tlingit Lullabies)* CD. ℗ 1998 Roby Littlefield. Used by permission.

♫ CD track #5. Listen to "The Spider Song," performed by John Pingayak (Cup'ik), from the Arctic region. This song tells about a singer's experience with a spider.

"The Spider Song," sung by John Pingayak. Recorded by Milt Lee. ℗ 2000 Oyate Productions. Used by permission.

♫ CD track #6. Listen to "E Komo," sung and played by Charles Ka'upu, from Hawaii. This is a dance song that pays homage to Pele, the Goddess of Fire, and her creative forces. Its melody is accompanied by an *ipu* (traditional gourd drum).

"E Komo," sung by Charles Ka'upu. Recorded by Milt Lee. ℗ 2000 Oyate Productions. Used by permission.

Lesson 1. Quiz

Name_____ Date_____

Traditional Native American Singing Quiz

Instructions: After reading the **Traditional Native American Singing** student handout, answer these questions (use back of the page if necessary).

1. What are **sacred songs?**

2. In what ways did Native Americans traditionally learn songs?

3. What kinds of songs are there in traditional Native American music?

4. What is the difference between **lyrics** and **vocables?**

Traditional Native American Singing Quiz:
Answer Key

1. What are **sacred songs?**

   SACRED SONGS ARE SPIRITUAL OR RELIGIOUS SONGS. THEY ARE LIKE PRAYERS. THEY MAY BE REQUESTS FOR GUIDANCE OR CALLS FOR HELP. THEY ARE TREATED WITH RESPECT AND OFTEN KEPT SECRET OR RESERVED FOR SPECIAL OCCASIONS.

2. In what ways did Native Americans traditionally learn songs?

   BY WORD OF MOUTH. THEY WERE PASSED THROUGH THE ORAL TRADITION FROM GENERATION TO GENERATION.

3. What kinds of songs are there in traditional Native American music?

   SACRED SONGS, SOCIAL SONGS, HERO AND HEROINE SONGS, WAR-RIOR SONGS, NATURE AND ANIMAL SONGS, LULLABIES, WOMEN'S SONGS.

4. What is the difference between **lyrics** and **vocables?**

   LYRICS ARE WORDS TO SONGS; THEY TELL A STORY OR DESCRIBE A SITUATION. VOCABLES ARE SYLLABLES WITHOUT RECOGNIZ-ABLE MEANING.

♫ Lesson 2. Traditional Native American Instruments

Lesson Overview

Traditional Native American cultures use musical instruments in ceremonies, rituals, games, social events, courting, and for communication. The most common rhythm instruments are drums, rattles, and rasps. Rhythm instruments traditionally played the accompaniment to the singing and dancing. In older times, they were rarely played by themselves and never played in orchestras. Pitched instruments include flutes, whistles, horns, and string bows. Flutes were commonly used by men to call and attract women. Whistles were used for calling long distances, sending warnings, and only occasionally during ceremonies. Horns imitated the calls of animals or scared away enemies. This lesson introduces a variety of traditional Native American instruments, what they are made of, how they make sound, and how they fit into larger families of instruments called membranophones, idiophones, aerophones, and chordophones.

Vocabulary. Rhythm, rhythm instruments, accompaniment, sacred, drums, amplify, resonator, vibration, rattles, shaker rattles, clapper rattles, rasps, pitch, pitched instruments, flute, melody, whistle, horn, vibrating, string bow, fiddle.

Purpose. To introduce instruments played in Native American music; to learn how these instruments fit into larger families of instruments called membranophones, idiophones, aerophones, and chordophones; to expose students to how sound is made with these instruments.

Preparation. Read the student handout **Traditional Native American Instruments** to familiarize yourself with the material. Preview the CD samples and have the CD ready for playing with the students. Be prepared to do some or all of the activities listed here. Also, make sure each student has a music notebook for keeping handouts, activity sheets, opinion pages, and so on.

Materials

- **Traditional Native American Instruments** student handout *(following)*
- **Traditional Rhythm Instruments Quiz** *(following)*
- **Traditional Rhythm Instruments Quiz Answer Key** *(following)*
- **Traditional Pitched Instruments Quiz** *(following)*
- **Traditional Pitched Instruments Quiz Answer Key** *(following)*

- **Traditional Rhythm Instruments Picture Page and Answer Key** *(following)*
- **Traditional Pitched Instruments Picture Page and Answer Key** *(following)*
- **Music Vocabulary** *(Appendix)*
- **Family of Instruments: Membranophones** activity sheet *(Appendix)*
- **Family of Instruments: Idiophones** activity sheet *(Appendix)*
- **Family of Instruments: Aerophones** activity sheet *(Appendix)*
- **Family of Instruments: Chordophones** activity sheet *(Appendix)*
- **Music notebooks**
- **CD music** examples on accompanying CD; cues in student handout
- **Additional music selections**

Activities

- Pass out the **Traditional Native American Instruments** handout for students to read silently or aloud or as a group. Afterwards, have students put the handout in their music notebooks. *(Link to language arts, history, geography, social studies.)*
- Give the **Traditional Rhythm Instruments Quiz** and the **Traditional Pitched Instruments Quiz** to assess student understanding of the lesson.
- Go over the music vocabulary at the top of the student handout before or after reading the text. See the glossary for definitions. *Suggestion:* Include these words in a regular class vocabulary lesson, or pass out flashcards with a vocabulary word on one side and the definition on the other and allow students to drill each other. Use the **Music Vocabulary** activity sheet to write out definitions. *(Link to language arts.)*
- Offer the **Vocabulary Challenge.** Students pick some or all of the words in this lesson's vocabulary list to use in a paragraph, essay, short story, or poem. *(Link to language arts.)*
- **Discuss.** Before and after reading the student handout, discuss the lesson topic as a group. Consider holding the discussion in a *talking circle* (see Lesson 1). Ask students what they know and what they've learned about Native American rhythm instruments. *(Link to language arts, social studies.)*
- Have students write in the correct names and instrument families under each picture on the **Traditional Rhythm Instruments Picture Page** and the **Traditional Pitched Instruments Picture Page.** See the answer keys for correct answers. Also see the **Science of Music** sections in the student handout and **Families of Instruments** in the extension activities for more understanding.

- The **Science of Music** sections in the student handout define and describe the families of instruments: membranophones make sound by beating a membrane stretched over a container; idiophones are instruments that are struck or shaken to make a sound; aerophones are wind-blown instruments; and chordophones are plucked or bowed. Directions for activities are in the **Science of Music** sections of the student handout. *[Link to science.]*
- Offer the **Bonus Challenge: Which Family of Instruments Does a Box Drum Belong In?** *Answer:* Idiophone, because it is hit, or beaten. It is not a membranophone because it has no membrane stretched over it. *Suggestion:* Consider offering extra credit to students who do this bonus challenge.

Extension Activities

For step-by-step directions and activity sheets, see the appendix.

- **Families of Instruments.** Divide the instruments mentioned in the lesson into "instrument families" grouped according to how they make sound (see the **Science of Music** sections in student handout for detailed explanations). *[Link to science.]*
- **Instrument Shuffle.** Deepen understanding and recognition of the instrument family groups by using picture flashcards. *[Link to language arts, science.]*
- **Research an Instrument.** Encourage students to become familiar with a Native American rhythm instrument and do research on its history, what it is made of, how it produces sound, and other interesting facts. *[Link to science, history, language arts.]*
- **Encyclopedia of Musical Instruments.** Have students create an "encyclopedia" of all the instruments mentioned in this lesson, and in this book. *[Link to science.]*
- **Invite a Music Expert.** Invite a Native American musician to visit your class and share his or her instrument and musical talent with the students. *[Link to social studies.]*
- Consider bringing in **additional selections of music** from other sources to expand the music examples for this lesson. Search the Internet, library, or local CD store to find them. Try *www.oyate.com.*

Name _____ Date _____

Yurok drummer. Photograph by Edward S. Curtis.
Courtesy of McCormick Library of Special Collections,
Northwestern University Library, Evanston, Illinois.
Used by permission.

Traditional Native American Instruments: Rhythm Instruments

Vocabulary: rhythm, rhythm instruments, accompaniment, sacred, drums, amplify, resonator, vibration, rattles, shaker rattles, clapper rattles, rasps, pitch, pitched instruments, flute, melody, whistle, horn, vibrating, string bow, fiddle

What is **rhythm?** What are **rhythm instruments?**

Rhythm is the beating of horses' hooves running across the prairie. Rhythm is the breaking of ocean waves on a beach. Rhythm is the steady beat of a drum.

In Native American music, rhythm instruments are drums, rattles, and rasps. They tap, slap, shake, scrape, and clap the beat of the music.

In traditional music, they were played as **accompaniment** to the singing and dancing. They were rarely played by themselves, and were never played in orchestras. Rhythm instruments were said to "help" the songs.

Like the songs themselves, Native American instruments are considered **sacred.** Great care is taken in gathering the materials, building them, decorating them, and playing them. The act of making and playing an instrument honors not only the music but the spirit of the material itself. For example, the leather drumhead, made from deerskin, honors the animal. The clay flute or carved wooden rattle honors the earth.

The Science of Music: Membranophones. Drums belong to a family of instruments called *membranophones.* These are instruments that have a stretchy layer of skin or paper (called a *membrane*) stretched over a container. Membranophones are played by hitting or striking the membrane. When the membrane is hit, it vibrates (moves fast) and this **vibration** sets the air around it in motion. It is the vibrating air that makes the sound! The bigger the container, the more air vibrates inside, and the louder and deeper the sound. Big drums sound louder and deeper than little drums. *Activity: Beat a drum and feel the vibration. Try drums of different sizes and notice the different sounds.*

Drums

Drums are instruments that you hit or strike to make a sound. Traditional Native American drums are made from animal skins or gut stretched over an open container. Native Americans in the forest stretched deer hide over the openings of hollowed-out logs. In the desert, they stretched animal skins over clay pots. In the Arctic, they stretched walrus gut over bentwood frames. Native Americans in different regions made instruments from materials unique to their environment.

Plains tribes built large drums from hollowed logs and hung them from stakes in the ground. They dug a hole underneath, which acted as a **resonator** to capture and **amplify** the sound. These drums were so loud that people could hear them ten miles away! In modern times, big powwow drums are played by a group of drummers who sit around a central drum and beat it.

The Arctic people traditionally made drums by stretching a thin membrane from a walrus stomach over a round wooden frame made from bent driftwood. Handles were made from walrus tusk ivory or wood. Today they stretch plastic or airplane fabric over a wooden frame and beat them with a thin willow stick.

The Yuman made "foot drums" with large planks over a hole in the ground, then stomped on the wood with their feet. The Nuuchanulth (Nootka) built box drums from pieces of wood; the drum was played by three men beating it with their feet.

The Navajo and Apache, in the Southwest, made "water drums" from clay or iron pots filled with water and covered with buckskin. The Iroquois and Chippewa made water drums from logs or wooden kegs half-filled with water. Other groups made water drums from gourds by cutting the fruit in half and filling it with water. The water serves as a resonator.

Copyright © 2004 by Teri Tibbett

Resonator. A **resonator** helps musical sounds get louder. A resonator is a hollow body, like a hollowed-out log or a clay pot. By striking the drumhead or body you make the drum vibrate, or shake. The air inside the hollow body vibrates too and it is the vibrating air that makes the sound! The bigger the hollow body, the more air vibrates inside and the louder the sound will be.

Frame drum (Plains)

Frame drum (Arctic)

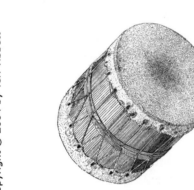

Log drum (Plains)

Box drum (Northwest Coast)

Gourd water drum (Southwest)

Skin drum (Hawaii)

The Science of Music: Idiophones. Instruments that are shaken, struck, clapped, or rubbed together to make a sound belong to a family of instruments called *idiophones*. Rattles and rasps are idiophones. Idiophones may be made from gourds, sticks, rocks, shells, animal hooves, or turtle shells. The sound is created by the objects slapping or clapping together—like seeds slapping against the inside of a gourd, shells beating against each other, or wooden sticks scraping together. Beating or rubbing causes the objects to vibrate and that causes the air around them to vibrate, and it's the vibrating air that makes the sound! *Activity: Play rattles and rasps made from a variety of materials. One group should use wood, one group should use metal, one group should use objects inside a container. Shake them, slap them, rub them, and compare their sounds.*

Rattles

Rattles are rhythm instruments that you shake or slap together to make a sound. Rattles also play the rhythm, or beat, of the music. The rattling sound is very important in many Native American ceremonies. Each kind of rattle has its own sound, and often, is believed to have its own power.

There are **shaker rattles** and **clapper rattles.** Shaker rattles are containers with small objects bouncing inside them, like seeds inside a gourd or pebbles inside a leather container. Native American shaker rattles are made from gourds, carved wood, clay, and turtle shells. Gourds are round, hard-shelled fruits that grow on a vine. When the fruit dies, the seeds inside come lose and rattle around. Seeds inside a gourd rattle make a "chich-chich" sound. Beads inside a metal rattle make a "clang-clang" sound. Pebbles in a wooden box rattle make a sound like knocking.

The Pueblo people of the Southwest shake painted gourd rattles. The Tsimshian of the Northwest Coast shake carved wooden totem rattles that feature important family designs carved on them. The Blackfoot, in the Plains region, traditionally used rattles made from animal skins. Hawaiians played feather gourd rattles. The Eastern Woodlands Iroquois made rattles by wrapping tree bark in the shape of a triangle, mounting it on a stick, and filling it with pebbles. Today they use leather cowhide instead of bark, and make other rattles from the horns of cows.

Clapper rattles are slapped or clapped together to make a sound. They are made from wood, bells, seashells, animal hooves, or any hard object strung together in a loop or sash. The Yaqui, in the Southwest, tie one hundred pairs of cocoons together on a leather string and shake them to make a sound. The Salish, in the Plateau region, use deer hooves strung together. Southwestern Pueblo tribes wear seashell sashes across their chests that shake as they dance. The Unangax̂ (Aleut), in the Arctic, dance with puffin beaks strung together. Hawaiians slap pebbles together and beat split bamboo wands against each other.

Bonus Challenge: Which Family of Instruments Does a Box Drum Belong In? Can you figure out which family of instruments a box drum belongs in? Write your answer.

Gourd rattle (Southwest)   Carved wood rattle (Northwest Coast)   Turtle shell rattle (Eastern Woodlands)

Leather rattle   Hoof rattle (Plains)   Seashell sash (Southwest)

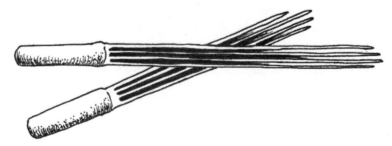

Split bamboo wands (Hawaii)

Unit One: Native American Music   **35**

Rasps

Rasps are instruments that you scrape or rub together to make a sound. One kind of rasp is a notched stick that is rubbed or scraped by another stick. Rasps may be made of wood, stone, or metal. Yaqui ironwood rasps are placed over a basket resonator and scraped against each other. The basket acts as a resonator, amplifying the sound. Rasps play the rhythm along with the drums and rattles.

Rasp

♪ CD track #5. Listen to John Pingayak (Cup'ik), from the Arctic region, play a walrus skin frame drum in "The Spider Song."

> "The Spider Song," sung by John Pingayak. Recorded by Milt Lee. Ⓟ 2000 Oyate Productions. Used by permission.

♪ CD track #2. Listen to Wilmer Mesteth (Lakota), from the Plains region, play a leather-head log drum in "I Had No Ears."

> "I Had No Ears," sung by Wilmer Mesteth. Recorded by Milt Lee. Ⓟ 2000 Oyate Productions. Used by permission.

♪ CD track #3. Listen to Sandoval Begay, a Diné (Navajo) from the Southwest region, chanting with rattles in "Dance Song of the Night Chant."

> *Recording:* "Dance Song of the Night Chant" (Navajo) by Sandoval Begay from the recording entitled *A Cry from the Earth: Music of the North American Indians,* Folkways 37777, provided courtesy of Smithsonian Folkways Recordings. © 1979. Used by permission.

♪ CD track #6. Listen to Charles Ka'upu, from Hawaii, play a drum made from a gourd fruit on "E Komo."

> "E Komo," sung by Charles Ka'upu. Recorded by Milt Lee. Ⓟ 2000 Oyate Productions. Used by permission.

Cree moose hunter with horn, 1928. Photograph by Edward S. Curtis.
Courtesy of McCormick Library of Special Collections, Northwestern
University Library, Evanston, Illinois.

Traditional Native American Instruments: Pitched Instruments

What is pitch? What are pitched instruments?

Pitch is the highness or lowness of sound. It's the part of the music that goes up and down. Pitches make up the song of a bird, or the wail of the wind. They form the yips of a coyote, or the howling of a wolf in the distance. Pitches make up the melody of a song.

Flutes are the most common pitched instruments in traditional Native American music. Whistles and horns were used for sending signals and for calling great distances. String bows were also played in some traditions.

Flutes

Flutes are hollow tubes with holes. If you put your fingers over the holes and blow, you can make the pitches move up and down, and thus make melodies. Native American flutes were traditionally made from hollowed-out bird bones, carved cedar wood, cane stalks, and other natural materials. Sometimes they were painted and decorated with hanging feathers and beads, or carved with designs. Sometimes they were plain.

Traditionally, flutes were played by men for the purpose of attracting women. In these cases, a man might hide some distance away from the camp and play a special **melody**, or tune, especially for the woman he wanted to attract.

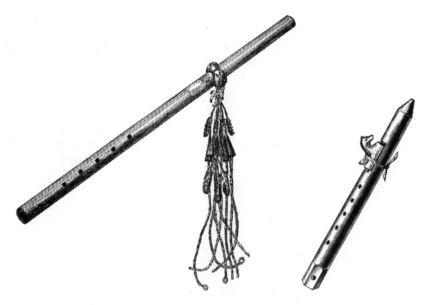

Native American flutes

In a Hopi ceremony called the *Flute Dance,* the flute is played for calling the corn maidens to bring the rain. In modern times, both men and women play Native American flutes.

Whistles

Whistles are hollow tubes with a hole at the top for blowing. An important difference between flutes and whistles is that whistles don't have holes for changing the pitch. They are simply tubes with a hole for blowing.

Traditionally, whistles were made from carved-out bird bones, wood, reeds, or clay molded into different shapes. Whistles were used for sending signals far away, or for calling out in an emergency, because their high pitches could be heard over far distances. Whistles are played in the *Sun Dance* ceremonies of the Plains region, where dancers blow high-pitched eagle-bone whistles above the sound of the drumming and dancing.

Bone whistle

Listen to Learn

The Science of Music: Aerophones. Instruments that use blown air to make a sound belong to the family of instruments called *aerophones.* Native American flutes, whistles, and horns are aerophones. *Aero* has to do with air, and *phone* has to do with sound. Air-sound! The thing all aerophones have in common is that you *blow* them to make a sound. Flutes and whistles have holes that you blow into. Horns have a hole you "toot" into. Either way, when you blow, you are sending a stream of air into a tube or pipe, creating **vibrating** air inside. It's the *vibrating* air that makes the sound. A long or fat tube has more air vibrating inside and so the sound is pitched *low.* A short or skinny tube has less air vibrating inside and so the sound is pitched *high.*

More air vibrating = lower pitch

Less air vibrating = higher pitch

The holes of the flute are used for changing the pitch. If you cover all the holes, the column of air will be long and the sound will be low (more air vibrating inside). But if you uncover the holes one by one, the tube of air will get shorter and the sound will get higher (less air vibrating inside). *Activity 1: Gather a variety of flutes, whistles, and horns. Practice blowing and listen to the sounds they make. Practice making the pitches go up and down by covering and uncovering the holes. Activity 2: Gather a variety of bottles and fill each with a different amount of water. Blow across the top of each one until you hear a sound. Notice the differences from bottle to bottle. Notice that the bottles with more air have a lower sound, and the bottles with less air have a higher sound.*

Horns

Horns were used by hunters to imitate the calls of animals, and by warriors to scare away enemies. They were made from seashells, horns of sheep and buffalo, or carved from wood. Horns have a small opening at one end that fans out to a larger opening, like a funnel. They are played by pursing the lips and "tooting" into the opening. Sometimes horns have holes—like flutes—that the player can use to change the pitch.

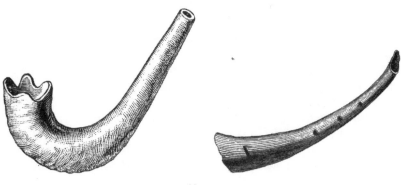

Horns

Unit One: Native American Music

String Bows

String bows are plucked. String bows used to be made by stretching an animal gut, or sinew, between two ends of a stick. Music was probably discovered when a hunter accidentally plucked the string of his hunting bow and heard a pleasant sound.

As the influences of the Europeans spread across North America, **fiddles** (violins) and other stringed instruments were introduced to Native Americans, who adapted these instruments into their music. The Apache fiddle is a one-stringed instrument made from an agave plant stalk, which is called "wood that sings." A string bow is rubbed across the string to make sound.

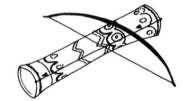

Gourd mouth bow   Apache fiddle with bow

♪ CD track #7. Listen to Mary Youngblood, who is Seminole-Aleut, perform "She Watches Them Play" on a wooden Native American flute.

"She Watches Them Play," written and performed by Mary Youngblood. From *The Offering* CD on Silver Wave Records. ℗ 1998. Courtesy of Mary Youngblood. Used by permission.

The Science of Music: Chordophones. Instruments that are plucked or strummed or rubbed to make a sound belong to the family of instruments called *chordophones*. *Chord* has to do with string, and *phone* has to do with sound. String-sound! When a string is plucked or strummed or rubbed (bowed), it vibrates, causing the air around it to vibrate. The vibrating string touches the box and causes the box to vibrate and the air inside the box to vibrate too. The box acts as a resonator and makes the sound get louder. *Activity: Take a small, thin branch, about a foot long, and bend it into an arch. Cut a rubber band to make one long strip. Tie the rubber band to each end of the stick, tight, bending it into a bow. Pluck it. Listen. Then touch the stick to your cheek, open your mouth, and pluck it again. Notice the sound gets louder as your mouth becomes a resonator. Try touching the stick to other resonators, like a table, plastic container, wooden container, metal container. Listen to the differences.*

Name _____ Date _____

Traditional Rhythm Instruments Quiz

Instructions: After reading the **Traditional Rhythm Instruments** student handout, answer these questions (use back of the page if necessary).

1. What are **rhythm instruments?**

2. Give an example of two traditional Native American **rhythm instruments.**

3. What is a **membranophone?** How do instruments in this family make sound? Give an example of a Native American membranophone.

4. What is an **idiophone?** How do instruments in this family make sound? Give an example of a Native American idiophone.

Traditional Rhythm Instruments Quiz: Answer Key

1. What are **rhythm instruments?**

   INSTRUMENTS THAT PLAY THE RHYTHM, LIKE DRUMS, RATTLES, RASPS.

2. Give an example of two traditional Native American **rhythm instruments.**

   LOG DRUM, FRAME DRUM, PLANK DRUM, GOURD DRUM, BOX DRUM, CLAY DRUM, WATER DRUM, GOURD RATTLE, LEATHER RATTLE, TREE BARK RATTLE, TURTLE SHELL RATTLE, SEASHELL RATTLE, HOOF RATTLE, BELL RATTLE, STONE RATTLE, WOOD RASP, BASKET RASP, METAL RASP.

3. What is a **membranophone?** How do instruments in this family make sound? Give an example of a Native American membranophone.

   MEMBRANOPHONES ARE INSTRUMENTS THAT HAVE A LAYER OF SKIN OR PAPER STRETCHED OVER A CONTAINER. YOU MAKE SOUND BY HITTING THE MEMBRANE. THE MEMBRANE VIBRATES, CAUSING THE CONTAINER AND THE AIR INSIDE THE CONTAINER TO VIBRATE. SOUND COMES FROM VIBRATING AIR. EXAMPLE: A DRUM, MADE WITH STRETCHED SKIN OVER IT.

4. What is an **idiophone?** How do instruments in this family make sound? Give an example of a Native American idiophone.

   IDIOPHONES ARE INSTRUMENTS THAT ARE SHAKEN, STRUCK, CLAPPED, OR RUBBED TOGETHER TO MAKE SOUND. EXAMPLES: RATTLES AND RASPS, STICKS HITTING TOGETHER, GOURDS WITH SEEDS SHAKING INSIDE, ROCKS HITTING TOGETHER, SEASHELLS CLANGING TOGETHER, ANIMAL HOOVES CLANGING TOGETHER.

Name _____   Date _____

Traditional Rhythm Instruments Picture Page

Instructions: Write the name of the instrument and the family group it belongs to on the lines provided under each picture.

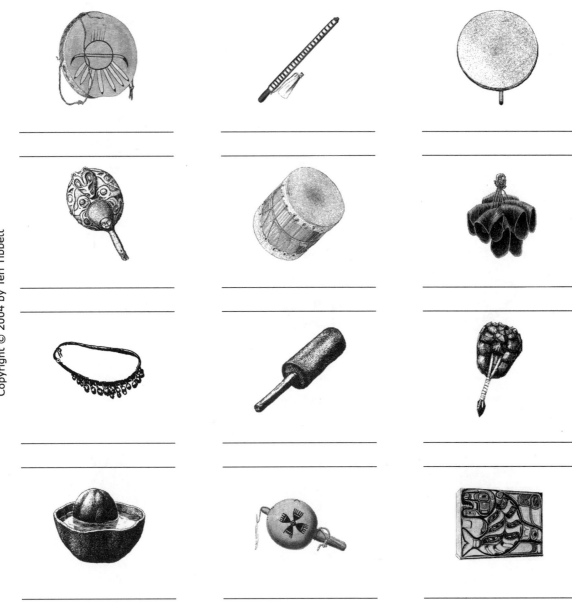

Traditional Rhythm Instruments Picture Page:
Answer Key

Frame drum

Membranophone

Rasp

Idiophone

Frame drum

Membranophone

Carved wood rattle

Idiophone

Log drum

Membranophone

Hoof rattle

Idiophone

Seashell rattle

Idiophone

Leather rattle

Idiophone

Turtle shell rattle

Idiophone

Gourd water drum

Idiophone

Gourd rattle

Idiophone

Box drum

Idiophone

Listen to Learn

Name _____ Date _____

Traditional Pitched Instruments Quiz

Instructions: After reading the **Traditional Pitched Instruments** handout, answer these questions (use back of the page if necessary).

1. What is pitch?

2. What is a **pitched instrument?** Give an example of a traditional Native American pitched instrument.

3. What is an **aerophone?** How do instruments in this family make sound? Give an example of a Native American aerophone.

4. What is a **chordophone?** How do instruments in this family make sound? Give an example of a Native American chordophone.

Traditional Pitched Instruments Quiz: Answer Key

1. What is pitch?

    PITCH REFERS TO THE HIGHNESS AND LOWNESS OF SOUND—THE PART OF THE MUSIC THAT GOES UP AND DOWN.

2. What is a **pitched instrument?** Give an example of a traditional Native American pitched instrument.

    PITCHED INSTRUMENTS USE PITCH TO MAKE SOUND; THEY CREATE HIGH PITCHES, LOW PITCHES, AND PITCHES IN BETWEEN. EXAMPLES ARE FLUTES, WHISTLES, HORNS, STRING BOWS.

3. What is an **aerophone?** How do instruments in this family make sound? Give an example of a Native American aerophone.

    AEROPHONES ARE INSTRUMENTS THAT USE BLOWN AIR TO MAKE SOUND. BLOWING SENDS A STREAM OF VIBRATING AIR INTO A TUBE OR PIPE. THE VIBRATING AIR MAKES THE SOUND. AEROPHONES WITH HOLES, LIKE FLUTES, CHANGE THE LENGTH OF THE TUBE OR PIPE AND SO CHANGE THE PITCH OF THE SOUND (HIGHER PITCHES COME FROM SHORTER/THINNER/ SMALLER TUBES; LOWER PITCHES COME FROM LONGER/WIDER/ BIGGER TUBES). EXAMPLES ARE FLUTES, WHISTLES, HORNS.

4. What is a **chordophone?** How do instruments in this family make sound? Give an example of a Native American chordophone.

    CHORDOPHONES ARE INSTRUMENTS THAT ARE PLUCKED OR STRUMMED OR RUBBED TO MAKE A SOUND. A VIBRATING STRING CAUSES THE AIR AROUND IT TO MOVE AND THE MOVING AIR MAKES THE SOUND. EXAMPLES ARE STRING BOWS AND FIDDLES.

Name _____   Date _____

Traditional Pitched Instruments
Picture Page

Instructions: Write the name of the instrument and the family group it belongs to on the lines provided under each picture.

_____   _____   _____

_____   _____   _____

_____   _____

_____   _____

_____   _____

_____   _____

Traditional Pitched Instruments
Picture Page: Answer Key

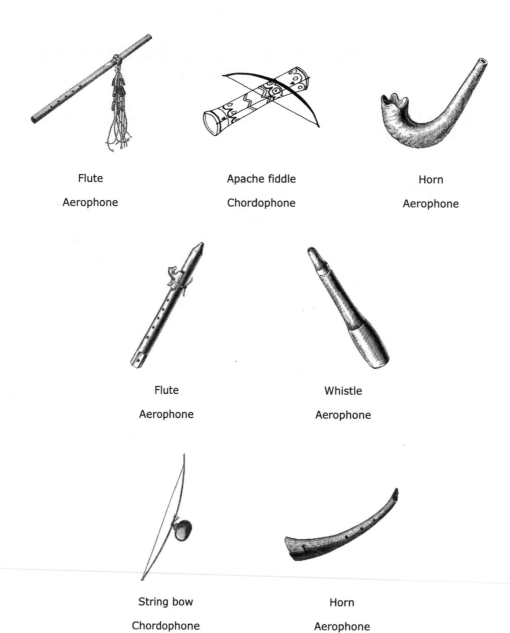

Flute

Aerophone

Apache fiddle

Chordophone

Horn

Aerophone

Flute

Aerophone

Whistle

Aerophone

String bow

Chordophone

Horn

Aerophone

Listen to Learn

♫ Lesson 3. Native American Music Regions

Lesson Overview

Over the centuries, Native American groups have developed individual singing styles, instruments, dances, rituals, and ceremonials. Ethnomusicologists have grouped Native American music into regions according to similarity of style. The regions are Eastern Woodlands, Plains, Southwest, Great Basin and Plateau, California, Northwest Coast, Subarctic, Arctic, and Hawaii. This lesson offers an overview of each region, with some examples of each. We highly recommend that you bring in additional music selections for these lessons, because the accompanying CD does not offer an example from each region.

Vocabulary. Tradition, ceremonial, ethnomusicologist, sacred songs, social songs, drum, rattle, rhythm, melody, throat singing.

Purpose. To offer an overview of Native American music by region, including songs, singing styles, instruments, and regional music styles.

Preparation. Read through the **Native American Music Regions** student handout to familiarize yourself with the information. Preview the CD samples (see cues in student handout) and have the CD ready for playing. Be prepared to do some or all of the following activities. Also make sure that each student has a music notebook for keeping handouts and activity sheets. *Suggestion:* Consider sitting in a *talking circle* for discussions. (See Lesson 1.)

Materials

- **Native American Music Regions** student handout *(following)*
- **Native American Music Regions Map** *(following)*
- **Native American Music Regions Quiz** *(following)*
- **Native American Music Regions Quiz Answer Key** *(following)*
- **Music Vocabulary** activity sheet *(Appendix)*
- **My Opinion Page** activity sheet *(Appendix)*
- **Great American Musicians!** activity sheet *(Appendix)*
- **Music on the Map** activity sheet *(Appendix)*
- **Music notebooks**
- **CD music** examples on accompanying CD; cues in student handout
- **Additional music selections**

Activities

- Pass out the **Native American Music Regions** student handout and have students read it silently or aloud in a group. Afterwards, have students put the handout in their music notebooks. *(Link to language arts, history, geography, social studies.)*

- Give the **Native American Music Regions Quiz** to assess student understanding of the lesson.

- Go over the music vocabulary at the top of the student handout before or after reading the text. Refer to the glossary for definitions. *Suggestion:* Include these words in a regular class vocabulary lesson, or pass out flashcards with a vocabulary word on one side and the definition on the other and allow students to drill each other. Use the **Music Vocabulary** activity sheet to write out definitions. *(Link to language arts.)*

- Offer the **Vocabulary Challenge.** Students pick some or all of the words in this lesson's vocabulary list to use in a paragraph, essay, short story, or poem. *(Link to language arts.)*

- **Discuss.** Before and after reading the student handout, discuss the lesson's topic as a group. Consider having the discussion in a *talking circle* (see Lesson 1). Ask students what they know and what they've learned about Native American music regions. *(Link to language arts, social studies.)*

- Offer the **Bonus Challenge: Which Native American Group Lived Closest to You?** After locating the region they live in on the **Native American Music Regions Map**, students use the Internet or library to research the customs and living arrangements of the Native American group or groups that used to live in their region or still live there and describe their musical traditions. Have students offer a written or oral report. *Answer examples:* People living in Juneau, Alaska, live in the Northwest Coast region. People in New York City live in the Eastern Woodlands region. Students describe the kinds of instruments they played, the kinds of songs they sang, their singing style, and their dances or ceremonies. *(Link to social studies, history, language arts, geography.)*

- Offer the **Bonus Challenge: What Is the Connection Between the *Ghost Dance* and the Massacre at Wounded Knee?** Students are invited to do research on the Internet, in an encyclopedia, or in books from the library, to learn more about the *Ghost Dance* and its connection to the Massacre at Wounded Knee, South Dakota; then they present a written or oral report. The *Ghost Dance,* from the Great Basin region, originated from a vision by a Paiute named Wovoka, who said that by dancing the dance the people could call on the ancestors and return life to the way it was before the settlers came. As the dance spread across the regions, more and more people began to dance it and it became a movement among many tribes. The fervor of the movement created fear and hysteria among non-Indian settlers and the military, who perceived the

Indians were dancing in preparation for war. On December 29, 1890, the U.S. Calvary reacted by attacking an encampment of sleeping men, women, and children at Wounded Knee. *Suggestion:* Consider offering extra credit to students who do the bonus challenge. *[Link to history.]*

Extension Activities

For step-by-step directions and activity sheets, see the appendix.

- **My Musical Traditions.** Investigate individual family traditions, including musical ones. *[Link to language arts, social studies.]*
- **Trace an Ancestor.** Help students experience cultural diversity by naming their own and seeing other students' cultural backgrounds. *[Link to language arts, social studies.]*
- **Call-and-Response Singing.** Practice call-and-response, or antiphonal singing. *[Link to singing.]*
- **Dogrib Hand Game.** This is a guessing game from the Dogrib First Nations tribe in the Subarctic. *[Link to rhythm.]*
- Consider bringing **additional selections of music** to expand the music examples for this lesson. Search the Internet, library, or local CD store to find them. Try *www.oyate.com.*

Name _____ Date _____

Nakoaktok dancers, 1914. Photograph by Edward S. Curtis.
Courtesy of McCormick Library of Special Collections,
Northwestern University Library, Evanston, Illinois.

Native American Music Regions

Vocabulary: tradition, ceremonial, ethnomusicologist, sacred songs, social songs, drum, rattle, rhythm, melody, throat singing

There are many ideas about when the first people settled in North America. Anthropologists say they walked across a "land bridge" from Russia to Alaska when the oceans were very low, and then migrated down the American continent. Many Native Americans believe their ancestors were always living in America, from the beginning of time.

When Christopher Columbus arrived in 1492, there were already six hundred tribes living in North America, each with its own culture, language, religion, system of government, **traditions,** and **ceremonials.** Each group had its own style of music, and these styles varied from region to region across North America.

Experts who study traditional music are called **ethnomusicologists.** These experts have noticed that people living close to each other tend to share their music and so their styles sound similar. They have grouped styles of Native American music into regions across North America and Hawaii. These regions are the Eastern Woodlands, Plains, Southwest, Great Basin and Plateau, California, Northwest Coast, Subarctic, Arctic, and Hawaii (see the **Native American Music Regions** map on page 69).

Ethnomusicology. Ethnomusicology is the study of music in a culture—for example, the study of sacred music in Native American cultures, or folk music in European-American cultures, or the blues in the African-American culture. *Ethno* refers to the ethnicity, or people, of a certain culture. *Musicology* is the study of music. Ethnomusicologists study the style, history, methods, and structures of a people's music. They record the songs and analyze them, listening closely to the words, rhythm, and melody in order to understand them. They learn the history of the music, where it came from, and what kind of influences it has picked up along the way.

Francis LaFlesche *(Omaha)* **(December 25, 1857–1932).** Francis LaFlesche, a Native American musicologist, anthropologist, and writer, was born in Nebraska. As a child, he attended a mission school where he learned to read and write in English and understand European-American customs. At home, his father taught him their native culture, including the Omaha dances, songs, and ceremonials. Francis practiced law, worked as an interpreter, was an adviser to the U.S. government, and wrote about what it was like to be a Native American living in two cultures. He wrote many important books, including a dictionary of the Osage language, a book of Osage ceremonials, and *A Study of Omaha Music* (1893), which he co-wrote with ethnomusicologist Alice Fletcher. He also composed an opera in 1912, *Da-o-ma.*

Eastern Woodlands Region

Eastern Woodlands tribes inhabit the eastern part of North America. They lived in settlements under the peaceful rule of organized nations before the arrival of the Europeans. The dense woodlands provided many animals, fish, and wild plants to eat. Many of these tribes were hunter-gatherers; many farmed corn, beans, and squash. Some lived in log houses or wood-frame houses covered with mud, bark, vines, and saplings. Others lived with other families in longhouses, where the people shared day-to-day living responsibilities and ceremonial duties. The settlements moved from time to time in order let the land replenish.

The Eastern Woodlands tribes sing both **sacred songs** and **social songs** and accompany the singing and dancing with **drums** and **rattles.** There are songs and dances for different occasions, including welcome songs, animal dances, hunting dances, social dances, and stomp dances.

A distinct feature of Eastern Woodlands music is the call-and-response style of singing: one person or group sings out (call) and another group answers back (response). Eastern Woodlands tribes have men's choruses and women's choruses who sing back and forth to each other.

Seneca false face dancer

"Gayowageenayho" is a traditional welcome song performed at social occasions.

Gayowajeenayho—Welcome Song

By Michele Stock

Gayo-wah-jee-nay-hay yah-ah hay-ay-oh
Gayo-wah-jee-nay-ay-ho *(Repeated)*

Michele Stock. Used by permission.

♫ CD track #1. Listen to "Gayowajeenayho—Welcome Song," a social song from the Eastern Woodlands, sung by Michele Stock.

"Gayowajeenayho—Welcome Song," sung by Michele Stock. Recorded by Milt Lee. ℗ 2000 Oyate Productions. Used by permission.

Michele Stock *(Seneca)* (October 3, 1955–). Michele Stock, a traditional Seneca singer, drummer, and rattle player, was born on the Allegheny Reservation in New York. As a child, she learned songs and dances of the Seneca people as they were performed in the traditional longhouse. She later received her master's degree in education and became a delegate at the White House Conference on Indian Education. Michele plays a cow horn rattle and water drum to accompany her singing. Her water drum is made from a hollowed-out log filled halfway with water, then covered with a wetted deer or cowhide skin stretched over the top. She performs the traditional songs and dances of her people in both sacred and social settings.

Plains Region

The huge Plains region stretches from the middle of the North American continent in present-day Mexico all the way into Canada. Before the arrival of the Europeans, the region was rich with buffalo (bison), which provided food and shelter for the Plains tribes. Most tribes traveled in small bands, following the buffalo herds' natural migratory patterns. Other tribes settled in communities and farmed, living in earthen houses, but also continued to hunt. The people performed *Buffalo Songs* and *Buffalo Dances* to bring good luck in hunting and to show their appreciation for these animals. The hooves and horns of the bison were made into tools and musical instruments.

Plains music is featured in war dances, round dances, grass dances, and more. Each dance has its own drumming patterns and singing style. Some songs tell stories about famous leaders and their great deeds. Others tell of victories in war or express sadness for those who were lost.

Plains drummer, 1927. Photograph by Edward S. Curtis.
Courtesy of McCormick Library of Special Collections,
Northwestern University Library, Evanston, Illinois.

"I Had No Ears" is a modern song composed by Wilmer Mesteth, an Oglala Lakota (Sioux). It tells about the Battle of Little Bighorn between the Lakota warriors and General Custer's U.S. Cavalry. Note that "the long knives" refers to the cavalry, "the long hair" refers to Custer. The phrase "I had no ears" means "I didn't listen."

I Had No Ears

By Wilmer Mesteth

(1) Mila hanska
(2) Pehin hanska
Wawakuwa ċa
ċeya inyanke
Ayuśtanśni
Nuġe mawaniċe

(1) The long knives
(2) The long hair
I chase down the long knives on the battlefield.
They are running on the battlefield.
I should have let them be,
I had no ears.

From Wilmer Mesteth. Used by permission.

♪ CD track #2. Listen to Wilmer Mesteth sing "I Had No Ears," a historical song describing the Lakota victory over General Custer at the Battle of Little Bighorn in 1876. Most Plains songs are sung in groups, so this one by a solo singer is unusual. Listen to the pulsing rhythm of the Plains style. The song begins with a melody of vocables, followed by the lyrics of the song, followed again by vocables. Try listening for this pattern of vocables and lyrics.

"I Had No Ears," sung by Wilmer Mesteth. Recorded by Milt Lee. ℗ 2000 Oyate Productions. Used by permission.

Wilmer Mesteth *(Lakota)* **(February 3, 1957–).** Wilmer Mesteth, a drummer and singer of traditional Lakota music and also a storyteller and flute player, was born in South Dakota. As a child, he learned the traditional songs of his tribe from his father, grandfather, and uncle, who had learned the same songs from their fathers and grandfathers. These old songs have passed through many generations. Wilmer also sings new songs from more recent times, like the songs about Chiefs Sitting Bull and Crazy Horse, or the victory song about the Battle of Little Bighorn. He has dedicated his life to preserving the culture of his people. He teaches history of the Oglala Lakota tribe, their culture, traditional music and dance, and art, including beadwork and quillwork. He presents music and teaches about these things at live performances and conferences around the world.

Southwest Region

Southwestern tribes live in the deserts and plateaus of present-day Arizona, New Mexico, California, Utah, and Mexico.

The Pueblo tribes built adobe structures in communities placed on the tops of mesas, in canyons, or even on cliff faces. Wild plants and animals are sparse in this dry climate, so these people learned to use scarce water to grow corn, beans, squash, melons, chili, tobacco, and cotton in small farms. Traditional clothing was made from handwoven cotton and sewed buckskin; sandals were made from plant fibers. Warmer winter clothes were made of rabbit skins or turkey feathers; moccasins were made from animal hides.

Many songs in this region call for rain or good crops. They can be sung by the women as they work or performed in elaborate ceremonials with dancers, drummers, and singers.

The Diné (Navajo) were a nomadic culture. They lived in circular shelters made from sticks and earth—called *hogans*—and later made structures of adobe. The Apache lived in brush-covered domes or Plains-style tepees made from animal hides. They too were nomadic and eventually settled into ranching and herding.

Navajo and Apache songs are sung at both formal and informal occasions, but most are saved for special occasions. *Blessingway* ceremonials are for ensuring good luck and abundance of food. *Enemyway* ceremonials are for protection. *Night Chants* are for purification and healing and last for many days and nights.

♩ CD track #3. Listen to "Dance Song of the Night Chant," by Sandoval Begay. Notice the rattles and high-pitched singing, which moves down to low-pitched singing in this traditional Navajo healing song.

Recording: "Dance Song of the Night Chant" (Navajo) by Sandoval Begay from the recording entitled *A Cry from the Earth: Music of the North American Indians,* Folkways 37777, provided courtesy of Smithsonian Folkways Recordings. © 1979. Used by permission.

Hosteen Klah *(Diné [Navajo])* **(1867–1937).** Hosteen Klah was born at Bear Mountain in present-day New Mexico. As a child, he was inspired by his uncle, a medicine man, who performed a healing ceremony on him and cured him from a sickness. Hosteen, who went on to become a medicine man himself, studied the ancient ceremonies, which included learning the complicated songs and music of the *Yeibichai* ritual and *Night Chant* ceremony. He was a gifted singer, weaver, and sandpainting artist who throughout his life remained an advocate for Navajo art and music.

Hosteen Klah. Photograph courtesy of Wheelwright Museum of the American Indian, Santa Fe, New Mexico.

Great Basin and Plateau Regions

The Great Basin and Plateau regions are located in the western-central part of the North American continent.

Great Basin people traditionally lived in homes made of poles covered with brush. They wore clothing made from rabbit skins, woven plant fibers, and shredded bark. They wove baskets from willow sticks and used them for gathering seeds and carrying water. Because of the scarcity of food, many families lived in small bands that gathered together only occasionally with larger groups for special hunting parties, social dances, and feasts when the food was plentiful.

One of the most famous song-dances to come from this region is the *Ghost Dance.* It began when Wovoka, a Paiute, received a vision that if his people would sing certain songs and perform a special *Round Dance,* they could call on the ancestors and return life to the way it was before the European settlers came. The *Ghost Dance* and songs became popular and spread among many North American native groups in the late 1880s. As more tribes joined the movement, the people added their own interpretations of the *Ghost Dance,* like the Plains tribes dancing to bring back their old way of life and the days of hunting buffalo. The movement died out after the Massacre at Wounded Knee in 1890.

The Plateau region includes parts of present-day Montana, Idaho, Washington, Oregon, and southern British Columbia. The river areas of this region provided plenty of fish and plants for food. The mountains offered deer, elk, moose, bear, rabbit, and mountain sheep. The deserts gave the people cactus, sage, and desert animals for food. Clothing was made from animal skins and plant fibers

Wovoka *(Paiute)* **(1859–1932).** Wovoka was born in the region now called Nevada. His name means "the cutter," but he was also known as *Wanekia,* "One Who Makes Life." He spent part of his childhood living with a European-American family where he received some religious training. When he was thirty years old, he had a vision that predicted the return of the land in its natural beauty if the people would perform the *Ghost Dance.* This led to a movement among Native American people that inspired a sense of renewal and hope for many.

Wovoka, circa 1915. Courtesy of Nevada Historical Society.

decorated with elk teeth, shells, bone, and porcupine quills. The Plateau tribes traveled to find food in the spring to fall seasons. During these times they lived in temporary shelters made of poles and woven mats. In the winter, they lived in permanent settlements with shelters made of logs built over pits and covered with sod.

The Plateau people sang songs to invite spirit guides to help them. The guides, who often appeared in the form of a dream or an animal, would teach the seeker a song that would then belong to that person and continue to guide him or her throughout life. The *Bear Dance* songs of the Noochew (Ute) show respect for the spirit of the bear and offer strength and help for the human spirit. The dance is said to have come from a young hunter who watched a bear dancing outside a cave in the spring. The bear told the hunter that if he performed the same dance, the man would gain strength in hunting. And so the hunter returned and taught that dance to his people.

California Region

Many cultures lived in the region that is present-day California. The land is varied—with steep mountains and wide rivers leading to ocean beaches, and lush green valleys and rolling yellow hills leading to vast dry deserts. An abundance of wild plants and game provided the original residents with plenty of food and materials for shelter. They ate pine nuts, berries, grass seeds, acorns, and mesquite beans. They made baskets from the fibers of plants and wove mats for sleeping, sandals for their feet, ropes to work with, and straps for carrying things. They made canoes from hollowed-out logs and rafts from woven reeds. The coastal people gathered seaweed and hunted seals, sea lions, and sea otters. They collected bird eggs and hunted waterfowl and other birds—like quail, pigeons, grouse, and woodpeckers. Houses were made of grass or reeds and earth, and were semipermanent. The mild weather allowed the people to wear light clothing, made from plant fibers and animal hides, or no clothing at all.

The *Bird Songs* of the Kuneyaay (Diegueño) are one of the musical traditions still alive in California today. Bird singers accompany dancers, who lift their feet to the rhythm of shaking gourd rattles. The songs teach the tribe's values and how to live a good life. The songs also tell the people's history and remind them of their ancient customs.

Did You Know? A special recording of Navajo *Night Chant* music was sent into outer space on the 1977 *Voyager* spacecraft in the hope that it would help represent our world if discovered by intelligent life elsewhere in the universe.

Yuman songs are often like poems. Yuman men use their voices to chant the **rhythm,** while the women sing the **melody** over the rhythm. The "Song of the Mockingbird" is a Yuman song that reflects on the singer's natural environment.

Arowp—Song of the Mockingbird

'Mai ah-ree-wah, 'ree-wah-ree
'Mai ah-ree-wah, 'ree-waht
'Mai ah-ree-wah, 'ree-wah-ree
'Mai ah-ree-wah, 'ree-wah-ree
'Mai ah-ree-wah, 'ree-wah
Shah-kwah tzah mee nah hee
Shah-kwah tza mee nah
Shah-kwah tza mee nah hee
Shah-kwah tza mee nah hee
Shah-kwah tza mee nah
O nyah kwah pai vah
Hu-nyah kwah hul pah
Hu-nyah kwah pai vah
Hu-nyah kwah hul pah
Hu-nyah kwah hul pah

Sky so thinly covered with clouds, with clouds,
Sky so thinly covered with clouds, with clouds.
The mockingbird, it is he who sings,
The mockingbird, it is he who sings.
I go up the mesa,
I go up the straight trail.

From *The Indians' Book,* by Natalie Curtis. Dover Publishing, New York, 1907. Used by permission.

The central tribes of California practiced the most elaborate ceremonies in the region. Dancers wore fancy clothing and danced in large dance houses for important occasions, such as a girl's or boy's passage into adulthood or to ask for good food and hunting. The musicians played flutes and whistles, drums, rattles, string bows, and large wooden foot drums, on which they both danced and stomped their feet.

Bonus Challenge: What Is the Connection Between the Ghost Dance and the Massacre at Wounded Knee? Do research on the Internet, in an encyclopedia, or in books from the library to learn about it. Write a brief report.

In Northern California, the Hupa, Yurok, and Karok tribes perform world-renewal ceremonies that include the *White Deerskin Dance* and the *Jump Dance.* In these ceremonies, sacred rites are performed through dance and song. *White Deerskin Dancers* wear regalia of deer hide and shell necklaces. *Jump Dancers* wear headdresses of feathers and shells.

Hupa White Deerskin Dancer. Photograph by Edward S. Curtis.
Courtesy of McCormick Library of Special Collections, Northwestern
University Library, Evanston, Illinois. Used by permission.

Sonny Pratt *(Hupa)* **(1942–), Ralph Miguelina** *(Hupa)* **(1952–).** Sonny Pratt and Ralph Miguelina were raised in the Hoopa Valley of Northern California. Sonny grew up singing the songs of his culture, inspired by his mother and his uncle. Ralph began singing and dancing when he was thirteen years old. His Indian name is *Goeeta,* after a beautiful singer. The two are singers and drummers of Hupa traditional music. They perform both sacred and social songs. They also sing their own songs and songs composed by others. Sometimes they both sing the melody together; at other times, one sings a melody while the other chants a rhythm with his voice.

Northwest Coast Region

Haida killer whale mask

The tribes of the Northwest Coast live near the ocean and along the inland waterways of present-day Oregon, Washington, British Columbia, and southeast Alaska.

The huge, dense forests of the region offered a bounty of wild game, plants, fish, and materials for shelter and clothing. Traditionally, the people hunted moose, deer, caribou, and elk. They fished for halibut, cod, trout, and salmon. They made clothes from animal hides and cedar bark, and wove baskets for hats to protect them from the rain. Winter robes were made from sea otter skins; ceremonial robes were made of mountain goat wool and cedar bark. Many of their homes were built of wooden planks because trees were abundant. From logs they made dugout canoes and carved wooden masks for ceremonies. In the central and northern regions, the people carved totem poles that displayed tribal and family histories. They placed these at the front of houses, gravesites, and other important places.

Northwest Coast people carved wooden shaker rattles to use in ceremonies. Some were plain, some were made into the shapes of animals. Some were carved with family crests and designs on them. Clapper rattles were made from seashells, deer hooves, or bird beaks strung together on a hoop.

The Tlingit song "Goo-soo Wa.e" ("Where Are You?") is owned by the Raven T'akdeintan clan. It is sung after the people of one village have trekked a long way to visit another village, or crossed a tough river, or made it though a rough storm in a canoe. It begins with a child from the Eagle clan standing and singing, "Where are you? Come to me!" and following with the names of the houses of the opposite Raven clan. A Raven would then stand to dance and sing, "Here I am, here I am." These call-and-response gestures offer social and spiritual balance among the people. Today, the song is used to acknowledge all clans who dance in honor of their fathers' clan.

As in all cultures, people of the Northwest sing lullabies to their children. "Haagú S'é" (A Boy's Lullaby) is a Tlingit song that encourages little boys to grow up to be good fishermen.

Charles Joseph, Kaal.átk' *(Tlingit)* (1892–1985). Born in Lituya Bay, Alaska, a child of the L'uknaxh.adi clan, Charles Joseph, Kaal.átk' became a Kaagwaantaan elder. His musical abilities were recognized at an early age, and he was trained to be a song carrier for many clans. He taught as many of these songs as he could to the children attending the Sitka Native Education Program from 1976 to 1985, which has allowed them to be passed by the oral tradition to the next generation of Tlingit people.

Haagú S'é—A Boy's Lullaby

From Charles Joseph, Kaal.átk'

Haagú s'é, Haagú s'é
K'isáani heeyahaa
téel' aaheix oowax'aká
wa.éich gwaa eeyataká
hee eenaa aa, hee eenaa aa
hee eenaa aa, hee eenaa aa

Come here a moment, little boys.
Dog salmon are resting
By the log jam in the stream.
You can go spear one!

From Charles Joseph, Kaal.átk'. Used by permission.

CD track #4. Listen to "Haagú S'é" (A Boy's Lullaby), performed by Roby Littlefield. This lullaby encourages little boys to grow up to be good fishermen.

"Haagú S'é," from Charles Joseph, Kaal.átk'. Recorded and sung by Roby Littlefield at Dog Fish Camp on the *Tlingit Dléigoox' (Tlingit Lullabyes)* CD. ℗ 1998 Roby Littlefield. Used by permission.

Subarctic Region

This region reaches across the middle of present-day Canada from the Atlantic coast to the interior of Alaska. The terrain includes woodlands in the East and flat, open tundra in the West.

Traditionally, the people were hunter-gatherers living in small bands, migrating to follow the food. They hunted small game—including rabbit, fox, mink, beaver, squirrel, muskrat, and porcupine, and large game—caribou, moose, deer, bear, and musk ox. The many rivers and streams of this region were home to salmon, trout, perch, sturgeon, and whitefish and gave habitat for migrating ducks, geese, and other waterfowl. Traditional houses were shaped like cones and covered with caribou hide and birch bark. Some included brush or tree branches;

others were made with logs and wooden planks. The earliest people wore leg-
gings, coats, hats, gloves, and boots made from animal skins. They made snow-
shoes from bent wood and stretched animal hide, and canoes from peeled bark.

Many groups in this region have social gatherings called *potlatches* that bring
people together for singing, dancing, and feasting. Potlatches are held at important times—like marriages, the naming of an infant, bestowing family crests,
raising social standing, or remembering someone who has died. The Tutchone
tradition holds potlatches to celebrate good fortune, or a person's recovery from
illness. Singers and dancers compose their own songs about love, beauty, loneliness, or sadness when someone has died.

Dance of the Kutchă-Kutchi, 1851. Lithograph by A. H. Murray.
From *Arctic Searching Expedition* by Sir John Richardson.
Courtesy of Rasmuson Library, University of Alaska, Fairbanks.

The Ingalik celebrate the *Feast of the Animals' Souls* ceremony, which has
been passed down over many generations and includes songs, dances, fancy
clothing, and masks. The masked dancers imitate fish, animals, and the act of
hunting.

Evelyn Alexander *(Athabascan)* **(December 25, 1916–).** Born in Alaska, Evelyn
Alexander is a singer and drummer. She grew up in the village of Minto, where she
lived a subsistence lifestyle—fishing, hunting, and gathering food from the land and
waterways. She was recognized as a talented singer when she was a little girl. She
learned songs from her father, friends, and family; as an adult, she sometimes makes
up her own songs. She sings at potlatches and dances and teaches children how
to sing and dance. She beats a solo drum with a stick to accompany her singing.
Evelyn's songs tell about the people she's known, experiences she's had, and experiences of other people. She continues to sing and live in the traditional way in a small
village on the Yukon River.

The Tanana potlatch begins with a feast. During the meal, the guests of honor are given special foods and gifts, while songs are sung and speeches are given to thank the host and express appreciation. A *Potlatch Song* is sung by the hosts and opens the celebration. This is followed by *Sorry Songs,* accompanied by drums, which express the singers' sadness for a lost loved one. Many join the circle of dancers and remember lost loved ones. The *Dance Songs* follow and are livelier and happier with dancers acting out the words. Potlatch songs are shared among groups who trade and visit with each other.

Arctic Region

Inupiat (Eskimo) drummers and dancers. Photo by Teri Tibbett. Used by permission.

The Arctic region is at the very top of North America, from the eastern coast of present-day Newfoundland to the western coast of Alaska. The land is buried in snow and ice during much of the year. The winters are long and dark. The first people hunted sea mammals using boats made of wood covered with animal skin and they fished through holes in the ice using ivory hooks. The land provided musk ox, caribou, and some small game, including rabbits and foxes. Ducks and geese migrated in the summer. Berries, roots, and greens were gathered and stored for the long winters.

The Inuit (Eskimo) of Canada traditionally lived in icehouses in winter and in tents made of skins in the summer. The Inupiat (Eskimo) and Yup'ik (Eskimo) of Alaska lived in sod houses made of earth and driftwood and bone. Sled dogs were used throughout the Arctic for transportation and to haul food and supplies.

Arctic songs are often sung by dancers who illustrate the lyrics with hand and body movements. A song about hunting a walrus might include pretending to throw a harpoon. A song about riding in a boat might use fancy caribou-hair

John Pingayak *(Cup'ik* [Eskimo]*)* (November 5, 1948–). John Pinagyak, born in Alaska, is a Cup'ik singer, drummer, and dancer. He grew up twenty miles from the Bering Sea, where he has lived a subsistence lifestyle—fishing on the river and hunting sea mammals in the ocean. Besides hunting, he and his people eat greens, roots, and berries gathered from the land. John learned to perform the music of his ancestors from his grandfather, who taught him to sing and drum. Today, he still sings and drums and teaches Native Alaskan culture at the public school in Chevak, Alaska. He often travels out of the village to teach and perform for other people. He has written plays and many songs that relate to the native lifestyle. He is highly respected in Alaska for his music and knowledge of the native traditions.

dance fans to imitate paddling motions. Dancers imitate seals diving, birds flying, wolves running, people picking berries or hunting, and other experiences from day-to-day life. Song "duels" allowed two angry people to vent their feelings through singing and dancing.

Dancers from the Unangax̂ (Aleut) tradition imitate the sounds of seagulls while gracefully dancing in a way that imitates their flying. Living close to the ocean offers plenty of opportunity to observe seagulls and practice their singing and flying movements. Unangax̂ musicians accompany their songs with rattles, sticks, and drum.

Throat singing is performed by Inuit women who stand facing each other, breathing and repeating low sounds in a fast, pulsing, rhythm-song. Throat singing is a game to see who can go the longest without smiling or laughing.

♪ CD track #5. Listen to "The Spider Song," performed by John Pingayak, playing the frame drum with a stick.

"The Spider Song," sung by John Pingayak. Recorded by Milt Lee. ℗ 2000 Oyate Productions. Used by permission.

Hawaii Region

The eight major and minor islands of Hawaii lie in the middle of the Pacific Ocean between North America and Asia. The land is lush with food and materials for shelter. Early Hawaiians fished from boats with nets and gathered food from trees and plants. They ate raw fish, bananas, sweet potato, poi (made from taro root), palm hearts, papaya, and other tropical fruits. Before European explorers and settlers came to the Islands, the native people performed chants and songs accompanied by drums and other percussion instruments made from the materials that were around them.

The native people sang songs that were thankful and paid homage to important spirits. They sang so that the plants would grow large and strong, and they played music at dances and celebrations. "E Komo" is a traditional Hawaiian dance song that pays homage to Pele, the Goddess of Fire, and her creative forces.

E Komo

E komo ma loko a'o halema'uma'u
E mauna e pu'u e ola ola nei
E pele e pele e pele e pele
E pele e pele hua'ina hua'ina ku
Pahu pahu 'uha ma'i o ka lani 'ani
Pahu pahu 'uha ma'i o ka lani 'ani
Pahu pahu 'uha ma'i o ka lani 'ani
A ma mau ana!

(Spoken) He inoa no hi'iakai ka poli o pele!

Queen Lili`uokalani ruled Hawaii in the late 1800s. She was also a musician who expressed her deepest feelings about Hawaii and her people in her songs. She composed many beautiful songs and poems, including one of Hawaii's most memorable songs, *Aloha 'Oe.*

Pele, Goddess of Fire

♪ CD track #6. Listen to "E Komo," sung by Charles Ka'upu. This traditional dance song pays homage to Pele, the Goddess of Fire, and her creative forces. It is accompanied by an *ipu* (traditional gourd drum).

"E Komo," sung by Charles Ka'upu. Recorded by Milt Lee. ℗ 2000 Oyate Productions. Used by permission.

Charles Ka'upu *(Hawaiian)* (October 21, 1957–). Charles Ka'upu, a singer and player of traditional Hawaiian music, was born on the island of Oahu. He grew up learning Hawaiian chants and has performed them throughout his life. He plays the traditional gourd drum, the *ipu,* and the skin drum, the *pahu.* He is also a historian of Hawaii and Hawaiian music, teaching these subjects in college. He has directed programming for a Hawaiian radio station featuring all Hawaiian music as well as a syndicated radio show called *Island Sounds.* Some of the traditional songs he sings are "The Blessing Chant," "The Planting Song," "Kamaekamea," "Pele Song," and "Ipu Song." His music is featured on the Quiet Storm recording label, *www.quietstorm.com.*

Aloha 'Oe

By Queen Lili`uokalani

Ha`aheo kah uah ee nah pali,
Ke nihi a`e la i ka nahele,
Eh uhai anah paha ee kah leeko,
Pua aheehee lehua ah oh ukah.

Chorus: Aloha `o-ee, aloha `o-ee,
Eh khe onaona noho ee-kah leepo,
One fond embrace a ho`ee ah`eh au,
Until we meet again.

Proudly by the rain in the cliff,
Creeping silently and softly up the forest,
Seeking perhaps the bud flower,
Ahihi lehua of the inland.

Chorus: Farewell to thee, farewell to thee,
Sweet fragrance dwelling in the dark forest.
One fond embrace before I leave now,
Until we meet again.

**Queen Lili`uokalani** *(Hawaiian)* **(1838–1917).** Queen Lili`uokalani was born in Hawaii, the daughter of High Chief Kapaakea and the Chiefess Keohokalole. As a child, she attended a school run by American missionaries and learned to speak English. She began studying music at an early age and played the piano, organ, ukulele, and guitar, and was an expert in sight-reading music. During her life she composed over 160 melodies and chants, including one of the four Hawaiian national anthems. She was inspired to write *Aloha 'Oe* after watching two people in love say goodbye to each other. It was also her farewell song to her people when the United States took control of her beloved islands in 1898.

Queen Lili`uokalani.
Courtesy of the Maui Historical
Society. Used by permission.

Bonus Challenge: Which Native American Group Lived Closest to You? Have you ever wondered what was going on two hundred years ago on the very spot where you are now standing? What did the land look like without houses, streets, or buildings? What kinds of trees and plants were growing? What kinds of animals roamed the land? Chances are, Native Americans were living nearby. Maybe they were passing through on their way to hunting grounds. Maybe they were setting up shelters in small camps. Maybe they were farming or forming a dance circle under the stars with singers and drummers. Discover which Native American group lived, or lives, closest to where you live now. Refer to the **Native American Music Regions** map to find out. Then search the Internet or library to answer the following questions: (1) What is the name of the tribe that lived (or still lives) nearest you? (2) What was their traditional language and what were some of their customs, traditional food sources, and shelter materials? (3) Describe the most interesting thing about this tribe or group. (4) Describe what you discovered about the music of the tribe. Present a written or oral report.

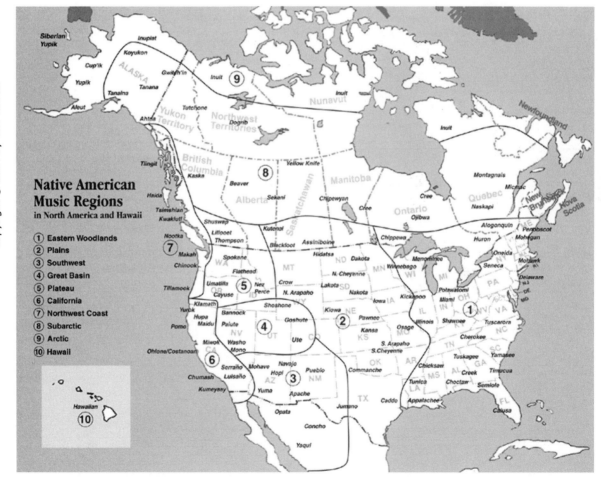

Name _____ Date _____

Native American Music Regions Quiz

Instructions: After reading the **Native American Music Regions** student handout, answer these questions (use back of the page if necessary).

1. What are the ten Native American music regions? Give one characteristic of each.

_____

_____

_____

_____

_____

_____

_____

_____

2. Which region seems most interesting to you? Explain why.

_____

_____

_____

_____

_____

Native American Music Regions Quiz:
Answer Key

1. What are the ten Native American music regions? Give one characteristic of each.

   EASTERN WOODLANDS
   PLAINS
   SOUTHWEST
   GREAT BASIN AND PLATEAU
   CALIFORNIA
   NORTHWEST COAST
   SUBARCTIC
   ARCTIC
   HAWAII

2. Which region seems most interesting to you? Explain why.

   STUDENTS PROVIDE REASONABLE ANSWERS.

♪ Lesson 4. Contemporary Native American Music

Lesson Overview

Contemporary Native Americans compose and perform many styles of music, including traditional music, country, jazz, rock, rap, and popular. Many have kept alive the songs of their ancestors and are still performing them today for sacred and other private occasions. Others are mixing traditional music and instruments with modern rhythms, chords, lyrics, and instruments. Native musicians today compose songs that express themes that reflect their concerns, lifestyle, and history.

Vocabulary. Contemporary music, hybrid, traditional, powwow, compose, melody, steel guitar, slack key, political songs, lyrics, accompaniment, genre.

Purpose. To introduce contemporary Native American music styles and musicians.

Preparation. Read the student handout **Contemporary Native American Music** to familiarize yourself with the material. Preview the CD samples (see cues in student handout) and have the CD ready for playing for the students. Consider bringing in additional selections of music from other sources to expand the music examples for this lesson. Be prepared to do some or all of the following activities. Also make sure that each student has a music notebook for keeping handouts and activity sheets.

Materials

- **Contemporary Native American Music** student handout *(following)*
- **Contemporary Native American Music Quiz** *(following)*
- **Contemporary Native American Music Quiz Answer Key** *(following)*
- **Music Vocabulary** activity sheet *(Appendix)*
- **My Opinion Page** activity sheet *(Appendix)*
- **How to Teach a Song** teacher guide *(Appendix)*
- **Songs as Poetry** activity sheet *(Appendix)*
- **Great American Musicians!** activity sheet *(Appendix)*
- **Music on the Map** activity sheet *(Appendix)*
- **Music notebooks**
- **CD music** examples on accompanying CD; cues in student handout
- **Additional music selections**

Activities

- Pass out the **Contemporary Native American Music** handout for students to read silently or aloud as a group. Afterwards, have students put the handout in their music notebooks. *(Link to language arts, history, geography, social studies.)*

- Give the **Contemporary Native American Music Quiz** to assess student understanding of the lesson.

- Go over the music vocabulary at the top of the student handout before or after reading the text. Refer to the glossary for definitions. *Suggestion:* Include these words in a regular class vocabulary lesson, or pass out flashcards with a vocabulary word on one side and the definition on the other and allow students to drill each other. Use the **Music Vocabulary** activity sheet to write out definitions. *(Link to language arts.)*

- Offer the **Vocabulary Challenge.** Students pick some or all of the words in this lesson's vocabulary list to use in a paragraph, essay, short story, or poem. *(Link to language arts.)*

- **Discuss.** Before reading the student handout, discuss what students already know about contemporary Native American music. Consider reviewing all the lessons in this unit. Read the student handout for this lesson and discuss it again, letting students add what they've learned. *(Link to language arts, social studies.)*

- Offer the **Bonus Challenge: Who Were Crazy Horse and Chief Joseph?** *Answer:* Crazy Horse (1845–1877), an Olagla Lakota (Sioux) born in present-day Nebraska, was a well-respected chief who earned a reputation as a skillful warrior passionate about preserving his people's traditional way of life. When the U.S. War Department ordered all Lakota bands to move to reservations in 1876, Crazy Horse led the resistance to avoid this, and later joined with Chief Sitting Bull to defeat General Custer at the Battle of Little Bighorn in 1876. Chief Joseph (1840–1904), Ni Míi Puu (Nez Percé) born in present-day Oregon, was a well-respected man who lived in peace with the nearby settlers. In 1877, when the U.S. government ordered his people to move to a reservation, Chief Joseph resisted and led his people away toward Idaho. The U.S. Cavalry followed and caught up with them, forcing Chief Joseph and his people to surrender and eventually move to a reservation in Oklahoma (called The Trail of Tears). Many years later Chief Joseph and his people returned to the Pacific Northwest but were spread out among many reservations and not allowed to live as they had. *Suggestion:* Consider offering extra credit to students who do the bonus challenge. *(Link to history.)*

Extension Activities

For step-by-step directions, see the appendix.

- **My Opinion Page.** Offer students a chance to freely express their own opinions about the music they hear. *(Link to language arts, critical thinking.)*

- **Sing a Song.** Students learn a song from this lesson. *Suggested song:* "Witchi Tai To." Play along with drums and rattles. *(Link to singing, language arts, rhythm, melody.)*

- **Songs as Poetry.** Examine the lyrics of songs for their poetic nature. *(Link to language arts.)*

- **Illustrate the Music.** Students illustrate a song or piece of music by drawing or painting their ideas of what the music "looks" like visually. *(Link to language arts, visual arts.)*

- **Great American Musicians!** Introduce students to American musicians whose talents have made them notable. *(Link to language arts, history.)*

- **Music on the Map.** Create a map and legend showing musically important places, such as musicians' birthplaces and music hot spots mentioned in the lesson. *(Link to geography.)*

- **Invite a Music Expert.** Invite a Native American musician to visit your class and share either traditional or contemporary music with the students. You may locate these musicians through the Internet, local tribal groups, local arts organizations, friends, and parents. Also consider taking students to hear a Native American music or dance performance, or to attend a powwow.

- Because of copyright issues, modern songs are difficult to obtain for the accompanying CD. Consider bringing in **additional selections of music** from other sources to expand the music examples for this lesson. Note the songs mentioned in each musician's biography for ideas. Search the Internet, library, local music store, or your own music collection for the music.

Name _____ Date _____

Contemporary Native American Music

Vocabulary: contemporary music, hybrid, traditional, powwow, compose, melody, steel guitar, slack key, political songs, lyrics, accompaniment, genre

In modern times, Native Americans perform both traditional music and **contemporary music.** Contemporary songs often reflect modern themes—remembering a famous person or event, describing what it's like to live on a reservation or work in a city, or expressing an opinion. Contemporary Native American music is country music, rock music, blues, jazz, popular, traditional, rap, and more. It might mix skin drums with electric drums, wooden flutes with saxophones, or string bows with electric guitars. Much of today's Native American music is a mixture, or **hybrid,** of musical styles that blend both **traditional** and contemporary elements.

Powwow Music

A **powwow** is a gathering of Native American tribes who get together to drum, sing, dance, feast, and give gifts. The people dress in regalia, perform traditional and contemporary dances, and spend time socializing. Powwows are held across America—in fairgrounds, convention centers, cow pastures, and open fields. They welcome people from all cultures. It is through these intertribal gatherings that many Native Americans stay in touch with their heritage and keep alive their traditions for future generations.

The Powwow Gathering. The powwow originated in the traditions of the Plains and Eastern Woodlands tribes. Powwows began as community events to express thanksgiving for abundance. In modern powwows there are contests for the best dances and the best dance clothing. Drum groups gather and beat large drums, singers sing both traditional and contemporary songs, and dancers dance. Socializing, feasting, and gift giving are important parts of the powwow.

Black Lodge Singers. *(Blackfeet).* The Black Lodge Singers are a twelve-member powwow drum group from Washington State who perform music from the northern plains. Their songs mix contemporary lyrics with traditional drumming and singing, and they sing in both their native language and English. The Black Lodge Singers beat a large sacred Buffalo drum to accompany their songs and the members **compose** their own music. Many of their songs tell about modern life; others are children's songs. Their leader, Kenny Scabby Robe, has composed many songs for children to help bring them back to the drum and their culture. Their albums include *Powwow Songs, Intertribal Powwow Songs, Round Dance Songs, Kids' Powwow Songs, Enter the Circle,* and *Tribute to the Elders.*

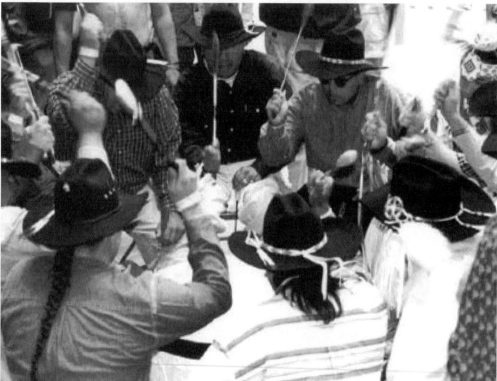

Powwow drummers. Photograph by Derek Matthews. Copyright © 2000 Derek Matthews. Courtesy of Gathering of Nations Powwow.

Arctic Music

People still gather in the Arctic on winter nights to dance, sing, drum, and socialize. Their songs tell of modern experiences—like getting stuck on the ice in a broken snowmobile, or taking a trip in a small plane to go play basketball, or winning at bingo. While the drummers drum and sing, the dancers tell stories with their hands and body movements.

At the Camai Festival in Alaska, singers, dancers, and drummers perform both their traditional and contemporary songs and dances. Native foods are served. Native-made arts, carvings, baskets, beadwork, and skin sewing are displayed and sold. The songs and dances make people happy. The festival is also an important social event for people of the region.

Native musicians from the Arctic are also combining traditional styles with modern instruments and styles. Susan Aglukark (born in 1971 in Manitoba, Canada) established a musical career by mixing traditional Inuk (Eskimo) chants with popular sounding **melodies.** *Pamyua,* from Alaska, combines elements of rock, funk, gospel, and rap, with traditional Yup'ik (Eskimo) influences.

Hawaiian Music

The **steel guitar** was invented by Hawaiian native Joseph Kekuku in the late 1890s. As its name implies, it is made of steel. It is played while being held on the lap. Players move a small bar up and down the strings to make the chords go up and down. Steel guitars make soothing and rhythmical music. This sound dominated Hawaiian music in the 1930s, and caught on later with mainland musicians who featured it in country music. It is still heard today in both Hawaiian and other contemporary music.

Slack key is a sweet and soulful finger-picking guitar style that draws from both Hawaiian and European traditions. The term *slack key* refers to when the strings of the guitar are loosened (or slackened) to change the pitch of the music. Slack key is said to be inspired by the oceans, volcanoes, mountains, and waterfalls of Hawaii. There are regional styles of slack key, with each island having its own style.

Gabby Pahinui was one of the most well-known modern slack key guitar players. His superb playing and sensitivity to the instrument created some of the most moving Hawaiian music in the last half of the twentieth century. Gabby Pahinui also helped to make slack key music popular all across America in the 1950s and 1960s.

Gabby Pahinui (Hawaiian) (April 22, 1921–1980). Gabby Pahinui, singer and slack key and steel guitar player, was born Charles Philip Pahinui in Hawaii. He learned to play music by ear (that is, by memorizing it) from a then-popular Hawaiian slack key guitar player. He later played in bands, both in Hawaii and on the mainland. Though he was well known as the Father of Modern Slack Key Guitar, Gabby was also master of the steel guitar and singer with a virtuosic singing voice. Some of his albums are *Brown Gabby, Best of Gabby Pahinui,* and *Gabby Pahinui Hawaiian Band.*

Native Women Musicians

Native American women also perform contemporary music. In the 1960s, Buffy Sainte-Marie became well known for her **political songs** that addressed the Vietnam War and the mistreatment of Native Americans. She has worked throughout her career to advocate for native people. Her song "Bury My Heart at Wounded Knee" addresses the relationship between the U.S. government and Native American people.

Joanne Shenandoah is a Native American singer, songwriter, performer, and composer. Her music blends ancient songs and chants of the Iroquois with traditional and contemporary instrumentation. Her **lyrics** reflect on Native American philosophy and culture. Shenandoah has performed at the White House, recorded several CDs, and was chosen Best Female Artist of 1998 and 1999 and Best Native Artist of the Year 2002 at the Native American Music Awards.

Joanne Shenandoah. Photograph by Jason Mashie.
Courtesy of Silver Wave Records.

Buffy Sainte-Marie *(Cree)* **(February 21, 1941–).** Buffy Sainte-Marie, singer-songwriter, activist, and digital artist, was born in Saskatchewan, Canada. She became famous for her protest songs in the 1960s, but in the mid-1970s she quit performing to raise her son and at that time became a regular guest on the children's show *Sesame Street.* She later returned to performing music and increased her efforts to help native people. She has performed around the world and at home in the cities, towns, and reservations of North America. She has written an award-winning film score and recorded many pieces of music. She teaches electronic music, songwriting, film scoring, Indian women's issues, and government, and has been recognized for her sophisticated digital art. Some of her songs are "Universal Soldier" (1963), "Now That the Buffalo's Gone" (1967), "I'm Gonna Be a Country Girl Again" (1968), and "Moonshot" (1973).

Lesson 4. Student Handout continued

> **Mary Youngblood** *(Seminole-Aleut)* **(June 24, 1958–).** California-born Mary Youngblood is a flutist. She learned to play piano, violin, classical flute, and guitar—all by the age of ten. She performed in choirs, musicals, bands, and orchestras throughout her school years. In her adult years she learned to play the sacred flute and has made CD recordings of Native American flute music, recorded soundtracks for movies and television, and won music awards, including Flutist of the Year at the Native American Music Awards. Her music has been described as "liquid poetry." Her albums include *The Offering* (1998) and *Heart of the World* (1999).

Mary Youngblood is a flute player. She was one of the first women to gain success performing on Native American flute, which was traditionally a man's instrument. Mary's playing is melodious and gentle. She weaves contemporary themes with traditional sounds, and composes her own music.

Country, Rock, Jazz, and Rap

Native American musicians perform a variety of contemporary styles from Navajo country musicians performing at fairs, rodeos, and dances to Muskogee blues musicians mixing native traditions with blues and jazz to Medicine Dream and Indigenous, two Native American rock bands.

In 1971, jazz saxophone player Jim Pepper recorded "Witchi-Tai-To," a chant he learned from his grandfather, mixing it with jazz chords and rhythms. The song was a hit on popular radio stations across America, one of the first Native American songs to do so.

Jerry Alfred and his group the Medicine Beat mix traditional singing and instruments with electric guitar, bass guitar, and harmonica. He was told at an early age that he would be "a keeper of the songs" and that his music would be heard around the world. He grew up to sing both traditional and contemporary native music and the prediction has come true: his music *is* heard around the world. One of his songs, "The Warrior Song," tells the story of a man whose grandmother put the spirit of the wolf and the bear into him.

> **Jim Pepper** *(Kaw-Creek)* **(June 18, 1941–1992).** Jim Pepper, born in Oregon, was a jazz saxophone player, singer, and songwriter. As a young boy he traveled with his father to powwow gatherings where he was exposed to the music and dancing of his father's tribe. At age fifteen he started playing saxophone and found that he liked jazz best. Jim made music his lifelong career, composing many songs with elements of both traditional and contemporary music. His great talent as a musician and composer gave him the opportunity to tour the world and play with other famous jazz musicians. His albums include *Pepper's Powwow* (1971), *Comin' and Goin'* (1983), *Art of the Duo* (1989), and *Remembrance* (1990).

Copyright © 2004 by Teri Tibbett

Jerry Alfred *(Northern Tutchone)* **(September 11, 1955–).** Jerry Alfred was born in the Yukon, Canada. He is a singer, songwriter, and guitar player. When he was three years old, a medicine man heard him singing and drumming on his tin plate and predicted that his music would be heard around the world. He was named "Song Keeper" and went on to learn the traditional songs of his people. While still a boy he sang in the choir at residential school, and taught himself how to play guitar. Jerry sings in his native language and through his music has helped preserve both his language and culture. With his band the Medicine Beat, he has produced albums of music and won several awards. His recorded collections include *Etsi Shon (Grandfather Song), Nendaa (Go Back),* and *Kehlonn (At the Foot of Grandmother's Bed).*

John Trudell is a Native American poet who uses the spoken word, backed by instrumental music, to express his views. He draws attention to political issues and issues affecting native people and plays on general themes in the human condition. His musical **accompaniment** includes traditional Native American drums and chants, as well as modern instruments—guitars, bass, and drums—with chords and rhythms from blues and rock music.

Litefoot is a Native American rap artist whose raps reflect images and realities of contemporary Native Americans, both in urban life and on the reservations. He has toured the world and made films, but he focuses particularly on performances for native youths living on reservations.

Vision Quest

Lyrics and music by Litefoot

I got a vision, it's more of a quest,
Cuz my people get arrested, my tribe is infested.
I lay my head down woke up in an ancient burial ground.
Don't make a sound.
It's scary in this sacred cemetery.
Go to the spot where Crazy Horse was buried,
I pray to our God rise up his spirit.
A faint voice becomes bold; I can hear it:
Litefoot, you must take heed.
Every Indian brought down I bleed.
Make an example everyone will follow:
Put down the bottle and never take a swallow.
Times have changed, the land looks strange,
And all of our people are bound in chains.
The path of righteousness is real narrow,
Your words are your bow, your pen is your arrow.

I woke up in a puddle of sweat,
Trippin' off the things that Crazy Horse said.

For instance, I feel the spirit's persistence,
Then I questioned my very existence.
Is there an ultimate plan? Am I the man?
A crutch for my nation so my people can stand?
Do I have the words to educate the youth?
Am I a fabricated hero or the burden of proof?
Then a powerful thought came to me:
The spirit of Crazy Horse ran through me.
I spoke his words; the vision was unblurred.
Powerful people pointed their fingers! Absurd!
I'm cured; healed to the fullest.
Fight with your mind, resist and we can do this.
No drugs. No gangs under arrest.
I had my vision. I begin my quest.

Let's sit in a sweat and all join hands,
And pray to these spirits all across the lands.
Show me the plan so I can lead,
Indeed stop the prejudice, hate, and greed.
Plant my seed, uplift hope to raise,
A child that gets praised and sees brighter days,
And teach him all of our beliefs.
Introduce him to Joseph the Chief.
Please my son, put down the gun.
Stand up and fight and refuse to run.
I make this your quest. It's your vision,
Your mission. Speak out to all the prisons,
And every Indian Nation,
Make a stop at every reservation.
Every minute of your time invest.
Litefoot, my son, that's your vision quest.

Litefoot. Copyright © 1998 Red Vinyl Records.

Litefoot (*Ani Yunwiya [Cherokee]*). Rapper, songwriter, musician, and actor, Litefoot was born G. Paul Davis in Oklahoma of Cherokee heritage. He began making his own records after a recording company turned down his Native American rap. He went on to make many recordings on his own label, Red Vinyl Records. Litefoot starred as Little Bear in the movie *Indian in the Cupboard* (1995), has been in other films and TV shows, and has made several albums of rap music. Litefoot's "no drugs, no alcohol" message encourages young people to grow up strong, with self-respect and honor. His recorded collections include *The Money* (1992), *Seein' Red* (1994), *Good Day to Die* (1996), *The Life & Times* (1998), *Rez Affiliated* (1999), *Tribal Boogie* (2000), and *The Messenger* (2002).

Since 1998 the Native American Music Awards have honored Native American musicians in **genres** ranging from traditional music to contemporary rock and rap. The Grammy Awards offered a Native American music category for the first time in 2000.

Bonus Challenge: Who Were Crazy Horse and Chief Joseph? Who were Crazy Horse and Chief Joseph, the people mentioned in Litefoot's song? Look for information on them in an encyclopedia, at the library, or on the Internet. Write a report on one or both of the men, presenting it either in written form or orally with pictures and props.

♪ CD track #7. Listen to "She Watches Them Play," composed and performed by Mary Youngblood, played on a contemporary Native American flute.

> "She Watches Them Play," written and performed by Mary Youngblood. From *The Offering* CD on Silver Wave Records. © and ℗ 1998 Mary Youngblood. Used by permission.

♪ CD cut #34. Listen to "Witchi-Tai-To," by Jim Pepper. This song mixes a traditional chant with jazz chords and saxophone.

> "Witchi-Tai-To," written by Jim Pepper. © 1968 Jim Pepper. Courtesy of Floy Pepper. ℗ Tutu Records. *www.jazzrecords.com*.

♪ CD track #35. Listen to "Vision Quest," by Litefoot, an example of Native American rap.

> "Vision Quest," written and performed by Litefoot. © and ℗ 1998 Red Vinyl Records. Used by permission.

Name _____   Date _____

Contemporary Native American Music
Quiz

Instructions: After reading the **Contemporary Native American Music** student handout, answer these questions (use back of the page if necessary).

1. What are the differences between Native American **traditional** and **contemporary music?**

2. How are contemporary Native Americans mixing traditional music with contemporary music?

3. Describe a powwow gathering.

4. How have Native Americans used **political songs** to communicate political issues?

Contemporary Native American Music
Quiz: Answer Key

1. What are the differences between Native American **traditional** and **contemporary music?**

   TRADITIONAL MUSIC HAS BEEN PASSED FROM GENERATION TO GENERATION. CONTEMPORARY MUSIC IS CREATED IN MODERN TIMES. TRADITIONAL INSTRUMENTS INCLUDE DRUMS, FLUTES, AND RATTLES. CONTEMPORARY INSTRUMENTS INCLUDE ELECTRIC GUITARS, SAXOPHONES, AND SO ON.

2. How are contemporary Native Americans mixing traditional music with contemporary music?

   THEY ARE MIXING SKIN DRUMS WITH ELECTRIC DRUMS, WOODEN FLUTES WITH SAXOPHONES, STRING BOWS WITH ELECTRIC GUITARS. THEY ARE MIXING TRADITIONAL CHANTS WITH MODERN LYRICS AND TRADITIONAL DRUMMING WITH ROCK OR JAZZ RHYTHMS.

3. Describe a powwow gathering.

   A POWWOW IS AN INTERTRIBAL GATHERING OF NATIVE AMERICANS WHO GET TOGETHER TO DRUM, SING, DANCE, FEAST, GIVE GIFTS. PEOPLE DRESS IN REGALIA AND PERFORM DANCES. CONTESTS ARE HELD FOR THE BEST DANCES AND CLOTHING. DRUMMERS SIT AROUND ONE DRUM AND BEAT IT WHILE THE DANCERS AND SINGERS PERFORM.

4. How have Native Americans used **political songs** to communicate political issues?

   BUFFY SAINTE-MARIE SANG POLITICAL SONGS ABOUT THE VIETNAM WAR AND THE MISTREATMENT OF NATIVE AMERICANS. HER SONG "BURY MY HEART AT WOUNDED KNEE" ADDRESSES THE RELATIONSHIP BETWEEN THE U.S. GOVERNMENT AND NATIVE AMERICAN PEOPLE. JOHN TRUDELL IS A NATIVE AMERICAN POET WHO USES THE SPOKEN WORD BACKED BY INSTRUMENTAL MUSIC TO EXPRESS HIS VIEWS AND DRAW ATTENTION TO POLITICAL ISSUES, ISSUES THAT AFFECT NATIVE AMERICANS, AND THEMES RELATED TO THE HUMAN CONDITION.

European-American Music

Contents

Unit Two: Overview

This unit explores the music of European-Americans, from its origins in North America in the seventeenth century through its evolution into the twenty-first century. The first European-American songs were brought to North America by the first explorers, who were followed by the early settlers and the many immigrants who have made this continent their home. Explorers brought songs from their homelands and composed new ones to describe the world they saw and the experiences they had in the Americas. Sailors sang sea songs and work songs and songs that reminded them of home. The early colonists sang sacred songs from *Psalters* (written books that contained the Psalms) brought from Europe. They also sang secular songs from the folk traditions of their homelands handed down to them through the oral tradition. After some time, the colonists began to compose their own sacred songs and secular songs, reflecting their language and sentiments about living in the new land.

Folk music expresses the experiences of ordinary people and what happens to them in their day-to-day lives. Folk songs may be love songs, work songs, lullabies, historical songs, or memorial songs. Music from the British Isles, which came to the Appalachian Mountains with the earliest settlers, was transformed into a style that came to be called mountain music. Early mountain music was played on fiddles, guitars, banjos, dulcimers, and mandolins, and it reflected not only the experiences of the people themselves but also their histories and legends.

Other folk styles developed throughout North America in places where people settled and became isolated. Cajun music, a lively style of folk music played with fiddles, guitar, accordion, and triangle, evolved in the bayou country of Louisiana based on the traditions of their French-Canadian forefathers. Klezmer is Jewish dance music that originated in Eastern Europe; it is played on a variety of wind and stringed instruments, often dominated by the clarinet. As North Americans divided into nations, they sang patriotic songs that expressed their sense of unity and pride.

Popular music was heard on the theatrical stages and in the homes of Americans as they gained more wealth and free time for entertainment. Early popular songs ranged in style from minstrel music to Broadway show tunes. Early popular and stage music expressed the feelings, ideas, and sentimental stories of a budding American culture.

Early American classical composers and musicians used the orchestral instruments of Europe and the rules of European music to compose American orchestral music and opera. They used American themes and landscapes to create classical music that was uniquely American. American operas became American stories told in song.

Over time, as the European influences began to fade and Americans developed their own way of doing things in their new land, American music became a melting pot of musical styles from around the world. Today, the music we call American has roots not only in European traditions but in African, Latin, Asian, and Middle Eastern traditions as well.

This unit explores the contributions made by European-Americans to North American music.

♪ Lesson 5. Colonial Music: Sacred and Secular

Lesson Overview

The first European settlements in North America were settled by both religious and nonreligious people. Thus, early colonial music was a mixture of both sacred and secular music. The first religious songs came from *Psalters* brought from Europe, but over time the songs changed as the American colonists composed their own hymns using language and themes familiar to them. Colonists also sang folk songs from their homelands; these too changed over time as they adopted American themes and attitudes.

Vocabulary. Sacred songs, Psalms, *Psalters,* line singing, Usual Way, Regular Singing, hymns, hymnals, shape-note singing, melody, unison, pitches, harmony singing, Sacred Harp singing, a cappella, secular songs, folk songs, ballads.

Purpose. To introduce some of the early music of colonial North America.

Preparation. Read the student handout **Colonial Music: Sacred and Secular** to familiarize yourself with the material. Preview the CD samples (cues in student handout) and have the CD ready for playing with the students. Be prepared to do some or all of the following activities. Also make sure that each student has a music notebook for keeping handouts and activity sheets.

Materials

- **Colonial Music: Sacred and Secular** student handout *(following)*
- **Colonial Music Quiz** *(following)*
- **Colonial Music Quiz Answer Key** *(following)*
- **Music Vocabulary** activity sheet *(Appendix)*
- **My Opinion Page** activity sheet *(Appendix)*
- **How to Teach a Song** teacher guide *(Appendix)*
- **Songs as Poetry** activity sheet *(Appendix)*
- **Music on the Map** activity sheet *(Appendix)*
- **Music notebooks**
- **CD music** examples on accompanying CD; cues in student handout
- **Additional music selections**

Activities

- Pass out the **Colonial Music: Sacred and Secular** handout for students to read silently or aloud as a group. Afterwards, have students put the handout in their music notebooks. *(Link to language arts, history, geography, social studies.)*

- Give the **Colonial Music Quiz** to assess student understanding.

- Go over the music vocabulary at the top of the student handout before or after reading the text. Refer to the glossary for definitions. *Suggestion:* Include these words in a regular class vocabulary lesson, or pass out flashcards with a vocabulary word on one side and the definition on the other and allow students to drill each other. Use the **Music Vocabulary** activity sheet to write out definitions. *(Link to language arts.)*

- Have students take the **Vocabulary Challenge.** Students pick some or all of the words in this lesson's vocabulary list to use in a paragraph, essay, short story, or poem. *(Link to language arts.)*

- **Discuss.** Before reading the student handout, discuss what students already know about the colonies and colonial music. Then read the student handout and discuss it again, letting students add what they've learned. *(Link to language arts, social studies.)*

- Experience **Regular Singing Versus Usual Way Singing.** The goal of this activity is to compare and contrast these two early American styles of learning and singing music. *Step 1:* Begin with a discussion, asking students to describe the Regular Singers' point of view and then the Usual Way point of view described in student handout. Regular Singing is reading and writing music. Usual Way Singing is listening and singing by memory or "by ear." Consider dividing the class into two groups to debate each method. *Step 2:* On the board or on a piece of paper, write the heading "Regular Singing" and list the pros and cons of learning to read and write music under it. Then write "Usual Way Singing" and list pros and cons of learning music by listening and repeating. *Suggestion:* Remind students that there is value in both styles of learning music. Musical masterpieces are created and performed by people who read and write music and by those who do not.

Extension Activities

For step-by-step directions and activity sheets, see the appendix.

- **My Opinion Page.** Offer students a chance to freely express their own opinions about the music they hear. *(Link to language arts, critical thinking.)*

- **Sing a Song.** Learn a simple colonial song from this lesson. *Suggested songs:* "Amsterdam No. 84" or "Old Man Who Lived in the Woods." *(Link to singing, language arts, rhythm, melody.)*

- **Songs as Poetry.** Examine the lyrics of songs for their poetic nature. *[Link to language arts.]*
- **Illustrate the Music.** Students illustrate a song or piece of music by drawing, coloring, or painting their ideas of what the music "looks" like visually. *[Link to language arts, visual arts.]*
- **Music on the Map.** Students create a map and legend showing musically important places, such as musicians' birthplaces and the music hot spots mentioned in the lesson. *[Link to geography.]*
- Consider bringing in **additional selections of music** from other sources to expand the examples for this lesson. Search the Internet, library, or local CD store.

Name _____ Date _____

Puritans singing

Colonial Music: Sacred and Secular

Vocabulary: sacred songs, Psalms, Psalters, line singing, Usual Way, Regular Singing, hymns, hymnals, shape-note singing, melody, unison, pitches, harmony singing, Sacred Harp singing, a cappella, secular songs, folk songs, ballads

The countries of Europe include England, Ireland, Scotland, France, Belgium, Denmark, Germany, Norway, Sweden, Spain, Italy, and Portugal. The first European visitors to America were explorers who traveled by ship to find new lands and resources for their native countries—resources like gold, fish, and spices. The early explorers sang songs about their homelands and about their experiences. Sailors sang about the sea and life on sailing ships. When the first permanent European settlers arrived in North America in the early 1600s, they brought with them the music of their birthplace. Over time, they began to compose new music that reflected their new lives in America.

Sacred Songs

Many of America's colonists were religious people who had left their homelands to live in a place where they could practice their religions freely. Their songs inspired and uplifted them as they built new lives in the new land. The first **sacred songs** sung by the colonists were called **Psalms;** these are songs taken from King David's poems in the Christian Bible. The Psalms were written in books called *Psalters* brought from Europe; the *Psalters* used old-fashioned language and difficult-to-read music notation.

Many colonists did not know how to read and write music, so they could not read the music written in the *Psalters.* Instead, they learned to sing "by ear," or by memory, using **line singing.** Line singing is when a leader sings out the first line of a song and the congregation (or chorus) echoes it back. Through line singing, people learned the music by hearing it and then repeating it. This style of singing became known as the **Usual Way.**

Eventually, some colonists formed music schools and traveled the countryside to teach others how to read and write music. Their style of singing became known as **Regular Singing,** based on a method of reading and writing music. However, there were plenty of people who liked line singing and didn't want to learn to read music. They preferred learning by listening and repeating, as they always had done. The two groups disagreed about which was the better way to learn music and this has been an argument ever since.

Regular Singing = reading and writing music
Usual Way = listening and repeating music

As American colonists left behind their European traditions, they developed new ways of doing things. They began writing their own sacred music, using simpler language to express their feelings and emotions. These new American-style sacred songs became known as **hymns.** American hymns used language that resembled more closely the way American people spoke. The hymns were soon published in books called **hymnals,** which became popular in early colonial churches.

Shape-Note Singing

One of the sacred music styles to develop with the colonists was **shape-note singing.** Shape-note music is written in different shapes to represent different pitches. For example, a triangle-shaped note represents *fa* in the musical scale, an oval-shaped note represents *sol,* a square shape represents *la,* and a diamond shape represents *mi.* Shape-note music was created by music teachers who wanted to make it easier for people to learn to read music. They published hymnals and delivered them throughout the colonies. The first shape-note book was printed in 1801. Titled the *Easy Instructor,* it was written by William Smith and William Little.

In the early days of shape-note singing, all the singers sang the **melody** of the song in **unison,** which means that everyone sang together on the same **pitches.** Over time, however, congregations began to practice **harmony singing,** which is when people sing on different pitches at the same time. *The Sacred Harp* book, compiled by Benjamin Franklin White in 1844, was the first hymnal to include harmony singing. Because of the book, the style became known as **Sacred Harp singing.** Traditionally, Sacred Harp singers sat in a group in the shape of a square, facing one another, so their voices could be heard by all. The singers took turns acting as leader, selecting songs from the *Sacred Harp* book, and standing in the middle of the room leading the rhythm with a hand. The people sang **a cappella,** which means there were no instruments to accompany them, and the sessions would last eight to ten hours at a time. After the singing, it was the tradition to serve a potluck dinner, with everyone sharing food and conversation. This tradition is still alive today in parts of North America.

"Amsterdam No. 84," composed in 1742 by Robert Seagraves, is an example of a Sacred Harp song popular among the colonists.

Amsterdam No. 84

By Robert Seagraves

Vocables
Rise my soul and stretch thy wings,
Thy better portion trace.
Rise from all terrestrial things
T'wards heav'n, thy native place.
Sun and moon and stars decay,
Time shall soon this earth remove.
Rise my soul and haste away
To seats prepared above.
Rivers to the ocean run
Nor stay in all their course.
Fire ascending seeks the sun,
Both speed them to their source.
So a soul that's born of God
Pants to view His glor'ous face,
Upwards tends to His abode
To rest in His embrace.

From *The Sacred Harp.* Copyright © 1991, Sacred Harp Publishing Company.
Used by permission.

"Amsterdam No. 84," an example of shape-note singing.
© 1991 Sacred Harp Publishing Company. Used by permission.

Secular Songs

Many settlers moved to America to be free to work where they wanted, live how they wanted, and make their own decisions about their lives. They sang the songs they knew from their homelands and their childhoods, describing the lives and histories they left behind. These nonreligious songs are called **secular songs.**

The earliest European-American secular songs were **folk songs.** Folk songs may best be described as music sung by everyday people about their everyday lives. They tell stories about falling in love or being betrayed in love. They tell about the person who made everyone laugh, or the one who made everyone angry. Folk songs are happy songs, sad songs, work songs, and songs about life.

The earliest folk songs sung in America were **ballads**—actually stories told in song. Ballads tell of sea battles and land battles and monsters defeated. They tell love stories and stories of courageous men and women. American scholar Francis James Child traveled throughout North America collecting the old folk ballads that originally came from the British Isles. He discovered 305 songs and put them into a book called *The English and Scottish Popular Ballads.* The book includes some of America's earliest European-American secular music.

Francis James Child (February 1, 1825–1896). Francis James Child, born in Massachusetts, grew up in a poor family and attended public schools. However, he was soon recognized for his intelligence and eventually attended Harvard University, where he later became Harvard's first professor of English and a specialist in early English language and literature. He collected ballad books in many languages and corresponded with scholars around the world on the subject. He also composed his own ballads. Francis Child is best known for his travels throughout rural America in the late 1800s, when he collected more than three hundred ballads that had originated in the British Isles. These ballads have come to be known as the "Child Ballads."

"The Old Man Who Lived in the Woods" is a song that originally came from the British Isles but changed over time to describe life in America. It was an early American favorite because it painted a humorous picture of the hard work the settlers had to do every day. The song tells the story of a settler who exchanged jobs with his wife for one day.

The Old Man Who Lived in the Woods

There was an old man who lived in the woods,
As you shall plainly see,
Who said he could do more work in a day
Than his wife could do in three.
With all my heart, the old woman said,
But then you must allow
That you must do my work for a day
And I'll go follow the plow.

You must milk the tiny cow,
Lest she should go dry,
And you must feed the little pigs
That live in yonder sty.
You must watch the speckled hen
For fear she lays astray.
And not forget the spool of yarn
That I spin every day.

The old woman took the staff in her hand
And went to follow the plow.
The old man took the pail on his head
And went to milk the cow.
But Tiny she winked and Tiny she blinked,
And Tiny she tossed her nose.
And Tiny she gave him a kick on the shins
'Til the blood ran down to his toes.

Lesson 5. Student Handout continued

Then whoa Tiny, and so Tiny
My little cow stand still.
If I ever milk you again he said
It will be against my will.

And then he went to feed the pigs
That lived within the sty.
The old sow ran against his legs
And threw him into the mire.

And then he watched the speckled hen
Lest she might lay astray,
But he quite forgot the spool of yarn
That his wife spun every day.

And the old man swore by the sun and the moon
And the green leaves on the trees,
That his wife could do more work in a day
Than he could do in three.
And when he saw how well she plowed
And ran the furrows even,
He swore she could do more work in a day
Than he could do in seven!

From *The Ballad of America.* Copyright © 1966 by John Anthony Scott.

♫ CD track #8. Listen to "Amsterdam No. 84," an example of shape-note singing.

Song: "Amsterdam No. 84," by Robert Seagraves. Copyright © 1991 Sacred Harp Publishing Company. Used by permission. *Recording:* "Amsterdam No. 84," by Robert Seagraves. From 2000 Minnesota Sacred Harp Convention, recorded by Tom Mitchell. ℗ 2000 Tom Mitchell (*www.LoudHymns.com*). Used by permission.

♫ CD track #9. Listen to "The Old Man Who Lived in the Woods," an example of a song sung by the earliest settlers.

Song: "The Old Man Who Lived in the Woods." From *The Ballad of America.* Copyright © 1966 by John Anthony Scott. Melody taken from a version by New England folklorist Bill Bonyun. Used by permission. *Recording:* "The Old Man Who Lived in the Woods," performed by Teri Tibbett. ℗ 2001 Migration Music. Used by permission.

Unit Two: European-American Music

Name _____   Date _____

Colonial Music Quiz

Instructions: After reading the **Colonial Music** student handout, answer these questions (use back of page if necessary).

1. What is the difference between a **sacred song** and **secular song?**

2. Describe **line singing.**

3. Describe differences between **Regular Singing** and the **Usual Way.**

4. What is **shape-note singing?**

5. What is a **ballad?**

Colonial Music Quiz: Answer Key

1. What is the difference between a **sacred song** and **secular song?**

   SACRED SONGS ARE OF A RELIGIOUS OR SPIRITUAL NATURE. SECULAR SONGS ARE NONRELIGIOUS.

2. Describe **line singing.**

   LINE SINGING IS WHEN A LEADER SINGS A LINE (OR PHRASE) OF A SONG AND THE GROUP ANSWERS BACK; IT IS SIMILAR TO CALL-AND-RESPONSE SINGING.

3. Describe differences between **Regular Singing** and the **Usual Way.**

   REGULAR SINGING IS SINGING BY READING THE MUSIC NOTATION. USUAL WAY IS SINGING BY EAR, MEMORY, OR BY LINE SINGING.

4. What is **shape-note singing?**

   SHAPE-NOTE SINGING RELIES ON WRITTEN NOTATION THAT TAKES THE FORM OF SHAPES TO REPRESENT THE DIFFERENT PITCHES—FOR EXAMPLE, SQUARES, OVALS, TRIANGLES.

5. What is a **ballad?**

   A BALLAD IS A STORY TOLD IN SONG.

♫ Lesson 6. Folk Music

Lesson Overview

European-American folk songs come from a variety of traditions, languages, and cultures. They are love songs, work songs, lullabies, historical ballads, battle songs, and songs about famous people. They have been sung in almost all languages, and come from all countries. Folk songs express the experiences of people, their histories, and legends. Mountain music evolved from traditions of the British Isles. Cajun and zydeco music developed from French-American and French-African traditions. Klezmer music developed from Eastern European Jewish traditions. As people from around the world have moved to and settled in America, they have brought the music of their homelands, and as time goes by, have slowly created new folk styles based on the influences found in the new land.

Vocabulary. Folk music, folk songs, oral tradition, sea chanteys, a cappella, medley, accompany, ethnomusicologist, mountain music, harmony singing, Cajun music, zydeco music, tempo, syncopated, genre, klezmer music, parody.

Purpose. To offer an overview of early European-American folk music.

Preparation. Read through the **Folk Music** student handout to familiarize yourself with the material. Preview the CD samples (cues in student handout) and have the CD ready for playing with the students. Be prepared to do some or all of the following activities. Also make sure that each student has a music notebook for keeping handouts and activity sheets.

Materials

- **Folk Music** student handout *(following)*
- **Folk Music Quiz** *(following)*
- **Folk Music Quiz Answer Key** *(following)*
- **Music Vocabulary** activity sheet *(Appendix)*
- **My Opinion Page** activity sheet *(Appendix)*
- **How to Teach a Song** teacher guide *(Appendix)*
- **Songs as Poetry** activity sheet *(Appendix)*
- **Great American Musicians!** activity sheet *(Appendix)*
- **Folk Instruments Picture Page** activity sheet *(following)*
- **Folk Instruments Picture Page Answer Key** *(following)*

- **Music on the Map** activity sheet *(Appendix)*
- **Compose a Song** activity sheet *(Appendix)*
- **Music notebooks**
- **CD music** examples on accompanying CD; cues in student handout
- **Additional music selections**

Activities

- Pass out the **Folk Music** handout for students to read silently or aloud as a group. Afterwards, have students put the handout in their music notebooks. *(Link to language arts, history, geography, social studies.)*
- Give the **Folk Music Quiz** to assess student understanding.
- Have students write the names and instrument families under each picture on the **Folk Instruments Picture Page.** See the answer key for correct answers. Also see **Families of Instruments** in other lessons and in the extension activities in the appendix for more understanding. *(Link to language arts, science.)*
- Go over the music vocabulary at the top of the student handout before or after reading the text. Refer to the glossary for definitions. *Suggestion:* Include these words in a regular class vocabulary lesson, or pass out flashcards with a vocabulary word on one side and the definition on the other and allow students to drill each other. Use the **Music Vocabulary** activity sheet to write out definitions. *(Link to language arts.)*
- Offer students the **Vocabulary Challenge.** Students pick some or all of the words in this lesson's vocabulary list to use in a paragraph, essay, short story, or poem. *(Link to language arts.)*
- **Discuss.** Before reading the student handout, discuss what students already know about folk music. Then read the student handout and discuss it again, letting students add what they've learned. *(Link to language arts, social studies.)*
- Offer the **Bonus Challenge: Compose a Folk Song.** Challenge students to compose a folk song. Some will feel guided on their own; others will need help. Guidelines are offered in the **Compose a Song** activity sheet. *Suggestion:* Encourage students to choose subjects that pertain to everyday life, like going to school, playing sports, dealing with girlfriends and boyfriends, pets, family, community, and so on. Encourage them to perform their songs, but don't require it. If some are shy about singing, offer the option to speak the song without a tune, or turn in a written piece. Ask students to give their songs a title, sign their name with the date, and put them away in their music notebooks. *To extend this activity:* Invite students to accompany themselves or each other with instruments, if they wish, or compile songs in a class songbook. *(Link to language arts.)*

Extension Activities

For step-by-step directions and activity sheets, see the appendix.

- **My Opinion Page.** Offer students a chance to freely express their own opinions about the music they hear. *[Link to language arts, critical thinking.]*

- **Sing a Song.** Learn one of the simple folk songs in this lesson. *Suggested songs to learn:* "Haul on the Bowline," "Old Joe Clarke," and "Jolie Blonde du Bayou." *[Link to singing, language arts, rhythm, melody.]*

- **Songs as Poetry.** Examine the lyrics of songs for their poetic nature. *[Link to language arts.]*

- **Illustrate the Music.** Students illustrate a song or piece of music by drawing, coloring, or painting their ideas of what the music "looks" like visually. *[Link to language arts, visual arts.]*

- **Great American Musicians!** Introduce students to American musicians whose talents have made them notable. *[Link to language arts, history.]*

- **Music on the Map.** Create a map and legend showing musically important places, such as musicians' birthplaces and the music hot spots mentioned in the lesson. *[Link to geography.]*

- **Research an Instrument.** Encourage students to become familiar with a specific instrument mentioned in the lesson and do research into its history, what it is made of, how it produces sound, and interesting facts about it. *[Link to science, history.]*

- **Invite a Music Expert.** Invite a folk musician to visit your class and share his or her instrument, singing, and musical style with the students. Some resources for locating musicians are local music and arts organizations, the Internet, friends, students, and parents. Also, consider taking students to hear a live performance or show a video.

- Consider bringing in **selections of music** from other sources to expand the examples for this lesson. Read the song selections mentioned in each musician's biography. For additional music ideas, search the Internet, library, or local CD store.

Name _____ Date _____

Folk musicians. American Tintype, ca. 1880. Courtesy Andrew Daneman Collection.

Folk Music

Vocabulary: folk music, folk songs, oral tradition, sea chanteys, a cappella, medley, accompany, ethnomusicologist, mountain music, harmony singing, Cajun music, zydeco music, tempo, syncopated, genre, klezmer music, parody

Folk music is found all over the world, in every culture, in every language. Folk music originates with ordinary people describing the events and experiences of their lives. **Folk songs** are love songs, work songs, lullabies, sea songs, historical songs, traveling songs, and memorial songs.

The earliest European-American folk songs came with the first explorers and settlers, who brought the music of their homelands. As people settled in America, their songs began to describe their new lives in the new land. American folk music today is a melting pot of many styles from many cultures around the world.

The Oral Tradition. Many European-American settlers did not read and write music, and so their songs were passed through the generations by way of the oral tradition. The oral tradition is passing information by word of mouth. For example, parents might teach their children a song about a flood that happened in the area. The song might describe the river rising, how the houses became full of water and the furniture floated, and how the people had to get away in boats. When the children grow up, they will teach that song and the history of that flood to their own children, who will remember the story too and pass it on to their children. As each generation teaches the song to the next generation, the song stays alive, the oral tradition continues, and the story of the flood will be remembered throughout time.

The Folk Tradition

In the strictest sense, folk songs are songs that pass from person to person through the **oral tradition**—that is, by telling or singing. Folk songs stayed alive in the minds and voices of people because not many people could read music or write the songs down. In modern times, however, folk songs are written down and recorded. The folk tradition lives on because people are still singing the old songs as well as new ones that describe everyday lives today and the events that happen.

Sea Chanteys

Sea chanteys are work songs and chants sung on sailing ships as they traveled the ocean. In old times, sailors were away from home for many months, sometimes years. The men depended on music for entertainment and to help them work.

Sailors sang about their wives and girlfriends left behind and the loneliness of being on the ocean. They sang about great sea battles and courageous captains. Singing helped the men stay focused on the rhythm of their work—like taking the slack out of a sail or hauling up the anchor. The "chantey man" was the lead singer. When the chantey man sang out, the others joined in on the chorus. They sang **a cappella**—without instrument accompaniment. "Haul on the Bowline" is a traditional sea chantey sung during "short haul" jobs. The men would pull hard on the ropes when they sang the word "Haul!"

Haul on the Bowline
Haul on the bowline, kitty is my darlin'
Haul on the bowline, the bowline—HAUL!

Haul on the bowline so early in the mornin'
Haul on the bowline, the bowline—HAUL!

Haul on the bowline top and mainsail bowline
Haul on the bowline, the bowline—HAUL!

Haul on the bowline, the bully mate is snarlin'
Haul on the bowline, the bowline—HAUL!

Haul on the bowline, haul for better weather
Haul on the bowline, the bowline—HAUL!

Haul on the bowline, the burly whips are rollin'
Haul on the bowline, the bowline—HAUL!

Haul on the bowline, a long time to pay day
Haul on the bowline, the bowline—HAUL!

Explorer Songs

In the early days of the American settlers, explorers and traders traveled across the continent to explore the new land. They found beautiful landscapes and waterways, they found animals and met the Native Americans who lived there. They traveled overland by foot and along the rivers in small boats.

"Fendez le Bois" is a traditional French-Canadian folk song that was popular among French explorers as they paddled in canoes along the waterways of Canada.

Fendez le Bois—Chop Some More Wood

A la claire fontaine
M'en allant promener
J'ai trouvé l'eau si belle
Que je m'y suis baigné.

Chorus: Fendez le bois, chauffez le four.
Dormez, la belle, il n'est point jour.

J'ai trouvé l'eau si belle
Que je m'y suis baigné.
Dans la plus haute branche,
Le rossignol chantait.

Repeat chorus.

Chante, rossignol,
Chante, toi qui a le coeur gai.
Tu as le coeur à rire,
Moi, je l'ai à pleurer.

Repeat chorus.

By the clear running fountain,
I wandered out one day.
I found the stream so lovely
I went there for to bathe.

Chorus: Chop some more wood, kindle the stove.
Sleep on, my love, it is not yet day.

I found the stream so lovely
I went there for to bathe.
Atop the highest branch,
A nightingale sang so happily.

Repeat chorus.

Sing, nightingale.
Sing on, you with the heart so happy.
You have a heart for laughter,
And I for tears they say.

Repeat chorus.

Mountain Music

As British settlers migrated across the eastern part of the new land, many traveled by foot and with packhorses into the mountains and valleys of Appalachia and settled there. They planted crops and built homes. Their families worked

> **Ethnomusicology.** Ethnomusicology is the study of music in a culture—the study of folk music in European-American culture, for example, or the study of blues in the African-American culture or ritual music in the Native American culture. *Ethno* is related to ethnic, or people of a certain culture. *Musicology* is the study of music. **Ethnomusicologists** study the style, history, methods, and form of a culture's music. They record the songs and analyze them. They listen to the words, the melodies, and harmonies to see what kind of structure is used. They learn the history of the music, where it came from, and what influences it picked up along the way. The practice of studying ethnic music didn't become popular in North America until the nineteenth century, when the phonograph record was invented, making it easier to record the music and then study it. Ethnomusicologist Cecil Sharp (1859–1924) collected American folk songs with English origins in the Appalachian Mountains in the early 1900s. He discovered many old songs that were no longer sung in England, but had been preserved in the Appalachian Mountains of North America.

on farms and socialized at dances. They sang old English folk ballads and sacred hymns from the new American hymnals. They sang a cappella and they also **accompanied** themselves with homemade instruments. But without roads or an easy way to travel distances, they remained isolated in the mountains and valleys for generations and so their music evolved in isolation too.

The music in the mountains was played on simple instruments made from the materials people found around them. Fiddles (or violins) were made of wood; washtub basses were made from old washtubs, with a broom handle and gut string to pluck; and dulcimers were made from wood boxes with strings. The music of this region came to be known as **mountain music.**

Fiddle

Mountain dulcimer

Mountain Dulcimer. The mountain, or "lap," dulcimer is a uniquely American instrument developed in the mountains of Appalachia. It is believed that a similar instrument (a box with strings) arrived with early settlers from northern Europe, but it quickly changed shape and design to become the instrument that is still played today. Mountain dulcimers are laid across the lap and plucked with a feather quill. For many generations, the dulcimer, like mountain music, was kept isolated in the mountains of Appalachia, where residents used it to accompany English ballads and other mountain music. Today it has wide-reaching appeal and is even played as an electric instrument.

Washtub bass

Mountain songs were considered common property when the original composer was not known. People sang the songs freely, changing the words and adding new verses as they wished. "Old Joe Clarke" has been a famous character in the mountains for at least a hundred years, even though no one can remember when he lived or who wrote the song!

Old Joe Clarke

I never cared for Old Joe Clarke,
Tell you the reason why.
He goes about the countryside
Eatin' shoofly pie.

Chorus: Fare thee well Old Joe Clarke
Fare thee well, I say.
Fare thee well Old Joe Clarke,
I'm a-goin' away.

Old Joe Clarke came to my house.
We were eatin' supper.
He stubbed his toe on the table leg,
And stuck his nose in the butter.

Repeat chorus.

Old Joe Clarke, he had a cow.
Her name was Betty Lou.
She had two great big brown eyes,
The other two were blue.

Repeat chorus.

Old Joe Clarke had a chicken coop
Eighteen stories high.
And every story in that coop,
Was filled with chicken pie.

Repeat chorus.

As railroads and paved roads were built across America and mountain people developed more contact with the outside world, new instruments came to the mountains. Banjos traveled with the minstrel shows of the mid-1800s. Guitars were introduced by the Spanish. The music changed as new instruments added new sounds and styles.

Banjo

Guitar

Sacred songs have always been an important part of mountain music. The people sang them in church and in their daily lives. Shape-note music, which had developed during colonial times, stayed alive in the southern mountains long after it had died out in the North. It is from this shape-note tradition that future American country-western and bluegrass musicians would develop their strong **harmony singing** style.

Cajun and Zydeco

Cajun music began with the French settlers in northeastern Canada living in Acadia, near present-day Nova Scotia. The Acadians sang folk ballads and sacred songs carried down through the oral tradition from their French ancestors. In the 1700s, when the British moved into the area, the French were forced to leave. Many migrated to the southern United States, where they found refuge in the swampy bayou country of Louisiana. *Bayou* is a Choctaw word meaning "creek" or "small river." Like the mountain musicians, the Acadians lived without roads or easy access to the outside world, and so they stayed isolated in the bayou for over a hundred years. Their traditions, language, and music stayed strong and distinct. Outsiders called them *Cajuns,* short for *Acadians.*

Cajuns played fiddle tunes that had Scottish influences, probably from their Scottish neighbors in Acadia. They developed the special characteristic of playing two fiddles at the same time to accompany their songs. This two-fiddle style is unique to Cajun music and is one of the characteristics that stands out when you hear the music. Later, when the Germans introduced the accordion, the Cajuns adopted that instrument too and began playing waltzes and one-step and two-step dances.

Accordion

The Balfa Brothers. The Balfa Brothers were born and raised in Louisiana: Will (1920–1979) on fiddle; Dewey (1927–1992) on fiddle, harmonica, accordion, and guitar; Harry (1931–) on accordion; and Rodney (1934–1979) on guitar, harmonica, and singing. Raised in a musical family, the boys began playing music at an early age. They played at local dances in the 1940s and made their first recordings in the 1950s on home recording equipment. In the 1960s they recorded "Drunkard's Sorrow Waltz," which became a hit across America. They also toured and performed nationwide, including at the Olympic Games in Mexico City in 1968. The band added new people over the years and recorded many more songs. The Balfa Brothers remain one of the most famous Cajun bands ever to perform. Their famous songs include "La Valse de Bon Baurche," "Le Two-Step de Ville Platte," and "La Valse de Bambocheurs."

In the 1920s, Cajun music made it into the mainstream through radio and phonograph recordings. The first records were French folk songs accompanied by fiddles, accordions, guitar, and triangle. The later recordings also included mandolins, string basses, and banjos. Besides being heard on the radio, Cajun music was heard throughout the southern United States on jukeboxes, at picnics and festivals, and in dance halls. It is happy music and audiences enjoyed dancing to it.

"Jolie Blonde du Bayou" is a well-known traditional Cajun song. It tells the story of a beautiful Cajun woman living on the bayou.

Jolie Blonde du Bayou

Jolie blonde, ma chère 'tite fille,
Gardez-donc quoi t'après faire,
T'après me laisser-moi tout seul dans les misères.
Quel espoir pour l'avenir que mon j'peux avoir?

Jolie blonde, tu croyais
Il avait juste toi dedans le pays.
Il y a pas juste toi dans tout le pays que mon j'peux aimer,
T'es la seule que mon j'voudrais dessus le bayou.

Pretty blonde, my dear little girl,
Look at what you have done.
Left me all alone in misery,
What hope for the future can I have?

Pretty blonde, you thought
That in all the country there was only you.
You're not the only one in the country I could love,
But you're the only one that I want on the bayou.

Like Cajun music, **zydeco music** also has its roots in French folk music. However, zydeco also has an African influence. Zydeco musicians are *Creoles*, people of both French and African ancestry, and their zydeco music is a blend of both cultures.

Early Creole musicians sang French sacred songs accompanied by handmade rhythm instruments—like bone castanets, wooden sticks, and washboards. Eventually, the handheld washboards were replaced by steel washboard vests worn on musicians' chests. Over time, as the music evolved, the **tempo** (speed of the music) became faster, African-American rhythm elements were added, and the music took on a **syncopated** style. *Syncopated* means that the rhythm highlights the "off-beats," and this was unusual in European styles of music. With the addition of the accordion, the music became known as *zydeco*—a pulsing, rhythmic, highly charged dance music. Though both zydeco and Cajun musicians share similar traditions, the two styles remain distinct American **genres**, or styles, of folk music.

Klezmer musicians

Klezmer Music

Klezmer is a Yiddish word meaning "folk instrumental musician." **Klezmer music** is Jewish dance music. It first came to North America in the late 1800s with Eastern European Jewish immigrants. It is a lively style of music played at celebrations and dances. The first klezmer musicians in North America played the *tsimbl* (hammered dulcimer), small accordion, and trombone. Their music was fun and upbeat.

During America's early jazz era, klezmer bands adopted American jazz instruments—including the coronet, clarinet, and saxophone. They also added violins, pianos, banjos, and drums. The music took on a new sound when clarinet players Naftule Brandwein (1897–1963), Dave Tarras (1897–1991), and Shloimke Beckerman (1889–1974) rose to fame, making the clarinet the most dominant instrument of klezmer music.

In the 1940s, Mickey Katz's *The Kosher Jammers* came along with a mixture of klezmer and jazz music, accompanied by trumpet, trombone, piano, and drums. His upbeat, funny songs were **parodies** of other songs. Some of his funniest parodies were the "Barber of Schlemiel" (parody of the "Barber of Seville"), "Borscht Riders in the Sky" (parody of "Ghost Riders in the Sky"), and "Yiddish Mule Train" (parody of "Mule Train").

In the 1970s, klezmer music experienced a revival among young musicians re-creating the music of their ancestors. Since then, klezmer musicians have been adding modern sounds with modern instruments including electric piano, guitar, and synthesizers. Today, klezmer, like other American folk music, has continued to evolve in the twenty-first century.

Bonus Challenge: Compose a Folk Song   Folk songs are not only old songs passed down by the oral tradition, they are also new songs composed by people living in modern times. Consider composing your own folk song about something that happened to you or someone else, or an important event in your community or family. It can describe a feeling or be about a favorite pet or friend. Be descriptive, paint a picture, describe what happened or is happening. Give your song a title, sign your name with the date. *Suggestion:* Sing or tell your folk song to someone—a friend, family, teacher, or class. Also, consider accompanying yourself on an instrument if you play one.

♪ CD track #10. Listen to "Haul on the Bowline," a traditional sea chantey sung by sailors as they sailed across the sea on sailing ships. It is sung a cappella.

> *Recording:* "Haul on the Bowline," performed by Steve Nelson, Greg Pease, and Robert Cohen.℗ 1988 Migration Music. Used by permission.

♪ CD track #11. Listen to "Fendez le Bois," a traditional French-Canadian song that was sung as early explorers paddled in canoes along the rivers of Canada.

> *Recording:* "Fendez le Bois," performed by Lynn Noel.℗ 2000 Lynn Noel. Used by permission.

♪ CD track #12. Listen to "Old Joe Clarke," a traditional mountain song about a shady character. The instrument accompanying the song is the mountain dulcimer.

> *Recording:* "Old Joe Clarke," performed by Teri Tibbett.℗ 2001 Migration Music. Used by permission.

♪ CD track #13. Listen to "Jolie Blonde du Bayou," a traditional Cajun song about a beautiful woman. Notice how the two fiddles play together; this is characteristic of Cajun music.

> *Recording:* Performed by Dewey Balfa, Marc Savoy, and D.L. Menard. From *Under a Green Oak Tree.*℗ 1976 Arhoolie Productions. *www.arhoolie.com.* Used by permission.

♪ CD track #14. Listen to "Wedding Dance," an example of klezmer music. Notice the strong clarinet that dominates the sound.

> *Song:* "Wedding Dance," performed by Robert Cohen. Copyright © 1994 Robert Cohen. *Recording:*℗ 1994 Zuvuya One Music, Migration Music.

Name _____   Date _____

Folk Music Quiz

Instructions: After reading the **Folk Music** student handout, answer these questions (use back of page if necessary).

1. What is the **oral tradition?**

2. What is an **ethnomusicologist?**

3. Describe **mountain music,** where it developed, and which ethnic group developed it.

4. Describe **Cajun music,** where it developed, and which ethnic group developed it. What is the difference between Cajun and **zydeco music?**

5. Describe **klezmer music** and which ethnic group developed it.

Folk Music Quiz: Answer Key

1. What is the **oral tradition?**

   SONGS OR STORIES ARE PASSED FROM GENERATION TO GENERA-
   TION THROUGH SINGING OR TELLING.

2. What is an **ethnomusicologist?**

   A PERSON WHO STUDIES ETHNIC MUSIC.

3. Describe **mountain music,** where it developed, and which ethnic group
   developed it.

   MOUNTAIN MUSIC EVOLVED FROM BRITISH ISLES FOLK MUSIC
   IN THE MOUNTAINS AND VALLEYS OF APPALACHIA. IT IS FROM
   BRITISH, SCOTTISH, AND IRISH ORIGINS.

4. Describe **Cajun music,** where it developed, and which ethnic group
   developed it. What is the difference between Cajun and **zydeco music?**

   CAJUN MUSIC EVOLVED FROM FRENCH-CANADIAN SETTLERS IN
   THE BAYOU COUNTRY OF LOUISIANA. CAJUN MUSIC IS FRENCH-
   CANADIAN IN ORIGIN. ZYDECO IS FRENCH-AFRICAN IN ORIGIN. IT
   HAS SYNCOPATED RHYTHMS AND FAST TEMPOS.

5. Describe **klezmer music** and which ethnic group developed it.

   KLEZMER MUSIC EVOLVED FROM EASTERN EUROPEAN JEWISH
   DANCE MUSIC TRADITIONS. IT IS FROM EASTERN EUROPEAN JEW-
   ISH ORIGINS.

Name_____   Date_____

Folk Instruments Picture Page

Instructions: Write the name of the instrument and the family group it belongs to on the lines provided under each picture.

_____   _____   _____

_____   _____   _____

_____   _____   _____

_____   _____   _____

_____

_____

Folk Instruments Picture Page: Answer Key

Mountain dulcimer

Chordophone

Guitar

Chordophone

Washtub bass

Chordophone

Clarinet

Aerophone

Banjo

Chordophone

Accordion

Aerophone and idiophone

Fiddle

Chordophone

♫ Lesson 7. Patriotic Music

Lesson Overview

Patriotic music expresses love for one's country. There are national anthems that express pride for a nation, and sentimental patriotic songs that express love for landscapes, liberty, the people of a country, and so on. This lesson explores these variations on the patriotic theme.

Vocabulary. Patriotic song, state song, national anthem, sentimental songs, compose.

Purpose. To offer an overview of patriotic music in North America.

Preparation. Read through the **Patriotic Music** student handout to familiarize yourself with the material. Preview the CD samples (cues in student handout) and have the CD ready for playing with the students. Be prepared to do some or all of the following activities. Also make sure that each student has a music notebook for keeping handouts and activity sheets.

Materials

- **Patriotic Music** student handout *(following)*
- **Patriotic Music Quiz** *(following)*
- **Patriotic Music Quiz Answer Key** *(following)*
- **Music Vocabulary** activity sheet *(Appendix)*
- **My Opinion Page** activity sheet *(Appendix)*
- **How to Teach a Song** teacher guide *(Appendix)*
- **Songs as Poetry** activity sheet *(Appendix)*
- **Great American Musicians!** activity sheet *(Appendix)*
- **Music on the Map** activity sheet *(Appendix)*
- **Compose a Song** activity sheet *(Appendix)*
- **Music notebooks**
- **CD music** examples on accompanying CD; cues in student handout
- **Additional music selections**

Activities

- Pass out the **Patriotic Music** handout for students to read silently or aloud as a group. Play CD examples and allow discussions. Afterwards, have students put the handouts in their music notebooks. *(Link to language arts, history, geography, social studies.)*

- Have students take the **Patriotic Music Quiz** to assess their understanding of the lesson.

- Go over the music vocabulary at the top of the student handout before or after reading the text. Refer to the glossary for definitions. *Suggestion:* Include these words in a regular class vocabulary lesson, or pass out flashcards with a vocabulary word on one side and the definition on the other and allow students to drill each other. Use the **Music Vocabulary** activity sheet to write out definitions. *(Link to language arts.)*

- Offer the **Vocabulary Challenge.** Students pick some or all of the words in this lesson's vocabulary list to use in a paragraph, essay, short story, or poem. *(Link to language arts.)*

- **Discuss.** Before reading the student handout, discuss what students already know about patriotic music. Then read the student handout and discuss it again, letting students add what they've learned. *(Link to language arts, social studies.)*

- Offer the **Bonus Challenge: Compose a Patriotic Song.** Challenge students to compose a patriotic song expressing their personal feelings or thoughts about their community, city, state, or country. Follow the guidelines offered in the **Compose a Song** activity sheet in the appendix. *(Link to language arts, music composition.)*

Extension Activities

For step-by-step directions and activity sheets, see the appendix.

- **My Opinion Page.** Offer students a chance to freely express their own opinions about the music they hear. *(Link to language arts, critical thinking.)*

- **Sing a Song.** Students learn a simple patriotic song from this lesson. *Suggested songs to learn:* "America, the Beautiful" or "This Land Is Your Land." *(Link to singing, language arts, rhythm, melody.)*

- **Songs as Poetry.** Students examine the lyrics of songs for their poetic nature. *(Link to language arts.)*

- **Illustrate the Music.** Students illustrate a song or piece of music by drawing, coloring, or painting their ideas of what the music "looks" like visually. *(Link to language arts, visual arts.)*

- **Great American Musicians!** Introduce students to American musicians whose talents have made them notable. *(Link to language arts, history.)*

- **Music on the Map.** Students create a map and legend showing musically important places, such as musicians' birthplaces and the music hot spots mentioned in the lesson. *(Link to geography.)*

- Consider bringing in **selections of music** from other sources to expand the music examples for this lesson.

Name _____ Date _____

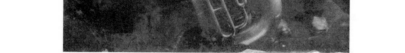

Brass band. American Tintype, ca. 1890. Courtesy Andrew Daneman Collection.

Patriotic Music

Vocabulary: *patriotic song, state song, national anthem, sentimental songs, compose*

When the revolutionary war ended in 1776, European-Americans were proud of their independence from England. They composed many songs for their new country. Songs about freedom were sung in the streets, at public gatherings, and in people's homes. When songs express pride and love for a country, they are called **patriotic songs.**

Patriotic songs can describe historical events—like great battles in war or noble acts of patriotism. Or they can tell about famous people and not-so-famous people. Patriotic songs may also simply express a feeling, or sentiment, about one's country.

Just after the American Revolution, performance troupes traveled from town to town singing patriotic songs to enthusiastic audiences, who cheered and sang along in great numbers. One of the most popular songs of the time was "Yankee Doodle." No one knows for sure who composed this song, but in 1776, it was the number one song in America! Today "Yankee Doodle" is the official **state song** of Connecticut.

National Anthems

An anthem is a song of praise or devotion. A **national anthem** is the official song of a country. The national anthem of the United States is "The Star-Spangled Banner," which was written during the War of 1812 when Francis Scott Key was held prisoner on a British ship in a port near Baltimore, Maryland. He watched from the ship as bombs exploded and fires burned around the American fort. He thought the fort was lost, but in the morning when the sun lit the land, he could see the American flag still flying on the flagpole. Feeling greatly inspired, he wrote a poem on the back of an envelope he had in his pocket. The poem was put to music and eventually became "The Star-Spangled Banner."

The Star-Spangled Banner

Lyrics by Francis Scott Key; Music attributed to John Stafford Smith

Oh, say can you see
By the dawn's early light
What so proudly we hailed
At the twilight's last gleaming?
Whose broad stripes and bright stars
Through the perilous fight,
O'er the ramparts we watched
Were so gallantly streaming?
And the rocket's red glare,
The bombs bursting in air,
Gave proof through the night
That our flag was still there.
Oh, say does that star-spangled
Banner yet wave
O'er the land of the free
And the home of the brave?

Francis Scott Key (1780–1843). Francis Scott Key was born in Maryland. A lawyer and a poet, he lived with his wife and eleven children near Washington, D.C., where he was a respected man in the community. During the War of 1812, Francis was asked to go aboard the British ship *Tonnant* to ask for the release of an American prisoner. He did so, and the British agreed to release the prisoner, but then he was told that they would have to wait to leave the ship until after the attack on Fort McHenry. The poem he wrote as he watched the battle was eventually named "The Star-Spangled Banner" and was put to the music of an old drinking song. It became the national anthem of the United States in 1931.

Francis Scott Key

The national anthem of Canada, "O Canada," came into the world as a poem written by Sir Adolphe-Basile Routhier, a poet and judge from Quebec. The music was later composed by Calixa Lavallée, a Canadian composer. It was first performed at the Congrès National des Canadiens-Français in 1880, but it waited one hundred years, until 1980, to become Canada's national anthem.

O Canada

French lyrics by Sir Adolphe-Basile Routhier

English lyrics by Robert Stanley Weir

Music by Calixa Lavallée

O Canada!
Terre de nos aieux,
Ton front est ceint de fleurons glorieux.
Car ton bras sait porter l'épée,
Il sait porter la croix.
Ton histoire est une épopée
Des plus brillants exploits.
Et ta valeur, de foi trempée,
Protégera nos foyers et nos droits.
Protégera nos foyers et nos droits.

O Canada!
Our home and native land!
True patriot love in all thy sons command.
With glowing hearts we see thee rise,
The True North strong and free!
From far and wide,
O Canada, we stand on guard for thee.
God keep our land glorious and free!
O Canada, we stand on guard for thee.
O Canada, we stand on guard for thee.

Calixa Lavallée (December 28, 1842–1891). Composer Calixa Lavallée was born in Quebec, Canada. He learned to play piano and organ at an early age. During his lifetime he worked and studied in many places, including the United States, France, England, Brazil, and the West Indies. In 1865 he composed a comic opera that was to debut at the New York Grand Opera House, but on the day before the opening, the owner of the theater was killed, the theater was closed, and Calixa's opera was not performed. He went on to compose operettas, a symphony, and many songs. He also founded the first Canadian Conservatory. In 1880 he was commissioned to compose the music for the poem "O Canada," which today is that country's national anthem.

Sir Adolphe-Basile Routhier (1839–1920). Sir Adolphe-Basile Routhier was born in Quebec, Canada. A poet and a lawyer, he eventually became the Chief Justice of Quebec. In 1880 he was asked by the Lieutenant Governor of Quebec to write the lyrics of a hymn for a convention of French-Canadians, the Congrès National des Canadiens-Français. The poem, "O Canada," was put to music by composer Calixa Lavallée, and eventually became Canada's national anthem.

Sentimental Songs

Songs that express feelings are called **sentimental songs.** Sentimental patriotic songs may describe the beauty of a place or its people, or respect and love for the freedoms available in the nation. "America, the Beautiful" (1895) was **composed** by Katharine Lee Bates after she visited the Rocky Mountains in Colorado. Her patriotic song tells about the beauty of America and the values on which it was founded.

America, the Beautiful

Lyrics by Katharine Lee Bates

Music by Samuel A. Ward

O beautiful for spacious skies,
For amber waves of grain,
For purple mountain majesties
Above the fruited plain.
America! America!
God shed His grace on thee,
And crown thy good with brotherhood,
From sea to shining sea.

O beautiful for pilgrim feet
Whose stern impassioned stress
A thoroughfare for freedom beat
Across the wilderness.
America! America! God mend thine every flaw,
Confirm thy soul in self-control,
Thy liberty in law.

O beautiful for patriot dream
That sees beyond the years,
Thine alabaster cities gleam,
Undimmed by human tears.
America! America! God shed His grace on thee,
And crown thy good with brotherhood,
From sea to shining sea.

Katharine Lee Bates (August 12, 1859–1929). Born in Massachusetts, Katharine Lee Bates was nine years old when she started writing in a little red book that was her diary. She grew up to be a scholar, poet, and writer, receiving degrees from Wellesley College and Oxford University. She was an instructor at Wellesley College from 1880 until she retired in 1925. Regarding her inspiration for writing "America, the Beautiful" at Pikes Peak in Colorado, she wrote, "It was then and there, as I was looking out over the sealike expanse of fertile country spreading away so far under those ample skies, that the opening lines of the hymn floated into my mind." Her poem was put to music and eventually became one of the most well-known patriotic songs in the United States.

Katharine Lee Bates. Photo by Charles W. Hearn. Courtesy of Wellesley College Archives.

In the mid-twentieth century, a traveling folksinger named Woody Guthrie composed songs out of his love for America. One of his most famous songs is "This Land Is Your Land." Written in 1956, this song expresses his appreciation and respect for America.

This Land Is Your Land

Lyrics and music by Woody Guthrie

Chorus: This land is your land, this land is my land
From California to the New York Island
From the Redwood Forest to the Gulf Stream waters,
This land was made for you and me.

As I went walking that ribbon of highway
I saw above me that endless skyway,
I saw below me that Golden Valley,
This land was made for you and me.

I roamed and rambled and followed my footsteps
To the sparkling sands of her diamond desert,
And all around me a voice was sounding,
This land was made for you and me.

When the sun came shining and I was strolling
The wheat fields waving and the dust clouds rolling,
A voice was chanting as the fog was lifting,
This land was made for you and me.

Repeat chorus.

Repeat third verse.

Copyright © TRO Richmond Organization, New York. Used by permission.

Bonus Challenge: Compose a Patriotic Song Make up your own patriotic song describing your feelings or thoughts about your community, city, state, or country.

Woody Guthrie (July 14, 1912–1967). Folksinger and songwriter Woody Guthrie was born in Oklahoma. As a child, he loved to entertain and made up his own songs, played harmonica, and danced for his friends and family. As an adult, he traveled across the United States during the Great Depression, meeting people who had lost their homes and jobs. He wrote songs about their desperate lives and sang them with his guitar for accompaniment. After he became famous, he was invited to sing his songs on the radio, where many people were able to hear his music. During his career he wrote many political songs that described the life and plight of poor people. His songs include "Talking Dust Bowl Blues," "Riding in My Car," "Hobo's Lullaby," and "Roll on Columbia."

♫ CD track #15. Listen to "America, the Beautiful." This patriotic song tells about the beauty of America, its people, and its liberties.

> *Recording:* "America, the Beautiful" performed by Teri Tibbett, Alex Nelson, Haley Nelson. ℗2001 Migration Music. Used by permission.

♫ CD track #16. Listen to "This Land Is Your Land." This patriotic song expresses sentimental appreciation and respect for America.

> *Song:* Composed by Woody Guthrie, © TRO Richmond Organization, New York. *Recording:* "This Land Is Your Land" by Woody Guthrie from the recording entitled *Folkways: The Original Version,* SF 40001, provided courtesy of Smithsonian Folkways Recordings. © 1989. Used by permission.

Name _____   Date _____

Patriotic Music Quiz

Instructions: After reading the **Patriotic Music** student handout, answer these questions (use back of page if necessary).

1. What are **patriotic songs?**

2. What is a **national anthem?**

3. What is the name of the **national anthem** of the United States?

4. What is the name of Canada's **national anthem?**

5. What are some of the subjects of **patriotic songs?**

6. If you were to compose a **patriotic song,** what would be the subject?

Patriotic Music Quiz: Answer Key

1. What are **patriotic songs?**

   SONGS THAT EXPRESS LOVE, PRIDE, APPRECIATION FOR ONE'S HOMELAND OR COUNTRY.

2. What is a **national anthem?**

   THE OFFICIAL SONG OF A NATION.

3. What is the name of the **national anthem** of the United States?

   "THE STAR-SPANGLED BANNER"

4. What is the name of Canada's **national anthem?**

   "O CANADA"

5. What are some of the subjects of **patriotic songs?**

   APPRECIATION OF BEAUTY, LIBERTY, PEOPLE, PRIDE IN BATTLE, AND SO ON.

6. If you were to compose a **patriotic song,** what would be the subject?

   STUDENTS PROVIDE ANY REASONABLE ANSWERS.

♫ Lesson 8. Early Popular Music

Lesson Overview

Popular music is music that pleases the general public. It is mainstream music. It is the music that plays on the radio and tops the music industry "charts" every week. Popular music changes over time as the styles, culture, and tastes of a society change. The first distinctly American popular music was the minstrel music of the mid-1800s; it was performed by European-Americans mimicking African-American dialect, lifestyle, and dress. Just before the turn of the century (1900), minstrel shows evolved into a new kind of stage entertainment called vaudeville. Besides providing stage show entertainment, popular music was printed on sheet music and sold for people to play at home in their parlors. Early popular music was the music people listened to before recordings and radio.

Vocabulary. Popular music, patriotic songs, ballads, comic opera, composer, minstrel song, minstrel shows, sentimental songs, verse, chorus, compose, political songs, rallying songs, humorous songs, melody, vaudeville.

Purpose. To offer an overview of popular music in America from the 1700s to the early 1900s.

Preparation. Read through the **Early Popular Music** student handout to familiarize yourself with the material. Preview the CD samples (cues in student handout) and have the CD ready for playing with the students. Be prepared to do some or all of the following activities. Also make sure that each student has a music notebook for keeping handouts and activity sheets.

Materials

- **Early Popular Music** student handout *(following)*
- **Early Popular Music Quiz** *(following)*
- **Early Popular Music Quiz Answer Key** *(following)*
- **Music Vocabulary** activity sheet *(Appendix)*
- **My Opinion Page** activity sheet *(Appendix)*
- **How to Teach a Song** teacher guide *(Appendix)*
- **Songs as Poetry** activity sheet *(Appendix)*
- **Great American Musicians!** activity sheet *(Appendix)*
- **Music on the Map** activity sheet *(Appendix)*
- **Music notebooks**
- **CD music** examples on accompanying CD; cues in student handout
- **Additional music selections**

Activities

- Pass out the **Early Popular Music** handout for students to read silently or aloud as a group. Afterwards, have students put the handout in their music notebooks. *(Link to language arts, history, geography, social studies.)*

- Give the **Early Popular Music Quiz** to assess student understanding of the lesson.

- Go over the music vocabulary at the top of the student handout before or after reading the text. Refer to the glossary for definitions. *Suggestion:* Include these words in a regular class vocabulary lesson, or pass out flashcards with a vocabulary word on one side and the definition on the other and allow students to drill each other. Use the **Music Vocabulary** activity sheet to write out definitions. *(Link to language arts.)*

- Have students take the **Vocabulary Challenge.** Students pick some or all of the words in this lesson's vocabulary list to use in a paragraph, essay, short story, or poem. *(Link to language arts.)*

- **Discuss.** Before reading the student handout, discuss what students already know about early popular music in America. Then read the student handout and discuss it again, letting students add what they've learned. *(Link to language arts, social studies.)*

Extension Activities

For step-by-step directions and activity sheets, see the appendix.

- **My Opinion Page.** Give students a chance to freely express their own opinions about the music they hear. *(Link to language arts, critical thinking.)*

- **Sing a Song.** Students learn a simple song from this lesson. *Suggested songs to learn:* "Oh Susanna," "Goober Peas," "Grandfather's Clock." *(Link to singing, language arts, rhythm, melody.)*

- **Songs as Poetry.** Students examine the lyrics of songs for their poetic nature. *(Link to language arts.)*

- **Illustrate the Music.** Students illustrate a song or piece of music by drawing, coloring, or painting their ideas of what the music "looks" like visually. *(Link to language arts, visual arts.)*

- **Great American Musicians!** Introduce students to American musicians whose talents have made them notable. *(Link to language arts, history.)*

- **Music on the Map.** Students create a map and legend showing musically important places, such as musicians' birthplaces and music hot spots mentioned in the lesson. *(Link to geography.)*

- **Invite a Music Expert.** Invite a popular-style musician to visit your class and share his or her instrument, singing, and musical style with the students. Some resources for locating musicians are local music and arts organizations, the Internet, friends, students, and parents. Also, consider taking students to hear a live performance, or show them a video of a popular artist.

- **Put on a vaudeville show.** Help students get to know vaudeville by putting on a vaudeville show themselves. *Step 1:* Discuss all the different types of acts usually included in a vaudeville show: singing, dancing, comedy, juggling, animal acts, clowning, magic, puppets, mimes, and so on (see the section on vaudeville in student handout). *Step 2:* Invite students to come up with an act, individually or in groups. *Step 3:* Have students research the type of act; find famous people who performed in that genre and read about them and their act. Consider having them compile the information for a written report. *Step 4:* Students design the acts and rehearse them. *Step 5:* Students gather costumes, props, scenery. *Step 6:* Create an order of acts. *Step 7:* Advertise the show on posters and handbills; as a class, research an authentic vaudeville poster to imitate (use the Internet, library, encyclopedia). *Step 8:* Perform the show for parents, friends, the entire school. *Suggestion:* Keep it fun! Make the "process" of creating the show as important as the "product," or performance. *(Link to language arts, history, performance art.)*

- Consider bringing in **selections of music** from other sources to expand the music examples for this lesson. Read the song selections mentioned in each musician's biography for additional music ideas. Search the Internet, library, or local CD store.

Name _____ Date _____

Three young women singing. American Tintype, ca. 1910. Photographer unknown.
Courtesy Andrew Daneman collection.

Early Popular Music

Vocabulary: popular music, patriotic songs, ballads, comic opera, composer, minstrel song, minstrel shows, sentimental songs, verse, chorus, compose, political songs, rallying songs, humorous songs, melody, vaudeville

Imagine a world without radio or television. Imagine no CDs or mini disc players. Instead, the only music you hear is live music made by other people, or the music you make yourself. This is what **popular music** was like in America before 1900. In those days, music was heard either in parlors—the living rooms of the day—where families would gather around the piano to sing popular songs, or on stages, where singers and actors performed for an audience of eager listeners.

Unit Two: European-American Music   **129**

Popular music is best described as music that pleases the general public. It's what's "popular" among most people. It includes songs, instrumental music, light opera, or almost any *style* of music. The common factor is that it is most listened to by the mainstream population.

Popular music changes over time as the styles and culture of a population change. What is popular with one generation will likely differ from what's popular with the next. For example, swing music was popular in the 1940s, and disco was popular in the 1970s.

Early Popular Songs

In 1776, when the United States became a nation, the popular songs of the day were **patriotic songs** that showed praise and support for the new country. "Free America" (1775), by Dr. Joseph Warren, and "The Liberty Song" (1768), by John Dickinson, were popular songs at the time of the American Revolution. People also sang **ballads** that told stories and expressed sentimental feelings, like "My Days Have Been So Wondrous Free" (1759), by Francis Hopkinson, and "The Lass of Richmond Hill" (1790), by James Hook.

Early in America's history, people attended stage shows and **comic operas** that told funny stories with funny songs. "The Disappointment or Force of Credulity" (1767), by Andrew Barton, and "The Poor Soldier" (1783), by John O'Keefe, are examples of early comic operas.

Francis Hopkinson (1737–1791) has been recognized as the first **composer** of American popular songs. He was friends with both George Washington and Thomas Jefferson, and a signer of the Declaration of Independence. His songs were simple and expressed his feelings. They were the first popular songs to be published and sold to Americans on sheet music for their home pianos.

Minstrel Songs

The first distinct style of popular song in America was the **minstrel song**, which developed in the 1840s. These songs were performed by European-Americans and mimicked African-American language, style, and dress. Minstrel performers sat on a stage in a half-circle, wearing blackface paint and torn clothes, and played banjo, fiddle, bones, and tambourine. Minstrel performers toured across America, joking, dancing, performing skits, and singing songs. In their day, **minstrel shows** were considered funny and entertaining. In modern times, however, they are seen as degrading to African Americans. One of the most popular minstrel songs of the day was "Dixie Land" (1860), composed by Daniel Emmett.

Daniel Decatur Emmett (October 29, 1815–1904). A songwriter and accomplished musician, Daniel Decatur Emmett was born in Ohio. Daniel grew up hearing church hymns and military music. He taught himself to play the fiddle and began composing his own tunes at an early age. At fifteen, he performed his first song at a Fourth of July celebration in Mt. Vernon. At seventeen, he joined the Army and became the leading fifer. Later, he traveled with various circus bands and began composing his own songs, playing banjo, fiddle, and fife. He helped form the Virginia Minstrels in 1843, the first minstrel-style stage band. His most famous composition, "Dixie Land," was adopted as the southern rallying song during the Civil War, even though Daniel himself was a Northerner. He composed many popular songs that are still sung today, including "Turkey in the Straw" (1834), "Old Dan Tucker" (1843), and "Jimmy Crack Corn" (1846).

Minstrel performer

Dixie Land

Lyrics and music by Daniel Emmett

I wish I was in the land of cotton,
Old times there are not forgotten,
Look away, look away, look away, Dixie land.
In Dixie land where I was born in, early on a frosty mornin',
Look away, look away, look away, Dixie land.

Chorus: Then I wish I was in Dixie, hooray! Hooray!
In Dixie land I'll take my stand, to live and die in Dixie,
Away, away, away down south in Dixie,
Away, away, away down south in Dixie.

Old Missus marry Will de Weaber,
Will-yum was a gay deceaber,
Look away, look away, look away, Dixie land.
But when he put his arm around her,
Smiled as fierce as a forty-pounder.
Look away, look away, look away, Dixie land.

Repeat chorus.

Dars buckwheat cakes an' ingen batter, makes you fat or a little fatter.
Look away, look away, look away, Dixie land.
Den hoe it down and scratch your grabble to Dixie's land
I'm bound to travel,
Look away, look away, look away Dixie land.

Repeat chorus.

Stephen Foster

By the 1850s, Stephen Foster was America's most popular songwriter. His lyrics were simple and easy to understand. His melodies had a gentle tone that appealed to many people and encouraged them to sing along. He was also popular for writing **sentimental songs** expressing sentimental feelings. Sentimental songs often remind people of their own personal feelings, experiences, and concerns.

Stephen Foster popularized a structure of songwriting that is still used in modern songwriting today. In this structure, a solo voice begins singing a **verse,** and this is followed by several voices joining in on the **chorus.** The structure moves from verse to chorus, verse to chorus throughout the song. The minstrel song "Oh Susanna" (1848) is an example of the verse-chorus structure.

Oh Susanna

Lyrics and music by Stephen Foster

I come from Alabama with my banjo on my knee.
I'm going to Louisiana, my true love for to see.
It rained all night the day I left, the weather it was dry.
The sun so hot, I froze to death, Susanna don't you cry.

Chorus: Oh Susanna, oh don't you cry for me
For I come from Alabama with my banjo on my knee.

I had a dream the other night when everything was still.
I thought I saw Susanna, a-coming down the hill.
The buckwheat cake was in her mouth, the tear was in her eye.
Says I, I'm coming from the South, Susanna don't you cry.

Repeat chorus.

Stephen Collins Foster (July 4, 1826–1864). Stephen Collins Foster was born in Pennsylvania on the fiftieth anniversary of the signing of the Declaration of Independence. He was best known as a songwriter, composing both lyrics and music for over two hundred songs. Stephen Foster enjoyed great success as the first American composer to earn his living composing songs. His first songs were minstrel songs, but later he composed songs that talked about the sadness of slavery. Some of his most remembered songs are "Oh Susanna" (1848), "Camptown Races" (1850), "Old Folks at Home (Swanee River)" (1851), "Jeannie with the Light Brown Hair" (1854), "Old Black Joe" (1860), and "Beautiful Dreamer" (1862).

Stephen Foster

Civil War Songs

When the Civil War broke out between the North and the South in 1861, Americans on both sides were pitted against each other over the issues of slavery and autonomy. Both sides wanted their ideas to be adopted and lived by. As battles were fought on the battlefields, the people at home **composed** songs that expressed their thoughts and feelings about the war. They composed political songs, rallying songs, humorous songs, love songs, and sad songs. During this time, the Hutchinson Family Singers traveled the countryside singing **political songs** that commented on social issues. "The Bereaved Slave Mother" is an antislavery song that stirred people's feelings.

The Bereaved Slave Mother

Lyrics by Judd Hutchinson

Oh! deep was the anguish of the slave mother's heart
When called from her darling for ever to part.
So grieved that lone mother, that heartbroken mother,
In sorrow and woe.

The lash of the master her deep sorrows mock
While the child of her bosom is sold on the block
Yet loud shrieked that mother, poor brokenhearted mother
In sorrow and woe.

Oh! list' ye kind mothers to the cries of the slave
The parents and children implore you to save.
Go rescue the mothers, the sisters and brothers
From sorrow and woe.

The most popular songs during the Civil War were the **rallying songs** that excited and inspired people's emotions. When these songs were sung in a crowd, the people raised their voices and sang along joyously. "Dixie Land" (1860) became the rallying song for the South. The rallying song for the North was an antislavery song written by Julia Ward Howe; it was called "The Battle Hymn of the Republic" (1862).

Life on the battlefield was often cold, wet, dirty, and uncomfortable. The soldiers were tired and sore from marching and fighting. Many times, their clothes were torn, their feet cold, and their stomachs empty. Sometimes they made up **humorous songs** to make themselves feel better. "Goober Peas" (ca. 1861) is a funny song about sitting in the fields eating the only thing the soldiers could find—peanuts! "Goober peas" is a nickname for peanuts.

> **Julia Ward Howe (May 27, 1819–1910).** Born in New York, Julia Ward Howe was a writer who published poetry, plays, and travel books, as well as many articles. Howe was also a social reformer who worked hard to help both women and African Americans gain more freedom. She is most remembered for composing "The Battle Hymn of the Republic," which became the most popular Civil War song in the North. She was inspired to write the song after visiting a Union Army camp where she watched soldiers march to battle. The words first came to her as a poem, which she scribbled on some paper. They were later put to the melody of a popular song of the time, "John Brown's Body."

Goober Peas

Lyrics by A. Pindar

Music by P. Nutt

Sittin' by the roadside on a summer day
Chattin' with my messmates, passin' time away
Lyin' in the shadow underneath the trees
Goodness how delicious eatin' goober peas!
Peas, peas, peas, peas, eatin' goober peas
Goodness how delicious eatin' goober peas!

When the horseman passes the soldiers have a rule
To cry out at their loudest, "Mister where's your mule?"
But then another pleasure, enchantin'er than these
Is wearin' out your grinders eatin goober peas!
Peas, peas, peas, peas, eatin' goober peas
Wearin' out your grinders eatin' goober peas!

Just before the battle the general hears a row
He says "The Yanks are comin.' I can hear their voices now."
He turns around in wonder and what do you think he sees?
The Georgia militia eatin' goober peas!
Peas, peas, peas, peas, eatin' goober peas
The Georgia militia eatin' goober peas!

I think my song has lasted almost long enough
The subject's interesting but the rhymes are mighty rough
I wish this war was over when free from rags and fleas
We'd kiss our wives and sweethearts and gobble goober peas!
Peas, peas, peas, peas, eatin' goober peas
We'd kiss our wives and sweethearts and gobble goober peas!

Turn of the Century

After the Civil War, a flood of sentimental songs were written and published by songwriters across the country. Many had adopted Stephen Foster's verse-chorus style and attempted to match his flare for tender **melodies.** Henry Clay Work's "Grandfather's Clock" (1876) is an example of a popular song about the life of an old man and his clock.

Grandfather's Clock

Lyrics by Henry Clay Work

My grandfather's clock was too large for the shelf,
So it stood ninety years on the floor;
It was taller by half than the old man himself,
And it weighed not a pennyweight more.
It was bought on the morn that my grandpa was born,
And was always his treasure and pride;
But it stopped short, never to go again
When the old man died.

Ninety years without slumbering (tick, tock, tick, tock)
His life seconds numbering (tick, tock, tick, tock)
But it stopped short, never to go again
When the old man died.

And watching its pendulum swing to and fro,
Many hours he had spent as a boy;
As he grew into manhood the clock seemed to know
For it shared every sorrow and joy.
And it struck twenty-four as he entered the door,
With his beautiful and blushing bride;
But it stopped short, never to go again
When the old man died.

My grandfather said, that of those he could hire,
Not a servant so faithful he found;
For it wasted no time and had but one desire
At the close of each week to be wound.
Yes it kept in its place not a frown upon its face,
And its hands never hung by its side;
But it stopped short, never to go again
When the old man died.

Then it rang an alarm in the dead of the night
An alarm that for years had been dumb;
And we knew that his spirit was pluming for flight
That his hour for departure had come.
Yes the clock kept the time with a soft and muffled chime,
As we stood there and watched by his side;
But it stopped short, never to go again
When the old man died.

Henry Clay Work (October 1, 1832–1884). Born in Connecticut, Henry Clay Work grew up in a family that helped to free slaves. Work became a printer and an inventor by trade, but he also wrote poetry. He taught himself music and published his first song when he was twenty-one years old. He wrote popular Civil War songs, many of which were outspoken against slavery. He continued to write popular songs after the war, including "Beautiful Rose" (1861), and "Grandfather's Clock" (1876), dedicated to his sister Lizzie. Some of his other songs are "Ring the Bell," "The Parrot and the Billy Goat," "The Monkey and the Mule," and "Watchman!"

Vaudeville

After the Civil War, a new style of stage show replaced minstrel shows. It was called **vaudeville.** There were some differences between the two. Where minstrel shows were performed by an entire troupe of people interacting with each other on the stage, vaudeville shows were made up of separate groups or "acts" that followed each other in a variety show that could include singers, dancers, comedians, jugglers, animal acts, clowns, magicians, puppets, mimes, rope spinners, horseback riders, escape artists, and daredevils—creating an extravaganza of high-energy, fast-moving entertainment. Vaudeville was performed in theaters, churches, bars, and barns all across America. It was the most popular form of American entertainment from 1875 to 1932.

Many actors, singers, comedians, and variety acts made their living traveling the vaudeville circuits. Some of vaudeville's greatest musicians were George M. Cohan (1878–1942), Sophie Tucker (1884–1966), Fanny Brice (1891–1951), and Eddie Cantor (1892–1964).

A typical vaudeville stage show might have opened with a high-energy visual act to get the audience's attention, like acrobats doing flips and jumps in the air. The second act might be a song-and-dance routine, where the performers told jokes and sang funny songs in front of the curtain (so the next act could set up behind the curtain). The following act might be a musical number with props and a chorus of singers. Then the star of the show would appear—a famous singer or comedian, for example. More acts followed and the show would end with an upbeat song or dance.

Fanny Brice
AP/World Wide Photos. Used by permission.

Fanny Brice (October 29, 1891–1951). Born Fania Borach in New York City, Fanny Brice became a stage performer of songs and comedy. She grew up wanting to be a performer and began working in vaudeville when she was still a teenager. She sang and danced in musical comedies on Broadway, performing humorous parodies of Jewish culture. Her loud voice and funny stage presence made her a charismatic stage performer and audiences flocked to see her. At nineteen, she was hired to perform with the *Ziegfeld Follies,* the grandest variety show of the time, where she became a comedy singing star. Over her career, Brice was most well-known for her humor, though her beautiful voice was occasionally called on for a "showstopper." Some of her famous songs are "Second Hand Rose," "I Found a Million Dollar Baby in a Five-and-Ten Cent Store," and "My Man."

During the Great Depression of the 1930s, theaters could no longer afford to put on vaudeville shows. It was cheaper to show movies, and soon the theaters stopped featuring live acts. This was the end of vaudeville, and the dawn of modern popular music.

Eddie Cantor (January 31, 1892–1964). Born Edward Israel Iskowitz in New York, Eddie Cantor was a stage performer and singer. As a boy, he liked to sing and juggle for his friends and family; as a teenager, he sang on street corners and won local talent contests. Eventually he moved into vaudeville and became well-known there before being hired by the *Ziegfeld Follies.* He performed in Broadway musicals, radio, movies, and television, and made many recordings over a long and productive career. During World War II he traveled to Europe and entertained troops. At home he helped create the March of Dimes and was president of the Screen Actors Guild and Jewish Theatre Guild. His songs include "If You Knew Susie," "Yes Sir, That's My Baby," "You Must Have Been a Beautiful Baby," and "Merrily We Roll Along."

♫ CD track #17. Listen to "Goober Peas." This humorous song was popular during the Civil War.

> *Recording:* "Goober Peas," performed by Teri Tibbett and Ford James.℗ 2001 Migration Music. Used by permission.

♫ CD track #18. Listen to "Grandfather's Clock," a popular song in the mid-1800s.

> *Recording:* "Grandfather's Clock," by Henry Clay Work. Performed by Doc Watson on *My Dear Old Southern Home.*℗ 1991. Courtesy of Sugar Hill Records. Used by permission.

Name _____ Date _____

Early Popular Music Quiz

Instructions: After reading the **Early Popular Music** student handout, answer these questions (use back of page if necessary).

1. What is **popular music?**

2. List at least four kinds of early American popular music.

3. Pick a famous songwriter or performer from the lesson and tell what you remember about him or her.

4. Describe a **vaudeville** show.

Early Popular Music Quiz: Answer Key

1. What is **popular music?**

   IT IS MUSIC THAT PLEASES THE GENERAL PUBLIC. MAINSTREAM MUSIC.

2. List at least four kinds of early American popular music.

   PATRIOTIC SONGS, BALLADS, COMIC OPERA, MINSTREL SONGS, STEPHEN FOSTER SONGS, POLITICAL SONGS, RALLYING SONGS, HUMOROUS SONGS.

3. Pick a famous songwriter or performer from the lesson and tell what you remember about him or her.

   FRANCIS HOPKINSON, DANIEL EMMETT, STEPHEN FOSTER, HUTCHINSON FAMILY SINGERS, JULIA WARD HOWE, HENRY CLAY WORK, FANNY BRICE, EDDIE CANTOR. STUDENTS SHOULD MAKE REASONABLE RESPONSES ABOUT THEIR CAREERS.

4. Describe a **vaudeville** show.

   IT OPENS WITH A HIGH-ENERGY ACT TO GET THE AUDIENCE'S ATTENTION, FOLLOWED BY SONG-AND-DANCE ROUTINES, JOKES, SINGERS, DANCERS, COMEDIANS, JUGGLERS, ANIMAL ACTS, CLOWNS, MAGICIANS, PUPPETS, MIMES, ROPE SPINNERS, HORSE-BACK RIDERS, ESCAPE ARTISTS, DAREDEVILS. THERE IS USUALLY A STAR OF THE SHOW, A FAMOUS SINGER OR COMEDIAN. SHOW ENDS WITH AN UPBEAT SONG OR DANCE.

♫ Lesson 9. Early Classical Music

Lesson Overview

Classical music, in the strictest sense, refers to European music composed between 1750 and 1820. Featured composers include Ludwig Van Beethoven, Wolfgang Amadeus Mozart, and Franz Joseph Haydn. This was the popular music at the time of the American Revolution. In more common terms, however, classical music has come to describe music played on orchestral instruments with European-based chords and rhythm structures. The first American classical composers composed in the European style. Eventually, some broke away and began composing in new forms, new scales, and with new instruments. *Opera* is a musical play in which the actors tell the story through singing. In grand opera, there are elaborate costumes, sets, and orchestral music. In light opera, the themes are funny and sentimental, and there is singing and dancing, with dialogue.

Vocabulary. Classical music, contemporary music, composer, conductor, instrumentalist, singer, composition, music notation, score, notes, tempo, dynamics, chamber music, string quartet, form, melody, symphony, concerto, opera, grand opera, light opera, overture, recitative, aria, solo, duet, trio, quartet, quintet, chorus.

Purpose. To introduce classical music performed in North America from the 1700s to the early 1900s.

Preparation. Read through the **Early Classical Music** student handout to familiarize yourself with the material. Preview the CD sample (cue in student handout) and have the CD ready for playing with the students. Be prepared to do some or all of the following activities. Also make sure that each student has a music notebook for keeping handouts and activity sheets.

Materials

- **Early Classical Music** student handout *(following)*
- **Early Classical Music Quiz** *(following)*
- **Early Classical Music Quiz Answer Key** *(following)*
- **Music Vocabulary** activity sheet *(Appendix)*
- **My Opinion Page** activity sheet *(Appendix)*
- **Great American Musicians!** activity sheet *(Appendix)*
- **Music on the Map** activity sheet *(Appendix)*
- **Music notebooks**
- **CD music** example on accompanying CD; cue in student handout
- **Additional music selections**

Activities

- Pass out the **Early Classical Music** handout for students to read silently or aloud as a group. Afterwards, have students put the handout in their music notebooks. *(Link to language arts, history, geography, social studies.)*

- Give students the **Early Classical Music Quiz** to assess their understanding of the lesson.

- Go over the music vocabulary at the top of the student handout before or after reading the text. Refer to the glossary for definitions. *Suggestion:* Include these words in a regular class vocabulary lesson, or pass out flashcards with a vocabulary word on one side and the definition on the other and allow students to drill each other. Use the **Music Vocabulary** activity sheet to write out definitions. *(Link to language arts.)*

- Offer the **Vocabulary Challenge.** Students pick some or all of the words in this lesson's vocabulary list to use in a paragraph, essay, short story, or poem. *(Link to language arts.)*

- **Discuss.** Before reading the student handout, discuss what students already know about early classical music in America. Then read the student handout and discuss it again, letting students add what they've learned. *(Link to language arts, social studies.)*

- Offer the **Bonus Challenge: Music in Numbers.** Musical ensembles are also called duos, trios, quartets, quintets, sextets, septets, octets, and so on. How far up can you go? Relate these terms to their mathematical counterparts. *Answer key:* 2 = duo, 3 = trio, 4 = quartet, 5 = quintet, 6 = sextet, 7 = septet, 8 = octet, 9 = nonet. *(Link to math.)*

Extension Activities

For step-by-step directions and activity sheets, see the appendix.

- **My Opinion Page.** Offer students a chance to freely express their own opinions about the music they hear. *(Link to language arts, critical thinking.)*

- **Great American Musicians!** Introduce students to American musicians whose talents have made them notable. *(Link to language arts, history.)*

- **Music on the Map.** Create a map and legend showing musically important places, such as musicians' birthplaces and music hot spots mentioned in the lesson. *(Link to geography.)*

- **Invite a Music Expert.** Invite a classical musician to visit your class and share his or her instrument, singing, and musical style with the students. Some resources for locating musicians are local music and arts organizations, the Internet, friends, students, parents. Also consider taking students to hear a live performance, or present a video performance.

- Consider bringing in **additional selections of music** to expand the musical offerings. Read composer biographies for ideas, or search the Internet, library, or CD store.

Name _____   Date _____

Early American music ensemble. American Tintype, ca. 1875.
Courtesy of Andrew Daneman Collection.

Early Classical Music

Vocabulary: *classical music, contemporary music, composer, conductor, instrumentalist, singer, composition, music notation, score, notes, tempo, dynamics, chamber music, string quartet, form, melody, symphony, concerto, opera, grand opera, light opera, overture, recitative, aria, solo, duet, trio, quartet, quintet, chorus*

Classical music, in the strictest sense, refers to a style of music that was popular in Europe between 1750 and 1820; it was created by composers such as Ludwig Van Beethoven, Wolfgang Amadeus Mozart, and Franz Joseph Haydn. Classical music was the contemporary music of early America.

However, the word *classical* has also come to mean music with European-style structures and chords played on European-style orchestral instruments. Classical music can be performed by a full orchestra or in small groups or by a solo instrument.

Classical music is composed by **composers,** directed by **conductors,** and performed by **instrumentalists** and **singers.**

Unit Two: European-American Music   **143**

Composers. Composers write music. They use their imaginations and write their musical ideas down on paper. It might take days, months, or even years to write an entire musical **composition.** Composers use **music notation**—the notes and symbols of music—to put their ideas on paper. The notes and symbols are arranged into a musical **score,** with all the parts for the musicians to play. The composer is the "author" of the score, while the conductor interprets and directs the score, and the instrumentalists and singers read and perform the score.

Conductors. Conductors direct the musicians. First, the conductor reads the score and decides how it will be performed. He or she talks to the musicians and also uses hand motions or a baton to direct them. Many conductors use their faces and whole bodies to show what they want the orchestra to do. It is the conductor's job to make sure the orchestra plays the correct **notes** (written symbols), **tempo** (speed), **dynamics** (loud and soft parts), and mood (gentle or lively) of the music.

Conductor

Bonus Challenge: Music in Numbers Musical ensembles are also called duos, trios, quartets, quintets, sextets, septets, octets, nonets, and so on. How far up can you go? Relate these terms to their mathematical counterparts. (*Example:* A "duo" refers to a group of "two.")

Instrumentalists and Singers. The people who perform the music are the instrumentalists and singers. There are pianists, violinists, flutists, trombonists, bassists, percussionists, and so on. The voice is the singer's instrument. Both singers and instrumentalists spend many years studying and practicing to develop their musical skills. They read and perform the music written in the score according to their own interpretation, and the interpretation of the conductor and composer.

Pianist and singer

Early Orchestral Music

Until the 1800s, few Americans had ever heard orchestral music performed—only a few American cities could afford to pay for an orchestra. However, many heard **chamber music** performed in parlors and at the homes of wealthy people. Chamber music is like orchestral music in that it is performed on the instruments of Europe. However, instead of being performed by a full orchestra, it is performed in small groups. A **string quartet** is an example of a chamber music group. String quartets play classical music on two violins, a viola, and a cello.

String quartet

Unit Two: European-American Music 145

The growth of full orchestral music in America might well begin with Theodore Thomas (1835–1905), a German-born violinist who spent the years after the Civil War traveling around North America performing and setting up permanent orchestras in America's major cities. He wanted Americans to hear classical music and to develop a taste for it. He gained the attention of audiences by performing popular music alongside classical music.

America's first classical superstar was Louis Moreau Gottschalk, who studied music in Europe and returned to North America to become a celebrity. His music was light and fun and characterized the spirit of America.

Louis Moreau Gottschalk

Gottschalk and other early American composers used European forms of composition in writing their music. A **form** is the structure, or way of organizing the music. For example, the form of a symphony includes sections called *movements,* and each movement has a different **melody** and tempo. Some other classical forms are the concerto and the string quartet.

Louis Moreau Gottschalk (May 8, 1829–1869). Born in Louisiana, Louis Moreau Gottschalk grew up in a neighborhood surrounded by the African-inspired and lively rhythms of Creole music. His first compositions included influences from this folk style of music. When he was thirteen years old he sailed to Europe to begin training in classical music, remaining there to study for more than ten years. When he returned to America, he traveled and performed throughout the United States and Canada to earn a living. He became well-known and respected as an American-born classical composer and pianist. Later in life, he traveled to and performed throughout South America. Some of his pieces are the "Union-Concert Paraphrase on National Airs," "Cuban Country Scenes," and "The Banjo."

Symphony. A **symphony** is a long composition for orchestra. Symphonies are divided into sections called *movements.* Each movement changes melody and tempo (speed) and contrasts with the one before it. For example, the first movement might be fast (*allegro*), the second movement slow (*andante, adagio, lento, largo*), and the third movement fast again (*allegro, presto*).

Concerto. Concertos are compositions for orchestra that feature a solo instrument. For example, a piano concerto features a solo piano with a full orchestra behind it, and a violin concerto features a violin backed by a full orchestra.

String Quartet. A string quartet is a composition for four stringed instruments—two violins, one viola, and one cello. String quartets may also have several movements.

By the turn of the century (1900), there were a handful of Americans composing in the European style of the day. They were John Knowles Paine (1839–1906), Arthur Foote (1853–1937), George Whitefield Chadwick (1854–1931), Horatio William Parker (1863–1919) and Amy Marcy Cheney Beach (Mrs. H.H.A. Beach) (1867–1944).

When European composer Antonin Dvorák lived in America in the late 1800s, he listened to the music of Native Americans and African Americans, and the folk songs of European-Americans. He encouraged American composers to use this music as a resource in composing their own music. Edward MacDowell (1860–1908) was one of the first to do this. He was called an *individualist* because he wrote music in a new style. He experimented with Native American themes in orchestral music. The symphony *Indian Suite* (1896) used a Kiowa chant. "Woodland Sketches" (1896) used the low hum of a string bass to represent the sounds of Indian drums.

John Knowles Paine (January 9, 1839–1906). Born in Maine, John Knowles Paine was a composer, musician, and educator. As a child he studied organ, piano, and music theory. He later studied music in Germany and returned to the United States where he was hired to play organ at a well-known Boston church. He became one of America's first successful composers and the first professor of music at Harvard University, the nation's oldest university. His works were performed in both America and Europe. He composed symphonies, chamber music, program music, and an opera. John Knowles Paine was inducted into the American Classical Music Hall of Fame in 1998. Some of his pieces are "Centennial Hymn," "Island Fantasy," and *Spring Symphony.*

Amy Marcy Cheney Beach (Mrs. H.H.A. Beach) (February 5, 1867–1944). A composer and pianist of classical music, Amy Marcy Cheney Beach was born in New Hampshire. She began playing the piano and composing music at four years old, and by seven she was giving public recitals. She studied music in Boston, and at age thirteen composed her first published piece, "Rainy Day." At seventeen she performed as a soloist with the Boston Symphony. After she married she gave up performing, but continued to compose until 1910 when she returned to the stage. In her lifetime, Mrs. Beach composed sonatas, symphonies, and concert songs that received widespread recognition in both America and Europe. Some of her pieces are "Festival Jubilee," "Gaelic Symphony," and "The Year's at the Spring."

Other composers also used American themes in their compositions. Rubin Goldmark (1872–1936) composed "Hiawatha Overture" in 1899 and "A Negro Rhapsody" in 1923. Harvey Worthington Loomis (1865–1930) composed "Lyrics of the Red Man" in 1903. Arthur Farwell (1872–1952) completed "American Indian Melodies" in 1900 and "Symphonic Song on Old Black Joe" in 1923. Henry F. Gilbert (1868–1928) wrote "Comedy Overture on Negro Themes" in 1905 and "Negro Dances" in 1914.

Early Opera

Opera is a musical play in which the actors tell the story by singing. In **grand opera,** the singers sing out over the orchestra. The costumes are lavish and the sets are elaborate. An orchestra plays on the floor in front of the stage (the pit), while the singers tell the story on the stage. The audience listens intently, respectfully. In **light opera,** the themes are funny and sentimental. The singing, dancing, and dialogue are much lighter and not so serious as grand opera.

A typical opera begins with an orchestral piece called the **overture.** The overture is the opening, the welcoming part of the opera. It is performed while the curtain is still closed and the actors are getting ready. When the curtain rises, the story begins. The actors move about the stage singing all their lines. The **recitative** (pronounced "reh-chee-ta-teef") is like a speech and tells the audience what is happening. **Arias** (pronounced "ah-ree-ah") are more songlike and comment on the character's feelings or emotions—perhaps love or jealousy. Arias are more melodious and pretty sounding.

An opera singer might perform alone as a **solo,** or with another person in a **duet** (two people). Sometimes opera singers perform in **trios** (three people), **quartets** (four people), **quintets** (five people), and so on. A large group with many singers is called a **chorus.** When the chorus sings, the music is louder and bigger.

The story in an opera may be magical or realistic. It may be about a famous person or an important event in history. There are serious operas with dramatic stories, and comic operas that tell funny stories.

History of Grand Opera. Opera began in Italy in the 1590s when a group of noble-men decided to perform the old Greek plays with music. In these plays, they sang the words instead of speaking them. After that, operas became more elaborate—with arias, recitatives, choruses, instrumental parts, comedy, and longer performances. The idea spread throughout Europe and though many serious operas were written in other countries, the most popular operas for over three hundred years were Italian. A typical Italian opera has three acts, with each scene having a recitative (telling what is happening in the story), followed by an aria (commenting on what happened). Operas told of famous legends or events in ancient history. By the 1800s, German opera had become popular as well. In German operas, the music was more expressive, with story lines often telling German histories, myths, and folklore. In the 1900s, opera styles branched out as composers experimented with new ideas and music, composing every-thing from serious operas to expressionist operas, ballad operas, folk operas, jazz operas, rock operas, and electronic operas. In the twenty-first century, operas con-tinue to evolve, telling old and new stories, in new and creative ways.

Grand opera *Aida* at the Metropolitan Opera, 1908–09. Courtesy of Metropolitan Opera Archives.

Unit Two: European-American Music

The first opera performed in America was in a tent in New Orleans in the late 1700s. By 1810, New Orleans was the first American city to have a permanent opera. New York saw its first grand opera open in 1825. By the 1870s, the finest European operas were being performed all over the United States.

The New York Metropolitan Opera House (the Met) opened in 1883, beginning a run of opera seasons that has continued over one hundred years into the twenty-first century. In the early days, only European singers performed the leading roles at the Met, and only European operas were performed there.

At the turn of the century (1900), more Americans were traveling to Europe to train in classical music and opera. As they returned, they began composing and performing for American audiences. Throughout the 1900s, Americans have proven to be as refined as Europeans and worthy of the world's attention.

♪ CD track #19. Listen to "Escensas Campetres" (Cuban Country Scenes), an example of early American classical music, performed by the Berlin Symphony Orchestra, Vienna State Opera Orchestra with Cary Lewis, Eugene List, conducted by Samuel Adler, Igor Buketoff.

Music: Composed by Louis Moreau Gottschalk (public domain). *Recording:* From *A Gottschalk Festival* CD. ℗1992 Vox Music Group. Used by permission.

Name _____   Date _____

Early Classical Music Quiz

Instructions: After reading the **Early Classical Music** student handout, answer these questions (use back of the page if necessary).

1. Describe **classical music.**

2. Describe the jobs of these musicians: **composer, conductor, instrumentalist, singer.**

3. What is a **string quartet?**

4. What is a **symphony?**

5. What is a **concerto?**

6. What is an **opera?**

Early Classical Music Quiz: Answer Key

1. Describe **classical music.**

   A PERIOD IN EUROPEAN MUSIC HISTORY FROM 1750 TO 1820; MORE COMMONLY TODAY THE TERM REFERS TO MUSIC WITH EUROPEAN-STYLE CHORDS AND STRUCTURES THAT IS PLAYED ON EUROPEAN ORCHESTRAL INSTRUMENTS.

2. Describe the jobs of these musicians:

   composer: PERSON WHO COMPOSES, OR WRITES, THE MUSIC.
   conductor: PERSON WHO DIRECTS THE MUSIC.
   instrumentalist: PERSON WHO PLAYS THE MUSIC ON AN INSTRUMENT.
   singer: PERSON WHO SINGS THE MUSIC.

3. What is a **string quartet?**

   A COMPOSITION FOR TWO VIOLINS, ONE VIOLA, AND ONE CELLO.

4. What is a **symphony?**

   A LONG COMPOSITION FOR ORCHESTRA, DIVIDED INTO MOVEMENTS, WITH EACH MOVEMENT HAVING A DIFFERENT TEMPO AND MELODY THAT CONTRASTS THE ONE BEFORE IT.

5. What is a **concerto?**

   A COMPOSITION FOR ORCHESTRA THAT FEATURES A SOLO INSTRUMENT.

6. What is an **opera?**

   A STORY TOLD IN SONG. GRAND OPERA IS LAVISH WITH ELABORATE SETS. LIGHT OPERA IS FUNNY OR SENTIMENTAL WITH SINGING AND DANCING; IT IS NOT SO SERIOUS AS GRAND OPERA.

♪ Lesson 10. Instruments of the Orchestra

Lesson Overview

The instruments of a European-style orchestra are divided into sections: strings, woodwinds, brass, and percussion. Music is written for the instruments of each section, creating the full sound of the orchestra. This lesson looks at each of these sections and divides the instruments into families called chordophones, aerophones, idiophones, and membranophones.

Vocabulary. Orchestra, sections, strings, woodwinds, brass instruments, percussion instruments, chordophones, vibrate, resonator, aerophones, low pitch, high pitch, idiophones, membranophones.

Purpose. To introduce the instruments of the orchestra, how they are divided into sections, how sound is made through them, and how they all fit into the larger families of instruments called membranophones, aerophones, idiophones, and chordophones.

Preparation. Read through the **Instruments of the Orchestra** student handout to familiarize yourself with the material. Preview the CD sample (cue in student handout) and have the CD ready for playing with the students. Be prepared to do some or all of the following activities. Also make sure that each student has a music notebook for keeping handouts and activity sheets.

Materials

- **Instruments of the Orchestra** student handout *(following)*
- **Orchestral Instruments Picture Page 1** *(following)*
- **Orchestral Instruments Picture Page 2** *(following)*
- **Orchestral Instruments Picture Page 1 and 2 Answer Keys** *(following)*
- **Music Vocabulary** activity sheet *(Appendix)*
- **Family of Instruments: Chordophones** activity sheet *(Appendix)*
- **Family of Instruments: Aerophones** activity sheet *(Appendix)*
- **Family of Instruments: Membranophones** activity sheet *(Appendix)*
- **Family of Instruments: Idiophones** activity sheet *(Appendix)*
- **Music notebooks**
- **CD music** example on accompanying CD; cue in student handout
- **Additional music selections**

Activities

- Pass out the **Instruments of the Orchestra** handout for students to read silently or aloud as a group. Afterwards, have students put the handout in their music notebooks. *(Link to language arts, history, geography, social studies.)*

- Have students write the correct names and instrument families under each picture on the **Orchestral Instruments Picture Page.** See the answer key for correct answers. Also see **Families of Instruments** in other lessons and in the extension activities in the appendix for directions. *(Link to language arts, science.)*

- Go over the music vocabulary at the top of the student handout before or after reading the text. Refer to the glossary for definitions. *Suggestion:* Include these words in a regular class vocabulary lesson, or pass out flashcards with a vocabulary word on one side and the definition on the other and allow students to drill each other. Use the **Music Vocabulary** activity sheet to write out definitions. *(Link to language arts.)*

- Offer students the **Vocabulary Challenge.** Students pick some or all of the words in this lesson's vocabulary list to use in a paragraph, essay, short story, or poem. *(Link to language arts.)*

- **Discuss.** Before reading the student handout, discuss what students already know about instruments of the orchestra. Then read the student handout and discuss it again, letting students add what they've learned. *(Link to language arts, social studies.)*

- **Sections of the Orchestra.** Learn the sections of the orchestra: strings, woodwinds, brass, and percussion. *Step 1:* Follow the teacher directions for cutting up the instruments in the **Families of Instruments** activity in the extension activities in the appendix. *Step 2:* Mix up the instrument pictures. *Step 3:* Ask students to divide the instrument pictures into sections of the orchestra, on their own, making a picture of a full orchestra. *Answer key:* Strings section = violin, viola, cello, double bass, harp. Woodwinds section = piccolo, flute, clarinet, oboe, bassoon. Brass section = trumpet, trombone, French horn, tuba. Percussion section = drum, kettle drum, triangle, cymbal, tambourine, xylophone, piano.

- Offer the **Bonus Challenge: Which Section Does the Piano Belong In?** *Answer:* The piano belongs in the percussion section.

- Offer the **Bonus Challenge: Which Family of Instruments Does the Piano Belong To?** *Answer:* The piano is both a chordophone *and* idiophone because it has both strings and hammers which tap the strings.

Extension Activities

For step-by-step directions and activity sheets, see the appendix.

- **My Opinion Page.** Offer students a chance to freely express their own opinions about the music they hear. *[Link to language arts, critical thinking.]*

- **Families of Instruments.** Divide the instruments mentioned in the lesson into instrument families grouped according to how they make sound. *[Link to science, language arts.]*

- **Instrument Shuffle.** Deepen students' understanding and recognition of the instrument family groups by calling out and holding up pictures of instruments and grouping them into families. For correct groupings, refer to the Orchestral Instruments Picture Pages 1 and 2 answer keys in this lesson. *[Link to language arts, science.]*

- **Research an Instrument.** Encourage students to become familiar with a specific instrument mentioned in the lesson and do research into its history, what its made of, how it produces sound, and interesting facts about it. As students complete their research, compile their work into an "Encyclopedia of Musical Instruments." *[Link to science, history.]*

- **Invite a Music Expert.** Invite an orchestral musician to visit your class and share his or her instrument, singing, and musical style with the students. Some resources for locating musicians are local music and arts organizations, the Internet, friends, students, parents. Also consider taking students to hear a live performance or present a video of a performance in the classroom.

- **The Science of Music.** The **Science of Music** sections in the student handout explore the science of sound. *[Link to science.]*

Name _____ Date _____

Juneau Symphony Orchestra. Photograph by Michael Penn.
Courtesy Juneau Symphony Orchestra.

Instruments of the Orchestra

Vocabulary: orchestra, sections, strings, woodwinds, brass instruments, percussion instruments, chordophones, vibrate, resonator, aerophones, low pitch, high pitch, idiophones, membranophones

When the kettle drums rumble and the violins play, when the cymbals crash and the horns shout over the tops of the flutes, violas, double basses, and cellos—this is the sound of an orchestra! It is a big sound, loud and dynamic; at other times, it is soft and gentle.

An **orchestra** is a group of instruments that are played together. It can be as raw as a batch of pots and pans beating together, or as sophisticated as one hundred orchestral instruments playing a symphony in a grand hall.

In European-style classical music, the instruments are divided into different groups called **sections.** The sections are the **strings, woodwinds, brass instruments,** and **percussion instruments.**

These instruments are played by musicians who train for many years. Each instrument in the orchestra is one part of a whole team of players, although there are times when individuals step out and play solos with the orchestra's backing.

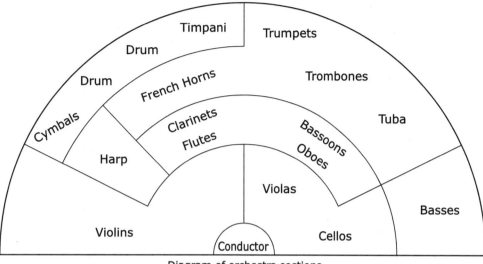

Diagram of orchestra sections

The Strings

Violin   Viola   Cello   Double bass   Harp

The Science of Music: Strings Are Chordophones. Chordophones are instruments with strings. They are plucked or rubbed (bowed) to make a sound. *Chord* has to do with string and *phone* has to do with sound. When a string is plucked or rubbed, it **vibrates** and makes a sound. When the vibrating string touches a hollow box or container, or **resonator,** it makes the container vibrate, as well as the air inside the container. It's the vibrating air that makes the sound. *Activity: Bring in stringed instruments to view and play; invite a local professional musician or student to demonstrate; visit the school orchestra; or make your own stringed instrument. If possible, pluck a string, watch it vibrate, feel the wood vibrating; imagine that the air vibrating inside is causing the sound; notice which instruments have a lower sound and which have a higher sound.*

Lesson 10. Student Handout continued

The Woodwinds

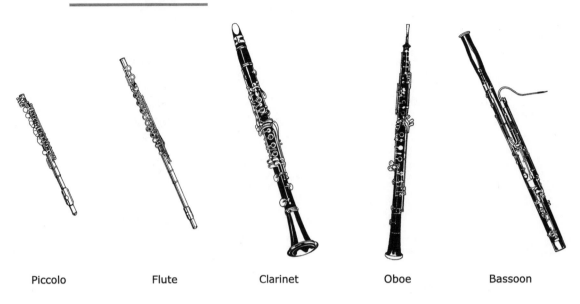

Piccolo   Flute   Clarinet   Oboe   Bassoon

The Brass

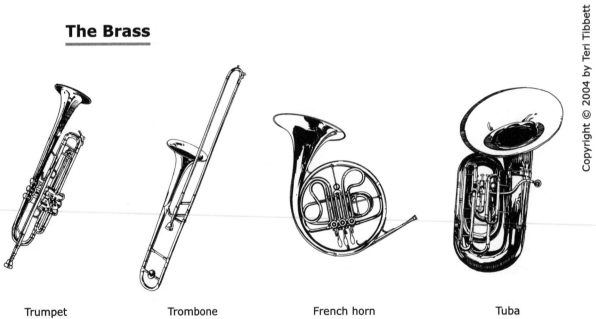

Trumpet   Trombone   French horn   Tuba

The Science of Music: Woodwinds and Brass Are Aerophones. Aerophones are instruments that are blown. In an orchestra, these are the wind instruments, both woodwinds and brass. *Aero* has to do with air. *Phone* has to do with sound. Air-sound! Blowing into an aerophone sends a stream of air into the tube or pipe, creating a vibrating column of air. It's the *vibrating* air inside the column that makes the sound. When the tube is long or fat, like a tuba, there is more air vibrating inside, and the sound is ***low-pitched.*** If the tube is short or skinny, like a piccolo, there is less air vibrating inside, and the sound is ***high-pitched.*** The holes in the tube allow the player to change the pitches by changing the length of the tube. For instance, covering all the holes makes a long tube and the pitch is low (more air vibrating inside). Opening all the holes shortens the column and the pitch is high (less air vibrating inside). *Activity: Bring in wind instruments to view and play; invite a local professional musician or student to demonstrate; visit the school orchestra or band class; or make your own wind instrument. If possible, blow into the instruments to test the different styles of blowing (be sure to have a sterilization system in place), or watch others blow them and observe. Note different ways of blowing, the different sounds, different shapes, and different materials. Imagine the instrument filled with vibrating air. Note the longer, bigger instruments have more air vibrating inside, creating lower pitches, and the shorter, thinner instruments have less air vibrating inside, creating higher pitches. Consider gathering a variety of bottles and fill each with a different amount of water. Blow across the top of each one until you create a sound. Notice the differences from bottle to bottle. Look for low and high pitches.*

The Percussion

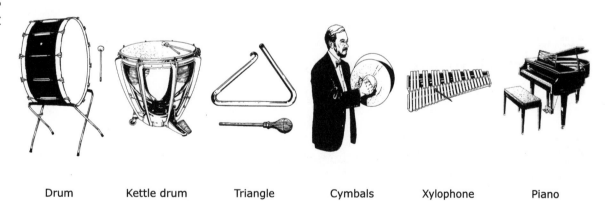

| Drum | Kettle drum | Triangle | Cymbals | Xylophone | Piano |

The Science of Music: Percussion Instruments Are Idiophones. Idiophones are instruments that are shaken, struck, clapped, or rubbed together to make a sound. They can be maracas, triangles, cymbals, xylophones, castanets, and guiros. Maracas are shakers with tiny seeds beating against the inside. Castanets are pieces of wood that clap together. Triangles and xylophones are struck with wands or mallets. Guiros are rubbed with sticks. When these materials come in contact with each other, they vibrate. Once again, it's the vibrating air in and around the vibrating object that makes the sound. *Activity: Bring in percussion instruments to view and play; invite a professional local musician or student to demonstrate; visit the school orchestra or band class; or make an idiophone. If possible, shake them, strike them, clap them, rub them, and compare their sounds.*

The Science of Music: Drums Are Membranophones. Membranophones are instruments that have a stretchy layer of skin or paper, called a membrane, stretched across a container. They are played by hitting or striking the stretched membrane. The striking causes the membrane to vibrate, setting the container and the air around it in motion. Vibrating air makes the sound. The bigger the container, the more air vibrates, and the louder and *lower* the sound. The smaller the container, the less air vibrates and the softer and *higher* the sound. *Activity: Bring in drums to view and play; invite a local professional musician or student to demonstrate; visit the school orchestra or band class; or make your own drum. Touch the drumhead or the container lightly to feel the vibration. Listen, too. Notice the difference between big and small drums.*

Bonus Challenge: Which Section Does the Piano Belong In? Write your answer in this space.

Bonus Challenge: Which Instrument Family Does the Piano Belong To? Write your answer in this space.

♪ CD track #19. Listen to "Escensas Campetres" (Cuban Country Scenes), an example of orchestral music, performed by the Berlin Symphony Orchestra, Vienna State Opera Orchestra with Cary Lewis, Eugene List, conducted by Samuel Adler, Igor Buketoff.

> *Music:* Composed by Louis Moreau Gottschalk (public domain). *Recording:* From *A Gottschalk Festival* CD. ℗1992 Vox Music Group. Used by permission.

Name_____ Date_____

Orchestral Instruments Picture Page 1

Instructions: Write the name of the instrument, the family group it belongs to, and the instrument section it belongs to on the lines provided under each picture.

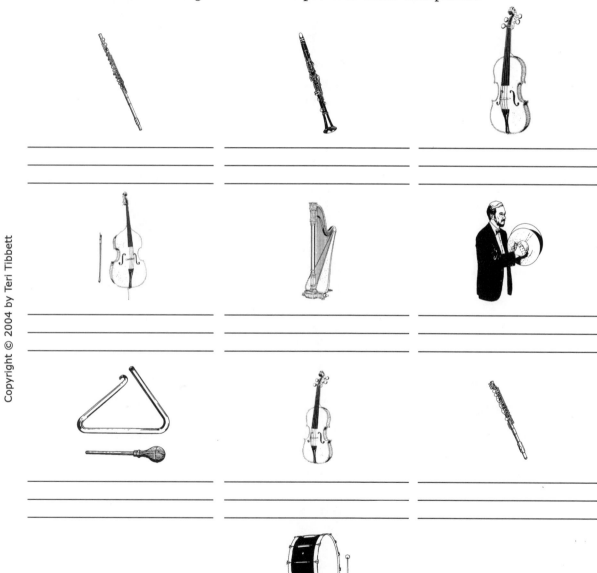

Orchestral Instruments Picture Page 1:
Answer Key

Flute
Aerophone
Woodwinds

Clarinet
Aerophone
Woodwinds

Viola
Chordophone
Strings

Double bass
Chordophone
Strings

Harp
Chordophone
Strings

Cymbals
Idiophone
Percussion

Triangle
Idiophone
Percussion

Violin
Chordophone
Strings

Piccolo
Aerophone
Woodwinds

Drum
Membranophone
Percussion

Name _____   Date _____

Orchestral Instruments Picture Page 2

Instructions: Write the name of the instrument, the family group it belongs to, and the instrument section it belongs to on the lines provided under each picture.

_____

_____

_____

_____

_____

_____

_____

_____

_____

_____

_____

_____

_____

_____

_____

_____

_____

_____

_____

_____

_____

_____

_____

_____

_____

_____

_____

_____

_____

_____

Orchestral Instruments Picture Page 2:
Answer Key

Cello
Chordophone
Strings

Trombone
Aerophone
Brass

Bassoon
Aerophone
Woodwinds

Oboe
Aerophone
Woodwinds

Trumpet
Aerophone
Brass

Xylophone
Idiophone
Percussion

Kettle drum
Membranophone
Percussion

Piano
Idiophone/chordophone
Strings

Tuba
Aerophone
Brass

French horn
Aerophone
Brass

Unit Three

African-American Music

Contents

Unit Three: Overview

This unit explores the heritage of African-American music in North America from its origins in early slave music to blues, jazz, soul, and funk. African-American slaves brought with them a rich tradition of African music and dance, which transformed into something new when mixed with the instruments and influences of the European-Americans. African-American slaves sang daily to accompany their work and worship. In the fields, they sang field calls to communicate with one another and to comfort themselves. At home, they played singing games and sang lullabies to their children. In their churches, they sang songs that helped give them a sense of hope. Music offered a means to express the intense emotions that were always a part of slave existence in America.

Spirituals and gospel music are sacred music. Spirituals are emotional songs; they expressed the sadness of the slave condition but also the hope of salvation. Singing spirituals was a way for slaves to make music that was acceptable to the plantation owners, who often forbade other forms of music expression. After emancipation in 1863, spirituals traveled with the people to the cities and towns they moved to. By the 1930s a new form of sacred music was taking shape: gospel music. Gospel is modern sacred music that mixes the soulful, heartfelt lyrics of spirituals with the rhythms, instruments, and upbeat tempos of modern urban music. Gospel music is the evolution of African-American spiritual music.

As African Americans moved away from the plantations, they carried with them the musical styles they had developed during over two hundred years of slave life. The field calls, spirituals, rhyming songs, singing games, and lullabies went with them and mixed with the traditions of the European-Americans. The musically inclined sang on street corners and in small clubs to earn a living. They composed their own songs based on the experiences of their lives, which were often sad or desperate. The songs reflected the hunger, poverty, and racism they encountered after gaining their freedom from slavery. This music came to be known as country blues. Early country blues players accompanied themselves on acoustic guitar, banjo, and piano. As time went by, as they moved north into the cities, they found work in clubs that featured blues singers and players. Over time more instruments were added, tempos were increased, and the blues transformed itself into a more modern-sounding urban style of blues, or dance music.

Dancing was always a part of African-American traditions—from dancing at church gatherings and after work on the plantations, to dancing in "juke joints" and African-American clubs and bars after emancipation. Ragtime music and New Orleans jazz were some of the first popular dance music forms to emerge from African traditions around the turn of the twentieth century. Eventually, as European-Americans heard the music and began performing it, these styles spread and became famous among mainstream audiences. By mid-century, as the civil rights movement swept across the country, opening more opportunities for African Americans to record and perform, their music finally came to the forefront of American culture.

Both soul and funk evolved from the blues, spirituals, gospel, and dance music of the 1950s. Soul mixes gospel music with rhythm and blues, creating a passionate, upbeat, rhythmic style of music. In the 1960s, the Motown Records label made music history by featuring African-American artists with a string of number one soul music hits over a period of many years. Funk music followed in the 1970s, mixing soul with rock and jazz. The result was a progressive, groove-oriented, highly danceable music.

♫ Lesson 11. Music of the Slaves

Lesson Overview

Before coming to North America, Africans sang and danced and played instruments to accompany their working, relaxing, celebrating, and worshipping. Once in America, most were not allowed to sing or dance in their traditional ways, but the drive to do so did not disappear. In the fields, they sang to communicate with one another and to soothe themselves. At religious gatherings, they sang sacred songs that expressed both joy and sadness, and the hope for salvation. At home, they played singing games and sang lullabies to their children. Music offered them a way to express the intense emotions that were so often a part of slave life.

Vocabulary. Traditional songs, oral tradition, field calls, call-and-response, antiphonal, work songs, rhythm, tempo, spirituals, lullaby, rhyming song, rhymes, banjo.

Purpose. To offer an introduction to the music performed by African-American slaves and the instruments they played.

Preparation. Read the student handout **Music of the Slaves** to familiarize yourself with the material. Preview the CD sample (cue in student handout) and have the CD ready for playing with the students. Be prepared to do some or all of the following activities. Also make sure that each student has a music notebook for keeping handouts and activity sheets.

Materials

- **Music of the Slaves** student handout *(following)*
- **Music of the Slaves Quiz** *(following)*
- **Music of the Slaves Quiz Answer Key** *(following)*
- **Early African-American Instruments Picture Page** activity sheet *(following)*
- **Early African-American Instruments Picture Page Answer Key** *(following)*
- **Music Vocabulary** activity sheet *(Appendix)*
- **My Opinion Page** activity sheet *(Appendix)*
- **How to Teach a Song** teacher guide *(Appendix)*
- **Songs as Poetry** activity sheet *(Appendix)*
- **Music notebooks**
- **CD music** example on accompanying CD; cue in student handout
- **Additional music selections**

Activities

- Pass out the **Music of the Slaves** handout for students to read silently or aloud as a group. Afterwards, have students put the handout in their music notebooks. *(Link to language arts, history, geography, social studies.)*

- Give the **Music of the Slaves Quiz** to assess student understanding of the lesson.

- Have students write in the correct names and instrument families under each picture on the **Early African-American Instrument Picture Page.** See the answer key for correct answers. *(Link to language arts, science.)*

- Go over the music vocabulary at the top of the student handout before or after reading the text. Refer to the glossary for definitions. *Suggestion:* Include these words in a regular class vocabulary lesson, or pass out flashcards with a vocabulary word on one side and the definition on the other and allow students to drill each other. Use the **Music Vocabulary** activity sheet to write out definitions. *(Link to language arts.)*

- Have students take the **Vocabulary Challenge.** Students pick some or all of the words in this lesson's vocabulary list to use in a paragraph, essay, short story, or poem. *(Link to language arts.)*

- **Discuss.** Before reading the student handout, discuss what students already know about African-American slave music. Read the student handout and discuss it again, letting students add what they've learned. *(Link to language arts, social studies.)*

- **Who Took the Cookie from the Cookie Jar?** This is an African-American ring game and rhyming song. It is played while sitting in a circle and chanting the lyrics while clapping hands and thighs alternately in a steady rhythm. The goal is to keep the rhythm going without stopping. *Step 1:* Students form a circle and each is given a number, or their names can be used. *Step 2:* The chant is begun by everyone together (see the words in the student handout). Keep it going until all the numbers (or names) have been called. *Suggestion:* If the exercise seems too easy, increase the tempo of the hand-clap–thigh-slap movements and use students' names instead of numbers. The faster it is, the more difficult it is to keep up.

- **Bonus Challenge: Families of Instruments.** Divide the instruments mentioned in this lesson into instrument families (see the **Science of Music** sections in Lesson 10 in Unit Two). *Answer key:* Chordophones = banjo, banjar, fiddle, harp, harp guitar, hunting bow. Idiophones = xylophone, bone castanet. Aerophones = flute, whistle, horn. Membranophones = drum. *(Link to science.)*

Extension Activities

For step-by-step directions and activity sheets, see the appendix.

- **My Opinion Page.** Offer students a chance to freely express their own opinions about the music they hear. *(Link to language arts, critical thinking.)*

- **Sing a Song.** Learn a simple early African-American song from this lesson. *Suggested songs to learn:* "Miss Mary Mack" and "Hambone." *(Link to singing, language arts, rhythm, melody.)*

- **Songs as Poetry.** Examine the lyrics of songs for their poetic nature. *(Link to language arts.)*

- **Illustrate the Music.** Students illustrate a song or piece of music by drawing, coloring, or painting their ideas of what the music "looks" like visually. *(Link to language arts, visual arts.)*

- **Families of Instruments.** Divide the instruments mentioned in the lesson into instrument families grouped according to how they make sound. *(Link to science, language arts.)*

- **Research an Instrument.** Encourage students to become familiar with a specific instrument mentioned in a lesson and do research into its history, what it is made of, how it produces sound, and interesting facts about it. As students complete their research, compile their work into an "Encyclopedia of Instruments." *(Link to science, history.)*

- Consider bringing in **additional selections of music** from other sources to expand the music examples for this lesson. Search the Internet, library, local music store, or your own collection.

- **The Oral Tradition.** Illustrate the oral tradition by playing the game "Telephone." *(Link to social studies.)*

- **My Musical Traditions.** Investigate individual family traditions, including musical ones. *Step 1:* Ask students to answer the questions on the **My Musical Traditions** activity sheet. *Step 2:* Discuss the students' answers. *Step 3:* Put sheets away in music notebooks. *(Link to language arts, social studies.)*

Name _____ Date _____

Music of the Slaves

Vocabulary: traditional songs, oral tradition, field calls, call-and-response, antiphonal, work songs, rhythm, tempo, spirituals, lullaby, rhyming song, rhymes, banjo

The first African Americans to live in North America came on ships from Africa and were sold as slaves. More than fifteen million Africans were carried across the seas over the course of 245 years, many settling in the southern United States. Most were forbidden to bring their traditional instruments or sing their **traditional songs,** and because of this much of their musical culture was left behind. The slaves eventually adopted the musical styles of their owners but they also remembered their own traditions, and so their music over time became a blending of the two.

African Traditions

Singing was a part of everyday life in Africa. People sang when they worked, rested, celebrated, got married, played games, or worshipped. As in many cultures of the world, Africans remembered their histories and traditions through music. Many of their legends, traditions, and values were stored in the words of their songs, which passed from generation to generation by the **oral tradition.**

The Oral Tradition. The oral tradition is passing information by singing or telling. African elders taught young people to sing songs that carried the legends and histories of the tribe. They taught them very carefully so that the young people would remember every word correctly. The children then grew up, and when they were adults, taught the songs to their children. In this way, stories and legends, which contain the values and morals of the culture, were passed on.

The most important instruments in the African tradition were rhythm instruments, usually drums and rattles. However, Africans also played wooden bars placed over boxes or gourds and hit with a mallet, and stringed instruments like harps, harp guitars, and hunting bows made from wood and gut. They played flutes and whistles made from bamboo, wood, and clay, and horns made from animal horns and tusks.

Music in the New Land

Most slaves were not allowed to speak their native languages or sing their native songs once they were in America. The drive to make music, however, did not stop. In spite of their hardships, the slaves sang in almost all situations. They sang on the ships coming over. They sang in the fields when they worked. They sang while tending the horses and cleaning the owner's house. They sang in the evenings in their homes. They sang lullabies to their children and singing games just for fun.

Field calls were sung in the field when the people worked. They were often sung in the **call-and-response** style—where one might "call out" to ask for water or food, or to greet a friend, or to express how he or she was feeling—and another would "respond" with an answer. The "Water Boy" song is an example of a field call. The water carrier was an important person in the fields, where slaves worked long hours under the hot sun. Songs that called for the water boy were common.

Water Boy

Water boy, water boy!
Water boy, water boy!
Water on the wheel.
How does the sun shine that I feel?
Little water time, hey, little water boy,
Little water time, hey, little water boy.
Water on the wheel.
How does the sun shine that I feel, little water boy?

From *Negro Folk Music U.S.A.*, by Harold Courlander.
Copyright © 1963, Columbia University Press, New York.
Copyright © 1991, Dover Publishing, New York.

> **Call-and-response** singing is common in African music. Call-and-response is when one person or group sings out (calls) and another person or group echoes (responds). Call-and-response is also known as **antiphonal** singing. *Anti* has to do with "opposite" and *phonal* has to do with sound. Opposite-sound! With call-and-response, the singing goes back and forth between opposing groups. This can mean two groups taking turns, like two choruses, or a leader singing first and a chorus responding.

The slaves sang **work songs** while they worked. They were sung to accompany repetitive tasks—like digging, picking, or pulling. The songs were rhythmical and helped the slaves keep a **rhythm** in their work. For example, a slow work song might be sung for hauling a heavy load, while a fast song might be sung for digging or hammering. The **tempo** (speed) of the song, then, would depend on the work being done. On the rice plantations, workers sang songs while beating the bundles of rice. In these cases, two men would take turns beating the sack, one right after another, which they did in a rhythmical way while singing a song. "Goin' to Beat This Rice" is an example of a work song.

Goin' to Beat This Rice

I goin' to beat this rice
Goin' to beat 'em so.
Goin' to beat 'em till the husks come off.
Ah Hannah, Ah Hannah!
Goin' to cook this rice when I get through.
Goin' to cook 'em so,
Ah Hannah, Ah Hannah!
Goin' to eat my belly full
Ah Hannah, Ah Hannah!

From *Negro Folk Music U.S.A.*, by Harold Courlander.
Copyright © 1963, Columbia University Press, New York.
Copyright © 1991, Dover Publishing, New York.

One of the styles of music that the slave owners allowed the slaves to sing was sacred music, or **spirituals.** These religious songs expressed emotions and feelings of hope. They were sung at church gatherings, at home, and during everyday life. Sometimes "moaning" or "groaning" happened in a song to express emotional feelings.

As in all cultures of the world, African Americans sang **lullabies** to their babies and children. Lullabies communicated stories, lessons, and affection. They could teach values, like patience and forgiveness or tolerance and respect. "Mama's Gonna Buy Him a Little Lap Dog" is a traditional lullaby with a hopeful message.

Mama's Gonna Buy Him a Little Lap Dog

Mama's gonna buy him a little lap dog.
Mama's gonna buy him a little lap dog.
Mama's gonna buy him a little lap dog,
Put him in his lap while she goes off.
Come up coffee, hey, hey!
Come up coffee, hey, hey!
Don't you fret and don't you cry.
Mama's gonna give you some apple pie.

From *Negro Folk Music of Alabama. Vol. 1: Secular.*
Recorded in Alabama by Harold Courlander for Ethnic-Folkways Library.

Rhyming songs were sung for games and dances. **Rhymes** are words that sound the same: "jump" and "bump" or "talk" and "walk," for example. There were rhyming songs for skipping and jumping, for ring games and circle games, and more. Many were passed from generation to generation, but children also made up their own verses to the rhyming songs and performed them with their own rhythms. "Miss Mary Mack" is an example of a traditional rhyming song.

Miss Mary Mack

Miss Mary Mack, Mack, Mack
All dressed in black, black, black
With silver buttons, buttons, buttons
Up and down her back, back, back.

And I love coffee, coffee, coffee,
And I love tea, tea, tea,
And the boys love me, me, me.

I went to the river, river, river
And I couldn't get across, 'cross, 'cross.
And I paid five dollars, dollars, dollars,
For the old gray horse, horse, horse.

And the horse wouldn't pull, pull, pull,
I swapped him for a bull, bull, bull.
And the bull wouldn't holler, holler, holler,
I swapped him for a dollar, dollar, dollar.

And the dollar wouldn't spend, spend, spend,
I put it in the grass, grass, grass,
And the grass wouldn't grow, grow, grow,
I got my hoe, hoe, hoe.

And the hoe wouldn't chop, chop, chop,
I took it to the shop, shop, shop,
And the shop made money, money, money,
Like the bees made honey, honey, honey.

See that yonder, yonder, yonder,
In the jaybird town, town, town,
Where the women got to work, work, work,
'Til the sun goes down, down, down.

Well, I eat my meat, meat, meat,
And I gnaw my bone, bone, bone,
Well goodbye honey, honey, honey,
I'm going on home.

From *Negro Folk Music U.S.A.*, by Harold Courlander.
Copyright © 1963, Columbia University Press, New York.
Copyright © 1991, Dover Publishing, New York.

Who Took the Cookie from the Cookie Jar? This African-American ring game is played standing (or sitting) in a circle, chanting the song, while clapping hands and thighs alternately in a steady rhythm. The goal is to keep the rhythm going and the song going without stopping. *Activity: Step 1: Students form a circle and each is given a number (or just use names). Step 2: Begin clapping: hands-thighs-hands-thighs, to establish the rhythm. Step 3: When the rhythm is established, begin chanting the following words and keep going until everyone's number or name has been called. If the game seems too easy, increase the tempo of the hands-thighs-hands-thighs rhythm. The faster it is, the more difficult it is to keep up.*

All together: *Who took the cookie from the cookie jar?*
Leader: *Number 1 (or the person's name) took the cookie from the cookie jar.*
Number 1: *Who me?*
Leader: *Yes you!*
Number 1: *Couldn't be!*
Leader: *Then who?*
Number 1: *Number 7 (or person's name) took the cookie from the cookie jar.*
Number 7: *Who me?*
Number 1: *Yes you!*
Number 7: *Couldn't be.*
Number 1: *Then who?*
Number 7: *Number 5 (or person's name) took the cookie from the cookie jar.*
And so on.

One African tradition to survive in America was call-and-response singing. Many of the songs the slaves sang were in this style. Field calls and work songs were often started by a solo singer and answered by a chorus of people. Rhyming and other game songs were also performed with a leader and a chorus. "Hambone" is a traditional African-American song that uses the call-and-response style.

Hambone

Call: Hambone! Hambone! Where ya been?
Response: Around the world and I'm back again.
Call: Hambone! Hambone! Where ya been?
Response: Around the world and I'm back again.
Call: Hambone! Hambone! Where's your wife?
Response: In the kitchen cookin' rice.

Hambone! Hambone! Have you heard?
Papa gonna buy me a mockingbird.
If that mockingbird don't sing,
Papa gonna buy me a diamond ring.
And if that diamond ring don't shine,
Papa gonna buy me a fishin' line,
Papa gonna buy me a fishin' line.

Call: Hambone! Hambone! Where ya been?
Response: Around the world and I'm goin' again.
Call: Hambone! Hambone! Where ya been?
Response: I'm goin' around and I'm goin' again.

Around the world and I'm goin' again.
Around the world and I'm goin' again.
Hambone! Hambone! Hambone!
Around the world and I'm goin' again.

Musical Instruments

African-American slaves had no money to buy musical instruments and so they made their own from materials they found around them. They made drums from hollowed-out tree trunks with stretched sheepskin or goatskin for a drumhead. They made thumb pianos from wood planks with metal tongs for plucking. They made xylophones from pieces of wood placed over boxes or gourds. They made whistles and flutes from bones and reeds. They made castanets from bones.

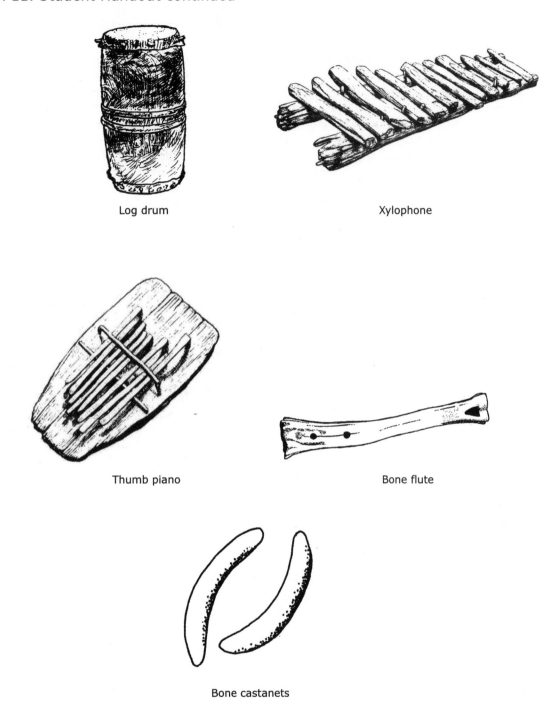

Log drum

Xylophone

Thumb piano

Bone flute

Bone castanets

One of the African instruments to reappear in the new world was a stringed instrument with a wooden neck and gourd body. In Africa, it was called a *banjar.* In America, the instrument was reworked with new materials and evolved into the present-day **banjo.**

Unit Three: African-American Music

The History of the Banjo. The banjo is basically a drum with strings that are attached to a neck. The strings can be plucked or strummed to make a sound. The American banjo is believed to have come from the *banjar,* an African instrument made of a gourd, wood, and gut. The slaves remembered banjars from their homelands and made them in America. The first American banjos were made by stretching an animal skin across a gourd body, adding a wooden neck, and stringing it with hemp or gut. Eventually, European-Americans began playing them in the minstrel shows of the mid-1800s. The instrument then traveled west during the Gold Rush and was played in the shows that entertained the miners of the late 1800s. Later, the banjo was played in early jazz and bluegrass music because it was a loud instrument that could be heard over the other instruments in the band. Today, the banjo is played in many different musical styles.

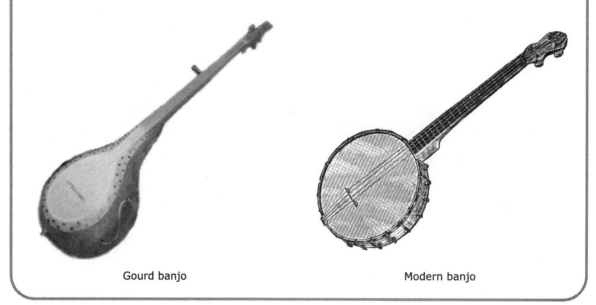

Gourd banjo   Modern banjo

Eventually, slaves learned to play fiddles (folk violins) for the plantation owners' dances. After the dances, the musicians took them home and played their own kind of music for themselves, changing the rhythms and chords to match their own styles and traditions.

♫ CD track #20. Listen to "Hambone," an African-American rhyming song, performed by Taj Mahal.

Recording: "Hambone," performed by Taj Mahal. From *Shake It to the One You Love the Best.* © 1986 Warren-Mattox Productions.

Bonus Challenge: Families of Instruments. Divide the instruments mentioned in this lesson into their instrument families: chordophones, membranophones, idiophones, and aerophones.

Name _____ Date _____

Music of the Slaves Quiz

Instructions: After reading the **Music of the Slaves** student handout, answer these questions (use back of page if necessary).

1. What were some of the music traditions of Africans before they came to America?

2. What were some of the ways the slaves made music in the new land?

3. What are **field calls**?

4. Tell about the history of the **banjo.**

Music of the Slaves Quiz: Answer Key

1. What were some of the music traditions of Africans before they came to America?

   SINGING; DRUMMING; DANCING; CALL-AND-RESPONSE SINGING; THE ORAL TRADITION; PLAYING INSTRUMENTS LIKE DRUMS, RATTLES, HARP GUITARS, HUNTING BOWS, WHISTLES, FLUTES, AND HORNS.

2. What were some of the ways the slaves made music in the new land?

   SINGING FIELD CALLS, WORK SONGS, CALL-AND-RESPONSE SONGS, SPIRITUALS, LULLABIES, RHYMING SONGS; PLAYING DRUMS, THUMB PIANOS, XYLOPHONES MADE FROM WOOD, WHISTLES AND FLUTES MADE FROM BONES AND REEDS, CASTANETS MADE FROM BONE, GOURD BANJOS.

3. What are **field calls?**

   SONGS OR CALLS THAT ASK FOR SOMETHING, OR RELAY A MESSAGE, OR EXPRESS A FEELING; THEY WERE SUNG IN THE FIELDS TO OTHER PEOPLE.

4. Tell about the history of the **banjo.**

   IT IS BELIEVED THAT THE MODERN-DAY BANJO CAME FROM AN AFRICAN INSTRUMENT CALLED THE BANJAR, WHICH IS BASICALLY A DRUM WITH STRINGS AND A NECK, SIMILAR TO A GUITAR. SLAVES PLAYED THEM, BUT SO DID MINSTREL MUSICIANS IN STAGE SHOWS DURING THE MID-NINETEENTH CENTURY. BANJOS TRAVELED WEST WITH THE MINERS OF THE GOLD RUSH, AND WERE FEATURED PROMINENTLY IN EARLY JAZZ AND BLUEGRASS MUSIC BECAUSE THEY WERE SUCH LOUD INSTRUMENTS AND COULD BE HEARD OVER THE REST OF THE BAND.

Listen to Learn

Lesson 11. Activity Sheet

Name _____ Date _____

Early African-American Instruments Picture Page

Instructions: Write the name of the instrument and the family group it belongs to on the lines provided under each picture.

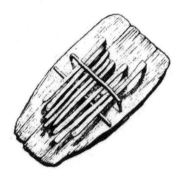

_____

_____

_____

_____

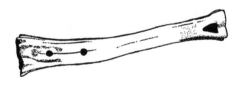

_____

_____

_____

_____

_____

_____

_____

_____

Early African-American Instruments
Picture Page: Answer Key

Thumb piano
Idiophone

Bone castanets
Idiophone

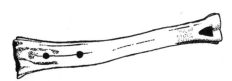

Bone flute
Aerophone

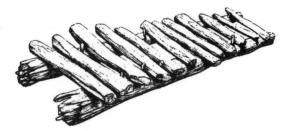

Xylophone
Idiophone

Gourd banjo
Chordophone and membranophone

Log drum
Membranophone

♪ Lesson 12. Spirituals and Gospel Music

Lesson Overview

Spirituals and gospel music are sacred music. Spirituals developed among the slaves on the plantations were based on a blend of African and European music traditions. These songs expressed the sadness of the slave condition, but also the hope for salvation. After emancipation, these songs went with the people to the cities and towns of North America. By the 1930s they had evolved into a new style of sacred music called gospel music. Gospel is modern sacred music that mixes the soulful, heartfelt lyrics of spirituals with rhythms, instruments, and the influences of urban popular music.

Vocabulary. Sacred songs, spirituals, melody, rhythm, call-and-response, signal songs, field holler, gospel music, improvise, compose, syncopated, tempo.

Purpose. To offer an introduction to the sacred music of African Americans from slavery times into the present.

Preparation. Read the student handout **Spirituals and Gospel Music** to familiarize yourself with the material. Preview the CD sample (cue in student handout) and have the CD ready for playing with the students. Be prepared to do some or all of the following activities. Also make sure that each student has a music notebook for keeping handouts and activity sheets.

Materials

- **Spirituals and Gospel Music** student handout *(following)*
- **Spirituals and Gospel Music Quiz** *(following)*
- **Spirituals and Gospel Music Quiz Answer Key** *(following)*
- **Music Vocabulary** activity sheet *(Appendix)*
- **My Opinion Page** activity sheet *(Appendix)*
- **How to Teach a Song** teacher guide *(Appendix)*
- **Songs as Poetry** activity sheet *(Appendix)*
- **Great American Musicians!** activity sheet *(Appendix)*
- **Music on the Map** activity sheet *(Appendix)*
- **Music notebooks**
- **CD music** example on accompanying CD; cue in student handout
- **Additional music selections**

Activities

- Pass out the **Spirituals and Gospel Music** handout for students to read silently or aloud as a group. Afterwards, have students put the handout in their music notebooks. *(Link to language arts, history, geography, social studies.)*

- Give the **Spirituals and Gospel Music Quiz** to assess student understanding of the lesson.

- Go over the music vocabulary at the top of the student handout before or after reading the text. Refer to the glossary for definitions. *Suggestion:* Include these words in a regular class vocabulary lesson, or pass out flashcards with a vocabulary word on one side and the definition on the other and allow students to drill each other. Use the **Music Vocabulary** activity sheet to write out definitions. *(Link to language arts.)*

- Offer the **Vocabulary Challenge.** Students pick some or all of the words in this lesson's vocabulary list to use in a paragraph, essay, short story, or poem. *(Link to language arts.)*

- **Discuss.** Before reading the student handout, discuss what students already know about spirituals and gospel music. Read the student handout and discuss it again, letting students add what they've learned. *(Link to language arts, social studies.)*

- **Syncopation.** Students practice three rhythms: (1) a steady rhythm pattern with no accents; (2) a rhythm pattern accenting the *downbeat* (first and third beats); and (3) a rhythm pattern accenting the *upbeat* (second and fourth beats) to create syncopation. Students practice each rhythm by tapping on a drum, book, their lap, or the desktop. Instructions and rhythm patterns are written in the student handout. *Suggestion:* Remind students to stay together and not speed up, and to *accent* (play louder) on the big boom and more softly on the small boom.

- **Bonus Challenge: Metaphors in Spirituals.** Look for metaphors in these spirituals: "Swing Low, Sweet Chariot," "Joshua Fought the Battle of Jericho," and "Sheep, Sheep, Don't You Know the Road?" Consider searching the Internet, library, and songbooks for other spirituals to analyze. Encourage students to write down the lines of these songs and then write the metaphor directly underneath each line of song, so interpretations can be read easily.

- **Bonus Challenge: Underground Railroad.** Read about the Underground Railroad and how it helped transport the slaves to freedom (use the Internet, library, or encyclopedia). Do a search for "signal songs" used to describe the plans for escaping, and investigate their meanings. Have students offer a report, either written or oral, or just read about it.

Extension Activities

For step-by-step directions and activity sheets, see the appendix.

- **My Opinion Page.** Offer students a chance to freely express their own opinions about the music they hear. *(Link to language arts, critical thinking.)*

- **Sing a Song.** Learn a simple song from this lesson. *Suggested songs to learn:* "Go Down Moses," "Swing Low, Sweet Chariot," and "He's Got the Whole World in His Hands." *(Link to singing, language arts, rhythm, melody.)*

- **Songs as Poetry.** Examine the lyrics of songs for their poetic nature. *(Link to language arts.)*

- **Illustrate the Music.** Students illustrate a song or piece of music by drawing, coloring, or painting their ideas of what the music "looks" like visually. *(Link to language arts, visual arts.)*

- **Great American Musicians!** Introduce students to American musicians whose talents have made them notable. *(Link to language arts, history.)*

- **Music on the Map.** Create a map and legend showing musically important places, such as musicians' birthplaces and music hot spots mentioned in the lesson. *(Link to geography.)*

- **Invite a Music Expert.** Invite a gospel musician to visit your class and share his or her musical talents with the students. Some resources for locating musicians are the Internet, local music and arts organizations, friends, students, parents.

- Consider bringing in **additional selections of music** from other sources to expand the music examples for this lesson. Note the songs mentioned in each musician's biography for ideas. Search the Internet, library, local music store, or your own music collection for the music.

Name _____ Date _____

Spirituals and Gospel Music

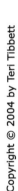

Vocabulary: sacred songs, spirituals, melody, rhythm, call-and-response, signal songs, field holler, gospel music, improvise, compose, syncopated, tempo

The lives of most slaves were not happy. They were taken from their homes, separated from their families, sold like property, and made to work without pay. They often lived in poor, dirty conditions, without opportunities to better their lives. Music was an acceptable way of expressing their emotions—especially grief and sadness. But music also felt good and helped people to feel better.

Spirituals

Spirituals are **sacred songs.** They express people's spiritual feelings and emotions. The earliest **spirituals** were sorrowful. They expressed sadness, suffering, pain, and the hope of freedom from suffering. "Nobody Knows the Trouble I Seen" expresses sadness—but adds a little hope at the end.

Nobody Knows the Trouble I Seen

Nobody knows the trouble I seen,
Nobody knows my sorrow.
Nobody knows the trouble I seen,
Glory hallelujah!

As the slaves adopted the European-American religions, they also learned to sing the European-American sacred songs. The slaves gathered in their own places of worship and sang the songs in their own ways. They sang in English and with European-influenced **melodies**, but introduced African **rhythms,** which were often livelier than the slave owners' versions.

Many spirituals are based on stories from the Christian Bible—in which people lived as slaves searching for freedom. In the song "Go Down Moses," the lyrics describe the Israelites who wanted their freedom from the Egyptian pharaoh. This song helped give the slaves hope for their own freedom.

Go Down Moses

Chorus: Go down Moses, way down in Egypt land.
Tell old pharaoh to let my people go.

Leader: When Israel was in Egypt land.
All: Let my people go.
Leader: Oppressed so hard they could not stand.
All: Let my people go.

Repeat chorus.

Leader: So Moses went to Egypt land.
All: Let my people go.
Leader: He made old pharaoh understand.
All: Let my people go.

Repeat chorus.

Other verses (with responses in parentheses) follow:

'Twas on a dark and dismal night. (Let my people go.)
When Moses led the Israelites. (Let my people go.)
When Israel reached the water side. (Let my people go.)
Commanded God, "It shall divide." (Let my people go.)
When they had reached the other shore. (Let my people go.)
They sang a song of triumph o'er. (Let my people go.)
Oh take your shoes off from your feet. (Let my people go.)
And walk onto the golden street. (Let my people go.)

Metaphors in Spirituals. Many early African-American spirituals were song-poems that used symbols and metaphors to illustrate the lives of slaves. A metaphor describes a thing as if it were another—for example, "The *world* is a *stage*" or "Her *face* is an *open book*." In "Go Down Moses" the metaphors are as follows: "Israel" = slaves; "Pharaoh" = slave owner; "Egypt" = America; "Moses" = deliverer.

Unit Three: African-American Music

Spirituals can be sung slowly and sadly, or in a lively, upbeat way, expressing a sense of hope and optimism. African-American slaves could be heard clapping their hands and stomping their feet and shouting out the words of songs, which were often sung in the **call-and-response** style, where the leader sings out and the congregation sings back. Spirituals allowed the slaves to express their deepest feelings in an acceptable way to the plantation owners, while also helping them to cope with their suffering. "Swing Low, Sweet Chariot" is a spiritual that expresses hope for a better life. Notice the call-and-response style of singing.

Swing Low, Sweet Chariot

Chorus: Swing low, sweet chariot,
Comin' for to carry me home.
Swing low, sweet chariot,
Comin' for to carry me home.

Call: I looked over Jordan and what did I see?
Response: Comin' for to carry me home.
Call: A band of angels comin' after me.
Response: Comin' for to carry me home.

Repeat chorus.

Call: If you get there before I do.
Response: Comin' for to carry me home.
Call: Tell all the folks that I'll be comin' there too.
Response: Comin' for to carry me home.

Repeat chorus.

Call: I'm sometimes up, I'm sometimes down.
Response: Comin' for to carry me home.
Call: But still my soul feels heavenly bound.
Response: Comin' for to carry me home.

Repeat chorus.

Bonus Challenge: Metaphors in Spirituals   Look for metaphors in these other spirituals: "Swing Low, Sweet Chariot," "Joshua Fought the Battle of Jericho," or "Sheep, Sheep, Don't You Know the Road?" "Swing Low, Sweet Chariot" is given here; search the Internet, the library, and songbooks for the lyrics of the other two. Write down the lines of these songs, and then write the metaphor directly underneath each line.

Signal Songs. Some spirituals had an important purpose acting as **signal songs** to give secret clues about how to escape to freedom. Signal songs used the words of sacred songs to send messages and give codes. With the development of the Underground Railroad, a society of people who secretly helped slaves to freedom, signal songs offered a way to communicate when and where they would meet, or the route to get to a meeting place. For example, in the spiritual "Steal Away," the words were actually codes for what to do:

I'm gonna steal away to Jesus. (*I'm going to escape to freedom.*)

I ain't got long to stay here. (*The time is coming to escape.*)

My Lord calls me. (*A message has come from a person with the Underground Railroad.*)

He calls me by the thunder, the trumpet sounds within my soul. (*A ringing bell or **field holler** will tell when it is time.*)

I ain't got long to stay here. (*The time is coming soon.*)

Gospel Music

After the turn of the twentieth century, as more African Americans moved into the cities of North America, they began to adopt city ways of doing things. To their music they added new instruments—like pianos, organs, drums, guitars, tambourines, and brass instruments. **Gospel music** emerged as a form that mixed spirituals with blues and jazz and other influences of urban (city) music. By the 1930s, African Americans who gathered in urban churches were singing sacred songs with upbeat tempos and an emotional fervor that inspired and shaped this new kind of music into modern-day gospel music. In gospel, the call-and-response style lives on as individual singers sing out over the group, followed by the response of the full group.

Fisk Jubilee Singers. Soon after emancipation in 1863—when the slaves were freed—the Fisk Jubilee Singers, a group of African-American students from Fisk University in Tennessee, traveled across the country singing African-American songs to help raise money for their school. They sang work songs that had come from the fields. They sang spirituals and sorrow songs. Their tour was a success because it raised money, but also because it raised awareness of the slaves and their music.

Bonus Challenge: Underground Railroad   Read about the Underground Railroad and how it helped transport slaves to freedom. Listen to a signal song and investigate its meaning. Offer a short presentation or written explanation of what you discovered.

Thomas Andrew Dorsey (July 1, 1899–1993). Singer, composer, and music arranger Thomas Andrew Dorsey was born in Georgia. He began playing and composing music at age eleven when he performed in a local theater to help support his family. While still a teenager, he moved to Chicago and attended the College of Composition and Arranging. There he began a career of composing and performing blues music. Eventually he played piano accompaniment for blues singers, including the famous Ma Rainey, but later quit that and began composing and performing only gospel music, which he continued to do for the rest of his life. Many of his songs are still sung by gospel choirs today. Some of his songs are "It's Tight Like That," "Precious Lord," "Take My Hand," and "Peace in the Valley."

Some gospel songs are traditional hymns or spirituals. Others are composed by modern composers. Still others are **improvised**—inspired by how people feel in the moment. Gospel songs can be shouted with joy and excitement, or sung slowly and expressively with deep reverence and feeling.

Thomas A. Dorsey was named the Father of Gospel Music because he was one of the first to **compose** contemporary gospel music. His songs used blues melodies and rhythms paired with sacred lyrics.

Mahalia Jackson was a modern gospel singer with a deep and powerful voice. On stage she expressed her feelings with her strong voice and rhythmic body movements. Through her music, people could feel the spirit in the words she was singing. Her version of "He's Got the Whole World in His Hands" expresses her deepest spiritual feelings.

He's Got the Whole World in His Hands

He's got the whole world in His hand.
He's got this whole world right in His hand.
He's got this whole world right in His hand.
He's got the whole wide world in His hand.

He's got the whole world right in His hand.
He's got this whole world in His hand.
He's got this whole world right in His hand.
He's got the whole wide world in His hand.

He's got everybody here right in His hand.
He's got everybody here right in His hand.
He's got everybody here right in His hand.
He's got the whole wide world in His hand.

Bridge: If religion was a thing money could buy.
(The whole wide world in His hand.)
The rich would live and the poor would die.
(The whole wide world in His hand.)

He's got the whole world right in His hand.
He's got this whole world right in His hand.
He's got this great big world right in His hand.
He's got the whole wide world in His hand.

He's got the little bitty baby in His hand.
He's got the little bitty baby right in His hand.
He's got the little bitty baby in His hand.
He's got the whole wide world in His hand.

From *Smithsonian Folkways Children's Collection,*
Smithsonian Folkways 45043.
Courtesy of Smithsonian Folkways Recordings.
Copyright © 1998. Used by permission.

By the 1940s, gospel groups were traveling and performing across the country. These tours helped to make this music popular in mainstream America. Record companies recorded more gospel music and radio shows played it over the airwaves. Gospel quartets became the rage, with members dressing stylishly as they performed on stage. The Spirit of Memphis, the Soul Stirrers, and the Dixie Hummingbirds were among the most popular gospel quartets.

In the 1950s, the Clara Ward Singers became the first gospel group to sell a million records. Their songs, written by leader Clara Ward, were lively and **syncopated,** with a fast **tempo.** The group's performances invited both audience and performers to dance and clap and sing along enthusiastically. The Clara Ward Singers sang in churches, auditoriums, festivals, and clubs all across North America, spreading gospel music and making it even more popular.

By the 1960s, larger groups formed called *gospel choirs.* These groups added electric guitars, bass, and drums, creating more of a rock 'n' roll sound. The Edwin Hawkins Singers made history with "Oh, Happy Day," a song that "crossed over" and was played on rock radio stations.

> **Mahalia Jackson (October 26, 1911–1972).** Mahalia Jackson, born in Louisiana, was a gospel singer and composer. She began singing at the age of four and sang in church choirs throughout her childhood. Her family was poor, and so she worked to help support them. She went on to create a career of singing and composing gospel music. Mahalia sang only songs she believed in. Her style of gospel music mixed blues, jazz, and ragtime. She performed in churches and concert halls throughout North America and Europe, made recordings, performed on radio, television, at jazz festivals, and at civil rights rallies. She sang for presidents, kings, and queens, and in 1968 sang an emotional rendition of "Precious Lord, Take My Hand" at the funeral of Dr. Martin Luther King, the civil rights activist. Her other songs include "Nobody Knows the Trouble I've Seen," "I'm Going to Move Up a Little Higher," and "Didn't It Rain."

Gospel singers: Virginia State University Gospel Choir.
AP/World Wide Photos. Used by permission.

As the decade of the 1960s came to a close, gospel music became even more sophisticated and polished. Gospel composers and arrangers created more complicated music, with singing parts and instrument parts that were interwoven in complex ways. Synthesizers and drum machines soon played a part as well, and over the years elements of country-western, hip-hop, rap, and New Age music have been added in. The mission of gospel music, however, has remained the same: to uplift people's spirits and express the deepest spiritual feelings.

"I Love to Praise His Name" is an upbeat gospel song. The lyrics reflect reverence and joy. The call-and-response singing adds energy and excitement.

I Love to Praise His Name

Call: I love to praise Him.
Response: I love to praise His name.
Call: I love to praise Him.
Response: I love to praise His name.
Call: I love to praise Him.
Response: I love to praise His name.

Syncopation is when the unexpected, or upbeats, are accented. In gospel music, accenting the upbeats creates a bouncy, lively feeling. Upbeats are the 2 and the 4 beats of a 4/4 rhythm. Here are three different rhythms. The first is a steady even rhythm pattern with no accents. The second accents the downbeat (the 1 and the 3 beats). The third accents the upbeats (the 2 and the 4 beats) to create syncopation. Practice each rhythm by tapping on a drum, book, or desktop. Don't speed up! Keep the rhythm steady and even. And if you're with a group, listen to one another! Stay together. Repeat each one for several minutes without stopping.

1. Steady Rhythm Pattern:

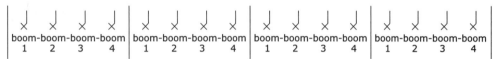

2. Accenting the *downbeat*:

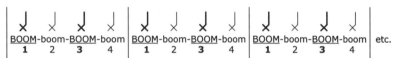

3. Syncopation. Accenting the *upbeat*:

All: I love to praise His holy name.
He's my rock, my rock, my sword and shield.
He's my wheel in the middle of the wheel.
I know He's never, never let me down.
He's just a jewel that I have found.

Call: I love to praise Him.
Response: I love to praise His name.
Call: I love to praise Him.
Response: I love to praise His name.
Call: I love to praise Him.
Response: I love to praise His name.

All: I love to praise His holy name.

CD track #21. Listen to "He's Got the Whole World in His Hands," an example of a spiritual song, and follow along with the lyrics as written in the student handout.

Song: Public Domain. *Recording:* "He's Got the Whole World in His Hands," by Mahalia Jackson, from the recording entitled *I Sing Because I'm Happy,* SF 90002, provided courtesy of Smithsonian Folkways Recordings, © 1992. Used by permission.

Unit Three: African-American Music   **193**

Name _____ Date _____

Spirituals and Gospel Music Quiz

Instructions: After reading the **Spirituals and Gospel Music** student hand-out, answer these questions (use back of page if necessary).

1. What kind of song is a **spiritual?**

2. What is **gospel music?**

3. What are **signal songs?**

4. What is **syncopation?**

Listen to Learn

Spirituals and Gospel Music Quiz: Answer Key

1. What kind of song is a **spiritual**?

   SPIRITUALS ARE SACRED SONGS THAT EXPRESS SPIRITUAL FEEL-
   INGS AND EMOTIONS. IN SLAVE TIMES, THEY WERE ALSO SORROW
   SONGS, EXPRESSING SADNESS, SUFFERING, PAIN, AND THE HOPE
   FOR FREEDOM. THEY TOLD STORIES FROM THE CHRISTIAN BIBLE.
   SOMETIMES THEY ALSO ACTED AS SIGNAL SONGS, HIDING MES-
   SAGES THAT WERE USED TO AID ESCAPE.

2. What is **gospel music**?

   GOSPEL MUSIC IS SACRED MUSIC THAT IS UPBEAT IN NATURE,
   OFTEN ACCOMPANIED BY PIANOS, GUITARS, TAMBOURINES,
   BRASS, BASS, AND DRUMS. THIS FORM FOLLOWED SPIRITUALS,
   DEVELOPING WHEN FREED SLAVES MOVED TO THE CITIES AND
   PICKED UP URBAN MUSICAL INFLUENCES.

3. What are **signal songs**?

   DURING SLAVERY, SLAVES MADE UP SIGNAL SONGS THAT USED
   THE WORDS OF THE SONG TO SEND MESSAGES AND SECRET CLUES
   FOR HOW TO ESCAPE TO FREEDOM.

4. What is **syncopation**?

   SYNCOPATION IS WHEN UNEXPECTED BEATS (UPBEATS) ARE
   ACCENTED. IN A 4/4 RHYTHM, THE 2 AND THE 4 BEATS ARE
   ACCENTED. THIS IS DIFFERENT FROM THE WESTERN MUSIC TRA-
   DITION OF ACCENTING THE 1 AND THE 3 BEATS. SYNCOPATION
   CREATES A LIVELY, BOUNCY RHYTHMIC FEEL.

♫ Lesson 13. The Blues

Lesson Overview

When the African-American slaves were freed, many moved away from the plantations into the towns and cities of the rural South. They carried with them the musical styles they had been developing for over two hundred years in America. The musically inclined found work on street corners and in small clubs, accompanying themselves on banjo, piano, or guitar. Many of these artists composed their own songs based on their personal experiences, which were often related to hunger, poverty, and racism. The music became known as the blues. As blues musicians moved into the cities and towns, they adopted instruments and influences that polished the music and created a newer "city" style of blues. *Note: Be cautious when introducing blues music to children. Many of the songs contain double meanings and allusions to adult-themed subjects.*

Vocabulary. Note-bending, guitar, country blues, syncopation, call-and-response, finger-picking, harmonica, lyrics, jukebox.

Purpose. To offer an introduction to the blues.

Preparation. Read the student handout **The Blues** to familiarize yourself with the material. Preview the CD sample (cue in student handout) and have the CD ready for playing with the students. Be prepared to do some or all of the following activities. Also make sure that each student has a music notebook for keeping handouts and activity sheets.

Materials

- **The Blues** student handout *(following)*
- **The Blues Quiz** *(following)*
- **The Blues Quiz Answer Key** *(following)*
- **Early Blues Instruments Picture Page** activity sheet *(following)*
- **Early Blues Instruments Picture Page Answer Key** *(following)*
- **Music Vocabulary** activity sheet *(Appendix)*
- **My Opinion Page** activity sheet *(Appendix)*
- **How to Teach a Song** teacher guide *(Appendix)*
- **Songs as Poetry** activity sheet *(Appendix)*
- **Great American Musicians!** activity sheet *(Appendix)*
- **Music on the Map** activity sheet *(Appendix)*
- **Music notebooks**

- **CD music** example on accompanying CD; cue in student handout
- **Additional music selections**

Activities

- Pass out **The Blues** handout for students to read silently or aloud as a group. Afterwards, have students put the handout in their music notebooks. *(Link to language arts, history, geography, social studies.)*
- Give **The Blues Quiz** to assess student understanding of the lesson.
- Go over the music vocabulary at the top of the student handout before or after reading the text. Refer to the glossary for definitions. *Suggestion:* Include these words in a regular class vocabulary lesson, or pass out flashcards with a vocabulary word on one side and the definition on the other and allow students to drill each other. Use the **Music Vocabulary** activity sheet to write out definitions. *(Link to language arts.)*
- Offer the **Vocabulary Challenge.** Students pick some or all of the words in this lesson's vocabulary list to use in a paragraph, essay, short story, or poem. *(Link to language arts.)*
- **Discuss.** Before reading the student handout, discuss what students already know about blues music. Read the student handout and discuss it again, letting students add what they've learned. *(Link to language arts, social studies.)*
- **Bonus Challenge: Instrument Families.** Challenge students to divide the instruments mentioned in this lesson into their instrument family groups: chordophones, idiophones, aerophones, membranophones. *Answer key:* Chordophones = guitar, banjo, piano, fiddle, mandolin, washtub bass. Idiophones = washboard, piano. Aerophones = harmonica, kazoo, jug, cornet. Membranophones = drum. *(Link to science.)*

Extension Activities

For step-by-step directions and activity sheets, see the appendix.

- **My Opinion Page.** Offer students a chance to freely express their own opinions about the music they hear. *(Link to language arts, critical thinking.)*
- **Sing a Song.** Learn a simple blues song from this lesson. *Suggested song to learn:* "Good Mornin' Blues." *(Link to singing, language arts.)*
- **Songs as Poetry.** Examine the lyrics of songs for their poetic nature. *(Link to language arts.)*
- **Illustrate the Music.** Students illustrate a song or piece of music by drawing, coloring, or painting their ideas of what the music "looks" like visually. *(Link to language arts, visual arts.)*

- **Great American Musicians!** Introduce students to American musicians whose talents have made them notable. *[Link to language arts, history.]*

- **Music on the Map.** Create a map and legend showing musically important places, such as musicians' birthplaces and music hot spots mentioned in the lesson. *[Link to geography.]*

- **Invite a Music Expert.** Invite a blues musician to visit your class and share his or her musical talents with the students. Some resources for locating musicians are the Internet, local music and arts organizations, friends, students, parents.

- Because of copyright issues, modern songs are difficult to obtain for the accompanying CD. Consider bringing in **additional selections of music** from other sources to expand the music examples for this lesson. Note the songs mentioned in each musician's biography for ideas. Search the Internet, library, local music store, or your own music collection for the music.

Name _____   Date _____

Memphis Minnie, Lead Belly, Bessie Smith, Blind Willie McTell

The Blues

Vocabulary: note-bending, guitar, country blues, syncopation, call-and-response, finger-picking, harmonica, lyrics, jukebox

When people use the term "the blues," it often communicates feeling sad or down. When someone says, "I'm feeling blue," it likely means that person isn't feeling too happy. But although the blues might describe a sad or down feeling, it is believed that the name for the music actually derives from the practice of playing blue notes. Blue notes are notes that "bend" or "slur" when they are played or sung, in a practice that is also called **note-bending.** Blues singers bend the notes with their voices, like a moan. Guitar players bend the strings when they play. Harmonica and other wind instrument players bend the notes by changing the airflow or the shape of their lips. This practice of note-bending creates blue notes, and the blues are full of blue notes.

Unit Three: African-American Music   **199**

Charley Patton (April 1891–1934). Born in Mississippi, Charley Patton was a singer, songwriter, and blues guitarist. He played guitar as a teenager and developed a country blues style that he learned from an old blues man. Charley expressed deep personal feelings through his music, which made for powerful performances. He was well-known in the Mississippi Delta region among African-American audiences, but he later toured and recorded his music and it spread his fame across America to a much larger audience. It is through his recordings that we can hear the original country blues style from the South. Some of his songs are "Banty Rooster Blues" (1929), "Pea Vine Blues" (1929), and "Mississippi Boweavil Blues" (1929).

Country Blues

It is likely that the blues began in the plantation fields where slaves worked hard and relieved some of their discomfort through singing. The blues often express misery and despair.

After the slaves were freed, those who could play instruments found work on street corners, in clubs, and in "juke joints," where African Americans gathered to socialize. Early blues musicians played a rural or "country" style of blues music, usually on the **guitar**, piano, or banjo, sung by a solo singer. The music was simple and straightforward. Early blues singers often sang about loneliness or being hungry, brokenhearted, or broke. Their music came to be called **country blues.** "World of Trouble" is a country blues song by Memphis Minnie.

World of Trouble

Lyrics by Memphis Minnie

It's a cold, cold morning,
I was out in the rain and snow.
It's a cold, cold morning,
I was out in the rain and snow.
Yes, in a world of trouble,
I couldn't find no place to go.

The wind was blowing
And the rain began to freeze.
The wind was blowing
And the rain began to freeze.
So much of trouble,
Lord, have mercy on me.

Standing on the corner,
My friends all was passing by.
Standing on the corner,
My friends all was passing by.

Memphis Minnie (June 3, 1897–1973). Born Lizzie Douglas in Louisiana but raised in Mississippi, Memphis Minnie was a singer, songwriter, and blues guitar player. She played guitar and banjo as a child and ran away at age thirteen to become a blues singer in Memphis. Her country blues style showed strong rhythm playing and a tough singing voice. Her songs were about love, hard times, and a hard life. Memphis Minnie made many recordings and became well known in the Chicago blues clubs. Some of her songs are "World of Trouble"(1925), "When the Levee Breaks" (1929), "Bumblebee" (1929), "Chickasaw Train Blues" (1934), and "Me and My Chauffer Blues" (1941).

Well, I cried so much,
Lord, I didn't have no tears to dry.

My brother, he's in trouble,
My dad, he just broke jail.
My man, he's in trouble,
And the law is on his trail.

It's a cold, cold morning,
And I'm out in the rain and snow.
Yes, in a world of trouble,
I had no place to go.

At the turn of the century (1900), as African Americans migrated north, country blues was heard by larger groups of people. From the Mississippi Delta region came Charley Patton, Son House, and Memphis Minnie. From Texas and Louisiana came Blind Lemon Jefferson and Huddie "Lead Belly" William Leadbetter. From Georgia, Blind Willie McTell and Blind Boy Fuller emerged.

Blues musicians often use syncopated rhythms in their music. **Syncopation** is when upbeats (weak beats) are accented (played louder) than the downbeats. Syncopated rhythms create excitement in a song and are very different from European-American rhythms, which tended to accent the downbeat (see the section on syncopation in Lesson 12).

Blind Lemon Jefferson (July 1897–1929). Born in Texas, Blind Lemon Jefferson was a singer, songwriter, and blues guitarist. Blind from childhood, he learned to play guitar at an early age and moved to Dallas, where he played on street corners for spare change. He performed in clubs and then traveled throughout the South playing for African-American audiences. He made close to one hundred recordings of his songs in his short life. Blind Lemon's music leaves us with a glimpse of the original country blues from the Texas-Louisiana region. Some of his songs are "Matchbox Blues," "Easy Rider Blues," and "See That My Grave Is Kept Clean."

Blind Willie McTell (May 5, 1901–1959). Born in Georgia, Blind Willie McTell was a blind guitar player, singer, and songwriter. He learned to play guitar from his mother when he was still a boy. After leaving home, he performed with traveling shows and carnivals, and later found work playing guitar at house parties and fish fries in Georgia. In this time he developed a syncopated finger-picking guitar style, influenced by ragtime music. After building a reputation as a fine guitar player, he recorded his music from 1927 to 1956. When not recording, Willie often played music on the streets of Atlanta for tips and spare change. Some of his songs are "Statesboro Blues" (1927), "Mama 'Tain't Long for Day" (1927), and "Broke-Down Engine Blues" (1929).

Early blues musicians also used **call-and-response** in their singing (a singer sings out the first line of a song and the guitar or another person's voice answers back). "Good Mornin' Blues," by Lead Belly, offers an example of this call-and-response style of singing in a blues song.

Good Mornin' Blues

Lyrics by Lead Belly

Good mornin' blues, blues how do you do?
Good mornin' blues, blues how do you do?
I'm doin' alright, good mornin', how are you?

I lay down last night, turnin' from side to side, oh
Turnin' from side to side.
I was not sick but I was just dissatisfied.

When I got up this mornin' with the blues walkin' round my bed, ah
With the blues walkin' round my bed.
I wouldn't eat breakfast, blues was all in my bread.

Good mornin' blues, blues how do you do?
Good mornin' blues, blues how do you do?
I'm doin' alright, good mornin', how are you?

Lead Belly (January 29, 1885–1949). Born Huddie William Ledbetter in Louisiana, Lead Belly was a blues guitar player, singer, and songwriter. He was born on a plantation, then moved with his family to Texas, where he grew up with an interest in music. His first instrument was an accordion, given to him by his uncle. He later learned to play the guitar, and by age twenty-one was making his living as a musician. He also worked as a laborer, picking cotton and working on railroad tracks. He spent seven years in jail before being pardoned after sending the governor a song that asked for the pardon. Record producers John and Alan Lomax discovered Lead Belly and began recording his music while he was still in jail. He went on to record hundreds of songs. Some of them are "Good Night Irene," "John Henry," "Bourgeois Blues," "Midnight Special," and "Linin' Track."

Lead Belly

Early Blues Instruments

At the turn of the century (1900), the guitar was the most common blues instrument. Besides strumming a background rhythm, guitar players used their fingers to pick the individual strings in a style called **finger-picking.** Blues musicians also used glass bottlenecks to slide up and down the strings to create note-bending.

Eventually, as other instruments were added, blues musicians formed "jug bands" and played lively, syncopated music on fiddles, guitars, mandolins, jugs, washtub basses, and washboards. Some played **harmonica,** using the instrument to imitate the human voice with bends and slurs.

Lesson 13. Student Handout continued

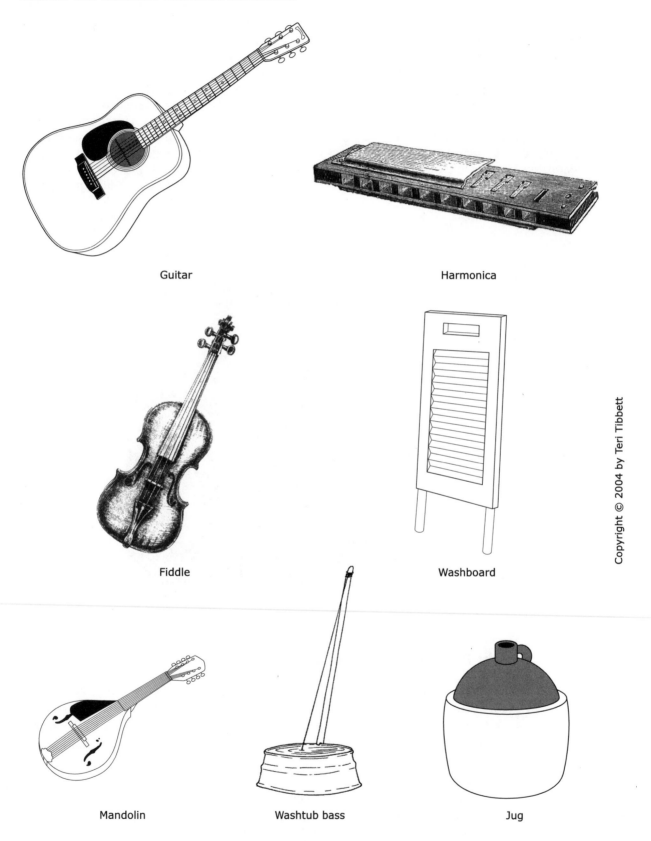

Guitar

Harmonica

Fiddle

Washboard

Mandolin

Washtub bass

Jug

Listen to Learn

W. C. Handy (November 16, 1873–1958). W. C. Handy, born in Alabama, was a blues singer and songwriter. His first musical experiences were in church, where he was attracted to the spirituals his friends and family sang. Early in life he studied music and played the cornet, and then performed in minstrel shows. In his travels he listened to the "Delta Blues" style of the South, and began composing his own blues music based on that style. His songs became popular, and over time he became known as the Father of the Blues. W. C.'s music helped bring the blues to mainstream audiences. Some of his songs are "Memphis Blues" (1912), "St. Louis Blues" (1914), "Yellow Dog Blues" (1914), and "Beale Street Blues" (1916).

City Blues

By the 1920s, record companies began recording blues musicians, which helped make the blues more popular across America. At the same time, country blues musicians were moving to the cities and picking up city influences. The rhythms became stronger, louder, more driving. The **lyrics** became more sophisticated and polished. The musicians added more instruments and formed into groups. In the larger cities, like Chicago and New York, audiences were hearing a new kind of blues music that reflected these changes. W. C. Handy, Ma Rainey, Bessie Smith, and Robert Johnson were the most popular "city" blues musicians of this era.

W. C. Handy

Unit Three: African-American Music

Robert Johnson (May 8, 1911–1938). Born in Mississippi, Robert Johnson was a blues guitar player, singer, and songwriter. He learned to play guitar as a teenager, imitating the styles of the old country blues musicians. During the Great Depression he traveled throughout the South, earning his living as an entertainer, performing at juke joints, country suppers, and levee camps. He also performed in the larger cities of St. Louis, Detroit, and Chicago. In his brief career he recorded twenty-nine of his own songs. Robert's music served as important inspiration to future blues and rock 'n' roll musicians. Some of his songs are "Walkin' Blues" (1936), "Come On into My Kitchen" (1936), "Crossroads Blues" (1936), "Ramblin' on My Mind" (1936), and "Sweet Home Chicago" (1936).

Robert Johnson

"St. Louis Blues," written by W. C. Handy, is one of the most famous city blues songs. The lyrics reflect the language style of African Americans of the era.

St. Louis Blues (abridged)

Lyrics by W. C. Handy

I hate to see de ev'nin' sun go down,
Hate to see de ev'nin' sun go down,
Cause ma baby, he done lef dis town.

Feelin' tomorrow lak Ah feel today,
Feel tomorrow lak Ah feel today,
I'll pack my trunk, make ma getaway.
St. Louis woman wid her diamon' rings
Pulls dat man roun' by her apron strings.
'Twant for powder an' for store-bought hair
De man I love would not gone nowhere.
Got de St. Louis Blues jes as blue as Ah can be,
Dat man got a heart lak a rook cast in the sea
Or else he wouldn't gone so far from me.

Spoken: Doggone it!

Been to de Gypsy to get ma fortune tole,
To de Gypsy done got ma fortune tole,
'Cause I'm most wile 'bout ma Jelly Roll.
Gypsy done tole me, "Don't you wear no black."
Yes she done tole me, "Don't you wear no black."
Go to St. Louis, you can win him back.
Help me to Cairo, make St. Louis ma-self.
Git to Cairo, find my ole friend Jeff.
Gwine to pin ma-self close to his side.
If Ah flag his train I sho' can ride.
I loves dat man lak a schoolboy loves his pie,
Lak a Kentucky col'nel loves his mint an' rye.
I'll love ma baby till the day Ah die.

Spoken: Doggone it!

In the 1930s and 1940s, as more blues music was recorded and heard on the radio, it became more popular across America. Blues musicians added electric guitars, saxophones, drums, and electric bass to their music. Chicago blues developed in Chicago, and other blues styles were developing on the stages of New York.

Ma Rainey (April 26, 1886–1939). Born Gertrude Pridgett in Georgia, Ma Rainey was a blues singer. She was raised in a showbiz family that performed in minstrel shows and vaudeville. She was fourteen years old when she sang on the stage for the first time. When she married "Pa Rainey," she became "Ma Rainey" and the two formed a vaudeville song-and-dance act that toured the country. In their act they performed blues and popular songs. Ma Rainey, came to be known as Mother of the Blues. She recorded over a hundred songs and sang with jazz musicians Louis Armstrong and Fletcher Henderson. Some of her songs are "Save 'Em Dry," "Jelly Bean Blues," and "Countin' the Blues."

Bessie Smith (April 15, 1894–1937). Born Bessie Anthony in Tennessee, Bessie Smith was a blues singer. As a young girl she sang on street corners for nickels and dimes; later she worked with a minstrel show as a dancer. She went on to perform in vaudeville and sang in clubs, tents, and theaters. At the height of her career, she made many recordings and performed in all the major cities, including Chicago and New York, as well as the small country towns of the South where she was raised. Known as the Empress of the Blues, she was a strong-willed woman who made her own decisions about her music and her career. Some of her songs are "Backwater Blues," "I Ain't Got Nobody," "Nobody Knows You When You're Down and Out," and "Lost Your Head Blues."

After the 1940s, the blues entered a new era. With electric instruments and up-tempo rhythms, the music was more danceable and attracted larger audiences. As European-Americans began to play versions of the music, it attracted these audiences as well. Blues was played on **jukeboxes** and in dance halls. The music evolved into rhythm and blues, and rhythm and blues was the foundation for rock 'n' roll.

♫ CD track #22. Listen to Lead Belly sing and play "Good Mornin' Blues." Hear how he bends the notes with his voice on the word "do" in the sentence "how *do* you do."

> *Song:* New words and new music arranged by Huddie Leadbetter. Edited and new additional material by Alan Lomax. TRO copyright © 1959 (renewed) Folkways Music Publishers, New York. *Recording:* "Good Mornin' Blues #2" by Lead Belly from the recording entitled *Bourgeois Blues: Lead Belly Legacy,* Vol. 2, SF 40045, provided courtesy of Smithsonian Folkways Recordings. © 1997. Used by permission.

Bonus Challenge: Instrument Families Read back through this lesson and list all the musical instruments mentioned, then divide them into their instrument family groups: chordophones, idiophones, aerophones, membranophones.

Name _____   Date _____

The Blues Quiz

Instructions: After reading **The Blues** student handout, answer these questions (use back of page if necessary).

1. What is the origin of **the blues?**

2. What is **note-bending?**

3. What are some early blues instruments?

4. Describe **early country blues** and **city blues** and how each developed.

The Blues Quiz: Answer Key

1. What is the origin of **the blues?**

    MOST LIKELY THE BLUES DEVELOPED IN THE WORK FIELDS OF
    THE PLANTATIONS AS SLAVES EXPRESSED THEIR DISCOMFORT, MIS-
    ERY, AND DESPAIR.

2. What is **note-bending?**

    THIS IS WHEN A NOTE IS SLURRED OR DIPPED AND SOUNDS LIKE
    A MOAN. GUITAR PLAYERS BEND THE NOTES BY STRETCHING A
    STRING, WIND INSTRUMENT PLAYERS BEND THE NOTES BY
    CHANGING THE SHAPE OF THEIR LIPS OR REGULATING AIRFLOW,
    AND SINGERS BEND THE NOTES BY DIPPING THEIR VOICES.

3. What are some early blues instruments?

    GUITAR, PIANO, HARMONICA, FIDDLE, WASHBOARD, MANDOLIN,
    WASHTUB BASS, JUG.

4. Describe **early country blues** and **city blues** and how each developed.

    EARLY COUNTRY BLUES WAS ACOUSTIC, WITH MUSICIANS USU-
    ALLY SINGING THEIR OWN SONGS AND ACCOMPANYING THEM-
    SELVES ON GUITAR, PIANO, OR BANJO. AS COUNTRY BLUES
    MUSICIANS MOVED INTO THE CITIES, THEY PICKED UP CITY
    INFLUENCES, WHERE MORE INSTRUMENTS WERE ADDED, MUSI-
    CAL GROUPS WERE FORMED, THE LYRICS AND MUSIC BECAME
    MORE SOPHISTICATED, AND EVENTUALLY ELECTRIC INSTRU-
    MENTS WERE ADDED.

Lesson 13. Activity Sheet

Name _____   Date _____

Early Blues Instruments Picture Page

Instructions: Write the name of the instrument and the family group it belongs to on the lines provided under each picture.

Early Blues Instruments Picture Page:
Answer Key

Guitar
Chordophone

Washboard
Idiophone

Jug
Aerophone

Fiddle
Chordophone

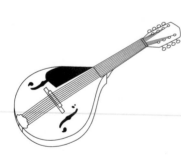

Mandolin
Chordophone

Harmonica
Membranophone

Washtub bass
Chordophone

♫ Lesson 14. Dance Music

Lesson Overview

Ragtime and New Orleans jazz were the first popular African-American styles of dance music to emerge around the turn of the century. By the 1930s and 1940s, African-American dance music was being heard and imitated by European-American musicians. Swing music, jump blues, and Chicago blues developed in this era and caught on with both African-American and European-American audiences. As the civil rights movement of the 1960s opened more opportunities for African Americans to record and perform, their music finally came to the forefront of American culture. Rhythm and blues, soul, and funk music are all incarnations of spirituals, the blues, and jazz.

Vocabulary. Syncopated, ragtime, player piano, jazz, early jazz, boogie-woogie, tempo, polyrhythmic, jump blues, rhythm and blues, Chicago blues, rhythm instrument, melody instrument, lead guitar, improvise, electrophone.

Purpose. To offer an introduction to stage and dance music created and performed by African Americans.

Preparation. Read the student handout **Dance Music** to familiarize yourself with the material. Preview the CD samples (cues in student handout) and have the CD ready for playing with the students. Be prepared to do some or all of the following activities. Also make sure that each student has a music notebook for keeping handouts and activity sheets.

Materials

- **Dance Music** student handout *(following)*
- **Dance Music Quiz** *(following)*
- **Dance Music Quiz Answer Key** *(following)*
- **Music Vocabulary** activity sheet *(Appendix)*
- **My Opinion Page** activity sheet *(Appendix)*
- **Great American Musicians!** activity sheet *(Appendix)*
- **Music on the Map** activity sheet *(Appendix)*
- **Music notebooks**
- **CD music** examples on accompanying CD; cues in student handout
- **Additional music selections**

Activities

- Pass out the **Dance Music** handout for students to read silently or aloud as a group. Afterwards, have students put the handout in their music notebooks. *[Link to language arts, history, geography, social studies.]*

- Give the **Dance Music Quiz** to assess student understanding of the lesson.

- Go over the music vocabulary at the top of the student handout before or after reading the text. Refer to the glossary for definitions. *Suggestion:* Include these words in a regular class vocabulary lesson, or pass out flashcards with a vocabulary word on one side and the definition on the other and allow students to drill each other. Use the **Music Vocabulary** activity sheet to write out definitions. *[Link to language arts.]*

- Offer the **Vocabulary Challenge.** Students pick some or all of the words in this lesson's vocabulary list to use in a paragraph, essay, short story, or poem. *[Link to language arts.]*

- **Discuss.** Before reading the student handout, discuss what students already know about African-American dance music since the mid-1900s. Read the student handout and discuss it again, letting students add what they've learned. *[Link to language arts, social studies.]*

- **The Science of Music: Player Pianos.** Try locating a player piano and look inside—notice the mechanisms that make it work, where the paper passes over the tracker bar, and the air channels to each key. Watch it play. If you can't find a real player piano, search the Internet, encyclopedia, or books in the library to locate diagrams and pictures.

- **The Science of Music: Electrophones.** Electronic instruments belong to a family of instruments called *electrophones*—instruments that use electronics to make sound. A section in the student handout describes electrophones and invites students to bring in instruments to explore. See the student handout for directions.

- **Bonus Challenge: Research an Electrophone.** Pick an electrophone and investigate its origins, how it works, and what kind of sound it makes. Some electrophones are the electric guitar, bass guitar, drum machine, organ, synthesizer, sampler, electric violin, electric flute, electric saxophone. Ask students to write a report on the subject or present an oral report.

- **Bonus Challenge: Families of Instruments.** The challenge is to read back through this lesson and list all the instruments mentioned. Divide them into families of instruments: chordophones, aerophones, idiophones, membranophones, electrophones. *Answer key:* Chordophones = piano, player piano, bass. Aerophones = saxophone, trumpet, clarinet, harmonica. Idiophones = piano, player piano. Membranophones = drums. Electrophones = electric guitar, electric bass guitar, electric piano, organ.

Extension Activities

For step-by-step directions and activity sheets, see the appendix.

- **My Opinion Page.** Offer students a chance to freely express their own opinions about the music they hear. *[Link to language arts, critical thinking.]*

- **Illustrate the Music.** Students illustrate a song or piece of music by drawing, coloring, or painting their ideas of what the music "looks" like visually. *[Link to language arts, visual arts.]*

- **Great American Musicians!** Introduce students to American musicians whose talents have made them notable. *[Link to language arts, history.]*

- **Music on the Map.** Create a map and legend showing musically important places, such as musicians' birthplaces and music hot spots mentioned in the lesson. *[Link to geography.]*

- **Invite a Music Expert.** Invite a ragtime, New Orleans jazz, swing, rhythm and blues, or Chicago blues musician to visit your class and share his or her musical talents with the students. Some resources for locating musicians are the Internet, local music and arts organizations, friends, students, parents.

- Because of copyright issues, modern songs are difficult to obtain for the accompanying CD. Consider bringing in **additional selections of music** from other sources to expand the music examples for this lesson. Note the songs mentioned in each musician's biography for ideas. Search the Internet, library, local music store, or your own music collections for the music.

Name_____ Date_____

Louis Jordan, King Oliver's Creole Jazz Band, Scott Joplin

Dance Music

Vocabulary: syncopated, ragtime, player piano, jazz, early jazz, boogie-woogie, tempo, polyrhythmic, jump blues, rhythm and blues, Chicago blues, rhythm instrument, melody instrument, lead guitar, improvise, electrophone

African-American dance music was played on the plantations, in the evenings, after the day's work was done. The people played bones and banjos and sang and danced to music they made themselves. As they moved off the plantations and into the cities and towns of America, they socialized in small juke joints, clubs, fish fries, and other gathering places, and they continued to play music and dance.

The first popular forms of African-American dance music to emerge stayed in the African-American communities. But over time, as European-Americans caught on to the music, the music slipped into the mainstream.

Stage Music

Some of the first African Americans to make a living in music performed in minstrel shows and vaudeville in the late 1800s. Minstrel shows were stage shows put on by European-Americans that mimicked African-American singing, dancing, dress, and language. Vaudeville shows were variety shows with a mix of acrobats, singers, comedians, magicians, and animal acts, among others.

Bert Williams was one of the first African Americans to become famous in American stage shows. In 1903, he and George Walker performed the first all-African-American musical show on Broadway, titled *In Dahomey,* by Paul Laurence Dunbar and Will Marion Cook. The show was about relocating slaves to Africa. Not many African Americans made it to the major stages of popular entertainment in America.

Bert Williams

Bert Williams (November 12, 1875–1922). Bert Williams was born in the West Indies. When he was a young boy, his family moved first to New York and then to California. As a child, he had a natural sense of humor and learned to play music by ear. He began performing in minstrel shows at age eighteen, when he was hired to tour and perform at the logging camps of Northern California. He later moved to San Francisco, and then to the East Coast, where he performed in minstrel shows and vaudeville. Bert was a great pantomimist and became famous for playing humorous characters. "Mr. Nobody" became his signature character. Eventually, Bert partnered with George Walker, and the two became a successful vaudeville team. He also performed with the *Ziegfeld Follies,* a famous New York variety show, where he became the highest paid act for many years. Some of his shows include *Bandana Land, Abyssinia, The Policy Players,* and *In Dahomey.*

The Science of Music: Player Pianos. The **player piano** is a piano that plays by itself. Here is how it works: foot pedals create suction when pumped, and this suction pulls down the black and white keys of the piano—taking the place of human fingers. Inside, a paper roll covers a "tracker bar" that has suction tubes leading to each key. When the paper roll travels across the tracker bar, the holes in the paper roll pass over the suction tubes, allowing air to pass through. The passing air creates suction, which causes the keys to pull down. The paper rolls are punched in a certain way to match the notes of a song so that when they roll, they play the song! The player piano was invented in 1896 by Edwin Votey of Detroit, who called it the *pianola*. The pianola was a wooden box that rolled up to a piano and "played" the keys with wooden "fingers." It too was powered by foot pedals and suction that made the "fingers" go up and down. *Activity: Locate a player piano and look inside—notice the mechanisms that make it work, where the paper passes over the tracker bar, and the air channels to each key. Watch it play. If you can't find a real player piano, search the Internet, encyclopedia, or books in the library to locate diagrams and pictures.*

Ragtime

At the turn of the century (1900), a new style of dance music evolved from the dance music of minstrel shows and vaudeville. It was played on piano and sounded very lively. The spirited pieces were called "rags." Rags used the chords and structures of European music, mixed with African **syncopated** rhythms. Eventually, the music came to be known as **ragtime.**

Scott Joplin was the most popular ragtime composer and performer of his time. His talent and vision led him to create some of the most complicated and lasting pieces of ragtime music ever written. The "Maple Leaf Rag" (1899) was his first famous "hit" and inspired many others to copy him. Joplin's rags were sold on sheet music, which people could read and play in their own homes. He also made piano rolls, which allowed people to play the music in their player pianos. Ragtime's popularity lasted until about 1910.

Scott Joplin (1868–1917). Scott Joplin was born in Texas. He was a composer, arranger, and piano player. His father had been a slave who knew how to play the violin. Scott learned to play piano at an early age, and by the time he was a teenager was playing in clubs and bars. He studied European music privately and at college, played cornet in a concert band, and arranged music for vaudeville shows. His first songs were marches and waltzes. He later composed music for piano, which evolved into ragtime. He also wrote music for ballet and opera. Scott believed that the music of both African and European traditions could come together into new American musical forms. His songs include "Maple Leaf Rag" (1899), "The Entertainer" (1902), which figured prominently in the 1970s movie *Butch Cassidy and the Sundance Kid,* "Pineapple Rag" (1908), and "Wall Street Rag" (1909).

Scott Joplin

Early Jazz

Jazz is a unique American musical style that began in the streets and small clubs of the southern United States. It developed after slavery ended, as the musically inclined added European wind instruments to their own singing and banjo and guitar playing. Jazz is a lively, upbeat style of music that emerged in dance halls, parties, parades, and funerals in the African-American communities around New Orleans. **Early jazz** blended European-American chords and structures with African-American syncopation, call-and-response, note-bending, and improvisation.

In the 1920s, a new era began for jazz in America. Phonograph records, radio, and microphones all contributed to a big change in how music was presented to the general public. Radio sent music over much greater distances. Records allowed it to be played in people's homes. Electric amplifiers made the instruments louder, and microphones helped singers to be heard in larger crowds and over the instruments of the band. Jazz singers and instrumentalists could now join in confidently with each other with a balance of sound. However, because of the laws and customs of the time, African Americans were segregated from European-Americans, and so they tended to perform their own music in their own clubs apart from the European-Americans.

From the 1920s to the 1940s, the African-American dance clubs that featured jazz provided a ripe environment for the music to grow and develop. The music of Louis Armstrong, Fletcher Henderson, Count Basie, and Duke Ellington came out of these underground venues. Eventually, their music caught on with European-Americans, who invited African-American musicians to play for them, arrange for them, and write for them. Many styles of jazz have emerged from the original New Orleans–style jazz music; this will be covered more in Unit Four, Lesson 18: Jazz.

King Oliver's Creole Jazz Band, 1921 (from left to right): Ram Hall, Honore Dutrey, King Oliver, Lil Hardin-Armstrong, David Jones, Johnny Dodds, Jimmy Palao, Ed Garland

Did You Know? In the early days of phonograph recording (the 1920s to the 1950s), many record companies refused to record the music of African Americans. For this reason, many talented and creative musicians could not be heard in mainstream America. Instead, European-Americans "copied" or "covered" the music of African Americans, making their own versions, which they recorded and performed in public. Mainstream audiences caught on and the music became popular. This was true both with many styles of music born in the African-American community.

Boogie-Woogie

Boogie-woogie is another form of piano music that evolved from the blues. Boogie-woogie is played with a fast **tempo** and syncopated rhythms. Where ragtime was more sophisticated with classical influences, boogie-woogie had a folk-blues influence. With boogie-woogie, the left hand plays a steady rhythm, while the right hand plays a lively melody. The effect is **polyrhythmic**—two rhythms playing at the same time. Meade Lux Lewis and Albert Ammons were experts in this style.

Jump Blues

Jump blues or *jumpin' jive* music is an up-tempo, lively dance music using screaming saxophones, loud trumpets, drums, bass, and guitars, with high-powered rhythms and fast tempos. It evolved in the 1940s, when dancers flocked to the dance floors to hear it and dance to it. Clubs featured it on their jukeboxes. Jump blues uses some elements of jazz, but adds blues chord patterns and a rhythmic beat that is highly danceable. Louis Jordan was famous for making jump blues popular. His funny lyrics and use of the twelve-bar blues pattern was a bridge between big-band jazz and rock 'n' roll music, which followed. Big Joe Turner was another popular jump blues musician.

Rhythm and Blues

In the 1940s and 1950s, African-American musicians continued to experiment with new rhythms and sounds. Where jump blues was "swinging" and used syncopated rhythms (emphasizing the *upbeat*), **rhythm and blues** used more straightforward rhythms that emphasized the *downbeat* (see the explanations of syncopation in Lesson 12 and the downbeat in Lesson 15). The music was lively, exciting, and highly danceable. Rhythm and blues (R&B) players formed smaller combos that featured piano, drums, guitar, and brass instruments. Probably the most popular style to come out of R&B music is rock 'n' roll, which also features straightforward rhythms and small combos of musicians.

Louis Jordan (July 8, 1908–1975). Louis Jordan was born in Arkansas. He was a bandleader, songwriter, and alto saxophone player. He learned music at the age of seven from his father, who taught him to play saxophone, clarinet, and other horns. Beginning at age fifteen, he played in clubs and with jazz bands for several years before branching off to form his own band. Louis Jordan and His Tympany Five was a small combo of musicians, very different from the "big bands" of the same era. His sound was exciting and his lyrics were funny and entertaining. He recorded and performed his own songs, many of which crossed over and become popular in the mainstream. He toured the world and was known as King of the Jukeboxes. His songs include "Let the Good Times Roll," "Caldonia," "Ain't Nobody Here But Us Chickens," "Beans and Cornbread," "Saturday Night Fish Fry," and "Blue Light Boogie."

Rhythm Guitar. The rhythm guitar player plays the rhythm of the music by strumming all the strings in a rhythmic way. The rhythm guitar plays the rhythm and so it is a *rhythm instrument.* The rhythm guitar is also a *harmonic instrument,* because when all the strings are strummed at once they make harmony (many notes are played at the same time).

Chicago Blues

In the 1940s, African-American dance music was cropping up all across the country. In the bars and clubs of Chicago's South Side, a new kind of music was gaining popularity: **Chicago blues.** Early Chicago blues was typically played by small groups of musicians, with electric guitar, electric bass, electric piano or organ, harmonica, and drums. The structure of the music and the lyrics to the songs were similar to country blues, but the rhythms were stronger and more danceable, and the presence of electric instruments made the music louder.

Country blues musicians Muddy Waters, Sonny Boy Williamson, Howlin' Wolf, and Elmore James moved from the rural South to Chicago to perform in the small blues clubs there. Over time, they added electric instruments and faster tempos and their music became more polished and "urban" sounding. Chicago blues was music people could dance to, and this helped make it very popular throughout the region.

Muddy Waters (April 4, 1915–1983). Born McKinley Morganfield in Mississippi, Muddy Waters was a blues guitar player, singer, and songwriter. He got his nickname as a child because he liked to play in a muddy creek. He grew up working in cotton fields, but by eighteen he had also learned to sing and play harmonica and guitar. He played in the country blues style and performed at local dances, juke joints, picnics, and fish fries before moving to Chicago at age twenty-eight. In Chicago he played at house parties and small taverns for African-American audiences. It was during this time that he learned to play electric guitar and later became famous performing the "electric" Chicago blues style that he became known for. In the 1960s and 1970s he re-emerged as a folk-blues musician, performing at folk festivals and touring across America and Europe—including a performance at the White House. His songs include "Long Distance Call," "Hoochie Coochie Man," "Walkin' Through the Park," and "Mannish Boy."

Lead Guitar. Lead guitar means the guitar is the featured instrument of the band, while the other instruments are the support, or "backup." The concept is similar to when a singer stands on stage and sings out over the rest of the band; this person is the lead singer. Lead guitarists play a melody one string at a time, instead of strumming all the strings at once. The effect is *melodic.* Their playing is usually **improvised**—made up on the spot—and not read from written music. The lead guitar plays melodies, and so it is a *melody instrument.*

Muddy Waters was one of the first blues players to make the electric guitar famous. He created a harder "industrial" sound that was new and attractive to players and listeners alike.

In the 1950s, a 25-year-old African-American guitar player named B. B. King joined the Chicago blues scene and added his own ideas to blues music. He played the electric guitar in a brand new way. Instead of strumming the strings like a **rhythm instrument**, he played them individually, like a **melody instrument**. This style of picking a melody is called **lead guitar** playing. B. B. King's lead guitar playing created a new direction in blues music that would one day inspire rock 'n' roll musicians and is still popular today.

The Science of Music: Electrophones. Instruments that use electronics to create or enhance their sound belong to a family of instruments called **electrophones.** Some electrophones use electronics to *create* sound—organs, synthesizers, samplers, vibraphones, and theremins are a few examples. Others use electronics to enhance or amplify the natural sound of an *acoustic instrument* (an instrument that makes sound without electricity); electric guitars, electric basses, electric violins, and electric flutes are some of these. The electric guitar is usually shaped like an acoustic guitar, with a body and neck and strings. However, where an acoustic guitar depends on the vibrating air inside its hollow body to make the sound get louder, an electric guitar depends on tiny microphones (called *pickups*) attached to its solid body to make its sound get louder. The pickups send sound signals to an amplifier, which, as its name implies, amplifies the sound through loudspeakers. Amplifiers help the guitar to be heard over the other instruments and create its own unique kind of sound. *Activity: Bring in an electric guitar, organ, synthesizer, keyboard, or any instrument that may be plugged in or is battery-operated. Listen to its sound. Compare it to an acoustic instrument. For example, compare an electric guitar to an acoustic guitar, an organ to a piano, an electric violin to an acoustic violin, and so on.*

B. B. King (September 16, 1925–). Born Riley B. King in Mississippi, B. B. King is a blues guitar player, singer, and songwriter. As a child he sang in gospel groups and learned to play blues guitar before he was sixteen. While still a teenager, he played on street corners for money. After moving to Memphis he worked at a radio station, eventually getting his own radio show under the name "Blues Boy King," which he later shortened to B. B. King. After that, he performed live, and his popularity spread. By the 1950s he was touring the country and recording songs that became number one hits on the rhythm and blues record charts. His unique style of playing lead guitar has been an influence to others ever since. His songs include "Three O'clock Blues" (1951), "Everyday I Have the Blues" (1955), "The Thrill Is Gone" (1970), and "My Guitar Sings the Blues" (1985).

B. B. King. AP/World Wide Photos. Used by permission.

Bonus Challenge: Research an Electrophone Pick an electrophone and investigate its origins, how it works, and what kind of sound it makes. Some electrophones are the electric guitar, bass guitar, drum machine, organ, synthesizer, sampler, electric violin, electric flute, electric saxophone. Offer a written or oral report.

Koko Taylor (September 28, 1935–). Born Cora Walton in Tennessee, Koko Taylor is a blues singer and songwriter. She learned to sing in church when she was a child. Listening to the radio, she heard the music of blues musicians, and with her brothers and sisters, would sneak into their backyard to play blues on homemade instruments. At age eighteen she moved to Chicago, where she timidly began to sit in and sing with famous blues bands. After being discovered, she recorded her music and soon became famous. She has performed on the radio, in movies, on television, and at jazz festivals all over the world. Koko Taylor has been called the Queen of the Blues. Her songs include "I Got What It Takes," "Let the Juke Joint Jump," and "Twenty-Nine Days."

Female blues singers Big Mama Thornton, Koko Taylor, and Etta James began singing rhythm and blues in the bars and clubs of Chicago. Their powerful voices and strong personalities helped carry the blues through the second half of the twentieth century.

Koko Taylor. Courtesy of Alligator Records.

Bonus Challenge: Families of Instruments Read back through this lesson and list all the instruments mentioned. Divide them into the families of instruments: chordophones, aerophones, idiophones, membranophones, electrophones.

♪ CD track #23. Listen to "Maple Leaf Rag," an example of ragtime music, by Scott Joplin.

> *Recording:* "Maple Leaf Rag," by Scott Joplin. From *Joplin Piano Rags.* Courtesy of The Scott Joplin Foundation. Used by permission.

♪ CD track #24. Listen to "When the Saints Go Marching In," an example of New Orleans jazz, performed by Louis Armstrong. Notice the upbeat, danceable rhythms.

> *Recording:* "When the Saints Go Marching In," performed by Louis Armstrong. From *Original Jazz Masters Series, Vol. 1.* Courtesy of 1201 Music. ℗ 1201 Music. Used by permission.

♪ CD track #25. Listen to "Boogie-Woogie," an example of a boogie-woogie piano music style, performed by Robert Cohen.

> *Recording:* "Boogie-Woogie," written and performed by Robert Cohen. ℗ 2001 Zuvuya One Music, Migration Music. Used by permission.

Name _____   Date _____

Dance Music Quiz

Instructions: After reading the **Dance Music** student handout, answer these questions (use back of page if necessary).

1. Who was Scott Joplin and what kind of music is he responsible for developing?

2. Describe **jump blues** or jumpin' jive music.

3. Describe **Chicago blues.**

4. How does the **lead guitar** player play the instrument?

5. How does the **rhythm guitar** player play the instrument?

Dance Music Quiz: Answer Key

1. Who was Scott Joplin and what kind of music is he responsible for developing?

   SCOTT JOPLIN WAS AN AFRICAN-AMERICAN COMPOSER AND PIANO PLAYER. HE IS RESPONSIBLE FOR DEVELOPING RAGTIME MUSIC.

2. Describe **jump blues** or jumpin' jive music.

   JUMP BLUES IS AN UP-TEMPO LIVELY STYLE OF DANCE MUSIC THAT USES SAXOPHONES, TRUMPETS, DRUMS, BASS, AND GUITARS. IT DEVELOPED IN THE 1940s IN AFRICAN-AMERICAN COMMUNITIES.

3. Describe **Chicago blues.**

   CHICAGO BLUES IS A DANCE MUSIC THAT EVOLVED IN THE 1940s IN THE CLUBS AND BARS OF CHICAGO, TYPICALLY PLAYED BY SMALL GROUPS OF MUSICIANS ON ELECTRIC GUITAR, ELECTRIC BASS, ELECTRIC PIANO OR ORGAN, HARMONICA, AND DRUMS, WITH SINGERS.

4. How does the **lead guitar** player play the instrument?

   LEAD GUITAR PLAYERS PLAY THE STRINGS INDIVIDUALLY LIKE A MELODY INSTRUMENT, RATHER THAN STRUMMING THE STRINGS LIKE A RHYTHM INSTRUMENT.

5. How does the **rhythm guitar** player play the instrument?

   RHYTHM GUITAR PLAYERS STRUM THE STRINGS ALL AT ONCE, CREATING CHORDS THAT SERVE BOTH AS HARMONIC BACKGROUND AND RHYTHMIC ACCOMPANIMENT.

♪ Lesson 15. Soul and Funk

Lesson Overview

Both soul and funk are African-American musical styles that evolved from the blues. Soul mixes gospel with rhythm and blues for a passionate, upbeat, rhythmic style of music. In the 1960s, as more recording and performing opportunities opened up for African Americans, their music moved to the forefront of American culture, filling the airwaves and concert halls of America. The Motown Records label made music history by featuring African-American artists, and enjoyed a string of number one radio hits over many years. Funk music followed in the 1970s, mixing soul with rock and jazz. The result was a progressive, groove-oriented, highly danceable music.

Vocabulary. Soul music, call-and-response, harmony, funk music, downbeat, upbeat, rhythm instrument, synthesizer, pitch, volume, sampler.

Purpose. To offer an introduction to and history of soul and funk music.

Preparation. Read the student handout **Soul and Funk Music** to familiarize yourself with the material. Be prepared to do some or all of the following activities. Also make sure that each student has a music notebook for keeping handouts and activity sheets.

Materials

- **Soul and Funk Music** student handout *(following)*
- **Soul and Funk Music Quiz** *(following)*
- **Soul and Funk Music Quiz Answer Key** *(following)*
- **Music Vocabulary** activity sheet *(Appendix)*
- **My Opinion Page** activity sheet *(Appendix)*
- **Songs as Poetry** activity sheet *(Appendix)*
- **Great American Musicians!** activity sheet *(Appendix)*
- **Music on the Map** activity sheet *(Appendix)*
- **Music notebooks**
- **Music selections**

Activities

- Pass out the **Soul and Funk Music** handout for students to read silently or aloud as a group. Afterwards, have students put the handout in their music notebooks. *(Link to language arts, history, geography, social studies.)*

- Give the **Soul and Funk Music Quiz** to assess student understanding of the lesson.

- Go over the music vocabulary at the top of the student handout before or after reading the text. Refer to the glossary for definitions. *Suggestion:* Include these words in a regular class vocabulary lesson, or pass out flashcards with a vocabulary word on one side and the definition on the other and allow students to drill each other. Use the **Music Vocabulary** activity sheet to write out definitions. *(Link to language arts.)*

- Offer the **Vocabulary Challenge.** Students pick some or all of the words in this lesson's vocabulary list to use in a paragraph, essay, short story, or poem. *(Link to language arts.)*

- **Discuss.** Before reading the student handout, discuss what students already know about African-American soul and funk music. Read the student handout and discuss it again, letting students add what they've learned. *(Link to language arts, social studies.)*

- **Playing on the Downbeat.** The downbeats are the first and third beats of a 4/4 rhythm. Funk music typically places a strong accent on the first downbeat. This is the opposite of syncopation, which accents the upbeats (second and fourth beats). In this activity students practice playing a rhythm that accents the first downbeat, so prevalent in funk music. *Activity:* Practice playing the rhythm written in the student handout on a drum, book, or desktop. Accent (play loudly) on the 1 and softly on the 2, 3, 4. Count aloud, almost shouting the 1, and saying more quietly the 2, 3, 4. *Advanced activity:* Bring in other percussion instruments, such as maracas or drums, to play in this exercise. Allow one group to drop out and not play on the 1 and only play on the 2, 3, 4 while anot her group plays on the 1 only. This is common in funk music. *(Link to rhythm, music theory.)*

- **Bonus Challenge: Important People from Many Cultures.** Students learn about important people and their contributions mentioned in the song "Black Man," by Stevie Wonder. *Step 1:* Research on the Internet, or other source, and print out the lyrics to "Black Man" from the *Songs in the Key of Life* CD. *Step 2:* Students pick one person mentioned in the song. *Step 3:* Students do research on this person and offer a report to the class, including biographical information, photographs, important contributions, and anecdotes if possible. *Step 4:* Compile the information gathered by students into a notebook titled "Famous People from Many Cultures." Include the lyrics to "Black Man" at the beginning of the book. Make copies for each student to take home. *Suggestion:* Consider this activity for Black History Month (February). *(Link to language arts, history, social studies.)*

- **Bonus Challenge: Families of Instruments.** Challenge students to group the instruments mentioned in the lesson into instrument families: chordophones, membranophones, aerophones, idiophones, and electrophones. *Answer key:* Chordophones = piano, guitar, bass. Membranophones = drums. Aerophones = saxophone, clarinet, horns, harmonica. Idiophones = piano. Electrophones = synthesizer, sampler, bass guitar. *(Link to science.)*

Extension Activities

For step-by-step directions and activity sheets, see the appendix.

- **My Opinion Page.** Offer students a chance to freely express their own opinions about the music they hear. *(Link to language arts, critical thinking.)*
- **Songs as Poetry.** Examine the lyrics of songs for their poetic nature. *(Link to language arts.)*
- **Illustrate the Music.** Students illustrate a song or piece of music by drawing, coloring, or painting their ideas of what the music "looks" like visually. *(Link to language arts, visual arts.)*
- **Great American Musicians!** Introduce students to American musicians whose talents have made them notable. *(Link to language arts, history.)*
- **Music on the Map.** Create a map and legend showing musically important places, such as musicians' birthplaces and music hot spots mentioned in the lesson. *(Link to geography.)*
- **Invite a Music Expert.** Invite a soul or funk musician to visit your class and share his or her musical talents with the students. Some resources for locating musicians are the Internet, local music and arts organizations, friends, students, parents.
- Because of copyright issues, modern songs are difficult to obtain for the accompanying CD. Consider bringing in **selections of music** from other sources to expand the music examples for this lesson. Note the songs mentioned in each musician's biography for ideas. Search the Internet, library, local music store, or your own music collection for the music.

Name _____   Date _____

Ray Charles, James Brown, Aretha Franklin

Soul and Funk Music

Vocabulary: soul music, call-and-response, harmony, funk music, downbeat, upbeat, rhythm instrument, synthesizer, pitch, volume, sampler

Soul Music

Throughout the 1950s, rhythm and blues music dominated the dance music scene with African-American audiences. In the 1960s, however, **soul music** took its place and brought together a mixture of gospel and blues to create a passionate new music that inspired both African-American and mainstream American audiences alike.

Ray Charles (September 23, 1930–). Born in Georgia, Ray Charles is a singer, songwriter, arranger, bandleader, and piano player. He became blind by age seven and attended a school for the deaf and blind, where he learned to play piano, saxophone, and clarinet. He also learned to read and write music in Braille and began composing music early in his life for jazz bands. Orphaned at age fifteen, he went out on his own, playing in bands around Florida. At seventeen he moved to Seattle, where he formed his own band, played in nightclubs, and began recording his music. Eventually his music became popular on mainstream radio and Ray Charles became a star. He sang in a blues style with gospel excitement, a style that came to be known as *soul.* In his career, he also "crossed over" and played country and jazz music, sometimes using a full orchestra and chorus of singers to accompany his songs. He continues to perform and create new music into his seventies. His songs include "What I Say" (1959), "Georgia on My Mind" (1960), "Hit the Road, Jack" (1961), "Born to Lose" (1962), and "Unchain My Heart" (1964).

Ray Charles, one of the pioneers of soul music, is known today as the Father of Soul Music. He sings with intense emotion, backed by a driving rhythm section and blues-style chord structures. His songs often used **call-and-response** singing between him and his backup chorus of singers, known as the Raylettes. "Hit the Road, Jack" is one of this group's most famous songs—a humorous call-and-response exchange between a man and a woman.

Aretha Franklin, known as the Queen of Soul, has a strong, passionate voice that she uses to express her deepest feelings and emotions. Her music offers a high-powered up-tempo mixture of gospel and blues music, also known as soul.

When Motown Records had its first hit in 1961, a new age dawned for African-American musicians. Motown Records signed recording contracts with previously unheard-of African Americans and distributed their music across America and the world. Groups like the Supremes, the Temptations, Gladys Knight and the Pips, and the Four Tops performed a blend of gospel and blues, with vocal **harmonies,** call-and-response singing, and dance music that crossed over and became popular among listening audiences of all ethnic groups.

Aretha Franklin (March 25, 1942–). Aretha Franklin was born in Tennessee. She is a gospel and soul singer. She began singing at an early age in her father's Baptist church, and also toured with him as he traveled the countryside. She began recording gospel songs at age fourteen. She soon moved into singing a mixture of gospel and blues, blending both into soul music. Her music has been popular with both African-American and European-American audiences. Aretha was the first woman to be inducted into the Rock and Roll Hall of Fame (1987) and the first African-American woman to appear on the cover of *Time* magazine. She continues performing and making recordings into the new millennium. Her songs include "Do Right Woman, Do Right Man" (1967), "Respect" (1967), "Natural Woman" (1967), "Chain of Fools" (1968), and "See Saw" (1968).

Stevie Wonder (May 13, 1950–). Born Steveland Judkins in Michigan, Stevie Wonder is a singer, songwriter, arranger, and player of many instruments, including harmonica, piano, synthesizers, and samplers. His earliest musical experiences were beating on pots and pans as he listened to the music on the radio. Blind from birth, he grew up in a protected environment where he was encouraged to learn music. At age seven he began playing the piano, and by nine he was playing drums and harmonica. He joined a church choir and learned gospel music, while still learning popular music from the radio. At age twelve he was "discovered" by Berry Gordy, owner of Motown Records, and began to record and sell records in great numbers. When he was twenty-one, he formed his own recording company and produced two successful albums before returning to Motown. Wonder developed a style that includes elements of rock, jazz, gospel, African, and Latin rhythms. In 1996, he received a Grammy Lifetime Achievement Award; he was also one of the first inductees into the Rock and Roll Hall of Fame. Stevie Wonder continues to perform on records, movie soundtracks, and live concerts into the new millennium. Some of his songs are "Uptight (Everything Is Alright)" (1965), "A Place in the Sun" (1966), "Superstition" (1973), "Living for the City" (1974), "Black Man" (1976), "Happy Birthday" (for Martin Luther King) (1980), and "For Your Love" (1995).

Stevie Wonder. AP/World Wide Photos.
Used by permission.

Listen to Learn

Playing on the Downbeat. The downbeat is the first and third beats of a measure in a 4/4 rhythm. Funk music usually places a strong accent on the first downbeat, as follows:

| 1 | 2 | 3 | 4 | 1 | 2 | 3 | 4 | 1 | 2 | 3 | 4 | 1 | 2 | 3 | 4 |

Activity: Practice playing the rhythm pattern written here on a drum, book, or desktop. Accent (play loudly) on the 1 and softly on the 2, 3, 4. Count aloud, almost shouting the 1, and speaking more quietly the 2, 3, 4. Advanced activity: Bring in percussion instruments, such as maracas or drums, to play in this exercise. Form into groups. Allow one group to drop out and not play on the 1 and play on the 2, 3, 4 while the other group plays on the 1 only. Repeat this pattern continuously for one to two minutes.

Soul music's widespread appeal was due, in part, to the opportunities that had finally opened to African Americans as a result of the civil rights movement, but it was also due to the music's fresh sound created by good songwriting and strong backup musicians.

Over a fourteen-year period, the backup music for Motown's lead singers was played by the Funk Brothers, a group of talented guitar players, drummers, bassists, saxophonists, and keyboardists who provided the foundation and the core of the *Motown sound.*

Motown singers often addressed urban (city) themes, accompanied by urban instruments, including electric guitar, piano, bass, horns, and drums. Later, as the style evolved, orchestral and electronic instruments were added. Stevie Wonder was one of the first African-American recording artists to use synthesizers and samplers in soul music (see accompanying sidebar for descriptions of synthesizers and samplers). He experimented with sounds and instruments, and his lyrics explored deep social issues. In his song "Black Man" (1976), Stevie Wonder draws attention to people from many cultures who have contributed to the world's most important discoveries, inventions, and events.

Bonus Challenge: Important People from Many Cultures Do a search on the Internet, at the library, or in songbooks for the lyrics to Stevie Wonder's song "Black Man" from the CD *Songs in the Key of Life.* Copy or print the lyrics. Pick one of the people mentioned in the song, and do research on this person. Then offer a report to the class. Include biographical information, photographs, and important contributions.

Unit Three: African-American Music

Funk Music

Funk music is a mixture of soul, rock, and jazz. It is groove-oriented music—music that establishes a steady rhythm, or "groove," throughout the song. The bass guitar is strong and loud and driving. Funk music is passionate and highly danceable.

In funk music, the rhythm emphasizes the **downbeat.** This is the opposite of syncopation, which emphasizes the **upbeat.** Playing the downbeat means the **rhythm instruments** (drums and bass) play hard on the downbeats and soft on the upbeats. Sometimes, to create a different kind of emphasis, the rhythm instruments will stop playing on the downbeat and let the horns and guitar play it instead. Regardless of who is playing it, the downbeat is strongest in this musical style.

Some early funk players were King Curtis, Junior Walker, Otis Redding, and the group Booker T and the MGs. In the 1960s, James Brown introduced a soulful kind of funk music. His rich, showman approach earned him the title Godfather of Soul.

By the 1970s, funk-rock bands, such as Sly and the Family Stone and Earth, Wind, and Fire, were popular with both African-American and European-American audiences. Sly's songs introduced social issues, like racism in "Everyday People" and believing in yourself in "Stand." The band Earth, Wind, and Fire performed a mixture of rhythm and blues, soulful ballads, and funky grooves—played on guitars, drums, and bass, with a sizzling horn section. The music was highly danceable and "funky."

Synthesizers and Samplers. A **synthesizer** is an electronic device that creates sounds by taking an electric signal and turning it into a musical sound. The first synthesizer, called the theremin, made in 1920, was played by waving hands in the air around two antennae—which made the **pitch** (high and low notes) and **volume** (loud and soft) go up and down. The Hammond organ followed in 1935 and was the first modern synthesizer. In the 1960s, synthesizers could play only one pitch at a time. By 1975, they could play many pitches at the same time, which allowed for music with harmony. By the 1980s, computer microprocessors could "sample" real sounds and play them back on a keyboard. These devices are called **samplers.** A "sample" is a digital recording of a sound assigned to a key on the keyboard. Pressing the key plays the "sampled" sound. Instruments of the orchestra can be sampled and played on a keyboard, as well as the human voice, percussion instruments, and stranger sounds like trash can lids, barking dogs, squealing children, and broken glass.

Bonus Challenge: Families of Instruments Group the instruments mentioned in this lesson into music families: chordophones, membranophones, aerophones, idiophones, and electrophones.

In the 1980s, funk music was overshadowed by disco. Synthesizers replaced horn sections, and drum machines replaced live drummers. Funk and soul musicians went underground, and parts of the sound reemerged later in the hip-hop culture and rap music.

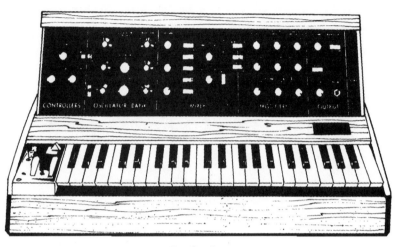

Synthesizer

Digital sampler. Courtesy of Emu Systems.

James Brown (May 3, 1928–). Born in South Carolina, James Brown is a singer, arranger, and songwriter. He grew up during the Great Depression, spending his early years picking cotton, shining shoes, and dancing for spare change. At age twenty he joined a gospel group that recorded and became popular on the radio. Eventually, he became his own bandleader, creating his own arrangements of songs. His backup music offered a steady, groove-oriented rhythm. His soulful singing was laced with shouts, screams, whoops, and vocal improvisations. James Brown's high-powered shows are his trademark and he has remained popular into the twenty-first century. His songs include "Please Please Please" (1956), "Papa's Got a Brand New Bag" (1965), "I Got You (I Feel Good)" (1965), and "It's a Man's World" (1966).

Name_____   Date_____

Soul and Funk Music Quiz

Instructions: After reading the **Soul and Funk Music** student handout, answer these questions (use back of page if necessary).

1. Describe **soul music.**

2. Describe **funk music.**

3. What did Motown Records contribute to soul and funk music?

Soul and Funk Music Quiz:
Answer Key

1. Describe **soul music.**

    SOUL MUSIC MIXES ELEMENTS OF BOTH BLUES AND GOSPEL, WITH SOME ROCK ELEMENTS ADDED IN MODERN TIMES. IT IS PASSIONATE AND "SOULFUL."

2. Describe **funk music.**

    FUNK MUSIC IS A MIXTURE OF SOUL, ROCK, AND JAZZ. IT IS GROOVE-ORIENTED MUSIC THAT ESTABLISHES A STEADY RHYTHM, OR "GROOVE," THROUGHOUT THE SONG. THE GUITAR IS STRONG, LOUD, DRIVING. THE DOWNBEAT IS EMPHASIZED (UNLIKE IN SYN-COPATION, WHICH EMPHASIZES THE UPBEAT). IT IS PASSIONATE MUSIC AND HIGHLY DANCEABLE.

3. What did Motown Records contribute to soul and funk music?

    IN THE 1960s MOTOWN RECORDS, BASED IN DETROIT, WAS THE MOST SUCCESSFUL RECORD COMPANY EVER TO MARKET THE MUSIC OF AFRICAN AMERICANS. MOTOWN'S HITS CROSSED OVER INTO EUROPEAN-AMERICAN RADIO AUDIENCES AND SPREAD THROUGH NORTH AMERICA AND AROUND THE WORLD, MAKING SOUL AND FUNK MUSIC SOME OF THE MOST POPULAR STYLES OF THE PERIOD. THE BACKUP MUSICIANS FOR MOST OF MOTOWN'S SINGERS WERE THE FUNK BROTHERS, WHO PROVIDED THE FOUN-DATION OF THE "MOTOWN SOUND."

New American Music

Contents

New American music synthesizes the traditions of many cultures into a variety of genres and musical styles—from blues to jazz, country to Tejano-conjunto, Cajun to rock and rap. These American hybrids developed from the traditions of Europeans, Africans, French, Spanish, and Native Americans. Just as the people of America make up a melting pot of cultures, American music is a melting pot of musical traditions. This unit introduces the major styles of music that developed in the twentieth century in North America.

Popular music is music that is popular with the general public. It is mainstream music, the music that plays on the radio and tops the record charts every week. Popular music changes over time as the styles, culture, and tastes of a society change. After the minstrel songs of the 1800s and vaudeville at the turn of the twentieth century, the era of Tin Pan Alley and Broadway musicals took over. Tin Pan Alley songs were published and sold by New York publishers. They were performed in people's living rooms, in the streets and pubs, and on the stages of America's musical theaters. By the 1940s, phonograph records, radio, and movies became the primary means by which Americans heard popular music. Because of this, the recording industry grew and became a multi-billion-dollar industry that controlled much of the music heard by Americans in the last half of the twentieth century.

American classical music and opera are heard on concert stages, in opera houses, in the soundtracks of movies, and behind popular singers. New American orchestral music is influenced by jazz, blues, folk, country, and the music of Native Americans, Latin Americans, African Americans, and Asian Americans.

Jazz was born on American soil based on the traditions of many cultures. The earliest jazz came out of the South, as freed African Americans picked up the instruments of European-Americans and began making music that mixed both traditions. What developed was New Orleans jazz, or Dixieland, as it is sometimes called. As more musicians picked up on the style, new forms of jazz emerged. Big band, or swing music, added new instruments and complex written arrangements. Bebop followed, taking standard songs and reworking them into up-tempo virtuosic renditions. Cool jazz reacted with slowed down tempos, softer dynamics, and understated melodies. Free jazz left behind many recognizable elements of Western music for a more open, free style of playing. Fusion incorporates jazz and rock for a groove-oriented music.

The earliest country music came from rural people and expressed mostly the experiences of rural life, but over time the music grew to express new American experiences. Pioneer songs and cowboy songs described life on the prairie, wagon trains, cattle drives, and loves left behind. Country music evolved when radio, phonograph records, and jukeboxes became widespread in America. Many branches of country music have evolved, including western swing, bluegrass, country-western, honky-tonk, Nashville country, outlaw country, and new country music.

Latin music was introduced in America with the first explorers and conquistadors from Spain, who brought guitars and Spanish folk songs with them.

Over time, as Spanish music mixed with the music of Native Americans, Africans, and Europeans and the music of the Caribbean, Latin American music has grown to be a hybrid of many styles. Mariachi music is country music describing country life and concerns. Tejano-conjunto is an upbeat music that developed in the southwestern United States and northern Mexico with strong European polka and accordion music influences. Salsa is a lively, rhythmical dance music developed in New York that mixes the traditions of Spanish, Caribbean, and African cultures.

Rock 'n' roll is one of the many incarnations of the African-American blues. The first rock 'n' roll and doo-wop bands were African American but in the 1950s, as rock 'n' roll became more popular, it tended to be recorded by European-Americans who covered the music of the original performers and made it famous with mainstream audiences. After the civil rights movement of the 1960s, more recording and performing opportunities opened for African Americans. Since then, many branches of rock have emerged, from many cultures—including folk rock, hard rock, surf music, country rock, jazz rock, punk rock, new wave, and grunge.

Rap music is street music that originated in New York. It developed in the 1970s out of the inner city hip-hop culture, expressing themes that reflected inner city issues. It was first played at house parties and street parties in African-American neighborhoods, but in the last part of the twentieth century it became popular across America and the world. East Coast "old school" was fun, honest, and raw. West Coast "gansta" rap reflected more violent themes. Southern rap offered a departure from the others with its own style of music and lyrics.

♪ Lesson 16. Modern Popular Music

Lesson Overview

Popular or "pop" music is mainstream music—the music that is most popular with the general public. It is the music that plays on the radio and tops the record charts every week. After the minstrel songs of the 1800s and vaudeville at the turn of the twentieth century, Tin Pan Alley and Broadway musicals followed that featured crafted songs published and sold by New York publishers and performed on New York stages. By the 1940s, records, radio, and movies became the primary means by which Americans heard popular music. The recording industry grew throughout the twentieth century into a multibillion-dollar industry selling popular music all over the world. Today popular music is influenced by many other genres, including jazz, folk, country, Latin, rock, rap, and more.

Vocabulary. Tin Pan Alley, music publishers, sheet music, popular music, lyrics, melody, refrain, popular song, Broadway musicals, compose, composition, microphone, radio broadcasting, phonograph record, jukebox, record company, record charts, parody.

Purpose. To offer an overview of popular music from the early 1900s into the twenty-first century.

Preparation. Read the student handout **Modern Popular Music** to familiarize yourself with the material. Consider reviewing Unit Two, Lesson 8: Early Popular Music as a prerequisite. Consider bringing music samples to enhance the lesson. Read the musician biographies in the student handout for recommended music selections. Be prepared to do some or all of the following activities. Also make sure that each student has a music notebook for keeping handouts and activity sheets.

Materials

- **Modern Popular Music** student handout *(following)*
- **Modern Popular Music Quiz** (following)
- **Modern Popular Music Quiz Answer Key** *(following)*
- **Charting the Charts** activity sheet *(following)*
- **Music Vocabulary** activity sheet *(Appendix)*
- **My Opinion Page** activity sheet *(Appendix)*
- **Songs as Poetry** activity sheet *(Appendix)*
- **Great American Musicians!** activity sheet *(Appendix)*

- **Music on the Map** activity sheet *(Appendix)*
- **Music notebooks**
- **Additional music selections**

Activities

- Pass out the **Modern Popular Music** handout for students to read silently or aloud as a group. Afterwards, have students put the handout in their music notebooks. *(Link to language arts, history, geography, social studies.)*

- Give the **Modern Popular Music Quiz** to assess student understanding of the lesson.

- Go over the music vocabulary at the top of the student handout before or after reading the text. Refer to the glossary for definitions. *Suggestion:* Include these words in a regular class vocabulary lesson, or pass out flashcards with a vocabulary word on one side and the definition on the other and allow students to drill each other. Use the **Music Vocabulary** activity sheets to write out definitions. *(Link to language arts.)*

- Offer the **Vocabulary Challenge.** Students pick some or all of the words in this lesson's vocabulary list to use in a paragraph, essay, short story, or poem. *(Link to language arts.)*

- **Discuss.** Before reading the student handout, discuss what students already know about modern popular music. Read the student handout and discuss it again, letting students add what they've learned. *(Link to language arts, social studies.)*

- **Charting the Charts.** The *Billboard* charts are one of the ways the music industry observes the public's changing taste in music. This activity tracks a song on the *Billboard* charts, charting its movement over a span of time. Read the section in the student handout. Use the **Charting the Charts** activity sheet to record the information. *Step 1:* Find a copy of *Billboard* magazine, or go to *www.billboard.com* and pick a chart to review. Some of the choices are the Billboard Top 40 (recommended), Modern Rock Tracks, Hot Latin Tracks, and Hot Dance Music. (On the Internet, click on Top 20 because you can't get into the complete chart without membership.) *Step 2:* Students write the name of the chart and the name of their song. *Step 3:* Using the graph on the activity sheet, students chart the number the song holds each week. For example, if the song is number 14, make a mark at 14 on the graph and write the date in the space below. Each week, mark the place number the song holds and write the date under it. See what happens over time, whether it goes up or down or stays the same. *Suggestion:* Consider exploring the idea that the music industry uses the *Billboard* chart information for demographic information and marketing. *(Link to math.)*

- **Bonus Challenge: Compose a Parody.** This activity introduces the concept of parody in music and challenges students to compose one. A parody is a humorous imitation of another song. Find examples of parodies to play for the students. *Suggestions:* Weird Al Yankovic's "Eat It," a parody of Michael Jackson's "Beat It," or Yankovic's "The Saga Begins," a *Star Wars* parody of Don McLean's "American Pie." Read the student handout for step-by-step directions. *To extend this activity:* Gather all student parodies into a class compilation called "Parodies" and make copies for each student to keep. *(Link to language arts.)*

Extension Activities

For step-by-step directions and activity sheets, see the appendix.

- **My Opinion Page.** Offer students a chance to freely express their own opinions about the music they hear. *(Link to language arts, critical thinking.)*

- **Songs as Poetry.** Examine the lyrics of songs for their poetic nature. *(Link to language arts.)*

- **Illustrate the Music.** Students illustrate a song or piece of music by drawing or painting their ideas of what the music "looks" like visually. *(Link to language arts, visual arts.)*

- **Great American Musicians!** Introduce students to American musicians whose talents have made them notable. *(Link to language arts, history.)*

- **Music on the Map.** Create a map and legend showing musically important places, such as musicians' birthplaces and music hot spots mentioned in the lesson. *(Link to geography.)*

- **Invite a Music Expert.** Invite a popular musician to visit your class and share his or her instrument and musical talent with the students. Some resources for locating musicians are the Internet, local music and arts organizations, friends, students, parents. Also consider taking students to hear a live performance, or show a video. *(Link to social studies.)*

- Consider bringing in **additional selections of music** from other sources to expand the music sample offerings. Read the song selections mentioned in each musician's biography for additional music ideas. Search the Internet, library, or local music store to find them.

Name _____   Date _____

Gloria Estefan, Rogers and Hammerstein, Michael Jackson, Madonna

Modern Popular Music

Vocabulary: Tin Pan Alley, music publishers, sheet music, popular music, lyrics, melody, refrain, popular song, Broadway musicals, compose, composition, microphone, radio broadcasting, phonograph record, jukebox, record company, record charts, parody

Tin Pan Alley

Tin Pan Alley is the name of a neighborhood in New York City where a group of **music publishers** began selling **sheet music** around the turn of the century (1900). They published and sold the music that people sang in their living rooms, around the family piano, or in a pub over a beer. These publishers helped develop today's modern popular music industry.

Tin Pan Alley songs fit the classic definition of **popular music**—music that pleases the general public. These songs are crafted and shaped to fit the tastes of the mainstream population. At first, Tin Pan Alley songs used the simple verse-chorus structure established by Stephen Foster; they were easy to sing

Dorothy Fields (July 15, 1905–1974). Dorothy Fields, born in New Jersey, became a popular songwriter. She grew up in a musical family. Her father performed in vaudeville and later produced musical shows. As a child, Dorothy was actively discouraged from growing up to work in show business. But she was drawn to it and found work writing songs with other musicians. She wrote for Fred Astaire and Ginger Rogers movies and collaborated on the songs for *Annie Get Your Gun* (1946) and other Broadway musicals. She was the first woman to be inducted to the Songwriters' Hall of Fame. Some of her songs are "I Can't Give You Anything But Love, Baby," "I'm in the Mood for Love," "Don't Blame Me," and "If My Friends Could See Me Now."

along with, and this added to their popularity. Songwriters also borrowed ideas from other genres—for example, using the rhythms of ragtime and jazz to make their music more popular and interesting.

Some of the earliest Tin Pan Alley songs are "The Sidewalks of New York" (1894), by Charles B. Lawlor and James W. Blaker, "My Wild Irish Rose" (1899), by Chauncey Olcott, "Swanee" (1919), by George Gershwin, and "Blue Moon" (1934), by Richard Rogers and Lorenz Hart. "In the Baggage Car Ahead" (1896), by Gussie Davis, was the first popular song by an African-American songwriter to sell a million copies of sheet music.

"On the Sunny Side of the Street" (1930), by Jimmy McHugh and Dorothy Fields, reflects the carefree, lighthearted nature of popular music. The **lyrics** are positive, the **melody** is upbeat, and the song invites listeners to sing along on the **refrain** (the part that is repeated).

Jimmy McHugh and Dorothy Fields. AP/World Wide Photos.
Used by permission.

Listen to Learn

Selling popular music became a big industry in North America. It includes a network of publishing houses, record companies, radio stations, and movie and television businesses, all working together to produce and sell a "musical product," which is the **popular song.** This business of music originated at Tin Pan Alley.

Broadway Musicals

Broadway is the name of a street in New York City where brightly lit theaters line the sidewalks and huge billboards display the names of famous musical shows. It is on this street that the **Broadway musical** became popular around the turn of the century (1900). Broadway musicals are musical plays that are performed on the stages of large New York theaters, with elaborate sets and costumes, singing, dancing, acting, and other visual entertainment. The stories are usually light in nature—unlike dramatic plays or grand opera.

The Broadway musical was likely born when George M. Cohan (1878–1942) left vaudeville and began composing for the theater. Where vaudeville had featured variety acts, George Cohen's shows were musical plays featuring songs with a story line. His musicals were upbeat and often patriotic, with songs like "Give My Regards to Broadway" (1904) and "You're a Grand Old Flag" (1906).

Give My Regards to Broadway

Lyrics and music by George M. Cohan

Did you ever see two Yankees
Part upon a foreign shore,
When the good ship's just around about
To start for Old New York once more?
With tear-dimmed eye they say goodbye,
They're friends without a doubt;
When the man on the pier
Shouts "Let them clear,"
As the ship strikes out.

Chorus: Give my regards to Broadway
Remember me to Herald Square,
Tell all the gang at Forty-Second Street
That I will soon be there;
Whisper of how I'm yearning,
To mingle with the old-time throng,
Give my regards to old Broadway
And say that I'll be there e'er long.

Say hello to dear old Coney Isle
If there you chance to be,
When you're at the Waldorf have a smile
And charge it up to me;
Mention my name ev'ry place you go,
As 'round the town you roam;
Wish you'd call on my gal,
Now remember, old pal,
When you get back home.

Repeat chorus.

Jerome Kern (January 27, 1885–1945) **composed** over seven hundred songs for Broadway shows. At times he teamed with Dorothy Fields or Oscar Hammerstein and composed award-winning songs with them. He composed the music for the famous musical *Showboat* (1927). Some of his most recognized songs are "How'd You Like to Spoon?" "Look for the Silver Lining," and "Smoke Gets in Your Eyes."

George Gershwin's **compositions** of the 1920s and 1930s brought many American themes to the Broadway stage. *Funny Face* (1929) is about an American fashion photographer and a model. His folk opera *Porgy and Bess* (1935) shows life in a South Carolina town and features hit songs like "Summertime," "It Ain't Necessarily So," and "I Got Plenty o' Nuttin'."

Irving Berlin's Broadway musical *Annie Get Your Gun* (1946) tells the story of Annie Oakley, a real-life sharpshooter who grew to fame performing in *Buffalo Bill's Wild West Show* in the late 1800s. Songs like "There's No Business Like Show Business" and "You Can't Get a Man with a Gun" paint a musical picture of this lively character in America's history.

Rogers and Hammerstein composed some of the most popular Broadway musical scores ever, including *Oklahoma!* (1943) about a woman in the American West and her courtships with a cowboy and a farmer. *South Pacific* (1949) is about an American nurse who falls in love with a plantation owner on an island in the South Pacific.

George Gershwin (September 26, 1898–1937). George Gershwin, who was born in New York, composed popular songs and musical scores for Broadway. He taught himself to play the piano at an early age and later took lessons and studied music. While still a teenager he composed songs and sold them on Tin Pan Alley. "Swanee" (1919), made famous by vaudeville performer Al Jolson, was one of his most popular early tunes. He pioneered mixing African-American jazz with classical music, and in 1924 his piece "Rhapsody in Blue" served to mark the beginning of a new jazz-inspired era in classical music. Working alone, or with his brother Ira and others on occasion, George created some of the most remembered popular music of the twentieth century. He also composed concertos, opera, and music for movies, television, and radio. Some of his songs are "Fascinatin' Rhythm" (1924), "Summertime" (1935), and "I Got Plenty o' Nuttin'" (1935).

George Gershwin. From *Great Composers in Historic Photographs,* Dover Publications.

Early Radio

The first radio program in America was broadcast on Christmas Eve, 1906, from a small station in Massachusetts. It broadcast two musical pieces, a poem, and a short talk. It was heard only by the crew of a ship out on the water, who had a radio receiver. By 1921, there were eight small radio stations broadcasting in the United States to only a few people with radio receivers. By 1922, there were 564 radio stations. Not long after that, radio companies started to build and sell home radios in huge quantities and people all over the country began tuning in.

Irving Berlin (May 11, 1888–1989). Born Israel Baline in Siberia, Russia, Irving Berlin emigrated to the United States with his family when he was four years old. He became a composer and piano player, composing some of America's most recognizable songs. At the age of fourteen, he was singing on street corners and in saloons to earn money for his family. He taught himself to play piano and found work as a singing waiter, and then sang and played piano in vaudeville. He wrote songs for successful vaudeville artists like Eddie Cantor and Fanny Brice. While serving in the Army in 1918, Irving Berlin composed the music for *Yip Yip Yaphank,* a patriotic musical performed by soldiers. When he returned to civilian life, his career soared; his music was heard on Broadway stages, on the radio, and in movie houses across America. Berlin lived to be 101 years old. Some of his songs are "Monkey Doodle Doo" (1925), "Cheek to Cheek" (1935), "Top Hat" (1935), "White Tie and Tails" (1935), "White Christmas" (1942), and "There's No Business Like Show Business" (1946).

Rogers and Hammerstein. Richard Rogers (June 28, 1902–1990) and Oscar Hammerstein (June 12, 1895–1960) were both born in New York. They became a songwriting team famous for popular Broadway musicals. Rogers composed the music, Hammerstein wrote the lyrics. Early in his career Rogers composed musical comedy and film scores with another partner, Lorenz Hart. Hammerstein studied law and wrote lyrics at Columbia University before writing for musical comedies and operettas. Rogers and Hammerstein began their collaboration in 1943 and composed a string of highly successful musical plays that have turned into some of Broadway's most popular all-time hits. After Hammerstein's death, Rogers continued composing for the Broadway stage, film, and television. Some of the collaborations between the two are "Oh What a Beautiful Morning" (1943) from *Oklahoma,* "I'm Gonna Wash That Man Right Out of My Hair" (1949) from *South Pacific,* and "My Favorite Things" (1959) from *The Sound of Music.*

The earliest radio shows of the 1920s and 1930s were broadcast live from studios—with singers, actors, and orchestras performing in front of **microphones** before live audiences. People all across America could, for the first time, sit in their living rooms and hear soap operas, news, popular music, orchestral music, and opera. The popular radio show *Your Hit Parade* aired the most popular songs of the day performed by the most popular singers. "Don't Fence Me In," by Cole Porter, "Do Nothin' 'Til You Hear from Me," by Duke Ellington, "Swingin' on a Star," by Johnny Burke and Jimmy Van Heusen, and "Besame Mucho," by Consuelo Velasquez and Sunny Skylar were all hits featured on *Your Hit Parade.*

In the beginning, radio stations were separate from each other. They broadcast their own news and music and other entertainment. But over time, as it became possible to send signals through telephone wires, radio stations started to link up and share programs. A New York radio station could now send a program through the telephone wire to a Chicago station, where it could be aired to a Chicago audience. As more radio stations linked together they started to form *networks* that evolved into broadcast companies. The earliest broadcasting companies were NBC (National Broadcasting Company), CBS (Columbia Broadcasting System), and ABC (American Broadcasting Company).

Cole Porter (June 9, 1891–1964). Cole Porter, a composer of popular songs, was born in Indiana. In his early years he played violin and piano. In 1901, when he was ten, he composed and published "Song of the Birds" and "The Cuckoo Tells the Mother Where the Bird Is." He studied music at Yale University and law at Harvard Law School. He also lived in Europe and studied music there before returning to the United States to make a career of composing music. Cole Porter wrote both the lyrics and the music to nearly a thousand songs, many of which became famous on the radio, on Broadway, and in the movies. He is still one of America's most remembered popular songwriters of the twentieth century. Some of his songs are "You Do Something to Me" (1929), "I Happen to Like New York" (1930), "Night and Day" (1932), and "Don't Fence Me In" (1934).

The Science of Music: Radio. A radio is a device that changes sound into electrical waves (transmitter) and sends the waves to another radio (receiver). The receiving set "reads" the waves and changes them back into sound that people can hear. How does a radio transmitter work? When a person talks into a microphone, the sound of the voice causes a vibration inside the microphone. The sound is changed into tiny electrical signals that pass from the microphone to another device, called a *modulator.* The modulator combines the electrical signals with radio waves and sends them to an aerial tower—a metal structure rising from the ground up into the air. The invisible signals move through the aerial tower and radiate out from it, just as light radiates from a lamp. This is called **radio broadcasting.** When the radio station plays a popular song, the music is changed into electric signals and transmitted out through the aerial tower to your radio. How does a radio receiver work? As the radio waves travel through the air, they can be "picked up" or received by smaller aerials, or antennae, attached to individual radios. The *receiver* then changes the electric radio waves back into sound waves, which are made louder by the *speakers* inside the radio box so people can hear them.

Early radio receiver

Phonograph Records

The first **phonograph record** was made by Thomas Edison in 1877 when he recorded his own voice speaking "Mary Had a Little Lamb" onto a spinning cylinder covered with tin foil. The first live recordings were of vaudeville skits, ragtime music, popular songs, opera, and concert band music from the turn of the century (1900).

Eventually, cylinders were replaced with flat plastic discs, called *records.* Records spun around on a turntable; a needle read the vibrations into the record player for playback. The early discs were called *78s* because they spun at 78 rpm (revolutions per minute).

The Science of Music: Phonograph Records. The verb *record* means to write down or register or remember permanently. A *phonograph record* "writes down" sound in a permanent way. The first phonograph record, called a "sound writer," was invented by Thomas Edison in 1877—the same person who invented the electric lightbulb. His first record was made on a cylinder covered with tin foil. He began by speaking into the large opening of a horn attached to a steel needle. The sound of his voice vibrated through the horn and down to the needle, which touched the cylinder covered with tin foil. As the cylinder cycled around, the needle made marks in the tin foil and "recorded" the vibrations. When it was time to play it back, the needle moved along the grooves of the tin foil, "reading" the tiny vibrations and sending them back out through the horn, where they could be heard again. Over time, Edison's machine was improved and expanded upon. The early ones were called *talking machines.* Modern phonograph systems use his basic idea, with a turntable for turning the disc, a needle for reading the vibration from the disc's grooves, a "pickup" for changing the vibration into electrical impulses, an amplifier for making the impulses louder, and a loudspeaker for changing the electrical impulses into sound waves so you can hear them.

Recording cylinder   Early "talking machine"

Phonograph

         Listen to Learn

Phonograph record

In the 1920s and 1930s, the Victor Company sent records to public schools in order to introduce orchestral music, operas, and popular music to students. This also served as a marketing tool to attract listeners who would one day grow up to purchase music from the record companies. Phonograph records introduced listeners across the country to music of many different styles performed by some of the country's most recognized musicians. By the 1940s, recordings of popular music were selling by the millions around the world. American songs were played in clubs, on the radio, in movies, on records and **jukeboxes,** and in people's homes.

By the 1960s, the average American home had a record player along with stacks of records of many styles. In the 1970s and 1980s, tape cassettes and CDs (compact discs) gradually replaced phonograph records as the medium for hearing recorded music. Records became nostalgia items held onto by a few collectors.

Recording Artists

The inventions of the radio and the record player changed the course of music in America. When people could hear recorded music in their own homes they stopped buying sheet music and singing around the piano in their living rooms. The buying and selling of records became a major American industry and **record companies** took on the role of finding talented musicians to feature. They spent millions of dollars on recording and promoting the artists, sending them on performance tours, buying ads on radio and television, and arranging for interviews with newspapers and magazines. Contests were held and "countdowns" were created to promote the most-listened-to songs of the week. Today, countdowns, concert tours, award ceremonies, CDs, and T-shirt sales all serve to promote the music and the artists, and so their popularity is assured.

Billboard Charts. *Billboard* is a music industry magazine that tracks entertainment news, including the "charts" that track the top-selling records. No. 1 on the *Billboard* charts means the song is the top-selling song of that week. These **record charts** reflect what is most enjoyed and purchased by the general public. The first "chart line" appeared in 1936 and listed the most played songs on the three major radio networks (CBS, NBC, ABC). In 1944, these chart lines became the *Billboard Music Popularity Chart.* In the 1950s, the *Top 40* was born, reporting the top forty most popular songs in North America. Today, *Billboard* charts music for many different popular music genres, including rock, country, R&B, hip-hop, jazz, Latin, and Top 40. *Activity: Track a song on the* Billboard *charts and analyze its movement over a span of time. Use a graph or the **Charting the Charts** activity sheet to record your information. This activity will show you one of the ways the music industry observes the public's tastes in music. Consider how chart information might be used for demographics and marketing music.*

JULY 5 2003

Billboard® MAINSTREAM ROCK TRACKS™

Airplay monitored by Nielsen Broadcast Data Systems

THIS WEEK	LAST WEEK	WEEKS ON	TITLE IMPRINT/PROMOTION LABEL	Artist
			☆ NUMBER 1 ☆	12 Weeks At Number 1
1	1	23	LIKE A STONE INTERSCOPE/EPIC	Audioslave
2	2	22	SEND THE PAIN BELOW EPIC	Chevelle
3	3	37	HEADSTRONG WARNER BROS.	Trapt
4	4	4	ST. ANGER ELEKTRA/EEG	Metallica
5	5	17	SOMEWHERE I BELONG WARNER BROS.	Linkin Park
6	8	17	STUPID GIRL FLIP/GEFFEN/INTERSCOPE	Cold
7	6	21	STRAIGHT OUT OF LINE REPUBLIC/UNIVERSAL/UMRG	Godsmack
8	7	12	PRICE TO PLAY FLIP/ELEKTRA/EEG	Staind
9	10	18	CAUGHT IN THE RAIN EPIC	Revis
10	9	14	THE ROAD I'M ON REPUBLIC/UNIVERSAL/UMRG	3 Doors Down
11	15	4	JUST BECAUSE CAPITOL	Jane's Addiction
12	11	14	FREE DREAMWORKS	Powerman 5000
13	13	16	DRIVEN UNDER WIND-UP	Seether
14	12	13	STILLBORN SPITFIRE	Black Label Society
15	14	40	WHEN I'M GONE REPUBLIC/UNIVERSAL/UMRG	3 Doors Down
16	17	9	MINERVA MAVERICK/REPRISE	Deftones
17	24	4	SHOW ME HOW TO LIVE INTERSCOPE/EPIC ◄ AIRPOWER ►	Audioslave
18	16	29	REMEMBER REPRISE	Disturbed
19	27	3	FAINT WARNER BROS. ◄ AIRPOWER ►	Linkin Park
20	20	12	FLY FROM THE INSIDE ATLANTIC	Shinedown
21	19	17	BRING ME TO LIFE WIND-UP	Evanescence Featuring Paul McCoy
22	21	10	MOBSCENE NOTHING/INTERSCOPE	Marilyn Manson
23	22	23	TIMES LIKE THESE ROSWELL/RCA/RMG	Foo Fighters
24	23	14	IMPRINT ROADRUNNER/IDJMG	doubleDrive
25	25	3	LIBERATE REPRISE	Disturbed
26	26	6	EVERYONE ELEKTRA/EEG	Socialburn
27	29	9	BOTTOM OF A BOTTLE LAVA	Smile Empty Soul
28	30	6	WORLD SO COLD EPIC	Mudvayne
29	39	2	SO FAR AWAY FLIP/ELEKTRA/EEG	Staind
30	NEW		SET ME FREE DECCA	Velvet Revolver
31	31	7	NOTHING SACRED COLUMBIA	Memento
32	28	10	GO WITH THE FLOW INTERSCOPE	Queens Of The Stone Age
33	NEW		SERENITY REPUBLIC/UNIVERSAL/UMRG	Godsmack
34	34	11	RED WHITE AND BLUE SANCTUARY	Lynyrd Skynyrd
35	32	7	RECTIFIER REPUBLIC/UNIVERSAL/UMRG	RA
36	36	5	OXYGEN'S GONE ISLAND/IDJMG	Die Trying
37	35	17	REST IN PIECES ISLAND/IDJMG	Saliva
38	38	3	SAFE PASSAGE AMERICAN/IDJMG	Manmade God
39	40	2	FIREPROOF FLICKER/MCA	Pillar
40	NEW		I DON'T WANNA BE ME ROADRUNNER/IDJMG	Type O Negative

Top 40 Billboard Chart. Copyright © 2003 VNU Business Media, Inc. Used with permission.

Did You Know? When a song sells a million copies, it is awarded a Platinum Record. Songs win a Gold Record for five hundred thousand copies sold, a Diamond Record for ten million.

In the end, what makes a person or song popular is how many recordings he or she sells. Most commonly, the more recordings an artist sells, the more famous he or she becomes.

One of the most popular recording artists of the late twentieth century was Michael Jackson, who began his musical career as a child. He was one of the first African Americans to reach superstar status and sell many millions of records.

In the last part of the twentieth century, the larger record companies, nicknamed *the majors,* traditionally controlled the recording industry's market by making sure their artists received most of the airplay on the radio and space on record store shelves. In the 1970s, however, artists began to leave the majors to market themselves.

In 1971, Stevie Wonder, who had had many hits with Motown Records in the 1960s, left that company, formed his own record company, and launched two successful albums of popular music. In the 1980s, Madonna entered the popular music mainstream with a clear idea of what she would do with her music and has remained in control of it ever since.

Independent record companies, nicknamed *the indies,* gained more airplay and more shelf space in music stores for their artists because the public developed a taste for alternative forms of music not recorded or promoted by the majors. The popularity of the indies has played a large role in bringing unknown performers into the mainstream without the sanction of major recording companies.

Parody Music

Throughout music history, parody songwriters have taken popular songs and made up their own funny versions of them. A **parody** is an imitation of a song written in a humorous way. For example, "The Ants Go Marching One by One" is a parody of the traditional song "When Johnny Comes Marching Home Again."

Michael Jackson (August 29, 1958–). Born in Indiana, Michael Jackson is a singer, songwriter, and dancer. He began performing at age four in his family's band, the Jackson Five. The group recorded with Motown Records in 1968 and followed with a string of popular hits that made it to the top of the record charts. Michael later recorded solo albums and made music videos, both of which became extremely popular in the 1980s. He has performed around the world to millions of people, with all-time record-breaking sales records, and has been called the King of Pop. Some of his songs are "ABC" (1968), "I Want You Back" (1968), "Billie Jean" and "Beat It" (1982), "Thriller" (1982), and "Bad" (1987).

Madonna (August 16, 1958–). Madonna was born Madonna Louise Ciccone in Michigan. She is a singer, dancer, songwriter, performer, and actor. As a young girl, she excelled in dance and drama and pursued these subjects in college. At nineteen years old she moved to New York, where she studied dancing and practiced singing. She promoted her music in dance clubs, which caught on, and soon was recording and selling her music. Madonna's songs eventually received national radio airplay, which led to greater popularity and more demand for her music. She has toured the world performing elaborate shows with costumes and choreography (dancing), and her songs have reached number one status many times on the record charts. She has performed on Broadway, made movies and music videos, and recorded music that continues to top the record industry charts in the new millennium. Some of her songs are "Who's That Girl" (1987), "Live to Tell" (1986), "La Isla Bonita" (1986), "Open Your Heart" (1986), and "Ray of Light" (1998).

Weird Al Yankovich is a singer-songwriter who is well-known for composing parodies. He wrote a song called "Eat It," which was a parody of Michael Jackson's "Beat It." Where Michael Jackson's song is about gangs, Weird Al's song uses the same melody and musical arrangement but changes the words to sing about food. Many other famous songwriters have written parodies of songs, including Michael Katz, Spike Jones, and Allen Sherman.

Bonus Challenge: Compose a Parody A parody is an imitation of a song written in a humorous way. Change the lyrics of a familiar song to make a new, funny parody. *Step 1:* Find examples of parodies. *Suggestions:* Weird Al Yankovic's "Eat It," a parody of Michael Jackson's "Beat It," or Yankovic's "The Saga Begins," a *Star Wars* parody of Don McLean's "American Pie." *Step 2:* Listen and compare the two versions. *Step 3:* Find and print the lyrics of a famous song, or any song of your choice. *Step 4:* Determine a theme for your parody (food, playground spoofs, sports humor, pets, famous events in history, for example). *Step 5:* Write the lyrics to the parody. Try to make the syllables of the parody match the syllables of the original lyrics in order to keep the rhythm and meter the same. *Step 6:* Edit and rework the parody. Keep reworking it until you are satisfied. *Step 7:* Consider performing it, or simply leave it as a written piece. *Step 8:* Put it away in your music notebook. *Suggestion:* Do an Internet search for parodies.

Name_____   Date_____

Modern Popular Music Quiz

Instructions: After reading the **Modern Popular Music** student handout, answer these questions (use back of page if necessary).

1. What is **Tin Pan Alley?** Describe some of its influences on modern popular music.

2. What is a **Broadway musical?**

3. What has been the influence of **radio** on popular music?

4. What are the *Billboard* **record charts?**

5. What is a **parody?**

Modern Popular Music Quiz: Answer Key

1. What is **Tin Pan Alley?** Describe some of its influences on modern popular music.

    TIN PAN ALLEY IS THE NAME OF A NEIGHBORHOOD IN NEW YORK CITY WHERE A GROUP OF MUSIC PUBLISHERS SET UP SHOP AND SOLD SHEET MUSIC AROUND THE TURN OF THE CENTURY. TIN PAN ALLEY SONGS FIT THE CLASSIC DEFINITION OF POPULAR SONGS—SONGS THAT PLEASE THE GENERAL PUBLIC.

2. What is a **Broadway musical?**

    BROADWAY MUSICALS ARE MUSICAL PLAYS PERFORMED ON THE STAGES OF THEATERS THAT LINE THE FAMOUS STREET NAMED "BROADWAY" IN NEW YORK CITY. THE MUSICALS HAVE SINGING, DANCING, ACTING, COSTUMES, AND ELABORATE SETS. THE MUSIC IN BROADWAY MUSICALS IS USUALLY POPULAR MUSIC.

3. What has been the influence of **radio** on popular music?

    RADIO SPREADS MUSIC TO LARGE AUDIENCES, INCREASING THE CHANCE THAT PEOPLE WILL HEAR IT AND BUY IT. THE MORE PEOPLE WHO BUY IT, THE HIGHER ITS RATING ON THE *BILLBOARD* CHARTS, THE MORE POPULAR IT BECOMES, THE MORE THE RADIO STATIONS WILL PLAY IT, AND THE MORE FAMOUS THE MUSIC WILL BECOME.

4. What are the *Billboard* **record charts?**

    BILLBOARD IS A MUSIC INDUSTRY MAGAZINE THAT TRACKS ENTERTAINMENT NEWS, INCLUDING "CHARTS" THAT TRACK THE TOP-SELLING RECORDS. NO. 1 ON THE *BILLBOARD* CHARTS MEANS A SONG IS THE MOST POPULAR TOP-SELLING SONG OF THAT WEEK. THE CHARTS REFLECT WHAT IS MOST ENJOYED AND PURCHASED BY THE GENERAL PUBLIC. THERE ARE CHARTS FOR MANY GENRES OF MUSIC, INCLUDING POPULAR, ROCK, COUNTRY, HIP-HOP, JAZZ, AND LATIN MUSIC.

5. What is a **parody?**

    A PARODY IS AN IMITATION OF A SONG WRITTEN IN A HUMOROUS WAY. AN EXAMPLE IS "THE ANTS GO MARCHING ONE BY ONE," A PARODY OF "WHEN JOHNNY COMES MARCHING HOME."

Listen to Learn

Name_____ Date_____

Charting the Charts

Instructions: The *Billboard* charts are one of the ways the music industry observes the public's tastes in popular music. This activity tracks a song on the *Billboard* charts and analyzes its movement for twenty weeks. See what happens over time, whether the song goes up or down or stays the same.

Step 1: Find a copy of Billboard magazine at a library or record store, or go to *www.billboard.com.*

Step 2: Pick a "chart" to review. Some of the choices are the *Billboard* Top 40 (recommended), Modern Rock Tracks, Hot Latin Tracks, and Hot Dance Music (on the Internet, click on Top 20 because you can't get into the complete chart without a membership). Write the chart name and song name on the blank lines here:

Name of the chart: _____

Name of the song: _____

Name of the performer: _____

Step 3: Using the following graph, chart the number your song holds each week. For example, if your song is number 14, make a mark in the Top 14 box in the graph and write the date in the space below it. Each week mark the place number (box) your song holds and write the date under it. If it falls below the Top 20, just put your mark in the 20+ box.

Name _____ Date _____

Top 1																				
Top 2																				
Top 3																				
Top 4																				
Top 5																				
Top 6																				
Top 7																				
Top 8																				
Top 9																				
Top 10																				
Top 11																				
Top 12																				
Top 13																				
Top 14																				
Top 15																				
Top 16																				
Top 17																				
Top 18																				
Top 19																				
Top 20																				
20+																				
Today's date																				

Listen to Learn

♫ Lesson 17. Contemporary Classical Music

Lesson Overview

American classical music is heard on concert stages and in opera houses, in the soundtracks of movies, in advertisements, on television, on the radio, and at home on CDs. Contemporary classical music is influenced by jazz, blues, folk, country, and the music of many cultures. The world began to take notice of American classical orchestral music and opera in the 1920s when American composers experimented with sounds and structures and expanded the boundaries of what was accepted in traditional European classical music. This lesson explores classical music in America as it evolved in the twentieth century.

Vocabulary. Orchestral music, dissonance, polyrhythm, chromatic scale, major scale, minor scale, scale, symphonic poem, composer, compose, light classic, film score, conceptual, synthesizer, acoustic, synthesized sound, digital sampler, electrophone, opera, recitative, aria, chorus, conceptual, symphony.

Purpose. To introduce contemporary American classical music, both orchestral and opera.

Preparation. Read the student handouts **Contemporary Orchestral Music** (Lesson 17a) and **Contemporary Opera** (Lesson 17b) to familiarize yourself with the material. Consider reviewing Lesson 9: Early Classical Music and Lesson 10: Instruments of the Orchestra in Unit Two as a prerequisite. Preview the CD sample (cue in student handout) and have the CD ready for playing with the students. Be prepared to do some or all of the following activities. Also make sure that each student has a music notebook for keeping handouts and activity sheets.

Materials

- **Contemporary Orchestral Music** student handout *(following)*
- **Contemporary Opera** student handout *(following)*
- **Contemporary Classical Music Quiz** *(following)*
- **Contemporary Classical Music Quiz Answer Key** *(following)*
- **Music in the Movies** activity sheet *(following)*
- **Pick an Opera** activity sheet *(following)*
- **Music Vocabulary** activity sheet *(Appendix)*
- **My Opinion Page** activity sheet *(Appendix)*
- **Great American Musicians!** activity sheet *(Appendix)*
- **Music on the Map** activity sheet *(Appendix)*

- **Music notebooks**
- **CD music** example on accompanying CD; cue in student handout
- **Additional music selections**

Activities

- Pass out **Contemporary Orchestral Music** and **Contemporary Opera** handouts for students to read silently or aloud as a group. Afterwards, have students put the handout in their music notebooks. *(Link to language arts, history, geography, social studies.)*
- Give the **Contemporary Classical Music Quiz** to assess student understanding of the lesson.
- Go over the music vocabulary at the top of the student handout before or after reading the text. Refer to the glossary for definitions. *Suggestion:* Include these words in a regular class vocabulary lesson, or pass out flashcards with a vocabulary word on one side and the definition on the other and allow students to drill each other. Use the **Music Vocabulary** activity sheets to write out definitions. *(Link to language arts.)*
- Offer the **Vocabulary Challenge.** Students pick some or all of the words in this lesson's vocabulary list to use in a paragraph, essay, short story, or poem. *(Link to language arts.)*
- **Discuss.** Before reading the student handouts, discuss what students already know about contemporary classical music. Read the student handouts and discuss them again, letting students add what they've learned. *(Link to language arts, social studies.)*
- **Bonus Challenge: Research a Synthesizer or Digital Sampler.** Have students choose a synthesizer or digital sampler to research. Investigate its origins, how it works, and any other interesting or important information. Have them prepare a written or oral report.
- **Bonus Challenge: Families of Instruments.** Group the instruments mentioned in this lesson into instrument families: chordophones, membranophones, aerophones, idiophones, and electrophones. (See Unit Two, Lesson 10: Instruments of the Orchestra.) *(Link to science.)*

Extension Activities

For step-by-step directions and activity sheets, see the appendix.

- **My Opinion Page.** Offer students a chance to freely express their own opinions about the music they hear. *(Link to language arts, critical thinking.)*
- **Illustrate the Music.** Students illustrate a song or piece of music by drawing or painting their ideas of what the music "looks" like visually. *(Link to language arts, visual arts.)*

- **Great American Musicians!** Introduce students to American musicians whose talents have made them notable. *(Link to language arts, history.)*

- **Music on the Map.** Create a map and legend showing musically important places, such as musicians' birthplaces and music hot spots mentioned in the lesson. *(Link to geography.)*

- **Invite a Music Expert.** Invite a classical musician to visit your class and share his or her instrument and musical talent with the students. *(Link to social studies.)*

- **Illustrate the *Grand Canyon Suite*.** Have students illustrate (draw, paint) a visual conception of Ferde Grofé's *Grand Canyon Suite*. *(Link to visual arts, geography.)*

- **Play Along with *Syncopated Clock*.** Play along with the ticking clock in *Syncopated Clock*, which offers a clear example of a steady beat. *(Link to rhythm.)*

- **Music in the Movies.** This activity invites students to listen to the background music in movies to discover how music creates mood and inspires emotion. *(Link to language arts, visual arts.)*

- **Pick an Opera.** The goal is to get to know an American opera—its story line, characters, music, and so on. *(Link to language arts.)*

- Because of copyright issues, modern music is difficult to obtain for the accompanying CD. Consider bringing in **additional selections of music** from other sources to expand the music examples for this lesson. Note the music mentioned in each composer's biography for ideas. Search the Internet, library, or local CD store, or your own music collection.

Name_____ Date_____

Composers Philip Glass, Glenn Gould, Leroy Anderson

Contemporary Orchestral Music

Vocabulary: orchestral music, dissonance, polyrhythm, chromatic scale, major scale, minor scale, scale, symphonic poem, composer, compose, light classic, film score, conceptual, synthesizer, acoustic, synthesized sound, digital sampler, electrophone, symphony

American **orchestral music** is heard on concert stages, in school auditoriums, on the soundtracks of movies, behind popular singers, and even in elevators! It is performed with large orchestras and small ensembles, on synthesizers and digital samplers. Sometimes it is even performed with electric buzzers and water pouring from pots! Contemporary orchestral music has many variations and many influences.

Modern Classical Music

When Charles Ives was experimenting with strange sounds and rhythms in the early 1900s, he was one of the first American classical composers to break away from European traditions and develop modern classical music. Ives intentionally

Listen to Learn

Charles Ives (October 20, 1874–1954). Composer Charles Ives was born in Connecticut. He grew up singing and playing piano and organ in a musical family. He composed his own music as a teenager and went on to study classical music at Yale University. Charles's compositions sounded different from the music being performed at the time, and later came to be called "modern music." His compositions include *Symphony No. 3: The Camp Meeting* (1904), *The Fourth of July* (1911–1913), *Fourth Symphony* (1916), and *Concord Sonata* (1939).

created **dissonance** (music that sounds harsh or unpleasant) in his compositions. Sometimes he would hold down a whole row of keys on the piano with a ruler to create dissonance. Sometimes he used **polyrhythms** (two or more rhythms at once) to build new sounds. His ideas seriously broke the rules of classical music composition.

By the 1940s, American composers were regularly "breaking the rules" of European composition. They used **chromatic scales** (twelve-tone scales) instead of the traditional **major** and **minor scales** (eight-tone scales). This sounded strange to people's ears. To really make things unusual, composers added the sounds of car horns, garbage cans, kitchen utensils, subway sounds, and crowd noises in their compositions.

Scales. Scales are patterns of notes (also called pitches, or tones) that are used to make up a song or other piece of music. For example, a major scale is a pattern of eight notes said to create a happy mood. A minor scale is a different pattern of eight notes said to create a sad mood. A chromatic scale is a pattern that uses twelve notes. Composers put together the notes from different scales to make music, like writers put together letters from the alphabet to make different words and sentences.

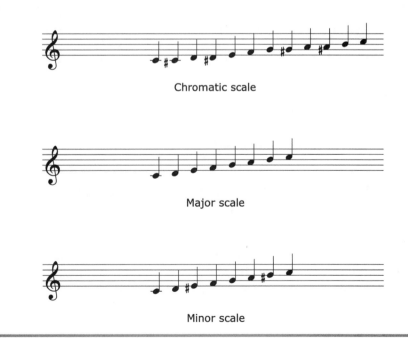

Chromatic scale

Major scale

Minor scale

Jazz Influences

At the turn of the century (1900), jazz was becoming very popular in America (see this unit's Lesson 18: Jazz). Jazz music used syncopated rhythms, upbeat tempos, and unusual chord patterns to create music that had never been heard before. By the 1920s, classical composers began to use jazz in their orchestral compositions.

When George Gershwin composed his piano concerto *Rhapsody in Blue,* it was billed as an "experiment in modern music" because it contained elements of jazz to illustrate musically the streets of New York City—from the opening wail of the clarinet reaching up like a city skyscraper, to the bustling rhythms and strutting piano moving like traffic through the boulevards. When George Gershwin performed it in public for the first time in 1924, it surprised audiences with its fresh sound. Many were awed by it, others were shocked, and still others criticized it for not being traditional classical music.

Ferde Grofé used music to illustrate the American desert in *Grand Canyon Suite* (1932). In the first movement, *Sunrise,* he used the soft roll of the tympani to create the moment just before dawn when everything is quiet and beginning to awaken, followed by woodwinds and other instruments to indicate the rising sun and explosion of sunlight in a new day. The second movement, *Painted Desert,* is silent and mysterious, played by the low tones of a bass clarinet and violas with unusual harmonies from the higher-sounding woodwinds and piano. In the third movement, the beating hooves of a donkey are created by percussion sounds in *On the Trail.* The fourth movement, *Sunset,* is played by bells and violins, oboes, cellos, and horns and flutes to create the image of sunlight slowly fading and nighttime coming on, with the horns

> **Ferde Grofé (March 27, 1892–1972).** Ferde Grofé, a composer and music arranger, was born in New York. He grew up in a musical family, learning to play piano and violin at the age of five. He also learned to play the viola and brass instruments. He performed with the Los Angeles Symphony Orchestra as a violist for ten years before leaving for New York and becoming an arranger of jazz-style music for the Paul Whiteman Orchestra. He composed his own symphonies, many of them illustrating American landscapes, including *Mississippi Suite* (1925), *Grand Canyon Suite* (1932), and *Hollywood Suite* (1935).

> **Aaron Copland (November 14, 1900–1990).** Composer Aaron Copland was born in New York. Early in his life, Aaron studied classical music in Europe. Upon returning to the United States, he composed music that used jazz rhythms combined with orchestral instruments. He composed for orchestra, opera, ballet, radio, and movie soundtracks. He also taught music and wrote books about music. His music often reflected American themes, like *Billy the Kid* (1938), about the famous cowboy bandit, and *Appalachian Spring* (1945), about a young pioneer couple. His other works include *Lincoln Portrait* (1942), *Rodeo* (1943), and the opera *The Tender Land* (1952–1956).

Listen to Learn

making the sounds of wild animal calls in the distance. The final movement, *Cloudburst,* begins with violins, indicating the approach of a storm, followed by more instruments playing loud and fast to indicate lightning flashing, thunder roaring, and rain pouring down.

Ferde Grofé. Photograph by Robert Tuggle.

Many modern composers have created **symphonic poems** that use unusual chord structures and instrument combinations to tell stories or paint musical pictures. A symphonic poem, or "tone poem," is one long movement for orchestra that tells a story or describes a scene. In a symphonic poem it is the *music* that illustrates the mood of the story, rather than lyrics (words). George Gershwin's *An American in Paris* (1928) is a symphonic poem that paints a musical picture of a tourist on the streets of Paris, France. Aaron Copland's *Rodeo* (1943) creates the image of life in the Wild West through music, dance, and western costumes.

Did You Know? In 1935, during the Great Depression, the Federal Music Project was created under President Franklin D. Roosevelt's Works Progress Administration (WPA). The project helped unemployed musicians find work. Over ten thousand musicians were commissioned to write, perform, and teach music for public organizations, such as schools, prisons, and hospitals. Part of the WPA's function, besides offering musicians a job, was to offer cultural exposure to Americans. Under this program, classical compositions were commissioned and performed, folk songs were collected and archived, and American audiences enjoyed affordable entertainment. The program ended in 1941.

Unit Four: New American Music

Leonard Bernstein (August 25, 1918–1990). Conductor and composer Leonard Bernstein was born in Massachusetts. He began taking piano lessons at age ten, and while still in high school produced his own version of the famous opera *Carmen.* During his years at Harvard University, he studied piano, composed, conducted, and performed classical music. He went on to conduct many great orchestras—including the Boston Pops, the New York Philharmonic, and the New York City Symphony Orchestra. Bernstein composed classical music for movies, television, and Broadway stage, and performed concerts commemorating humanitarian causes. Some of his works are *Peter Pan* (1950), *On the Waterfront* (1954), *Candide* (1956), and *West Side Story* (1957).

Popular Influences

By the 1940s, orchestras and opera companies were established in every major American city, offering affordable live music to more Americans than ever before. As moving pictures became popular, classical **composers** were hired to **compose** the music for the background scores. As more people became exposed to classical music, the more popular it became.

In the 1950s, Leonard Bernstein emerged as one of America's major composer-conductors of the twentieth century. He composed for orchestras, operas, film scores, Broadway musicals, television, and conducted the New York Philharmonic Orchestra. His music was well known throughout the world because it was catchy and easy to listen to.

Leonard Bernstein. Photograph
by Lim M. Lai.

Glenn Gould (September 25, 1932–1982). Pianist and composer Glenn Gould was born in Ontario, Canada. When he was three, it was discovered that he had strong musical talents. At five, he was composing his own pieces for family and friends. His mother gave him lessons until the age of ten, when he began studying at the Royal Conservatory of Music in Toronto. Two years later he debuted as a soloist with the orchestra at a Royal Conservatory concert. Glenn traveled to New York and was soon signed on by a recording company, and his recordings became best-sellers. During his career he performed in the United States and Canada, Europe, and the former Soviet Union. He also performed on television and live in concerts until 1964, when he gave his last public piano performance. He then pursued his other interests of composing, recording, conducting, experimenting with technology, and broadcasting. His compositions include *String Quartet, Op. 1, Two Pieces for Piano,* and *Sonata for Bassoon and Piano.*

Leroy Anderson composed **light classics** for the Boston Pops Orchestra. Light classics are musical compositions that are usually fun as opposed to serious, easy to listen to, and enjoyable to many people. Leroy Anderson used strange sounds, like typewriters and cats meowing, to make his music fun. He was best known for using gadgets in his music, like percussion blocks and strings to make the sound of a ticking clock, or a real alarm clock in his piece *Syncopated Clock* (1945). He used an actual typewriter as a solo instrument in *The Typewriter* (1950), and the sounds of violins to imitate cats meowing in *The Waltzing Cat* (1950). In *Plink Plank Plunk* (1951) the string players of the orchestra pluck the strings and rub their fingers on the backs of the instruments to make squeaking sounds.

Movies and Television

Since the first "talkie" films of the 1930s, movies have almost always had soundtracks playing music in the background. The soundtrack is the music that plays in the background to create mood and enhance the action on-screen. Car chases are enlivened with crashing cymbals and fast tempos. Love scenes or sad scenes are softened with violins playing gently. Scary scenes are made more tense with screeching high-pitched instruments.

Leroy Anderson (June 19, 1908–1975). Composer Leroy Anderson was born in Massachusetts. His father was an amateur musician; his mother was a church organist and his first piano teacher. He played piano as a child and went on to study music at Harvard University, where he played trombone. He worked as an organist, bassist, and choirmaster before being hired to arrange and compose for the Boston Pops Orchestra, which he did for twenty-five years. He was a guest conductor of many symphony orchestras throughout the United States and Canada, and recorded his music from 1952 to 1960. His piece *Blue Tango* was the first instrumental piece to reach number one on the popular radio show *Your Hit Parade* in 1951. Leroy Anderson was well known for creating unusual and exciting classical music that appealed to many people. His compositions include *Syncopated Clock* (1945), *Blue Tango* (1951), *The Pennywhistle Song* (1951), *The Typewriter* (1953), and *Clarinet Candy* (1962).

Since the first Disney cartoon *Steamboat Willie* in 1928, cartoons have used musical accompaniment. In the Warner Brothers cartoon *Back Alley Uproar* (1948), Sylvester the Cat is featured sitting on a fence singing the operatic aria *Figaro* from Rossini's *Barber of Seville*. *The Whale Who Wanted to Sing at the Met* features well-known arias and concert songs by opera singers. *Fantasia* (1940) and *Fantasia 2000* (2000) both use animation to paint vivid descriptions of the music. In the feature *Who Framed Roger Rabbit?* (1988), loud percussion instruments stir up the excitement as Roger chases Baby Herman around the kitchen amidst falling dishes and flying knives.

Check out almost any Hollywood soundtrack and you will most likely hear music playing, whether it is a large-scale production with orchestra and choir, or a simple background featuring solo guitar, violin, or piano.

John Williams is probably the most well-known composer of **film scores** for movie soundtracks. A film score is the musical composition performed as background to the action in a film. He has written the music for movies and television shows for over fifty years. His compositions follow the action of the characters and the story line and help create the mood that the audience will feel as they watch what is happening on the screen.

John Williams. Photograph by Bachrach. Courtesy of Gorfaine/Schwartz Agency.

Did You Know? The method of using music to follow the on-screen action is called "Mickey Mousing" because it was first used in Mickey Mouse cartoons. The movie *Spy Kids* (2001) has lots of it.

John Williams (February 8, 1932–). Composer John Williams was born in New York. As a child he played piano, trombone, trumpet, and clarinet. He studied music at the University of California, Los Angeles, and at the Juilliard School of Music in New York. Early in his career he worked as a jazz pianist in nightclubs. He began composing music for television in the 1950s and for film in the 1960s. In the 1980s, he conducted the Boston Pops Orchestra, and over his career has composed classical symphonies and concertos, as well as fanfare music for Prince Philip of England and for the Olympic Games. His television themes include the music for *Lost in Space* (1965) and *NBC News* (1985). His film scores include *Jaws* (1975), *Star Wars* (1977), *Raiders of the Lost Ark* (1981), *Jurassic Park* (1993), and *Harry Potter and the Chamber of Secrets* (2002).

Conceptual Music

In the 1950 to 1960s, many American composers continued to create new and unusual sounds in classical music. Their music came to be called **conceptual** because it used "ideas" and "concepts" instead of traditional rhythms, structures, and chord patterns. For example, in *Imaginary Landscape No. 4 (March No. 2)*, composer John Cage put twelve radios on a stage, each tuned to a different radio station, and let them play their different shows, from news to music to just static. At every performance, each radio broadcasts a different station and so the composition is unique every time it is performed. In *Changes for Piano* (1951), he used mathematical laws of chance to create the structure for the music.

John Cage

Unit Four: New American Music

John Cage (September 5, 1912–1992). Composer John Cage was born in California. Early in his career he composed music for dance and played for dancers. He later experimented with unpitched sounds—using items like electric buzzers and flowerpots—and fitted pianos with bolts, screws, paper clips, and bottle caps between the strings to change the sound. He also composed with electronic music, computer sounds, and taped sounds of real-life noises. In *Water Music* (1952) he used a deck of cards, whistles, and water pouring from pots. In *4'33* the performance was the audience sitting in the auditorium, and the pianist sat quietly at the keyboard. His other works include *Sonatas and Interludes for Prepared Piano* (1946–1948) and *Concerto for Prepared Piano and Chamber Orchestra* (1951).

Electronic Orchestral Music

In the 1960s, many classically trained composers began using **synthesizers** to create new and unusual sounds in their music. Synthesizers are played like a keyboard or a piano. However, the sounds are not natural *acoustic* sounds, like those coming from a piano, but instead are *synthesized* (created) by electronics. An **acoustic** sound is the natural sound created by a physical object vibrating, like a wooden violin, brass trumpet, or silver flute. A **synthesized sound** is created by an electronic device that changes electronic signals into musical sounds.

Milton Babbitt composed *Composition for the Synthesizer* (1961) and *Ensembles for Synthesizer* (1963) using synthesized electronic sounds. Wendy Carlos recorded the popular *Switched-On Bach* (1968), an album of classical pieces played on the Moog synthesizer. In the 1983 film *Koyaanisgatsi,* Philip Glass used electronic instruments to play patterns over and over, speeding up and slowing down and changing in a variety of unusual ways throughout the film. Synthesized musical compositions changed the way classical music was heard across the world.

In the 1970s, **digital samplers** replaced synthesizers in popularity. *Samplers* are machines that make a digital "sample" or "copy" of a sound and play it back on a keyboard. With digital samplers, musicians can compose classical music on their home computers and use sampled sounds of the orchestra to play their entire compositions, all while sitting alone at a desk!

The Science of Music: Synthesizers and Digital Samplers. A synthesizer is an electronic device that creates music by turning an electric signal into a musical sound. The first synthesizer, the theremin, created in 1920, was played by waving your hands in the air around two antennae to make the sound go up and down. The Hammond organ appeared in 1935 as the first modern synthesizer. By the 1980s, digital samplers began taking the place of synthesizers. A digital sampler is a computer microprocessor that records, or takes a "sample" of a live sound and then plays it on a keyboard. The process involves first recording a natural sound and changing it into a digital impulse called a "sampled sound," then assigning it to a key on the keyboard. Instruments of the orchestra can be sampled and played on a keyboard, as can the human voice, percussion instruments, and stranger sounds like trash can lids, barking dogs, squealing children, and breaking glass. One composer sampled street sounds in New York City and "played" them in a composition. Synthesizers and digital samplers belong to the family of instruments called *electrophones*—instruments that use electronics to make sound.

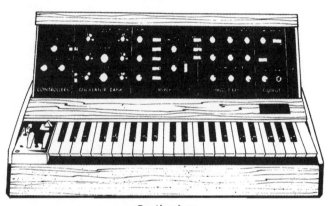

Synthesizer

Digital sampler (courtesy of Emu Systems)

Bonus Challenge: Research a Synthesizer or Digital Sampler Choose a synthesizer or digital sampler to research. Investigate its origins, how it works, and any other interesting or important information. Offer a written or oral report.

Unit Four: New American Music

Women Composers

When Amy Marcy Cheney Beach (1867–1944) was composing classical music at the turn of the century (1900), she was the first widely recognized American woman composer. In her time, it was not common for women to study or perform music. In fact, when she married, she stopped performing because it was not acceptable for a married woman to continue her career. However, she continued to compose at home and her works were eventually acknowledged in both Europe and America. (See Lesson 9 in Unit Two.)

Joan Tower. Photograph by Steve J. Sherman. Courtesy of Associated Music Publishers, Inc. (BMI). All rights reserved.

Joan Tower (September 6, 1938–). Composer Joan Tower was born in New York. She grew up in South America, where she learned to play piano. She later studied musical composition at Columbia University in New York and has been composing since that time. Her music is descriptive. In *Platinum Spirals* (1976), the image of long platinum threads spiraling upward and unfolding is created by the expressive bowing of the violins. Her orchestral piece *Sequoia* (1981) illustrates the contrast between the tree's massive height and its tiny needles. Joan's works are performed internationally. Her other pieces include *Silver Ladders* (1986) and *For the Uncommon Woman* (1992).

Listen to Learn

Since the 1950s, more American women have studied, composed, and performed music as a profession. The social rules have changed, and women are not only free to pursue music as a career but their works are regularly recognized and respected both internationally and at home. The works of Joan Tower, Ellen Taafe Zwilich, and Libby Larsen are some examples.

Libby Larsen. Photograph by Ann Marsden.
Courtesy of Libby Larsen.

Libby Larsen (December 24, 1950–). Composer Libby Larsen was born in Delaware. She grew up influenced by popular music, Broadway musicals, and boogie-woogie piano, which led her to study composition at the University of Minnesota and other institutes across the country. Libby has written for orchestras, opera, stage, dance, choral pieces, and anthems. She has used electric basses in the bass section and synthesizers in the percussion section. Her piece *Four on the Floor* (1983), inspired by boogie-woogie music, uses a walking bass rhythm, piano, strings, and instrumental solos, as in blues music. Some of her other pieces are *Missa Gaia: Kyrie* and *Symphony: Water Music.*

African Americans

After the Civil War, many African Americans began to attend college and study the music of Europe, learning to compose in the European style. Harry Thacker Burleigh (1866–1949) composed *Plantation Melodies for Violin and Piano* (1901) and *Songs for the Southland* (1914), which drew on the influences of African-American spirituals. Samuel Coleridge Taylor (1875–1912) composed *Hiawatha's Wedding Feast* (1898). William Grant Still (1895–1978) drew from African-American folk songs and themes in *Afro-American Symphony* (1930) and *Lenox Avenue* (1937), about life in Harlem, New York. Still's *They Lynched Him on a Tree* (1940) addressed racism in the rural South. African-American composer Ulysses Kay (1917–1995) composed *The Quiet One* (1948), *Serenade* (1954), and *Suite* (1945), which received some acclaim.

William Grant Still. Photograph by Lim M. Lai.

William Grant Still (May 11, 1895–1978). Born in Mississippi, William Grant Still was a composer and concert performer. His mother played piano besides writing and directing plays, and his father was the leader of a community brass band. Both parents encouraged their son's interest in music. He first arranged popular music for nightclub orchestras and musical shows. He studied classical music and then composed symphonies, operas, and scores for movies and television. His *Afro-American Symphony* debuted in 1931 and was the first performance of a **symphony** by an African-American composer by a leading orchestra, and also the first time an African-American composer conducted a major orchestra. His opera *Troubled Island* (1949) was the first African-American opera to be performed by a major opera company. His other pieces include *They Lynched Him on a Tree* (1940), *The American Suite* (1957), and *Little Red Schoolhouse* (1957)

Native Americans

Hawaiian composer Dai-Keong Lee (1911) studied on mainland United States with Aaron Copland, among others, and composed classical music for orchestra, chamber music, opera, and ballet. Some of his pieces are *Hawaiian Festival Overture* (1940), *Pacific Prayer* (1943), and *Tropical Overture* (1948).

Asian Americans

Asian-American composers, instrumentalists, singers, and conductors are performing regularly in America and around the world. Japanese-American Seiji Ozawa (b. 1935) is the conductor who was music director of the Boston Symphony Orchestra for twenty-eight years. Chinese-American Bright Sheng (b. 1955) composes for solo pipa (four-stringed Chinese lute) and full orchestra in *Nanking! Nanking!* Master cellist Yo Yo Ma (b. 1955), also Chinese-American, has collaborated on many music projects, including *Lulie the Iceberg,* a musical tale for children, and *The Silk Road Project,* which explores cross-cultural influences between East and West cultures.

Bonus Challenge: Families of Instruments   Group the instruments mentioned in this lesson into families: chordophones, membranophones, aerophones, idiophones, and electrophones.

Bright Sheng (December 6, 1955–). Composer and pianist Bright Sheng was born in Shanghai, China. He began to play piano at the age of four, studying under his mother. During the Cultural Revolution in China, Bright lived for seven years near the Tibetan border, playing piano and percussion in a Chinese folk music and dance troupe. While there, he continued to pursue his studies on his own, as well as collect the folk music of the region. After the Cultural Revolution ended, Sheng moved back to Shanghai and studied music composition at the Shanghai Conservatory of Music. He moved to New York in 1982 and studied music at Queens College and Columbia University, where his teachers included George Perle, Hugo Weisgall, Chou Wen-Chung, and Jack Beeson. He also studied composition and conducting with Leonard Bernstein. In 1999, he was commissioned by U.S. President Bill Clinton to compose a piece for a state dinner honoring the premiere of China. Bright Sheng has composed music for both orchestra and opera, including the compositions *The Song of Majnum, China Dreams, Flute Moon, Postcards,* and *Madame Mao.*

Bright Sheng. Photograph by Wah Lui. Courtesy of
G. Schirmer, Inc. (ASCAP). All rights reserved.

Yo Yo Ma (October 7, 1955–). Cellist Yo Yo Ma was born in Paris, France. He began playing cello at the age of four, encouraged by his parents. Shortly after that time his family moved to New York, where he grew up and continued his music studies. He attended the Juilliard School and Harvard University, graduating in 1976. Yo Yo Ma performs recital and chamber music, and is also a soloist with orchestras worldwide. He performs music as collaborations with composers, dancers, and filmmakers. He has studied both European and Chinese traditions in music, as well as rural African music. He has recorded with many musicians, and his CDs frequently top the *Billboard* charts in classical music. His works and collaborations include *The Silk Road Project, Inspired by Bach, Hush, Appalachia Waltz, Appalachia Journey,* and *Solo.*

Yo Yo Ma. Photograph by J. Henry Fair.

Composer Tan Dun (b. 1957) composed the music for the 2001 film *Crouching Tiger, Hidden Dragon,* mixing Chinese and Western traditions. His *2000 Today: A World Symphony for the Millennium* led a musical celebration that was broadcast around the world with a message of peace. Vietnamese-American composer P. Q. Phan (b. 1962) taught himself to play piano before studying music formally. His opera *Tragedy at the Opera* (1998) had no voices; the instruments were used to play the roles. Midori (b. 1971) is a Japanese-born violinist who at the age of eleven was a guest soloist at the New York Philharmonic's traditional New Year's concert, for which she received a standing ovation. Her lively personality and

Erik Santos (October 21, 1961–). Erik Santos was born in Washington, D.C. A Filipino-American composer and pianist, he has composed music for symphony orchestras and smaller chamber groups. He brings together the elements of music, dance, theater, art, poetry, and video into his performance pieces, which are intended to break down barriers between audience and performer. He teaches composition and music technology at the University of Michigan School of Music. His latest projects include *Star Rising,* which was commissioned by the American Guild of Organists for their national convention in Philadelphia in 2002. His other compositions include *Zauberkraft, Con Curces de Fuego, Sun Dogs,* and *Guernica Dances.*

superb violin playing have graced the stages of North America, Europe, and the Far East. Erik Santos (b. 1961) is a Filipino-American composer who has received national and international recognition. In 1998, he premiered *Guernica Dances* for two pianos and four hands clapping.

Erik Santos. Courtesy of Erik Santos.

Latin Americans

Mexican Carlos Chávez (1899–1978) was a composer, conductor, and educator who conducted for every major orchestra in the United States, Europe, and Latin America. He composed music that was influenced by Native American and Spanish traditions. His piece *Xochipilli: An Imagined Aztec Music* was written for winds, percussion, and traditional Mexican instruments.

Carlos Chávez. Photograph by Lim M. Lai.

Carlos Chávez (June 13, 1899–1978). Composer, conductor, and educator Carlos Chávez was born in Mexico. In his youth he trained as a pianist, and he spent time investigating the music of Native Americans and their cultures, folk instruments, and dances, which he later incorporated into orchestral pieces. He composed symphonies, ballets, concertos, a cantata, and an opera, and he also composed for voice, piano, and chamber groups. He was music director of the National Symphony Orchestra of Mexico and director of the National Conservatory in Mexico. Carlos was respected for his highly percussive, Latin-influenced classical music, which he performed across America and throughout the world. His compositions include *Sinfonía de Antígona,* *Sinfonía de India,* and *La Hija de Cólquide.*

♪ CD track #26. Listen to *Old Folks Quintet,* an example of electronic classical music made with a digital sampler, performed by Robert Cohen, based on the Stephen Foster song "Old Folks at Home."

> *Recording: Old Folks Quintet,* arranged by Robert Cohen. ℗ 2001 Zuvuya One Music, Migration Music. Used by permission.

Name_____   Date_____

Scene from the folk opera *Porgy and Bess,* by George Gershwin.
Photograph by James Heffernan. Courtesy of Metropolitan Opera.

Contemporary Opera

Vocabulary: opera, recitative, aria, chorus, conceptual

The first American **opera** performed in North America was *The Pipe of Desire,* by Frederick Shepherd Converse. It debuted in Boston in 1906 and at the New York Metropolitan Opera in 1910. It is the fanciful story of a feisty elf named *Iolan* who takes a magic pipe from the *Old One,* and when he plays it brings misfortune to himself. In the end, he learns a hard lesson, but is the better for it.

By the 1920s more American operas were performed, including *The Canterbury Pilgrims* (1917) and *Rip Van Winkle* (1920), written by Reginald de Koven, and *Cleopatra's Night* (1920), written by Henry Kimball Hadley. At this time, American opera managers began to let Americans sing the major operatic roles, where previously only European singers were invited to sing them.

The first American-born, American-trained woman to sing a major role at the New York Metropolitan Opera was Rosa Ponselle, who debuted in 1918. She was discovered by Italian opera star Enrico Caruso, who saw her performing on a vaudeville stage and insisted she leave vaudeville and train for opera. She went on to be one of the most famous singers the Metropolitan Opera has ever known.

The first American-born, American-trained man to sing a major role at the Metropolitan Opera was Lawrence Tibbett, a young man from a cattle town in California. He joined the Metropolitan Opera in 1923, and in 1925 performed the role of Ford in *Falstaff* so beautifully that the audience would not let the opera continue until Tibbett came out and took several bows. This performance launched his career and opened the door for many more American opera singers to perform on American stages.

Rosa Ponselle. Courtesy of the Rosa Ponselle Foundation.

Rosa Ponselle (January 22, 1897–1981). Rosa Ponselle was born in Connecticut. She was an opera singer (dramatic soprano) who began singing and playing piano in a local store demonstrating sheet music for customers. As a teenager she sang in motion picture houses, restaurants, and vaudeville. When she was twenty-one she was "discovered" by opera singer Enrico Caruso, who brought her to the Metropolitan Opera to sing—with no previous opera training or experience. Traditionally, singers had to gain much practice on the stages of Europe before they were allowed to sing at the Met. Rosa was given the chance with just five months' rehearsal because, as Caruso had said, her voice was too naturally beautiful not to let her sing. She sang leading roles at the Met until she retired. She went on to teach, record, and perform in concerts.

Lawrence Tibbett (November 16, 1896–1960). Born in California, Lawrence Tibbett was an opera singer (baritone). When he was six years old, his father, a deputy sheriff, was shot and killed by a bandit, forcing his family to move to Los Angeles where the boy studied music and sang as a paid soloist in church choirs. He eventually moved to New York, where he trained before becoming an overnight success at the Metropolitan Opera. He went on to create the roles for six new American operas at the Met, in a career that spanned twenty-seven seasons. He also sang on live radio, made movies, and performed in concerts for American presidents and European royalty. *Note: Lawrence Tibbett was the author's grandfather!*

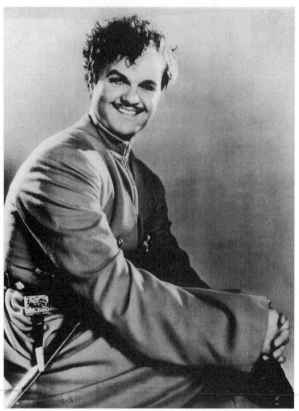

Lawrence Tibbett. Courtesy of Tibbett Family Collection.

Folk Opera

Folk operas feature themes that reflect rural, or folk life. In 1935, George Gershwin premiered *Porgy and Bess,* a folk opera about African-American life in a South Carolina town. Gershwin used **recitatives** (story songs), **arias** (emotional songs), and **choruses** (group songs), as in classic opera, but set them to rural themes with blues and jazz music, which was very unusual in opera. Other examples of folk operas are Kurt Weill's *Down in the Valley* and Douglas Moore's *The Devil and Daniel Webster.*

Scene from the folk opera *Porgy and Bess,* by George Gershwin. Simon Estes and Grace Bumbry singing. Photograph by James Heffernan. Courtesy of Metropolitan Opera.

Popular Opera

By the 1940s, opera was becoming popular across America. Weekly radio broadcasts from the Metropolitan Opera in New York introduced the music to millions of Americans in their living rooms. Concert tours and live performances in churches, theaters, and colleges brought the music directly to the people. Previously, if people wanted to see opera, they had to travel to the big cities, which many could not afford to do.

The themes of American opera began to reflect American life. Ernst Bacon's (1898–1990) opera *A Tree on the Plains* (1942) depicts the singers hitchhiking and chewing gum. *Street Scene* (1947), by Kurt Weill (1900–1950), shows life in a New York neighborhood. William Schuman's *The Mighty Casey* (1953) is about a great American baseball player, with the song titles "Peanuts," "Popcorn," "Soda," and "Crackerjack."

In 1943, the New York City Center of Music opened its doors and offered opera, ballet, and musical theater at affordable prices. The center presented music by American composers, performed by American musicians, with sets and costumes designed by American designers. Americans flocked to the performances. The operas were sung in English, so the average audience member could follow along—which added to its popularity.

Scene from the opera *The Great Gatsby* by John Harbison.
Photograph by Winnie Klotz. Courtesy of Metropolitan Opera.

African Americans in Opera

In the 1940s, opera companies began to allow African Americans to sing the major parts. The first all-African-American production of *Aida* was performed at the Chicago Opera House (1942), followed by an all-African-American production of *La Traviata* in New York's Madison Square Garden (1944).

In 1955, Marian Anderson was the first African American to sing a major role at the Metropolitan Opera. She was later invited to sing for kings and queens in Europe and presidents in the United States.

Did You Know? In 1939 Marian Anderson was denied the privilege of performing at Constitution Hall in Washington, D.C., because the sponsors of the concert refused to let African Americans perform there. First Lady Eleanor Roosevelt, and other notable people, rallied and opened the Lincoln Memorial for Marian's concert instead. From the John F. Kennedy Center for the Performing Arts Web site *(www.kennedy-center.org)*: "As Abraham Lincoln's statue watched over her from behind, Anderson gave an extraordinary performance that will go down in history as one of the most dramatic civil rights spectacles ever." In her quiet way, Anderson was an important pioneer in the civil rights movement for African Americans.

Marian Anderson (February 27, 1897–1993). Marian Anderson was born in Pennsylvania. She was an opera singer (contralto). As a child she played violin and sang in church choirs. Her studies in opera began at age nineteen, both in Europe and North America, and were followed by tours and performances around the world. She had an extensive career as a recitalist and radio performer before singing opera. During her career she was often not allowed in restaurants, hotels, and concert halls because of her skin color. But during her lifetime the civil rights movement helped open the way to perform in places that had previously barred her. At fifty-seven she was invited to sing the role of Ulrica in Giuseppe Verdi's *Un Ballo in Maschera* (1955) at the New York Metropolitan Opera, marking the first time an African American would sing at the Met. She retired in 1965 with a final concert in Philadelphia.

Marian Anderson

Leontyne Price (b. 1927) sang in church choirs as a child. She played Bess in the European performance tour of Gershwin's *Porgy and Bess* and debuted at the Metropolitan Opera in 1961, receiving a standing ovation that lasted forty-two minutes! Leontyne Price went on to become one of the most prominent African-American singers of opera in the twentieth century. Shirley Verrett (b. 1933) also became a major opera star in the United States and Europe. Like others before her, she spent many years of her career barred from certain places because of her race, but enjoyed many more opportunities after the civil rights movement.

Philip Glass (January 31, 1937–). Philip Glass, a composer, was born in Maryland. He grew up listening to recordings of great classical music at his father's radio repair shop. As a child he played the violin, flute, and piano. When still in high school, he moved to Chicago where he found work waiting tables and loading airplanes while studying mathematics and philosophy at the University of Chicago. He later studied Western music in New York at the Juilliard School of Music and in Europe, and Eastern music in North Africa, India, and the Himalayas. Philip Glass blends the techniques of many traditions in his own compositions, which have been called "avante-garde" and "minimalistic." He has composed for orchestra, music theater, film scores, dance pieces, and opera. His operas include *Einstein on the Beach* (1976), *The Making of the Representative for Plant 8* (1986), *Hydrogen Jukebox* (1990), and *The Voyage* (1992).

Conceptual Opera

In the second half of the century, composers were coming up with new ideas that pushed opera to the edge of what was considered "normal." **Conceptual** opera uses "ideas" or "concepts" rather than plot or dialogue to express the story.

In *Einstein on the Beach* (1976), Philip Glass used abstract musical patterns repeated over and over to honor the great mathematician. The opera uses saxophone, spoken words, popular songs, and synthesizers. It is a conceptual piece because it illustrates the story through movement and song, not through dialogue or plot.

John Adams's *Nixon in China* (1987) is about President Richard Nixon's historic visit to China to meet the Chinese leader Mao Tse-Tung. It too uses unusual ideas to illustrate the story, including ballet dancers with rifles dressed like soldiers of the People's Revolutionary Army.

John Adams (February 15, 1947–). Composer John Adams was born in Massachusetts. He began studying music theory, composition and the clarinet at the age of ten, and as a teen performed in marching bands with his father. He composed and conducted his first orchestral piece at fourteen, which was performed by a community orchestra. He went on to study at Harvard University for six years before moving to California where he taught, composed, and conducted music for orchestra and opera. In 2002, he composed *On the Transmigration of Souls* for the New York Philharmonic to commemorate the first anniversary of the World Trade Center attacks. For this work he received the 2003 Pulitzer Prize for Music. In 2003, John became Composer in Residence at Carnegie Hall in New York City. His operas include *Nixon in China* (1987), *The Death of Klinghoffer* (1991), *I Was Looking at the Ceiling and Then I Saw the Sky* (1995), and *El Niño* (2000).

Name _____   Date _____

Contemporary Classical Music Quiz

Instructions: After reading the Contemporary Classical Music student hand-outs, answer these questions (use back of page if necessary).

1. What is a **symphonic poem?**

2. What are **light classics?**

3. How is **orchestral music** used in movie soundtracks?

4. What is **conceptual** classical music?

5. What is a **digital sampler** and how does it work?

Contemporary Classical Music Quiz: Answer Key

1. What is a **symphonic poem?**

   A SYMPHONIC POEM, OR "TONE POEM," IS ONE LONG MOVEMENT FOR ORCHESTRA THAT TELLS A STORY OR DESCRIBES A SCENE THROUGH MUSIC RATHER THAN LYRICS (WORDS). SYMPHONIC POEMS PAINT A MUSICAL PICTURE.

2. What are **light classics?**

   LIGHT CLASSICS ARE MUSICAL COMPOSITIONS FOR ORCHESTRA THAT ARE CONSIDERED "LIGHT" BECAUSE THEY ARE FUN AND EASY TO LISTEN TO, NOT SERIOUS.

3. How is **orchestral music** used in movie soundtracks?

   MOVIES HAVE ALWAYS USED MUSIC BEHIND THE ACTION IN ORDER TO ENHANCE THE ACTION AND TO CREATE MOOD. VIOLINS CAN CREATE A SAD OR SENTIMENTAL MOOD, HIGH-PITCHED INSTRUMENTS CAN MAKE A SCARY SCENE SCARIER. CRASHING CYMBALS AND FAST TEMPOS CAN ENLIVEN A CAR CHASE SCENE.

4. What is **conceptual** classical music?

   MUSIC THAT USES IDEAS OR CONCEPTS INSTEAD OF, OR IN ADDITION TO, TRADITIONAL RHYTHMS, STRUCTURES, AND CHORD PATTERNS. FOR EXAMPLE, JOHN CAGE USED RADIOS TUNED TO DIFFERENT STATIONS TO CREATE A NEW SOUND AT EACH PERFORMANCE. SOME CONCEPTUAL COMPOSITIONS INCLUDE SOUNDS OTHER THAN FROM ORCHESTRAL INSTRUMENTS, SUCH AS POURING WATER, ELECTRIC BUZZERS, AND PIANOS WITH BOLTS, SCREWS, PAPER CLIPS, AND BOTTLE CAPS ATTACHED TO THE STRINGS.

5. What is a **digital sampler** and how does it work?

   A DIGITAL SAMPLER IS A COMPUTER MICROPROCESSOR THAT RECORDS, OR TAKES A "SAMPLE," OF A LIVE SOUND, THEN CHANGES IT INTO A DIGITAL IMPULSE SO IT CAN BE PLAYED ON A KEYBOARD.

Name _____   Date _____

Music in the Movies!

Music is used all the time to create "mood" in movies and television. Fighting scenes have loud, crashing music to make the fighting seem more exciting. Car chases have fast-paced music to go along with the speeding cars. Love scenes have soft, tender music. Mood in the movies is created by what you see and what you hear. In this activity, notice how music creates mood. Watch a movie or television show that has music in the background, then answer the following questions; use the back of the page if necessary.

1. What is the name of the movie?

2. What does the music do in a quiet scene?

   What are the actors doing? What's happening on the screen?

   What instruments are playing?

   Describe the mood.

3. What does the music do in a loud scene?

   What are the actors doing? What's happening on the screen?

   What instruments are playing?

   Describe the mood.

4. Notice any scene in the movie you liked.

   What were the actors doing? What's happening on the screen?

   What instruments are playing?

   Describe the mood.

Name _____ Date _____

Pick an Opera

The goal of this activity is to get to know an American opera—its story line, characters, music, and so on. *Suggested operas: Amahl and the Night Visitors,* by Menotti; *The Tender Land,* by Aaron Copland; *Porgy and Bess,* by George Gershwin; *The Second Hurricane,* by Aaron Copland; *Where the Wild Things Are, The Fantastic Mr. Fox,* and *Higglety Pigglety Pop!* by Oliver Knussen. Listen to the music if possible before writing your answers to the following questions.

1. What is the name of the opera?

2. Write a paragraph describing the story from beginning to end. Use the back of the page if necessary.

3. List the characters.

4. List the recitatives and arias.

5. Write any interesting information or stories about the opera or characters.

6. Write your opinion of the opera.

♫ Lesson 18. Jazz

Lesson Overview

Jazz is music that was born on American soil. It mixes the traditions of many cultures with a broad range of players who also come from varying cultural backgrounds. The earliest jazz came out of the South, as freed slaves picked up the instruments of European-Americans and began making their own style of music with them. What developed was New Orleans jazz, or as it is sometimes called, Dixieland jazz. Early jazz featured wind and rhythm instruments played in an upbeat, syncopated style, with collective improvisation (everyone improvising at the same time) one of its main characteristics. As more musicians experimented with the music, new forms emerged. Swing music, or big band music, of the 1930s and 1940s saw the musical form become more sophisticated, with written arrangements and new instruments. Bebop followed, taking standard songs and reworking them into up-tempo, virtuosic renditions. Cool jazz reacted with slowed-down tempos, softer dynamics, and understated melodies. Free jazz left behind many recognizable elements of music for a more open, free style of playing. Fusion incorporates both jazz and rock for a "groove"-oriented sound. All of these styles of jazz are still played today to pockets of fans around the world.

Vocabulary. Melody, rhythm, New Orleans jazz, Dixieland jazz, virtuoso, scat singing, improvise, swing music, big band, bebop, vocables, lyrics, cool jazz, free jazz, atonal, arrhythmic, fusion.

Purpose. To offer an overview of jazz music as it developed in North America.

Preparation. Read the student handout **Jazz** to familiarize yourself with the material. Preview the CD samples (cues in student handout) and have the CD ready for playing with the students. Consider bringing in additional music samples from other sources to enhance the lesson. Be prepared to do some or all of the following activities. Also make sure that each student has a music notebook for keeping handouts and activity sheets.

Materials

- **Jazz** student handout *(following)*
- **Jazz Quiz** *(following)*
- **Jazz Quiz Answer Key** *(following)*
- **Music Vocabulary** activity sheet *(Appendix)*
- **My Opinion Page** activity sheet *(Appendix)*
- **Great American Musicians!** activity sheet *(Appendix)*

- **Music on the Map** activity sheet *(Appendix)*
- **Music notebooks**
- **CD music** examples on accompanying CD; cues in student handout
- **Additional music selections**

Activities

- Pass out the **Jazz** handout for students to read silently or aloud as a group. Afterwards, have students put the handout in their music notebooks. *(Link to language arts, history, geography, social studies.)*
- Give the **Jazz Quiz** to assess student understanding of the lesson.
- Go over the music vocabulary at the top of the student handout before or after reading the text. Refer to the glossary for definitions. *Suggestion:* Include these words in a regular class vocabulary lesson, or pass out flashcards with a vocabulary word on one side and the definition on the other and allow students to drill each other. Use the **Music Vocabulary** activity sheets to write out definitions. *(Link to language arts.)*
- Offer the **Vocabulary Challenge.** Students pick some or all of the words in this lesson's vocabulary list to use in a paragraph, essay, short story, or poem. *(Link to language arts.)*
- **Discuss.** Before reading the student handout, discuss what students already know about jazz music. Read the student handout and discuss it again, letting students add what they've learned. *(Link to language arts, social studies.)*
- **Bonus Challenge: Pick a Jazz Style.** Students investigate a jazz style. Individually or in groups, students pick one of the jazz styles mentioned in this lesson—for example, New Orleans jazz (Dixieland), swing, bebop, cool jazz, free jazz, or fusion—and investigate it. They read more about its roots, how it developed, some of the musicians who played in that style. They listen to the music. They offer a written or oral report with illustrations, photos, and CD samples. Compile everyone's written work into a "Jazz Notebook." *(Link to language arts.)*
- **Bonus Challenge: Families of Instruments.** Group the instruments mentioned in this lesson into instrument families: chordophones, membranophones, aerophones, idiophones, and electrophones. *Answer key:* Aerophones = clarinets, saxophones, trombones, trumpets. Membranophones = drums. Chordophones = guitars, banjos, string bass, piano. Idiophones = piano. Electrophones = synthesizers, electric pianos, digital samplers, electric guitars. (See Unit Two, Lesson 10: Instruments of the Orchestra.) *(Link to science.)*

Extension Activities

For step-by-step directions and activity sheets, see the appendix.

- **My Opinion Page.** Offer students a chance to freely express their own opinions about the music they hear. *[Link to language arts, critical thinking.]*

- **Illustrate the Music.** Students illustrate a song or piece of music by drawing or painting their ideas of what the music "looks" like visually. *[Link to language arts, visual arts.]*

- **Great American Musicians!** Introduce students to American musicians whose talents have made them notable. *[Link to language arts, history.]*

- **Music on the Map.** Create a map and legend showing musically important places, such as musicians' birthplaces and music hot spots mentioned in the lesson. *[Link to geography.]*

- Because of copyright issues, modern songs are difficult to obtain for the accompanying CD. Consider bringing in **additional selections of music** from other sources to expand the music examples for this lesson. Note the songs mentioned in each musician's biography for ideas. Search the Internet, library, local music store, or your own music collection.

- **Invite a Music Expert.** Invite a jazz musician to visit your class and share his or her instrument and musical talent with the students. Some resources for locating musicians are the Internet, local music and arts organizations, friends, students, parents. Plan ahead, because musicians' schedules are often established far in advance. Tell the musician about the content of your lesson, how much time to plan for, and what you'd like him or her to do. Many professional musicians already work with students and have a planned program to offer—ask about this. Also, remember that professional musicians might ask for a fee, because this is how they earn their living. Consider taking students to hear a live performance, or show a video performance. *[Link to social studies.]*

Name _____ Date _____

Benny Goodman, Duke Ellington, Louis Armstrong, Billie Holiday

Jazz

Vocabulary: *melody, rhythm, New Orleans jazz, Dixieland jazz, virtuoso, scat singing, improvise, swing music, big band, bebop, vocables, lyrics, cool jazz, free jazz, atonal, arrhythmic, fusion*

Long before it was called *jazz,* it was a lively style of dance music performed in rural communities across the southern United States, just after the Civil War. It was played on European instruments with European chord structures, but the rhythms and the "feel" of the music came from African musical traditions.

Early Jazz

By the early 1900s, New Orleans musicians were playing an exciting, upbeat style of music in the city's streets, dance halls, bars, and on riverboats along the Mississippi River. The musicians mixed influences from African, French, Spanish, and English traditions. The **melodies** were played on trumpets, trombones, clarinets, and tubas. The **rhythms** were played with guitar, banjo, piano, and drums.

The earliest jazz musicians were African American. They played at events that ranged from fish fries to funeral processions. Sidney Bechet and King Oliver's Creole Jazz Band, from New Orleans, were some of the first to spread the music to larger audiences. Later, the movement of African Americans to the North carried the music to Chicago, where it attracted even larger audiences and became even more popular. European-Americans, like Bix Biederbeck and the Original Dixieland Jass Band, formed jazz groups and the music spread across the country. By the 1920s, jazz was heard from New Orleans to Chicago, from New York to Kansas City. Sometimes called **New Orleans jazz**, it is also known more commonly today as **Dixieland jazz.**

Louis Armstrong was one of the first New Orleans jazz musicians to become famous in America. He played trumpet with King Oliver's Creole Jazz Band in the 1920s and later with Fletcher Henderson and His Orchestra in New York. Louis Armstrong, a true trumpet **virtuoso**, developed a style of "solo" or "improvised" playing, in which he altered the rhythms, bent the notes, and made new and unusual sounds with his trumpet. When he sang he used his voice like an instrument, improvising and experimenting with syllables, also known as **scat singing.**

Memphis Jug Band

When the Saints Go Marchin' In

Call: Now, when the saints
Response: Oh when the saints
Call: Go marchin' in
Response: Marchin' in
Call: Now when the saints
Response: Go marchin' in
Call: Yes, I want to be in that number
When the saints go marchin' in!

Louis Armstrong (August 4, 1901–1971). African-American cornet and trumpet player—and master showman—Louis Armstrong was born in Louisiana. He learned to play the bugle as a child while attending a "waif school," and later took trumpet lessons from King Oliver of New Orleans. In 1922 he moved to Chicago with King Oliver's Creole Jazz Band, and in his career played with Fletcher Henderson and His Orchestra and formed the Hot Fives and the Hot Sevens, featuring New Orleans jazz–style music. He traveled around the world, made movies, performed on Broadway, and recorded many albums of music. Louis Armstrong is one of the most respected musicians in jazz history. Some of his best-known recordings are "Heebie Jeebies," "Ski-Dat-De-Dat," "West End Blues," "When the Saints Go Marching In," and "Hello, Dolly."

One of the main features of jazz is playing a solo during a song. This is when a musician steps out in front of the band and becomes the featured player while the other musicians play in the background as support. Jazz musicians **improvise** their parts—making up much of the music as they go along. Rather than reading music, they let their memory and the structure of the music, and what they feel at the moment, steer the way.

Swing Music

In the 1930s, jazz musicians formed larger bands and created more complicated arrangements for the musicians to play, each having his or her own musical part to read. The arrangements were written for instrument groups called *sections* of the jazz orchestra. The sections were the reed instruments (clarinets and saxophones), brass instruments (trumpets, cornets, trombones), and rhythm instruments (drums, string bass, and piano). Fletcher Henderson and His Orchestra were among the first to perform this lively dance style, which came to be known as **swing music.**

The laws and customs of the time restricted African Americans from performing in many clubs and concert halls across the United States. Some rose in popularity anyway, like Count Basie, Cab Calloway, Mary Lou Williams, and Duke Ellington, who arranged their own music and hired their own musicians to perform it. They toured the country and the world, and their music became ambassadors of the big band swing sound.

Fletcher Henderson (December 18, 1897–1952). Fletcher Henderson was born in Georgia. He was an African-American piano player, arranger, composer, and bandleader. He earned a degree in chemistry, but instead of pursuing that career found work performing songs for sheet music companies and managing a record company. Eventually, he gathered musicians and formed a band, and performed his own swing music in the New York club scene. He pursued this for over a decade before joining Benny Goodman's orchestra as arranger and piano player. Many of Fletcher's arrangements for Benny Goodman became hits, although Fletcher was not fully recognized for them. His arrangements were interesting and innovative, and served as a model for other big bands. Some of his arrangements include "St. Louis Shuffle" (1927), "Sing Sing Sing" (1936), and "Mary Had a Little Lamb" (1936).

Duke Ellington (April 29, 1899–1974). Born Edward Kennedy Ellington in Washington, D.C., Duke Ellington was an African-American composer, arranger, piano player, and bandleader. The Duke learned to play piano as a child, when he also studied music formally. While still in his teens, he began playing with bands, and formed his own band in 1924. He was hired to work in New York's Cotton Club, a place where African Americans performed for European-American audiences. His raw style, with exotic rhythms, trumpet growls, and unusual harmonies, were recorded and performed regularly on the radio live from the club, which increased his popularity and gained him more opportunities. He performed in the United States and other countries to enthusiastic audiences. His arrangements were upbeat, rhythmic, and highly danceable. He was a showman with a talent for making the music exciting. Duke Ellington also composed classical pieces and sacred music later in his life. Some of his famous pieces include "Mood Indigo" (1930), "It Don't Mean a Thing If It Ain't Got That Swing" (1932), "Take the A Train" (1941), "Don't Get Around Much Anymore" (1942), and "Do Nothin' Til You Hear from Me" (1943). (*Note:* Although "Take the A Train" was Duke Ellington's theme song, it was actually composed by his longtime friend, partner, and collaborator Billy Strayhorn.)

Mary Lou Williams. Image courtesy of the Dave E. Dexter, Jr. Collection. Department of Special Collections, Miller Nichols Library, University of Missouri-Kansas City. From *Club Kaycee: Sights and Sounds of the Golden Age of Kansas City Jazz* (http://www.umkc.edu/orgs/kcjazz/).

Mary Lou Williams (May 8, 1910–1981). Born in Georgia, Mary Lou Williams was an African-American jazz piano player, composer, arranger, and bandleader. She was playing and performing on the piano by the age of six, and in her teenage years played and arranged music for jazz bands. By the time she was twenty in 1930, she had recorded her first solo jazz album. In her career she arranged music for bands led by Tommy Dorsey, Benny Goodman, Duke Ellington, and Dizzy Gillespie. She started her own band in 1942 and produced her first successful hit, *Zodiac Suite,* which covered an array of styles from boogie-woogie to blues to bebop and was eventually performed by the New York Philharmonic Orchestra. She later composed sacred music and continued to perform jazz for the rest of her life. Her *History of Jazz,* recorded in 1970, featured the history of jazz told through playing and talking. Some of her pieces are "Mess-a-Stomp," "Froggy Bottom," "Little Joe from Chicago," "Camel Hop," "Roll 'Em," "In the Land of Oo-Bla-Dee," and "Black Christ of the Andes."

Paul Whiteman of the Paul Whiteman Orchestra listened to the music of African Americans, reworked it, and performed it for European-American audiences who went wild for it. Other bandleaders hired African Americans to write the arrangements for their **big bands**, because it was much easier for European-Americans to be heard than African Americans. And so it was the European-American bands that became popular.

By the 1930s, bandleaders were playing the popular music of Tin Pan Alley (see this unit's Lesson 16: Modern Popular Music) all across the country. These were popular songs with huge appeal. Audiences listened to it on the radio, bought it in sheet music, and flocked to dance halls to hear it live. Bing Crosby, Frank Sinatra, Doris Day, Nat "King" Cole, and Dinah Shore became superstars singing the most popular songs of the day to the accompaniment of big band orchestras. The invention of microphones allowed them to be heard over the instruments.

Billie Holiday (April 7, 1915–1959). Billie Holiday was born Eleanora Harris in Pennsylvania. She was an African-American blues and jazz singer and a songwriter. She grew up in poverty, with little schooling and no musical training, teaching herself to sing as a teenager. She sang in bars and clubs before being discovered by a record producer who brought her into the limelight to make records and perform with famous bands. In 1933 she recorded with the Benny Goodman Orchestra, and later with Duke Ellington's and Count Basie's big bands, before striking out her own to become a solo performer. From there Billie performed across Europe and North America to huge audiences. Her singing style was sincere, emotional, and unique. She was highly respected for her exceptional talent and skill as a jazz singer. Some of her songs include "Good Morning Heartache," "God Bless the Child," "Them There Eyes," and "Pennies from Heaven."

Benny Goodman (May 30, 1909–1986). Benny Goodman was born in Illinois. He was a European-American clarinet player and bandleader. He learned to play the clarinet as a child and performed in jazz bands as a teenager. By the time he was twenty he was making records and performing on the radio. At twenty-five he formed his own dance band and worked in dance halls. By 1935 he was so popular that he became known as the King of Swing. He hired both European-American and African-American players and arrangers for his music and was one of the first to do so. His band, like other bands of the era, featured popular lead singers and a group of highly professional, well-respected musicians. Later in life he performed and recorded classical music. Some of his famous pieces are "Sentimental Journey," "After You've Gone," "One O'Clock Jump," "Goody Goody," "Sing, Sing, Sing," and "On the Sunny Side of the Street."

Benny Goodman

Tommy Dorsey (November 19, 1905–1956). Born in Pennsylvania, Tommy Dorsey was a European-American trombone and trumpet player and a bandleader. He grew up in a musical family; his father was a music teacher. His first instrument was trumpet and later he took up the trombone. He and his older brother Jimmy first played in local bands, then formed their own bands. In 1934 they formed the Dorsey Brothers Orchestra, which lasted only a year, before the brothers argued and the younger man left to form his own band. Tommy hired excellent musicians and arrangers and created some of the most popular music of the era. His fame lasted throughout the 1930s and 1940s, during which time he recorded, had numerous number one hits, made movies, and traveled widely. In the 1950s, toward the end of their lives, he and his brother reunited and carried on the swing tradition, both live and in a television series called *Stage Show.* Some of his pieces are "Marie," "The Dipsy Doodle," "All the Things You Are," and "I'll Be Seeing You."

Frank Sinatra. Courtesy of Tibbett Family Collection.

Bonus Challenge: Families of Instruments Group the instruments mentioned in this lesson into instrument families: chordophones, membranophones, aerophones, idiophones, and electrophones.

Listen to Learn

Frank Sinatra (December 12, 1915–1998). Frank Sinatra was born in New Jersey. He was a singer and an actor. Early in life he wanted to be a journalist, but after winning an amateur music contest he began to make music his career. He first worked in small clubs and bars, made records, and performed on the radio. As his popularity grew, he became a featured singer with big bands, including Harry James and His Orchestra and the Tommy Dorsey Orchestra, singing popular music. He became a teenage idol singing in a smooth "swing" style that captivated young listeners and made him a star. He later appeared in movies and on television. Frank continued to record and perform throughout his life with a string of number one hits that have remained popular into the twenty-first century. Some of his songs are "Jeepers Creepers" (1938), "Fools Rush In" (1940), "Come Fly with Me" (1959), "Strangers in the Night" (1966), and "Something Stupid" (1961).

Bebop

In the 1940s in small nightclubs in New York City, small combos of musicians were departing from swing music and creating a new up-tempo style of jazz that came to be called **bebop**. The structures of bebop songs were often based on "standards," or popular tunes, but were reworked and played faster. Bebop musicians performed complicated technical pieces requiring great musical skill. Emphasis was placed on solo playing and improvising rather than following written arrangements. Innovators of bebop included Dizzy Gillespie on trumpet, Charlie Parker on alto saxophone, and Thelonius Monk on piano.

Charlie Parker (August 29, 1920–1955). Charlie Parker was born in Kansas. He was an alto saxophone player. Even as a child, Charlie knew he wanted to be a musician. He played in the high school band and at age fifteen began working with local jazz bands. He moved between New York, Chicago, Kansas City, and Los Angeles to play jazz. He recorded a great deal, formed his own band, and played with other great jazz musicians such as Dizzy Gillespie and Thelonius Monk. Nicknamed "Bird," Charlie Parker's musical genius brought him fame throughout America and Europe, where he recorded and played on the radio, in clubs, and concerts. His strong technical and improvisational abilities, coupled with a tremendous creative spirit, made him an innovator in the evolution of bebop. Some of his better-known recordings include "Donna Lee" (1945), "Salt Peanuts" (1945)," "Ornithology" (1946–47), "A Night in Tunisia" (1946–47), "Scrapple from the Apple" (1946–47), and "La Cucaracha" (1953).

Charlie Parker. Photograph © Herman Leonard.
Courtesy of Herman Leonard Photograph *(www.hermanleonard.com).*

In the 1940s and 1950s, the vocal group Lambert, Hendrix, and Ross imitated the solo improvisations of jazz saxophone and trumpet players, putting words to them. The melodies they sang sometimes sounded more like instrument solos than singing.

Ella Fitzgerald sang in the bebop style and popularized scat singing (when the singer, or vocalist, sings **vocables** or nonsense syllables) in place of **lyrics.** With scat singing, singers improvise the notes they sing, just like jazz instrument players improvise their parts.

Bonus Challenge: *Pick a Jazz Style* Individually, or in groups, pick one of the jazz styles mentioned in this lesson—New Orleans jazz (Dixieland), swing, bebop, cool jazz, free jazz, or fusion—and investigate it. Read more about its roots, how it developed, some of the musicians who played in that style. Listen to the music. Consider offering a written or oral report with illustrations, photos, and CD samples.

Miles Davis (May 25, 1926–1991). Miles Davis was born in Illinois. He was an African-American trumpet player, keyboardist, and composer. He was raised in a family that valued music. He began playing trumpet at age thirteen and played in high school bands while still a teenager. He moved to New York to study music at the Juilliard School of Music, but eventually joined other musicians who were experimenting with new sounds and styles. Miles's innovative playing was paired with such other creative jazz players as Charlie Parker, Coleman Hawkins, John Coltrane, Dizzy Gillespie, and Herbie Hancock in the course of his career. In his later years he picked up elements of rock and funk music, which he incorporated into his music. He was known for always experimenting with new sounds and musical ideas. He remained a creative inspiration for many musicians who followed him. His recordings include *Kind of Blue, Birth of the Cool, Miles Ahead,* and *Milestones.*

Cool Jazz

In the 1950s, a new style of jazz emerged. Some musicians decided to slow it down and play it more "laid back" or understated. The music featured piano, bass, drums, and a solo instrument—like saxophone, trumpet, vibes, or flute—with improvisational playing. Musicians who broke into this style, which came to be called **cool jazz,** include Miles Davis, Stan Getz, Gerry Mulligan, Art Farmer, Chet Baker, Paul Desmond, the Modern Jazz Quartet, and Dave Brubeck.

Dave Brubeck (December 6, 1920–). Born in California, Dave Brubeck is a European-American composer and a piano player. His mother taught him to play piano, and he went on to perform in jazz groups beginning at age fifteen. He studied music in college and by 1949 his trio was regularly performing on the West Coast jazz scene. In 1951, he formed a quartet with alto saxophonist Paul Desmond. The quartet played together until 1967. Their jazz instrumental piece "Take Five" (1959) became a worldwide jazz standard. Since 1967 he has continued to perform as leader of his own groups with, among other musicians, Gerry Mulligan, Bill Smith, and Bobby Militello. In addition to jazz, he has composed classical music, ballets, a musical, and music for movies and television. He has performed for audiences around the world, including presidents, the pope, kings and queens. He has recorded over 150 albums of music. Some of his albums are *Time Out, Jazz Impressions of Japan, Jazz Impressions of Eurasia,* and *The Real Ambassadors.* Some of his songs are "Blue Rondo à La Turk," "In Your Own Sweet Way," and "The Duke."

Paul Desmond (November 25, 1924–1977). Paul Desmond was born in California. He was a European-American alto saxophonist and composer. Paul played clarinet in high school and college, switching to alto saxophone a few years later. During World War II he played in the Army band while stationed in San Francisco. In 1951 he helped form the Dave Brubeck Quartet, staying with the group for sixteen years. In that time they performed on college campuses, in clubs, and in concert halls and made recordings of their music. He was especially known for his cool, melodic playing and dry sense of humor. In 1959, he composed "Take Five," the first million-selling jazz record, which featured the rarely used 5/4 meter and expanded the limits of jazz. His albums include *Desmond Blue, Easy Living,* and *Summertime.*

Dave Brubeck Quartet. From left to right: Paul Desmond, Gene Wright, Joe Morello, and Dave Brubeck. Courtesy of Dave Brubeck Collection, Hold-Atherton Special Collections, University of the Pacific Libraries. Copyright © Dave Brubeck.

Free Jazz

Free jazz represents another step in the evolution of jazz music. Where bebop was based on popular songs, free jazz players wanted few or no recognizable elements in their music. Free jazz avoids predictable chord progressions and rhythms, resulting in music that is open, unstructured, **atonal,** and **arrhythmic.** *Atonal* means without a central key, or tone center. *Arrhythmic* is without a specific rhythm. The music can sound dissonant, or chaotic, but it allows the

Ornette Coleman (March 19, 1930–). Ornette Coleman, an African-American alto saxophone, trumpet, and violin player, was born in Texas. His earliest influences were big band swing and church music. He is mostly self-taught, learning to read music and play alto saxophone while still in high school. Early on he developed a desire to experiment with sounds and styles of playing. He found work in dance clubs, but his unusual improvisations turned people away and it was difficult for him to find work. After moving to Los Angeles in the 1950s, he met other musicians with similar musical interests and formed a quartet and studied music theory. He retired for a short time in the early 1960s when he learned to play trumpet and violin. He later added electric guitars, basses, and rock rhythms to his music, and composed in classical styles. He wrote music for film, but has continued playing jazz into the new millennium. Two of his most famous albums are *Free Jazz* and *The Shape of Jazz to Come.* Some of his pieces are "Beauty Is a Rare Thing," "Focus on Sanity," "Ramblin'," "When Will the Blues Leave?," "Saints and Soldiers," and "Skies of America."

players to experiment freely with little or no preconceived structure to stay within. Ornette Coleman, John Coltrane, and Cecil Taylor experimented with free jazz in their careers.

Fusion

In the 1960s and 1970s, new combinations of instruments changed the sound of jazz. Synthesizers, electric guitars, electric pianos, and electric percussion all came together in another branch of jazz called **fusion,** or jazz-rock. Fusion mixes jazz chord structures and improvisation with rock rhythms and instruments. The rhythm section may create a "groove" of repeated syncopated notes, played over and over, on top of which a vocalist or instrumentalist might sing or play. Some well-known fusion players are Larry Coryell, the Brecker Brothers, Stanley Clarke, Chick Corea, Herbie Hancock, and later, Jaco Pastorius, Spyro Gyra, and Weather Report.

Chick Corea (June 12, 1941–). Chick Corea was born Armando Anthony Corea in Massachusetts. He is a composer, piano player, and bandleader. He grew up in a musical home where he was exposed to jazz and classical music. He began studying piano at age four. In his early twenties he performed in Latin bands and developed a Latin style that has stayed with him throughout his career. As piano accompanist for jazz singer Sarah Vaughn, and during a period with jazz great Miles Davis, Chick moved further into the limelight. He later formed his own bands featuring improvisational jazz-fusion. His band Return to Forever often played Latin rhythms in a fusion style. He has been an innovator in jazz and classical music, focusing on experimentation and creativity with new ideas and new sounds. In the 1990s he began a series of live recordings from a club in New York, saying that the music "flows more freely" in a live setting. His classical work includes pieces for piano and orchestra, including *Piano Concerto No. 1,* which he performed and recorded with the London Philharmonic Orchestra. Some of his pieces are "Spain" (1971), "Sometime Ago–La Fiesta" (1972), "My Spanish Heart" (1976), "Children's Songs" (1983), "Cool Weasel Boogie" (1984), and "Wigwam" (2000).

Today there are jazz festivals, record labels featuring jazz musicians, and clubs all over the world that feature jazz music. As times goes on, and as musicians continue to break away from tradition and experiment with new sounds and structures, the evolution of jazz will continue. Jazz came about because of the creative minds and spirits of many great musicians, and it will likely continue in the same way.

Chick Corea. Photograph courtesy of *www.chickcorea.com.*

♫ CD track #24. Listen to "When the Saints Go Marching In," performed by Louis Armstrong, an example of New Orleans–style jazz.

Recording: "When the Saints Go Marching In," performed by Louis Armstrong. From *Original Jazz Masters Series Vol. 1.* Provided courtesy of 1201 Music. ℗ 1201 Music. Used by permission.

♫ CD track #27. Listen to "La Cucaracha," arranged by Robert Cohen in the bebop style.

Recording: "La Cucaracha," arranged by Robert Cohen. ℗ Zuvuya One Music, Migration Music. Used by permission.

♫ CD track #28. Listen to "Take Five," performed by the Dave Brubeck Quartet, an example of cool jazz.

Song and Recording: "Take Five," by Paul Desmond. © and ℗ 1966, 1988 Desmond Music Company (U.S.) and Derry Music Company (worldwide outside U.S.). Used with permission of the copyright owners.

♫ CD track #34. Listen to "Witchi-Tai-To," performed by Jim Pepper, an example of jazz-rock.

Song: © 1968 Floy Pepper. *Recording:* "Witchi-Tai-To," performed by Jim Pepper. ℗ Tutu Records. Used by permission.

Name _____   Date _____

Jazz Quiz

Instructions: After reading the **Jazz** student handout, answer these questions (use back of page if necessary).

1. Where in North America did jazz begin?

2. What does it mean for a jazz musician to **improvise?**

3. Give a brief description of the following styles of jazz:

    New Orleans jazz (Dixieland)

    Swing music

    Bebop

    Cool jazz

    Free jazz

    Fusion

Jazz Quiz: Answer Key

1. Where in North America did jazz begin?

   NEW ORLEANS, LOUISIANA.

2. What does it mean for a jazz musician to **improvise?**

   IMPROVISATION IN JAZZ IS WHEN MUSICIANS MAKE UP THEIR PARTS AS THEY GO ALONG (COMPOSE SPONTANEOUSLY) AS OPPOSED TO READING THE MUSIC OR MEMORIZING THE PART.

3. Give a brief description of the following styles of jazz:

   New Orleans jazz (Dixieland): THE EARLIEST JAZZ PLAYED IN THE STREETS, CLUBS, DANCE HALLS, AND RIVERBOATS ON TRUMPETS, TROMBONES, CLARINETS, TUBAS, GUITAR, BANJO, PIANO, AND DRUM. IT IS MOSTLY IMPROVISED. MIGRATED FROM NEW ORLEANS TO CHICAGO WITH THE MIGRATION OF AFRICAN AMERICANS FROM THE SOUTH AFTER THE END OF SLAVERY.

   Swing music: A LIVELY STYLE OF DANCE MUSIC THAT WAS MADE BY BIGGER BANDS, AND FEATURED WRITTEN ARRANGEMENTS OF THE MUSIC RATHER THAN IMPROVISATION. ALSO CALLED BIG BAND MUSIC.

   Bebop: AN UP-TEMPO STYLE OF JAZZ THAT IS PLAYED WITH SMALLER COMBINATIONS OF MUSICIANS AND FASTER TEMPOS; FEATURES IMPROVISATION. EARLY BEBOP MUSICIANS OFTEN TOOK POPULAR SONGS AND REWORKED THEM IN THE BEBOP STYLE.

   Cool jazz: A MORE LAID-BACK, UNDERSTATED STYLE OF JAZZ THAT WAS POPULAR IN THE 1950s AND 1960s. TEMPOS WERE SLOWER THAN BEBOP AND ALSO FEATURED IMPROVISATION.

   Free jazz: A STYLE OF JAZZ THAT AVOIDS PREDICTABLE CHORD PROGRESSIONS AND RHYTHMS, RESULTING IN MUSIC THAT IS OPEN, UNSTRUCTURED, ATONAL, ARRHYTHMIC.

   Fusion: FUSION BLENDS JAZZ WITH ROCK ELEMENTS. IT FEATURES SYNTHESIZERS, ELECTRIC GUITARS, ELECTRIC PIANOS, ELECTRIC PERCUSSION. THE RHYTHM CAN BE "GROOVE"-ORIENTED, WITH SYNCOPATED NOTES REPEATED OVER AND OVER. ALSO CALLED JAZZ-ROCK.

♫ Lesson 19. Country Music

Lesson Overview

American country music might well have begun with the songs of the early European settlers, both sacred and secular. Folk songs describe the lives of ordinary people and tell stories, legends, histories, loves, tragedies, hopes, and fears. Pioneer songs and cowboy songs describe life on the prairie, the wagon trains and cattle drives, and moving west. Old-time music came from European folk traditions of the eastern mountain people. Mariachi music describes country life of rural Mexico. Since the 1920s, many branches of country music have evolved from these rural styles into country-western, western swing, bluegrass, honky-tonk music, Nashville country, outlaw country, and new country.

Vocabulary. Country music, pioneer songs, compose, cowboy songs, roots music, polka, old-time music, harmony singing, country-western music, repertoire, acoustic, virtuosic, bluegrass music, western swing, contemporary, honky-tonk music, country rock.

Purpose. To offer an overview of country music as it has developed in North America.

Preparation. Read the student handout **Country Music** to familiarize yourself with the material. Consider reviewing Unit Two's Lesson 6: Folk Music as a prerequisite. Preview the CD samples (cues in student handout) and have the CD ready for playing with the students. Consider bringing in additional music samples from other sources to enhance the lesson. Be prepared to do some or all of the following activities. Also make sure that each student has a music notebook for keeping handouts and activity sheets.

Materials

- **Country Music** student handout *(following)*
- **Country Music Quiz** *(following)*
- **Country Music Answer Key** *(following)*
- **Music Vocabulary** activity sheet *(Appendix)*
- **My Opinion Page** activity sheet *(Appendix)*
- **How to Teach a Song** teacher guide *(Appendix)*
- **Songs as Poetry** activity sheet *(Appendix)*
- **Great American Musicians!** activity sheet *(Appendix)*
- **Music on the Map** activity sheet *(Appendix)*
- **Music notebooks**

- **CD music** examples on accompanying CD; cues in student handout
- **Additional music selections**

Activities

- Pass out the **Country Music** handout for students to read silently or aloud as a group. Afterwards, have students put the handout in their music notebooks. *(Link to language arts, history, geography, social studies.)*
- Give the **Country Music Quiz** to assess student understanding of the lesson.
- Go over the music vocabulary at the top of the student handout before or after reading the text. Refer to the glossary for definitions. *Suggestion:* Include these words in a regular class vocabulary lesson, or pass out flashcards with a vocabulary word on one side and the definition on the other and allow students to drill each other. Use the **Music Vocabulary** activity sheets to write out definitions. *(Link to language arts.)*
- Offer the **Vocabulary Challenge.** Students pick some or all of the words in this lesson's vocabulary list to use in a paragraph, essay, short story, or poem. *(Link to language arts.)*
- **Discuss.** Before reading the student handout, discuss what students already know about country music. Read the student handout and discuss it again, letting students add what they've learned. *(Link to language arts, social studies.)*
- **Bonus Challenge: Visit the Grand Ole Opry.** Have students go to the Grand Ole Opry Web site *(www.opry.com)* and click on "history" to learn more. Have them listen to a broadcast over the radio or the Internet or watch a Grand Ole Opry show (broadcast on Saturday nights) on one of the country cable networks. Students report back about what they saw or heard. They describe the musicians, their instruments, clothing styles, style of music, or anything else they notice. Consider having students fill out a **My Opinion Page** for a song.
- **Bonus Challenge: Pick a Country Style.** Individually, or in groups, students pick one of the country styles mentioned in this lesson—for example, pioneer songs, cowboy songs, old-time music, country-western, bluegrass, western swing, honky-tonk, women in country, outlaw country, new country. They read more about its roots, how it developed, some of the musicians who played in that style. They listen to the music. They then offer a written or oral report with illustrations, photos, and CD samples. Compile everyone's written work into a "Country Music Notebook." *(Link to language arts.)*
- **Bonus Challenge: Families of Instruments.** Group the instruments mentioned in this lesson into instrument families: chordophones, membranophones, aerophones, idiophones, and electrophones. (See Unit Two, Lesson 10: Instruments of the Orchestra.) *(Link to science.)*

Extension Activities

For step-by-step directions and activity sheets, see the appendix.

- **My Opinion Page.** Offer students a chance to freely express their own opinions about the music they hear. *(Link to language arts, critical thinking.)*

- **Sing a Song.** Learn a simple country song from this lesson. *Suggested songs to learn: "Oh Susanna," "Whoopi Ti-Yi-Yo," "Old Joe Clarke." (Link to singing, language arts, rhythm, melody.)*

- **Songs as Poetry.** Examine the lyrics of songs for their poetic nature. Use the **Songs as Poetry** activity sheet. *(Link to language arts.)*

- **Illustrate the Music.** Students illustrate a song or piece of music by drawing or painting their ideas of what the music "looks" like visually. *(Link to language arts, visual arts.)*

- **Great American Musicians!** Introduce students to American musicians whose talents have made them notable. *(Link to language arts, history.)*

- **Music on the Map.** Create a map and legend showing musically important places, such as musicians' birthplaces and music hot spots mentioned in the lesson. *(Link to geography.)*

- **Invite a Music Expert.** Invite a country musician to visit your class and share his or her instrument and musical talent with the students. Also consider taking students to hear a live performance, or show a video. *(Link to social studies.)*

- Consider bringing in **additional selections of music** from other sources to expand the music sample offerings. Note the songs mentioned in each musician's biography for ideas. Search the Internet, library, local music store, or your own music collection for the music.

Name _____ Date _____

Earl Scruggs, Merle Haggard, Carter Family, Gene Autry

Country Music

Vocabulary: *country music, pioneer songs, compose, cowboy songs, roots music, polka, old-time music, harmony singing, country-western music, repertoire, acoustic, virtuosic, bluegrass music, western swing, contemporary, honky-tonk music, country rock*

American **country music** covers a broad spectrum—from old-time mountain music to contemporary country rock.

As early American settlers moved west over the mountains, across the plains and deserts and onto the fertile soils of the West Coast, their music traveled with them. People built homes and formed small settlements. They built railroads and cities and towns. Their music changed with their surroundings to describe their new lives.

Pioneer Songs

Life on the frontier was not easy. Moving west meant traveling over harsh terrain, under a hot beating sun, in bitter cold winds and snow, crossing rushing rivers, losing livestock and wagons to mud and sweeping currents. Early **pioneer songs** described the rough life of the settlers. Singing helped ease the burden and gave people something to do when the work was done.

The song "Peter Emberley" tells about a lumberjack who leaves his family and friends to go logging in the forests of New Brunswick. "Sioux Indians" describes a battle between a wagon train settlement and a band of Lakota (Sioux) on the western plains. "Skip to My Lou" and "Turkey in the Straw" were popular dance tunes played at pioneers' social gatherings.

In the 1840s, gold seekers rushed to California, and later to Alaska and the Yukon, in the hopes of striking it rich in the gold fields. They carried the popular songs of the day and sang them in their camps. "Betsy from Pike" tells of a tough woman who crossed the plains with a guy named Ike. "Oh Susanna," a mid-1800s minstrel song by Stephen Foster, was very popular with the gold diggers. "The Fools of the '49" describes the harsh conditions of traveling over land and sea to get to the gold.

Cowboys and covered wagons. Lithograph by A. R. Waud. Dover Publications.

Unit Four: New American Music

The Fools of the '49 (abridged)

When gold was found in '48, the people said 'twas gas,
And some were fools enough to think the lumps were only brass.
But they soon were satisfied and started off to mine.
They bought a ship came round the horn in the fall of '49.

Chorus: Then they thought of what they had been told
When they started after gold
That they never in this world would make a pile.

The poor, the old, the rotten scows were advertised to sail
To New Orleans with passengers, but they must come and bail.
The ships were crowded more than full, but some hung on behind
And others dived off from the wharf and swam 'til they were blind.

Repeat chorus.

With rusty pork and stinking beef and rotten wormy bread,
With captains too that never were as high as the mainmast head.
The steerage passengers would rave and swear they'd paid their passage.
They wanted something more to eat besides the lowly sausage.

Repeat chorus.

And they began to cross the plains with oxen, holler and haul.
And steamers they began to run as far as Panama.
And there for months the people stayed that started after gold
And some returned disgusted with the lies they had been told.

Repeat chorus.

From *The Ballad of America: The History of the United States in Song and Story,* collected by John Anthony Scott. Southern Illinois University Press.

After the Civil War, as railroad tracks were put down across the continent, songs were **composed** about railroad work and life. The folk song "John Henry" tells about a railroad worker who competed against a steam drill. John Henry won the competition, but he died from the strain, a hero. "Casey Jones" tells about a brave railroad engineer who carried the mail to Mississippi and died when his train hit another train. "Paddy on the Railway" tells about an Irishman's adventures on the railroad.

Cowboy Songs

The cattle drives of the late 1800s inspired new songs about cowboy life. As the men rode their horses, driving the cattle across the plains, sometimes they would sing to the rhythm of their horses' hooves. "The Chisholm Trail" tells about the troubles of a cowboy along the trail between Texas and Kansas. Some **cowboy songs** used cattle calls in them. "Whoopie Ti-Yi-Yo, Git Along Little Dogies" (*dogies* is cowboy slang for young cattle) uses a cattle call in the chorus and is repeated throughout the song. Cattle calls are nonsense syllables used to direct the cattle during the drives.

Whoopie Ti-Yi-Yo, Git Along Little Dogies

Adapted by John A. Lomax and Alan Lomax

As I was a-walking one morning for pleasure
I spied a young cowboy a-ridin' along.
Well, his hat was shoved back and his spurs was a-jinglin'
And as he was riding he was singing this song.

Chorus: Whoopie-ti-yi-yo, git along little dogies.
It's your misfortune and none of my own.
Whoopie-ti-yi-yo, git along little dogies.
You know that Wyoming will be your new home.

Early in the springtime we round up the dogies
We cut 'em out, brand 'em and bob off their tails,
Round up the horses, load up the chuck wagon,
And then throw the dogies out on the north trail.

Repeat chorus.

Your mother was raised way down in Texas
Where the jimson weed and the cholla is grown.
But we'll fill you up on those prickly pear briars
Until you are ready for Idaho.

Repeat chorus.

Collected, adapted, and arranged by John A. Lomax and Alan Lomax.
TRO copyright © 1938 (renewed) Ludlow Music,
New York. Used by permission.

At night, when the cattle were resting, the cowboys rode in circles around the herd, singing to calm them. "The Night Herding Song" is one of these songs.

The Night Herding Song

Oh, slow little dogies quit your rovin' around.
You wandered and trampled all over the ground.
Oh, slow up dogies and feed kinda slow.
And don't forever be on the go.
Move slow little dogies, move slow.
Hay-o, hay-o, hay-o.

Famous cowboy outlaws like Jesse James were forever remembered in ballads passed down through the generations. The "Ballad of Jesse James" tells of the blue-eyed, teenage bank robber who became a folk hero in the Wild West.

Cisco Houston (August 18, 1918–1961). Cisco Houston was born Gilbert Vandine in Delaware. He was raised in a musical family whose influences came from the folk traditions of North Carolina and the Appalachian Mountains. At age sixteen he began traveling across America, and by twenty was singing on the radio with folksinger Woody Guthrie. The two remained lifelong friends and musical partners. Besides singing and playing music, Cisco worked as a cowboy, lumberjack, potato picker, and actor. Over time, as his fame grew, he began making records, performing on television, playing at folk festivals, and touring the world. His recordings include *Cisco Houston: The Folkways Years 1941–1961, The Songs of Woody Guthrie,* and *Best of Vanguard Years.*

Roots Music

Roots music is music that comes from the experiences of regular people from all cultures. American roots music includes folk songs, country songs, blues, gospel, Cajun, zydeco, Tejano-conjunto, klezmer, old-time, bluegrass, and Native American songs.

As people from different cultures settled in America, their music began to take on characteristics of the music around them. For example, when the Germans and Czechs settled in Mexico, their accordion **polka** music mixed with Spanish folk songs and Native American rhythms, and the result was Tejano-conjunto, or Tex-Mex music.

Before radio and records, the music of a region tended to stay in the region and be played in the culture it belonged to. After radio, records, television, and movies, the music from each region would start to spread, and as it spread, it would pick up influences along the way.

Musician Taj Mahal plays roots music from his African-American heritage, including the blues, folk, African, Caribbean music, and jazz. The group Los Lobos mixes Spanish lyrics with blues, rock, and country music. Blues guitar player and singer Bonnie Raitt mixes blues, country, folk, and rock. Native American singer Buffy Sainte-Marie has written songs with both traditional and nontraditional themes. Singer Linda Ronstadt mixed country and rock and has crossed over to the mariachi music of her Mexican heritage.

Roots music is music that has tradition attached to it. It is ethnic music, with as many styles as there are cultures.

Taj Mahal (May 17, 1942–). Taj Mahal was born Henry St. Clair Fredricks in New York. He is a singer, songwriter, and musician. He grew up in Massachusetts listening to the music of blues and early rock musicians. His mother sang gospel and his father composed and arranged Caribbean jazz. As a boy, Taj Mahal taught himself to play over twenty instruments, including guitar, banjo, dobro, piano, bass guitar, mandolin, harmonica, and dulcimer. He played with a rhythm and blues band in the early 1960s, performing in coffeehouses and on college campuses, and eventually began to record his own music and tour. His interest in cultures inspired him to study and perform from a variety of traditions, including Caribbean, West African, African-American, zydeco, blues, folk, country, and jazz. He has written music for movie soundtracks, acted in movies, recorded and toured the world, and provided voices for cartoons. His recordings include *Taj Mahal* (1968), *Giant Step* (1969), *Mo' Roots* (1974), *Shake Sugaree* (1984), and *The Best of Taj Mahal* (2000).

Taj Mahal. Photograph by Skip Gray. Courtesy of Skip Gray.

Listen to Learn

Old-Time Music

In Nashville, Tennessee, in the 1920s, the people at Okeh Records began recording the music of mountain people. Okeh first recorded a harmonica player named Henry Whitter, followed by Fiddlin' John Carson. Their music was called *hillbilly music.* It was played on the radio, at barn dances, medicine shows, music contests, political rallies, and other public events in the rural mountains and valleys of Appalachia. The music was a lively blend of folk-style songs that featured fiddle, banjo, and guitar. In time it became known as **old-time music** because it featured old folk-style songs but newly composed songs as well.

One of the first old-time music groups to become famous was the Carter Family. Sara Carter was the lead singer, and her husband, A. P., and sister-in-law, Mother Maybelle, sang harmony on the choruses. They accompanied themselves with guitar and autoharp, and three-part **harmony singing.**

Carter Family. The members of the original Carter Family were Alvin Pleasant (A. P.) Carter and his wife, Sara. Both A. P. and Sara were born and raised in the Clinch Mountains of Virginia during the 1890s. After they married in 1915, they began performing together and later welcomed their sister-in-law, Maybelle, into their group. The Carter Family signed their first recording contract in 1928 and recorded hundreds of songs over the next decade. They did some traveling and performing for live audiences, but it was difficult to make a living during the Depression when people didn't have the extra money to spend for entertainment. By 1939 the group had broken apart, but reformed again in the 1950s with A. P. and Sara's daughter, Janette. The Carter Family was the first group inducted into the Country Music Hall of Fame in 1970. Some of their famous songs are "Keep on the Sunny Side," "Wabash Cannonball," "Will the Circle Be Unbroken," and "Wildwood Flower."

Jimmie Rodgers (September 8, 1897–1933). Jimmie Rodgers was born in Mississippi. He was a singer and songwriter. As a child he learned to play guitar and banjo. As a teenager he organized traveling shows, performing in a tent and charging admission. He later found work as a water boy, and then as a brakeman on the railroad. Jimmie went back and forth as a performer and a railroad worker until 1927, when his records became popular, selling in the millions. He performed for sold-out live shows and toured with cowboy comedian Will Rogers. His movie short *The Singing Brakeman* was shown across the country. Jimmie Rodgers has been called the Father of Country Music and was the first musician inducted into the Country Music Hall of Fame in 1961. Some of his songs are "T for Texas (Blue Yodel)" (1928), "Waitin' for a Train" (1929), "Yodeling Cowboy" (1930), "Hobo Bill's Last Ride" (1930), and "Years Ago" (1933).

Jimmie Rodgers, the "Singing Brakeman," wrote songs about the everyday life of rural Americans. He sang about cowboys, girls, trains, and hobos. He played solo guitar and yodeled between verses, which became his trademark. "T for Texas" is about a woman named Thelma who "made a fool out of me" and "Waitin' for a Train" follows the life of a hobo riding the railroad.

As radio became more popular during the 1920s and 1930s, live radio shows became some of America's most popular entertainment. In the South, radio stations featured live "barn dances" with old-time music. Uncle Jimmy Thompson, a fiddler, was a regular on the Saturday night Grand Ole Opry broadcast beginning in 1925. Over time, the Opry's weekly radio broadcasts expanded to include comedy teams and ballad singers.

Stage of the Grand Ole Opry. Photograph by Randy Piland. Courtesy of Grand Ole Opry.

Bonus Challenge: Visit the Grand Ole Opry Go to the Grand Ole Opry Web site (*www.opry.com*) and click on "history" to learn more. Listen to a broadcast over the radio or Internet, or watch a Grand Ole Opry show (broadcast on Saturday nights) on one of the country cable networks. Report back about what you saw or heard. Describe the musicians, their instruments, clothing styles, style of music, or anything else you notice.

History of the Grand Ole Opry. The Grand Ole Opry began as a radio show broadcast from Nashville, Tennessee, on WSM Radio in 1925. The first shows were "barn dances" or variety shows featuring fiddlers, square dance callers, and string bands. By 1928 it was named the Grand Ole Opry, and live shows occurred every Saturday night featuring singers, guitar players, comedians, and bluegrass music. Deford Bailey, Uncle Dave Macon, the Possum Hunters, and the Fruit Jar Drinkers were some of the stars to perform in the early years. By the 1940s, the Grand Ole Opry was broadcast across the entire country and the numbers of country music fans grew. Stars like Roy Acuff, Bill Monroe and His Blue Grass Boys, Lester Flatt and Earl Scruggs, Hank Williams, Hank Snow, Minnie Pearl, Kitty Wells, Patsy Cline, Loretta Lynn, Ernest Tubb, Porter Wagoner, Dolly Parton, Garth Brooks, Reba McEntire, and Trisha Yearwood would perform there in the last half of the century. In 1974, the Grand Ole Opry moved to a larger hall. In 2000, the Opry celebrated its seventy-fifth anniversary to a packed house of 4,400 people in the audience. The Opry still broadcasts every weekend, and has stayed an institution in country music into the new millennium.

Country-Western

Country-western music developed in the 1950s and 1960s. It is a blend of songs from the European folk tradition (see Unit Two, Lesson 6: Folk Music) and popular music from Tin Pan Alley (see Unit Two, Lesson 8: Early Popular Music). Country-western features cowboys and cowboy themes and acoustic instruments like guitar, and is performed by musicians and singers who dress up in the cowboy style.

Roy Rogers (1911–1998) from Ohio, and his wife Dale Evans (1912–2001) from Texas, rose to fame singing country songs together. Roy Rogers also performed Tin Pan Alley songs, like "Don't Fence Me In" and "I'm an Old Cowhand." His partner Bob Nolan (1908–1980), of the group Sons of the Pioneers, composed the standard country-western songs "Tumbling Tumbleweeds" and "Cool Water."

Gene Autry rose to fame composing his own songs and making movies, playing the guitar-playing cowboy hero who always had time for a song. He sang about the cowboy lifestyle and helped make the image of the country cowboy an international icon.

Did You Know? Before there was recorded music, country music was played live and passed by word of mouth through the oral tradition. When the mountain people moved into the cities, they brought the old-time songs they'd learned from their parents and grandparents. Their songs were common property, meaning anyone could sing them and they belonged to no one. When these songs came to the city and were recorded and published, the songs became "copyrighted," or assigned an owner, and were now someone's personal property. For more information on what a copyright is, do a search on the Internet or in the library.

Gene Autry (September 29, 1907–1998). Gene Autry was born in Texas. He was a singer, songwriter, actor, and guitar player. He grew up in Texas and Oklahoma and got his start in the 1920s singing on the radio as "Oklahoma's Yodeling Cowboy." He was one of the earliest country musicians to record his music and perform on the radio. In the 1930s, Gene began making movies, starring as a singing cowboy in eighty-nine films and costarring in several more. In 1940, he starred in *Gene Autry's Melody Ranch* radio show and in the 1950s *The Gene Autry Show* on television. He also produced several popular television shows, among them *Annie Oakley* and *The Range Rider.* Gene Autry has been inducted into the Country Music Hall of Fame, the Nashville Songwriters' Hall of Fame, and the National Cowboy Hall of Fame. His songs include "Back in the Saddle Again," "Cowboy's Heaven," "Home on the Range," "Deep in the Heart of Texas," and "Yellow Rose of Texas."

Gene Autry. Courtesy of Gene Autry Entertainment.

Did You Know? Gene Autry, America's Favorite Singing Cowboy, is the cowriter of the song "Here Comes Santa Claus," and his version of "Rudolph the Red-Nosed Reindeer" is the second most popular Christmas song of all time.

Listen to Learn

Hank Snow (1914–1999), the Singing Ranger from Nova Scotia, Canada, became a country star writing and performing his own songs. He entertained audiences with his horse, Shawnee, who performed stunts and tricks at their shows. Hank Snow's **repertoire** included popular songs, train songs, gospel, and songs about his homeland.

Patsy Montana (1914–1996), from Arkansas, recorded "I Wanna Be a Cowboy's Sweetheart" (1935), which featured her yodeling and beautiful singing. She became the first woman in country music to sell a million records.

Patsy Montana. Courtesy *www.montanarose.com.*

Patsy Montana (October 30, 1914–1996). Pasty Montana was born Ruby Blevins in Arkansas. She was a country singer, songwriter, and guitar player. She grew up singing and yodeling and played violin, organ, and guitar as a child. As a teenager she performed on the radio and at rodeos with a group called the Montana Girls. She also rode rodeo. Patsy appeared in movies and on the radio with Gene Autry, the Sons of the Pioneers, and the Lightcrust Doughboys. Her songs were of western subjects and her cowgirl image was enhanced with western dress, hat, boots, and guitar in hand. In 1996, she was inducted into the Country Music Hall of Fame. Her songs include "I Wanna Be a Cowboy's Sweetheart," "Old Nevada Moon," and "Back on the Montana Plains."

Bluegrass

By the 1940s a new kind of country music was becoming popular on the radio and stages across America. It was faster and very upbeat. It was performed on **acoustic** instruments—guitar, banjo, mandolin, fiddle, and bass guitar, and featured **virtuosic** players. The style became known as **bluegrass music.** Bluegrass groups featured "breakdowns"—when every member of the band takes a turn being the feature performer. In a breakdown a player can play whatever he or she wants while the other musicians play in the background. Bluegrass music's verse-chorus song structure and strong harmony singing are carryovers from the sacred music of early mountain musicians.

Bill Monroe (1911–1996) and his Blue Grass Boys introduced this style. Bill's mandolin sound was new and unusual. The rhythms were fast. The harmony singing was strong and virtuosic. Bill Monroe became known as the Father of Bluegrass. Earl Scruggs (b. 1924) on banjo and Lester Flatt (1914–1979) on guitar eventually left the group to form their own group called the Foggy Mountain Boys, and stayed together over twenty years. Lester Flatt and Earl Scruggs continued to develop the fast-paced, finger-picking style that is one of the highlights of bluegrass music.

"Rocky Top" is a bluegrass song that was popular in the 1960s and remains well-played even today.

Rocky Top

By Boudleaux Bryant and Felice Bryant

I wish that I was on old Rocky Top
Down in the Tennessee hills.
Ain't no smoggy smoke on Rocky Top,
Don't pay no telephone bills.
Corn won't grow at all on Rocky Top,
Dirt's too rocky by far.
That's why all the folks on Rocky Top
Get their corn from a jar.

Chorus: Rocky Top you'll always be
Home sweet home to me.
Good ol' Rocky Top,
Rocky Top, Tennessee, Rocky Top, Tennessee.

Now, I've had years of cramped-up city life,
Trapped like a duck in a pen.
All I know is it's a pity life,
Can't be simple again.

Once I had a girl on Rocky Top
Half bear, the other half cat.
Wild as a mink, but sweet as soda pop,
I still dream about that.

Repeat chorus.

Composed by Boudleaux and Felice Bryant. Copyright © 1967
House of Bryant Publishers. Used by permission.

Western Swing

Western swing is an upbeat style of country music that "swings" like big band music. The rhythms and chords are influenced by jazz; the singing and lyrics are influenced by country. It is played on fiddles, guitars, piano, drums, electric guitar, bass guitar, Hawaiian steel guitar, and wind instruments. Western swing became popular in roadhouses, county fairs, and dancehalls in Texas and Oklahoma in the 1930s. Bob Wills (1905–1975) and his Texas Playboys created the style with fourteen members in his band at one time! They performed both old-time fiddle tunes, like "Goodbye Liza Jane" and "Cotton-Eyed Joe," and **contemporary** songs, like "San Antonio Rose" and "Take Me Back to Tulsa."

Honky-Tonk Music

Having grown up in the rural South, Hank Williams was exposed to the blues music of his African-American neighbors. His own musical style blended blues chord changes with country guitar and country themes. His band members played fiddle, guitar, steel guitar, dobro, and bass. Hank Williams sang lyrics that were honest and straightforward. This kind of country music came to be called **honky-tonk music.** Honky-tonk songs are about heartbreak and breakups, good times and bad times, finding love and losing it.

Hank Williams (September 17, 1923–1953). Hank Williams was born in Alabama. He was a singer, songwriter, and guitar player. By the age of fourteen he was performing live in his own band and on the radio. In 1937 he won an amateur contest that inspired him to pursue music as a career. He played in bars, theaters, clubs, and medicine shows and made a few records until 1949, when he recorded "Lovesick Blues" and it became a hit. From there he recorded more hits, toured the United States, Canada, and Germany, and was a regular guest on the Grand Ole Opry. His band, the Drifting Cowboys, recorded and traveled with him. Hank's style was honest and down-to-earth. He sang about regular things in life—love, heartbreak, courting, and having a good time. He was inducted into the Country Music Hall of Fame in 1961 and is still known today as one of the fathers of honky-tonk music. Some of his hits were "Move It on Over," "Mind Your Own Business," "Hey, Good Lookin'," "Jambalaya," "Honky-Tonk Blues," and "Your Cheatin' Heart."

Hank Williams. Courtesy of Hank Williams Museum.

Ernest Tubb (1914–1984) was a musician from Texas who recorded the honky-tonk hit "Walking the Floor Over You" in 1941. Lefty Frizzel (1928–1975), also from Texas, recorded and sold millions of copies of the song "If You've Got the Money, I've Got the Time" (1950). Kitty Wells (b. 1919), from Nashville, sang "It Wasn't God Who Made Honky-Tonk Angels" (1952), a woman's answer to another popular song "The Wild Side of Life" (1952), by Hank Thompson.

The Nashville Sound

In the late 1950s and early 1960s, much of the music coming out of Nashville, Tennessee, had an orchestral sound. Several major record companies set up recording studios and signed contracts with some of the best country singers and musicians. The music at this time was more polished and popular sounding, with orchestral instruments and written arrangements.

Jim Reeves (1923–1964), from Texas, crooned country ballads to the accompaniment of piano, bass guitar, and orchestral instruments playing in the background. His songs "Four Walls" (1957), "He'll Have to Go" (1959), and "Welcome to My World" (1964) were big hits in this genre.

Patsy Cline (1932–1963), from Virginia, also sang with orchestral backup. When her song "Walking After Midnight" became a hit in 1957, she followed with many more, including "I Fall to Pieces" (1961) and "Crazy" (1961, by Willie Nelson).

Tennessee singer Eddy Arnold (b. 1918) sang "Don't Rob Another Man's Castle" (1949). His signature song "Cattle Call" (1955) and "Make the World Go Away" (1965) added orchestral instruments and background singers.

Women in Country

Patsy Montana, Kitty Wells, and Patsy Cline were not the first women in country music, but they will be remembered for creating a path for women in the country music industry. Their songs described the woman's point of view in relationships. Where many of the early songs described heartaches and being "cheated" or "jilted," a new trend developed in the 1960s showing the women to be stronger, smarter, and wiser partners.

Loretta Lynn (b. 1935), from Kentucky, writes songs showing a self-determined, no-nonsense attitude: "You Ain't Woman Enough to Take My Man," "Fist City," and "Coal Miner's Daughter."

Tammy Wynette (1942–1998), from Mississippi, recorded "D.I.V.O.R.C.E.," a song showing the child's perspective in a family divorce. "'Til I Can Make It on My Own" and "Alive and Well" painted the picture of a woman surviving the traumas of life.

Dolly Parton (b. 1946), from Tennessee, recorded "Coat of Many Colors," telling her own story of growing up poor and the coat her mother made of cloth scraps. "Jolene" (1974) kindly asks another woman to leave her man alone, and "Eagle When She Flies" (1991) is a celebration of international womanhood.

Reba McEntire (b. 1955), from Oklahoma, shows a full range of emotions in her songs. "Can't Even Get the Blues No More" (1982) expresses the sadness of breaking up and the pain of getting over it. "Good Friends" (1986) shows the value of friendships, and "Climb That Mountain High" (1989) offers hope for reaching your dreams.

Trisha Yearwood (b. 1964), from Georgia, shows compassion in the face of a hurt man in "The Woman Before Me." "You Can Sleep While I Drive" (1989) is hopeful about moving on.

Shania Twain (b. 1965), from Ontario, Canada, co-wrote "When" (1997) about the unlikely prospect of two people getting together again and "You're Still the One" (1997) about being in love with someone for life.

In country music, women have always had a voice in song—from the earliest mountain grandmas at home with their families, to the sequined-studded singers on the stages of country music concerts worldwide.

Loretta Lynn (April 14, 1935–). Born Loretta Webb in Kentucky, Loretta Lynn is a country singer, songwriter, and guitar player. She grew up in an Appalachian Mountains family of eight children, and her earliest exposure to popular music was listening to the radio. At age thirteen she married, and at fourteen she started raising children. She and her husband Dolittle Lynn jumpstarted her career by driving from radio station to radio station across the South to promote her records. Their efforts paid off, and Loretta's music became popular. She went on to make many records, perform on stages across the country and around the world, star at the Grand Ole Opry, and remain a respected member of the country music family for over forty years. Some of her songs are "You Ain't Woman Enough to Take My Man," "Blue Kentucky Girl," "Coal Miner's Daughter," "On My Own Again," and "Working Girl."

Loretta Lynn. Courtesy of Loretta Lynn Enterprises.

Outlaw Country

The *outlaws* are a group of country singer-songwriters who did not fit the mold of the popular *Nashville sound* of the 1960s. They did not use orchestral instruments, or wear sequins on their clothes. They played a rougher style of music, less polished, which featured singing, guitar, bass, pedal steel, and drums. They came to be called outlaws because their music was outside the mainstream of country music.

Willie Nelson (b. 1933), from Texas, sang "Mamas Don't Let Your Babies Grow Up to Be Cowboys" (1978, by Ed Bruce), warning mothers about the downfalls of cowboy life. He also composed "On the Road Again" (1980), which describes the lifestyle of a touring country music singer, and "My Heroes Have Always Been Cowboys" (1979), which reflects on his heroes.

Johnny Cash (1932–2003), from Arkansas, sang "Five Feet High and Rising," which told the story of a Mississippi flood that occurred during his childhood. He also wrote "Folsom Prison Blues" about life in prison and "I Walk the Line." His music has inspired many generations of new country musicians, and has always "crossed the line" of what was standard in country music.

Waylon Jennings (1937–2002), from Texas, wrote songs that hovered on the edge of country music. He wrote a protest to popular country music in his song "Are You Sure Hank Done It This Way?" In his career, he teamed up with other country music outlaws Willie Nelson, Johnny Cash, and Kris Kristofferson.

Merle Haggard (April 6, 1937–). Merle Haggard was born in California. He began playing guitar at age twelve and performing in clubs at age fifteen. After serving some time in prison, he joined a country band and became well known in his hometown of Bakersfield. In 1964, he had his first hit called "Sing a Sad Song," which sold many records and was played on the radio. From there he began a solo career that has resulted in many hits. Writing songs about his "troubled past" helped group him with other "outlaw" musicians throughout his fifty-year career. In 1996, he was inducted into the Country Music Hall of Fame. Some of his songs are "The Fugitive," "Okie from Muskogee," "Mama Tried," "Workin' Man Blues," "Pancho and Lefty," and "That's the Way Love Goes."

Merle Haggard (b. 1937), from California, wrote songs that reflected a hard life. His song "The Fugitive" tells about a man who is always on the run from the law. "Ramblin' Fever" is about a man who wanders and doesn't settle down.

New Country

In the 1980s, the country band Alabama took the spotlight in modern country music. Where it had been the tradition for a singer to be a star backed by a group of musicians, Alabama featured the entire band as the star. Their songs became hits, one after the other, and for many years they swept the Country Music Awards with their winnings. Their songs were inspired by country life, including "My Home's in Alabama," "High Cotton," and "Song of the South."

Alabama. Courtesy of Alabama.

Garth Brooks (b. 1963), from Oklahoma, became a superstar in the 1990s, performing to the largest audiences in country music history. His song and video "We Shall Be Free" premiered at the 1993 Super Bowl—broadcast to over eighty-seven countries—with a message of tolerance and brotherhood. His rodeo songs "Rodeo" and "Wild Horses" offer glimpses into the lives of rodeo riders.

In the 1990s, there was a trend to play country music on electric guitars, bass, and drums, with hard rhythms and themes. The music came to be called **country rock** and ended up "crossing over" and becoming popular with mainstream audiences. Country-rockers the Kentucky Headhunters really crossed the line of both country and rock. They recorded "Country Life" and "Walk Softly on This Heart of Mine"—two of their tamer songs.

Grand Ole Opry seventy-fifth anniversary. Photograph by Randy Piland.
Courtesy of Grand Ole Opry.

Bonus Challenge: Pick a Country Style Individually or in groups, pick one of the country styles mentioned in this lesson: pioneer songs, cowboy songs, old-time music, country-western, bluegrass, western swing, honky-tonk, women in country, outlaw country, or new country. Read more about its roots, how it developed, and some of the musicians who played in that style. Listen to the music. Offer a written or oral report with illustrations, photos, and CD samples.

♫ CD track #29. Listen to "Turkey in the Straw," performed by Bob Banghart and Robert Cohen. Written by Daniel Emmett in 1834 as a minstrel song, it became popular with the pioneers.

> *Recording:* "Turkey in the Straw," performed by Bob Banghart (fiddle) and Robert Cohen (piano). ℗ 1994 Zuvuya One Music, Migration Music.

♫ CD track #30. Listen to "Whoopie Ti-Yi-Yo, Git Along Little Dogies," performed by Cisco Houston. This is an example of a cowboy song.

> *Song:* "Whoopie Ti-Yi-Yo, Git Along Little Dogies" collected, adapted, and arranged by John A. Lomax and Alan Lomax. TRO © 1938 (renewed) Ludlow Music, New York. *Recording:* "Whoopie Ti-Yi-Yo," by Cisco Houston from the recording entitled *Smithsonian Folkways Children's Collection*, SF 45043, provided courtesy of Smithsonian Folkways Recordings. © 1998. Used by permission.

♫ CD track #20. Listen to "Hambone," performed by Taj Mahal. This is an example of roots music in the African-American tradition.

> *Recording:* "Hambone," performed by Taj Mahal. From *Shake It to the One You Love the Best*. ℗ 1986 Warren-Mattox Productions.

♫ CD track #12. Listen to "Old Joe Clarke," sung by Teri Tibbett. This is an example of an old-time country song from the mountain tradition.

> *Recording:* "Old Joe Clarke," performed by Teri Tibbett. ℗ 2002 Migration Music. Used by permission.

♫ CD track #31. Listen to "Rocky Top," a bluegrass song, performed by David Sause, Teri Tibbett, Christina Seaborn, Andy Ferguson, and Joe Karson.

> *Song:* "Rocky Top," composed by Boudleaux and Felice Bryant. Copyright © 1967 House of Bryant Publishers. *Recording:* "Rocky Top" ℗ 1988 Migration Music. Used by permission.

Bonus Challenge: Families of Instruments Group the instruments mentioned in this lesson into instrument families: chordophones, membranophones, aerophones, idiophones, and electrophones.

Name _____   Date _____

Country Music Quiz

Instructions: After reading the **Country Music** student handout, answer these questions (use back of page if necessary).

1.   What are some of the origins of **country music?**

2.   Write something about as many of the styles of **country music** as you can:

Country-western

Bluegrass

Western swing

Honky-tonk music

Nashville sound

Women in country

Outlaw country

New country

Country Music Quiz: Answer Key

1. What are some of the origins of **country music?**

   PIONEER SONGS, COWBOY SONGS, OLD-TIME MUSIC, MOUNTAIN MUSIC, ROOTS MUSIC.

2. Write something about as many of the styles of **country music** as you can:

   Country-western: COUNTRY-WESTERN MUSIC DEVELOPED IN THE 1950s AND 1960s, A BLEND OF EUROPEAN FOLK MUSIC AND THE POPULAR MUSIC OF TIN PAN ALLEY. COUNTRY-WESTERN MUSICIANS DRESSED IN COWBOY CLOTHES, PLAYED GUITARS, RODE HORSES, AND SANG ABOUT COWBOY LIFE. GENE AUTRY AND ROY ROGERS AND DALE EVANS WERE SOME OF THE MORE FAMOUS COUNTRY-WESTERN MUSICIANS.

   Bluegrass: BLUEGRASS IS AN UP-TEMPO FORM OF OLD-TIME MUSIC PLAYED ON GUITAR, BANJO, MANDOLIN, FIDDLE, AND BASS GUITAR. TWO IMPORTANT FEATURES ARE THE VERSE-CHORUS-VERSE STRUCTURE AND STRONG HARMONY SINGING. BILL MONROE AND HIS BLUE GRASS BOYS, AND LESTER FLATT AND EARL SCRUGGS ARE THE MOST WELL-KNOWN BLUEGRASS MUSICIANS.

   Western swing: WESTERN SWING IS AN UPBEAT STYLE OF COUNTRY MUSIC THAT "SWINGS" LIKE BIG BAND MUSIC BUT HAS LYRICS AND SINGING INFLUENCED BY COUNTRY MUSIC. IT IS DANCEABLE AND FEATURES MUSIC ON FIDDLES, GUITARS, PIANO, DRUMS, ELECTRIC GUITAR, BASS GUITAR, HAWAIIAN STEEL GUITAR, AND SOME WIND INSTRUMENTS. BOB WILLS AND HIS TEXAS PLAYBOYS PLAYED WESTERN SWING.

   Honky-tonk music: HONKY-TONK WAS POPULAR IN "HONKY-TONKS" (BARS), WHERE THE SONGS WERE OFTEN ABOUT HEARTBREAK, BREAKUPS, GOOD TIMES, BAD TIMES, FINDING LOVE, AND LOSING IT. HANK WILLIAMS, ERNEST TUBB, LEFTY FRIZZELL, KITTY WELLS, AND HANK THOMPSON PLAYED HONKY-TONK MUSIC.

Country Music Quiz: Answer Key (continued)

Nashville sound: IN THE LATE 1950s AND EARLY 1960s MUCH OF THE MUSIC COMING OUT OF NASHVILLE HAD ORCHESTRAL INSTRUMENTS IN THE BACKGROUND. IT WAS A POLISHED SOUND AND THE SINGERS USUALLY "CROONED" OVER THE LUSH INSTRUMENTAL PARTS. JIM REEVES, PATSY CLINE, AND EDDY ARNOLD WERE SOME OF THE MAJOR SINGERS IN THIS GENRE.

Women in country: AS LONG AS THERE HAS BEEN COUNTRY MUSIC THERE HAVE BEEN WOMEN COUNTRY SINGERS AND MUSICIANS. THEIR SONGS DESCRIBE A WOMAN'S POINT OF VIEW. WHERE EARLIER SONGS DESCRIBED HEARTACHES AND BEING CHEATED OR JILTED, MODERN COUNTRY SHOWS A STRONGER, SMARTER, AND WISER WOMAN. PATSY CLINE, KITTY WELLS, PATSY MONTANA, LORETTA LYNN, TAMMY WYNETTE, DOLLY PARTON, REBA McENTIRE, TRISHA YEARWOOD, AND SHANIA TWAIN ARE SOME OF THE FEW WHO HAVE RISEN TO FAME IN COUNTRY MUSIC EXPRESSING A WOMAN'S POINT OF VIEW.

Outlaw country: THE "OUTLAWS" WERE A GROUP OF COUNTRY SINGER-SONGWRITERS WHO DID NOT FIT THE MOLD OF THE POPULAR NASHVILLE SOUND OF THE 1950s and 1960s. THEY PLAYED A ROUGHER STYLE OF MUSIC AND WERE CALLED OUTLAWS BECAUSE THEIR MUSIC WAS A STEP OUTSIDE THE MAINSTREAM. WILLIE NELSON, JOHNNY CASH, MERLE HAGGARD, AND WAYLON JENNINGS WERE CONSIDERED OUTLAWS.

New country: IN THE 1980s, A COUNTRY BAND CALLED ALABAMA TOOK THE SPOTLIGHT AND SHOWED THAT AN ENTIRE BAND COULD BE THE STAR, NOT JUST THE FRONT PERSON, AS HAD BEEN THE TRADITION. IN THE 1990s, SUPERSTARS LIKE GARTH BROOKS PERFORMED TO THE LARGEST AUDIENCES IN COUNTRY MUSIC'S HISTORY.

♫ Lesson 20. Latin American Music

Lesson Overview

Latin music was introduced in America by the first explorers and conquistadors from Spain, who brought guitars and Spanish folk songs with them. Spanish music mixed with the music of Native Americans, Africans, and Europeans to create the many styles that are included in Latin American music today. In North America, the most popular styles are Tejano-conjunto, or Tex-Mex, which evolved in the southwestern United States and northern Mexico; mariachi, which developed in Mexico; salsa, which came from the Caribbean and thrived in New York City dance clubs in the 1960s before spreading out from there; and Latin popular music, which is winning music awards and sweeping mainstream radio, movies, and television across America.

Vocabulary. Folk songs, Tejano-conjunto music, bajo sexto, mariachi music, syncopated, arrangement, salsa music, Latin popular music.

Purpose. To offer an overview of Latin music as it has developed in North America.

Preparation. Read the student handout **Latin American Music** to familiarize yourself with the material. Preview the CD samples (cues in student handout) and have the CD ready for playing with the students. Be prepared to do some or all of the following activities. Also make sure that each student has a music notebook for keeping handouts and activity sheets.

Materials

- **Latin American Music** student handout *(following)*
- **Latin American Music Quiz** *(following)*
- **Latin American Music Quiz Answer Key** *(following)*
- **Music Vocabulary** activity sheet *(Appendix)*
- **My Opinion Page** activity sheet *(Appendix)*
- **How to Teach a Song** teacher guide *(Appendix)*
- **Great American Musicians!** activity sheet *(Appendix)*
- **Music on the Map** activity sheet *(Appendix)*
- **Music notebooks**
- **CD music** examples on accompanying CD; cues in student handout
- **Additional music selections**

Lesson Activities

- Pass out the **Latin American Music** handout for students to read silently or aloud as a group. Afterwards, have students put the handout in their music notebooks. *(Link to language arts, history, geography, social studies.)*

- Give the **Latin American Music Quiz** to assess student understanding of the lesson.

- Go over the music vocabulary at the top of the student handout before or after reading the text. Refer to the glossary for definitions. *Suggestion:* Include these words in a regular class vocabulary lesson, or pass out flashcards with a vocabulary word on one side and the definition on the other and allow students to drill each other. Use the **Music Vocabulary** activity sheets to write out definitions. *(Link to language arts.)*

- Offer the **Vocabulary Challenge.** Students pick some or all of the words in this lesson's vocabulary list to use in a paragraph, essay, short story, or poem. *(Link to language arts.)*

- **Discuss.** Before reading the student handout, discuss what students already know about Latin American music. Read the student handout and discuss it again, letting students add what they've learned. *(Link to language arts, social studies.)*

- **Bonus Challenge: Pick a Latin Style of Music.** The goal of this activity is for students to investigate a genre of Latin American music. Individually or in groups, students pick one of the styles mentioned in this lesson—for example, Tejano-conjunto, mariachi, salsa, Latin popular. Students read more about the style's roots, how it developed, some of the musicians who played in that style. They listen to the music. Then they offer a written or oral report with illustrations, photos, and CD samples. Compile everyone's written work into a "Latin Music Notebook." *(Link to language arts.)*

- **Bonus Challenge: Families of Instruments.** Group the instruments mentioned in this lesson into instrument families: chordophones, membranophones, aerophones, idiophones, and electrophones. (See Unit Two, Lesson 10: Instruments of the Orchestra.) *(Link to science.)*

Extension Activities

For step-by-step directions and activity sheets, see the appendix.

- **My Opinion Page.** Offer students a chance to freely express their own opinions about the music they hear. *(Link to language arts, critical thinking.)*

- **Sing a Song.** Students learn a simple song from this lesson. *Suggested songs: "La Bamba" or "Amor Bonito." (Link to singing, language arts, rhythm, melody.)*

- **Illustrate the Music.** Students illustrate a song or piece of music by drawing, coloring, or painting their ideas of what the music "looks" like visually. *(Link to language arts, visual arts.)*

- **Great American Musicians!** Introduce students to American musicians whose talents have made them notable. *(Link to language arts, history.)*

- **Music on the Map.** Create a map and legend showing musically important places, such as musicians' birthplaces and music hot spots mentioned in the lesson. *(Link to geography.)*

- **Invite a Music Expert.** Invite a Latin American musician to visit your class and share his or her instrument or musical talent with the students. Some resources for locating musicians are the Internet, local music and arts organizations, friends, students, parents. Plan ahead because musicians' schedules are often planned far in advance. Tell the musician the content of your lesson, how much time to plan for, and what you'd like him or her to do. Many professional musicians already work with students and have a planned program to offer—ask about this. Remember that professionals may ask for a fee because this is how they earn a living. Also consider taking students to hear a live performance, or show a video. *(Link to social studies.)*

- Consider bringing in **additional selections of music** to expand the music sample offerings. Read the song selections mentioned in each musician's biography for additional music ideas. Search the Internet, library, or local music store to find them.

Name _____   Date _____

Mariachi Vargas, early 1900s

Latin American Music

Vocabulary: *folk songs, Tejano-conjunto music, bajo sexto, mariachi music, syncopated, arrangement, salsa music, Latin popular music*

Latin music was introduced in North America by the first explorers and conquistadors from Spain, who brought guitars and Spanish **folk songs**. Over time, as Spanish music mixed with the music of Native Americans, Africans, and Europeans, it grew to be a hybrid of many styles. From mariachi to Tejano-conjunto to salsa and cumbia, Latin American music is integral to the evolution of North American music.

Tejano-Conjunto

Tejano-conjunto, Norteño, or Tex-Mex music all originated in the region of the southwestern United States and northern Mexico. It is a lively, upbeat music that evolved from Spanish folk songs, Mexican Indian traditions, and European accordion and polka music.

Listen to Learn

Early Tejano and conjunto groups played accordion with ***bajo sexto*** (twelve-string bass guitar), *tololoche* (string bass), and drum. They played in cantinas and at weddings, parties, fiestas, and celebrations. Their music featured polkas (Czech dance music), *boleros* (Spanish dance music), and *cumbias* (Spanish music with African rhythms).

In the 1930s, Tejano and conjunto musicians moved into the recording studio and their music was heard on radio and jukeboxes across the country. Accordion player Narciso Martínez (1911–1992) joined with Santiago Almeida (1911–1999) on the *bajo sexto* and the two created a lively performance style that became the basis of today's Tejano-conjunto music.

Tex-Mex musician

Eventually, the bands welcomed singers who sang songs about love and rural life, called *rancheras,* and songs about historical events, people, and controversies, called *corridos.* Accordionist Valerio Longoria (1924–2000) introduced singing into Tejano-conjunto music when he recorded the *cancion ranchera,* a polka style with lyrics and harmony. Lydia Mendoza (b. 1916) did a lot to spread Tejano-conjunto music throughout the region with her beautiful singing and twelve-string guitar playing.

Amor Bonito—Beautiful Love

Lyrics and music by Lydia Mendoza

El mundo estará muy lleno
De amor y de amores
Pero pa' mi hay solo uno
Que da luz a mi existencia.
Mi amor es retebonito
Brillante como un lucero
Que en las tristezas de mi alma
Me alegro con su recuerdo
Doy gracias a mi diocito
Por lo bueno que es conmigo
Que siempre oye mis plegarias
A todo lo que le pido
Amor bonito, bonito
Cariño mi cariñito
Te quiero porque te quiero
Cariño mi cariñito
Porque eres mi amor
Tu amor es retebonito
Radiante como una estrella
Que pensando en tu cariño
Se acaban todas mis penas
Doy gracias a mi diocito
Que siempre oye mis plegarias.

The world may be
Full of love and loves,
But for me there is only one
That gives light to my life.
My love is so beautiful and
Bright as a morning star,
So bright that when my soul is sad
Only his memories make me happy again.
I thank God who is so good to me
And listens to my prayers
And everything that I ask for.
Beautiful love, beautiful
Dear, my little dear.
I love you because I love you
Because you are my love.
Your love is so beautiful
Shining as a star,
And thinking of you, love
I put an end to all my sorrows.
I thank God who always
Listens to my prayers!

Lydia Mendoza (May 21, 1916–). Lydia Mendoza was born in Texas. She is a singer, songwriter, and guitar player. She grew up in a musical family that performed in a group called La Familia Mendoza. The family sang in variety shows and made many recordings. Lydia sang and played mandolin and made her first recording at twelve years old. In 1934, she stepped out on her own with a twelve-string guitar and began recording songs by herself, which became hits with Latin American audiences. The music was called Tejano music. She was called *La Cancionera de los Pobres* (the Poor People's Songstress) because she performed for poor farm workers. In 1950, she sang for the president of Mexico, and in 1977 at the inauguration of U.S. President Jimmy Carter. Some of her most popular songs are "Mal Hombre," "Amor Bonito," "Besando La Cruz," "Silverio Perez" (about the famous Mexican bullfighter), and "Margarita Margarita."

Lydia Mendoza. Photograph courtesy of Arhoolie Records (*www.arhoolie.com*).

In the 1950s, Tejano-conjunto musicians began adding orchestral instruments to their music, which made it sound bigger and more polished. They also added elements of blues, jazz, and rock. Conjunto Bernal was one of the most well-known groups to branch out into this new style. They featured orchestral instruments with well-blended harmonies and uplifting melodies that kept the original flavor of traditional conjunto music, but added a more modern sound.

In the 1960s and 1970s, new musicians added rhythm and blues, pop, rock, country, and disco sounds to Tejano-conjunto. One of the most popular modern musicians to emerge was Selena Quintanilla Perez (1971–1995) who became famous when she was still a teenager. She mixed traditional music with modern popular music, singing in both Spanish and English, backed by guitar, drums, bass, and keyboards. Her music featured songs that reflected her Latin heritage, and over time she had twelve Top 40 singles on the *Billboard* charts and a Grammy Award. Her popularity spread not only among Latin audiences but among mainstream audiences as well.

Mariachi Music

Mariachi music is a blend of Spanish and Indian folk traditions. When the Spanish arrived in America, they brought violins, harps, and guitars. The Native American people living there were already playing drums, rattles, flutes, and conch shell horns. The two blended styles and later added the rhythms of African Americans to create a music that is now called **mariachi music.**

Mariachi music is Mexican country music. It is a lively, happy music that reflects country life, the people and their experiences, love, and the legends of the region. It is dance music that sometimes uses the tapping of feet to create a **syncopated** beat against the rhythm of the instruments playing. Early mariachi music featured violins, harp, *vihuela* (a high-pitched, round-backed guitar) and the *guitarrón* (a big-bodied bass guitar).

By the 1800s, each region of Mexico had its own style of mariachi music. In the region of Jalisco it is called *son jalisciense.* In Veracruz it is *son veracruzano.* In northeastern Mexico it is called *son huasteco.* The "Mexican Hat Dance," or *Jarabe Tapito,* is a traditional mariachi dance from the Jalisco region. In this dance, the man wears a *charro* or classic outfit of the Jalisco horseman, and the woman wears a handwoven shawl over a colorful sequined shirt.

"La Bamba" is a tropical song from the coastal region of Veracruz. It is a traditional song, but it became popular in the United States in the 1950s when Mexican-American singer Richie Valens recorded it and sold millions of records to American teenagers.

La Bamba

Para bailar la bamba.
Para bailar la bamba.
Se necesita una poca de gracia,
Una poca de gracia y otra cosita.
Y arriba, y arriba,
Y arriba, y arriba, y arriba iré.
Yo no soy marinero,
Yo no soy marinero,
Por ti seré, por ti seré, por ti seré.

Chorus: Baila bamba, baila bamba,
Baila bamba, baila bamba.
En mi casa me dicen,
En mi casa me dicen,
El inocente porque tengo chicas.
Porque tengo chicas,
De quince a viente.
Y arriba, y arriba,
Y arriba, y arriba, y arriba iré.
Yo no soy marinero.
Yo no soy marinero.
Soy capitán, soy capitán, soy capitán.

Repeat chorus.

In order to dance the bamba,
In order to dance the bamba,
You need a little bit of grace,
A little bit of grace and other things.
And up and up,
Up and up I'll go.
I'm not a sailor,
I'm not a sailor.
But for you I'll be
For you I'll be.

Chorus: Dance the bamba, dance the bamba
dance the bamba, dance the bamba.

In my house they say about me
In my house they say I'm the innocent.
Because I have girlfriends,
Because I have girlfriends,
From fifteen to twenty,
And up and up.
Up and up I'll go.
I'm not a sailor,
I'm not a sailor.
I'm a captain,
I'm a captain.

Repeat chorus.

One of the first mariachi groups to gain popularity was Mariachi Vargas de Tecalitlán, which was formed by Gasper Vargas in 1898, and carried on by his son Silvestre Vargas. They helped spread the music with their happy, upbeat style.

Unit Four: New American Music

Mariachi Vargas de Tecalitlán. The band Mariachi Vargas de Tecalitlán was formed by Gasper Vargas in 1898 in Jalisco, Mexico. In the first part of the 1900s, they were a regional band popular only in the nearby rural areas. In 1934, however, they were invited to perform at the inauguration of Mexican President Lázaro Cárdenas and their popularity spread throughout Mexico. Gasper's son, Silvestre, took over as leader of the group and helped them take a leading role in spreading the popularity of mariachi music. The group recorded dozens of records, performed live, and appeared in over two hundred films. Other important mariachi musicians to play with Mariachi Vargas include arranger Rubén Fuentes, trumpet player Miguel Martínez, and composer-singer Jose Alfredo Jimenez. In 1976, Pepe Martinez became the musical director and helped to keep the group's music fresh and innovative in the world of mariachi music. Some of their recordings are *El Mejor Mariachi del Mundo* (1959), *Fiesta en Jalisco* (1970), *Viva el Mariachi* (1996), and *Antologia* (2003).

As time went on, mariachi music took on a more "polished" flair. New instruments were added and **arrangements** of traditional songs were written down, thus leaving behind the tradition of playing by ear, or by memory. Mariachi singers sang *corridos* (story songs), *rancheras* (country songs), and *boleros* (romantic songs). "Allá en el Rancho Grande" is a typical mariachi song performed in the *ranchera* style.

Allá en el Rancho Grande—Over at the Big Ranch

Chorus: Allá en el rancho grande.
Allá donde vivía.
Había una rancherita,
Había una rancherita.
Que alegre me decía,
Que alegre me decía.

Te voy a hacer los calzones,
Como los usa el ranchero.
Te los comienzo de lana,
Y te los acabo de cuero.

Repeat chorus.

El gusto de los rancheros,
Es tener un buen caballo.
Ensillarlo por las tardes,
Y darle vuelta al varado.

Repeat chorus.

El gusto de una ranchera,
Es tener un buen comal.
Echar las tortillas grandes,
Y sin darle al caporal.

Repeat chorus.

Chorus: Over at the big ranch
Where I used to live.
There was this cowgirl,
There was this cowgirl,
Who happily said to me,
Who happily said to me,
I will make you trousers
Like cowboy trousers.
I'll begin with yarn
And finish with leather!

Repeat chorus.

Happiness for the cowboys
Is having a good horse
Saddling up in the afternoons
And riding around in the fields.

Repeat chorus.

Happiness for the cowgirl
Is having a good hearth stone
Making big tortillas
Without giving any to the boss.

Repeat chorus.

By the 1960s, mariachi music gained even more popularity when radio stations started playing it across Mexico and the United States. It became the national music of Mexico and was played at public events, holidays, baptisms, weddings, funerals, and birthdays. Modern mariachi groups feature trumpets, violins, guitar, *vihuela,* and *guitarrón,* and strong singing.

In the United States, it gained popularity with both Hispanic and non-Hispanic audiences. The bands Los Camperos from California and Mariachi Cobre from Arizona were some of the first to make it popular north of Mexico. Mexican-American singer Linda Ronstadt helped popularize mariachi music in the United States by her collaborations with mariachi musician Rubén Fuentes.

Today, groups like Sol de México and Campanas de América perform traditional mariachi music, but add contemporary styles to make the music innovative and new.

Linda Ronstadt (July 15, 1946–). Singer and actress Linda Ronstadt was born in Arizona. She grew up in a musical family, influenced by her father who taught her songs from his Mexican heritage. She sang with her sisters in the group the Three Ronstadts and later formed a rock band called the Stone Poneys that became popular on rock radio stations in the 1960s. Linda's solo career has ventured through a variety of styles, including folk, country rock, big band jazz, and Broadway show tunes, but her mariachi music was most expressive of her heritage. She has recorded albums and CDs, made movie soundtracks, and performed in concert and on Broadway. Her two collections of mariachi music are *Canciones de Mi Padre* (1990) and *Mas Canciones* (1991).

Salsa Music

Salsa means "sauce" in Spanish. **Salsa music** is a spicy dance music that became popular in New York in the 1960s. Salsa evolved from the traditions of immigrants from Puerto Rico, Cuba, Colombia, and Venezuela, and other Caribbean peoples.

Tito Puente

Listen to Learn

Tito Puente (April 20, 1923–2000). Born Ernesto Antonio Puente Jr., in New York, Tito Puente was a Latin percussionist and arranger. He began taking piano lessons at age six, and then learned drums and percussion at the age of ten. His earliest influences include the big band music of the 1930s and 1940s, which he listened to on the radio. In the 1930s, Tito joined the Noro Morales Orchestra as a drummer, and later concentrated on the *timbales,* a pair of shallow cylindrical drums played with sticks. He also studied at the Juilliard School of Music. In the late 1940s, he formed a band, Tito Puente and His Orchestra, which he stayed with throughout his career. The band played Latin music that mixed elements of *mambo,* an African-Cuban style of dance music, and big band swing music. His song "Albaniquito" was one of the first *mambo* hits to cross over to mainstream audiences. In the 1950s and 1960s, Tito's orchestra became quite famous in the genre of Latin jazz, and in the 1970s and 1980s, he combined the music traditions of Africa, Cuba, Puerto Rico, and other Caribbean cultures into a new style of music that came to be called salsa. He earned many awards and toured throughout the world in this career. Some of his albums include *Puente Goes Jazz* (1956), *Dance Mania* (1958), *Best of Tito Puente Vol. 1* (1992), and *Oye Como Va: The Dance Collection* (1997).

Salsa's roots can be traced to the music of Africans, who were brought to the Caribbean as slaves in the 1600s. Over time, the traditions of the Africans blended with the traditions of the Spanish and a hybrid was created. This music has strong percussion rhythms played on *congas* (drums), *claves* (sticks), and *guiros* (wooden rasps), with trumpets, guitars, and bass guitars. Salsa gained popularity when Fania Records recorded salsa singers and musicians and introduced them to the rest of the world. Tito Puente (1923–2000) and His Orchestra, with singer Celia Cruz (1925–2003) and percussionist Mongo Santamaria (b. 1922) set the stage for salsa music in North America.

El Gran Combo and the Apollo Allstars with Robert Rohena followed, and more recently Marc Anthony (b. 1969) rose to fame performing popular salsa music.

Latin Popular Music

Latins brought to North America the *tango, mambo,* and *cha-cha.* These popular dance music styles swept across America in the late 1900s and are still performed today.

Songs like "Besame Mucho" (1941), by Consuelo Velasquez, "La Bamba" (1958), performed by Richie Valens, "Feliz Navidad" (1973), performed by Jose Feliciano, and "Oye Como Va" (1969), performed by the rock group Santana, were some Latin songs to cross over and become popular with mainstream audiences.

Gloria Estefan (b. 1957) introduced Latin songs and rhythms to mainstream audiences in the 1980s with her band the Miami Sound Machine. They performed upbeat tropical music with lyrics in both Spanish and English, and put on high-powered shows across the continent.

Gloria Estefan (September 1, 1957–). Born Gloria Maria Milagrosa Fijardo in Havana, Cuba, Gloria Estefan is a Latin American singer and performer. Her family moved to Miami, Florida, when she was two. As a child there she learned to play guitar and sing. While still in high school she sang with a band, but she pursued and received a college degree before joining any bands permanently. In the late 1970s, she began singing with the Miami Sound Machine and recorded several Spanish-language albums before her international success with North American, European, and Latin American audiences. She has performed throughout the world—including at the Super Bowl in 1992 and the Olympic Games in 1996. She has acted in films and recorded music for movie soundtracks. Some of her songs are "Rhythm Is Gonna Get You" (1986), "Coming Out of the Dark" (1991), and "Music of the Heart" (1997).

Gloria Estefan

Bonus Challenge: Families of Instruments Group the instruments mentioned in this lesson into families: chordophones, membranophones, aerophones, idiophones, and electrophones.

In 1999, "Mambo No. 5," by Lou Bega, with its danceable mambo beat and catchy chorus, gained such popularity that it became an international hit on radio and in dance clubs around the world.

Latin popular singers Ricky Martin (b. 1971), Christina Aguilera (b. 1980), and Jennifer Lopez (b. 1970) became superstars in the world of Latin popular music throughout the 1990s into the new millennium, selling millions of records and performing at the most prestigious music events in North America.

The first Latin Grammy Awards were held in 2000 and featured a host of Latin categories—including Best Latin Song; Best Latin Male and Female Pop Singers; Best Latin Albums in Tejano, Salsa, Merengue, Rock, Rap, Jazz, Classical, and more.

♫ CD track #32. Listen to "Amor Bonito," an example of Tejano-conjunto music. Notice the upbeat rhythms and joyful singing of this Spanish love song.

> *Song:* "Amor Bonito," by Lydia Mendoza. Copyright © 1984 San Antonio Music Publishers. *Recording:* From the CD entitled *Lydia Mendoza: First Queen of Tejano Music.* ℗ 1996 Arhoolie Productions, *www.arhoolie.com.* Used by permission.

♫ CD track #33. Listen to "Allá en el Rancho Grande," an example of mariachi music.

> *Recording:* "Allá en el Rancho Grande," performed by Adelita Reyes, Angel "El Cuervo," and Valente Pastor. ℗ Producciones Mexicanas Discograficas. Used by permission.

Bonus Challenge: Pick a Latin Style of Music   Individually or in groups, pick one of the styles mentioned in this lesson: Tejano-conjunto, mariachi, salsa, or Latin popular. Read more about its roots, how it developed, some of the musicians who played in that style. Listen to the music. Offer a written or oral report with illustrations, photos, and CD samples.

Name _____   Date _____

Latin American Music Quiz

Instructions: After reading the **Latin American Music** student handout, answer these questions (use back of page if necessary).

1. Describe **Tejano-conjunto music.** What are some of the origins and influences? What instruments are played?

2. Describe **mariachi music.** What are some of its origins and influences? What instruments are played?

3. Describe **salsa music.** What are some of its origins and influences? What instruments are played?

4. Describe **Latin popular music.** Who are some of the major popular Latin performers?

Latin American Music Quiz: Answer Key

1. Describe **Tejano-conjunto music.** What are some of the origins and influences? What instruments are played?

   TEJANO-CONJUNTO, NORTEÑO, AND TEX-MEX ALL DEVELOPED IN THE SOUTHWESTERN UNITED STATES AND NORTHERN MEXICO. IT IS A LIVELY, UPBEAT MUSIC THAT EVOLVED FROM SPANISH FOLK SONGS, MEXICAN INDIAN MUSIC TRADITIONS, GERMAN, POLISH, AND CZECH ACCORDION AND POLKA MUSIC. EARLY GROUPS PLAYED ACCORDION WITH *BAJO SEXTO* (TWELVE-STRING BASS GUITAR), *TOLOLOCHE* (STRING BASS), AND DRUM. ADDED LATER WERE ORCHESTRAL INSTRUMENTS AND ROCK AND JAZZ INSTRUMENTS, INCLUDING GUITAR, DRUMS, BASS, AND KEYBOARDS.

2. Describe **mariachi music.** What are some of its origins and influences? What instruments are played?

   MARIACHI IS A BLEND OF SPANISH AND INDIAN FOLK TRADITIONS. IT IS MEXICAN COUNTRY MUSIC. IT IS LIVELY, HAPPY MUSIC THAT SINGS ABOUT COUNTRY LIFE, THE PEOPLE AND THEIR EXPERIENCES, LOVE, AND LEGENDS OF THE REGION. DIFFERENT MARIACHI STYLES HAVE EVOLVED IN DIFFERENT REGIONS OF MEXICO. MODERN MARIACHI GROUPS PLAY TRUMPETS, VIOLINS, GUITAR, *VIHUELA* (HIGH-PITCHED ROUND BACK GUITAR), AND *GUITARRÓN* (BIG BODIED BASS GUITAR).

3. Describe **salsa music.** What are some of its origins and influences? What instruments are played?

   SALSA IS A SPICY DANCE MUSIC THAT BECAME POPULAR IN NEW YORK IN THE 1960s AND IS STILL POPULAR TODAY. IT EVOLVED FROM MUSIC TRADITIONS OF IMMIGRANTS FROM PUERTO RICO, CUBA, COLOMBIA, VENEZUELA, AND OTHER CARIBBEAN PEOPLES, WHO BROUGHT INFLUENCES FROM SPANISH MUSIC AND AFRICAN RHYTHMS. SALSA IS PLAYED ON *CONGAS* (DRUMS), *CLAVES* (STICKS), *GUIROS* (WOODEN RASPS) AND WITH TRUMPETS, GUITARS, AND BASS GUITARS.

4. Describe **Latin popular music.** Who are some of the major popular Latin performers?

   SOME OF THE EARLIEST POPULAR LATIN MUSIC IN NORTH AMERICA WAS THE TANGO, MAMBO, AND CHA-CHA-CHA, WHICH WERE POPULAR IN THE MID-1900s. GLORIA ESTEFAN AND THE MIAMI SOUND MACHINE HELPED LATIN MUSIC CROSS OVER TO MAINSTREAM AUDIENCES IN THE 1980s. LATIN PERFORMERS TO FOLLOW WERE LOU BEGA, WITH "MAMBO NO. 5," RICKY MARTIN, CHRISTINA AGUILERA, AND JENNIFER LOPEZ. THE LATIN GRAMMY AWARDS BEGAN IN 2000.

♪ Lesson 21. Rock Music

Lesson Overview

When African Americans were playing rhythm and blues in small clubs across America, they were crafting a style of music that would one day be called rock 'n' roll. Rock 'n' roll is one of the many incarnations of the blues. The first rock 'n' roll and doo-wop bands were African American, but in the 1950s, when rock 'n' roll became increasingly popular, it tended to be recorded by European-Americans who "covered" the music of African Americans and made it famous with mainstream audiences. After the civil rights movement of the 1960s, recording and performing opportunities opened up for African Americans. Since then, many branches of rock have emerged, including folk rock, surf music, hard rock, country, jazz rock, punk rock, new wave, and grunge.

Vocabulary. Rock 'n' roll, record charts, rhythm, melodic, harmony singing, vocables, lyrics, Motown music, acoustic guitar, electric guitar, folk rock, country rock, hard rock, disco, jazz-rock, punk rock, rap music, grunge music.

Purpose. To offer an overview of rock music as it developed in North America.

Preparation. Read the student handout **Rock Music** to familiarize yourself with the material. Consider having music samples available to enhance the lesson. Be prepared to do some or all of the following activities. Also make sure that each student has a music notebook for keeping handouts and activity sheets.

Materials

- **Rock Music** student handout *(following)*
- **Rock Music Quiz** *(following)*
- **Rock Music Quiz Answer Key** *(following)*
- **Music Vocabulary** activity sheet *(Appendix)*
- **My Opinion Page** activity sheet *(Appendix)*
- **Great American Musicians!** activity sheet *(Appendix)*
- **Music on the Map** activity sheet f *(Appendix)*
- **Music notebooks**
- **Music selections**

Activities

- Pass out the **Rock Music** handout for students to read silently or aloud as a group. Afterwards, have students put the handout in their music notebooks. *(Link to language arts, history, geography, social studies.)*

- Give the **Rock Music Quiz** to assess student understanding of the lesson.

- Go over the music vocabulary at the top of the student handout before or after reading the text. Refer to the glossary for definitions. *Suggestion:* Include these words in a regular class vocabulary lesson, or pass out flashcards with a vocabulary word on one side and the definition on the other and allow students to drill each other. Use the **Music Vocabulary** activity sheets to write out definitions. *(Link to language arts.)*

- Offer the **Vocabulary Challenge.** Students pick some or all of the words in this lesson's vocabulary list to use in a paragraph, essay, short story, or poem. *(Link to language arts.)*

- **Discuss.** Before reading the student handout, discuss what students already know about rock music. Read the student handout and discuss it again, letting students add what they've learned. *(Link to language arts, social studies.)*

- **The Science of Music: Electric Guitars Are Electrophones.** Instruments that use electronics to create or enhance their sound belong to a family of instruments called electrophones. A section in the student handout describes guitars as electrophones. Invite students to bring in an electronic guitar and experiment making sounds with it. Compare the sound of an electric guitar to an acoustic guitar. *Suggestion:* Consider inviting a local professional musician, parent, or student who plays electric guitar to demonstrate. *(Link to science.)*

- **Bonus Challenge: Bo Diddley Beat.** Bo Diddley was an early rock 'n' roll musician who popularized an unusual rhythm pattern, sometimes called the "Bo Diddley beat." This challenge invites students to play the pattern written in the student handout. Ask a student or parent who reads music to demonstrate or teach it. Practice on drums, laps, or table-tops. The goal is to play for several minutes and allow a "groove" to develop.

- **Bonus Challenge: Research an Electrophone.** Pick an electrophone and investigate its origins, how it works, and what kind of sound it makes. Some electrophones are electric guitar, bass guitar, drum machine, organ, synthesizer, digital sampler, electric violin, electric flute, electric saxophone. Have students offer a written or oral report.

- **Bonus Challenge: Pick a Rock Style.** Students investigate a branch of rock music. Individually or in groups, students pick one of the branches mentioned in the lesson: rock 'n' roll, doo-wop, folk rock, country rock, hard rock, disco, jazz-rock, punk rock, rap. They read more about its roots, how it developed, some of the musicians who played in that style. They listen to the music. Students then offer a written or oral report with illustrations, photos, and CD samples. Compile written work into a "Rock Music Notebook." *(Link to language arts.)*

- **Bonus Challenge: Families of Instruments.** Group the instruments mentioned in this lesson into instrument families: chordophones, membranophones, aerophones, idiophones, and electrophones. (See Unit Two's Lesson 10: Instruments of the Orchestra.) *(Link to science.)*

Extension Activities

For step-by-step directions and activity sheets, see the appendix.

- **My Opinion Page.** Offer students a chance to freely express their own opinions about the music they hear. *(Link to language arts, critical thinking.)*

- **Great American Musicians!** Introduce students to American musicians whose talents have made them notable. *(Link to language arts, history.)*

- **Music on the Map.** Create a map and legend showing musically important places, such as musicians' birthplaces and music hot spots mentioned in the lesson. *(Link to geography.)*

- **Invite a Music Expert.** Invite a rock musician to visit your class and share his or her instrument and musical talent with the students. Some resources for locating musicians are the Internet, local music and arts organizations, friends, students, parents. Plan ahead because musicians' schedules are often established far in advance. Tell the musician the content of your lesson, how much time to plan for, and what you'd like him or her to do. Many professional musicians already work with students and have a planned program to offer—ask about this. Also, remember that professional musicians might request payment, because this is how they earn their living. Also consider taking students to hear a live performance, or show a video. *(Link to social studies.)*

- Because of copyright issues, modern songs are difficult to obtain for the accompanying CD. Consider bringing in **selections of music** from other sources to expand the music sample offerings. Read the song selections mentioned in each musician's biography for other music ideas. Search the Internet, library, or local music store to find them.

Name_____   Date_____

Janis Joplin, the Ramones, Chuck Berry, Bob Dylan

Rock Music

Vocabulary: *rock 'n' roll, record charts, rhythm, melodic, harmony singing, vocables, lyrics, Motown music, acoustic guitar, electric guitar, folk rock, country rock, hard rock, disco, jazz-rock, punk rock, rap music, grunge music*

Rock 'n' Roll

Blues musician Muddy Waters once said, "The blues had a baby and they named it rock 'n' roll." Another blues musician, Willie Dixon said, "The blues are the roots, the rest are the fruits."

There seems to be little argument that **rock 'n' roll** music evolved from the rhythm and blues music of African Americans. When Bill Haley's "Rock Around the Clock" reached number one on the **record charts** in 1955, many said it was the beginning of rock 'n' roll music. More truthfully, it was the beginning of rock

Bill Haley (July 6, 1925–1981). Bill Haley was born in Michigan. He was a singer, songwriter, saxophone player, and bandleader. He began his musical career as a yodeling cowboy, and his first popular songs were country songs. But when he started to blend country music with blues music, he came up with a new sound all together. He formed the band Bill Haley and His Comets in 1953 and the band went on to record many hits. Their music, coupled with their high-powered stage act that included acrobatics and gimmicks, attracted a huge following around the world. Bill Haley continued to tour and perform as an "elder" rock musician into the 1970s. His songs include "Rock Around the Clock" (1954), "Shake, Rattle, and Roll" (1954), "See You Later Alligator" (1956), and "Don't Knock the Rock" (1957).

'n' roll music "crossing over" into mainstream American audiences. Rock 'n' roll had been playing in African-American clubs and on African-American radio stations for a few years before Bill Haley's song. Bill Haley, a European-American, helped start the craze that would go on to influence an entire generation.

Many laws and customs of the 1950s imposed segregation, which served to keep African Americans and European-Americans separated in many public places. In the music world, this meant fewer opportunities for African Americans to perform or record their music at clubs, concerts, and on the radio.

Bill Haley and His Comets. AP/World Wide Photos. Used by permission.

Elvis Presley (January 8, 1935–1977). Elvis Presley was born in Mississippi. He was a singer, guitar player, and actor. He grew up singing gospel music in church. At age eight he won a local song contest and continued to sing throughout his school years. Sun Records producer Sam Phillips hired Elvis to record for him after hearing a demo recording Elvis had made for his mother. He had many hits at Sun Records, which led to more recording and touring and more exposure. Eventually, Elvis came to be one of the most popular performers of the twentieth century. In his career, he acted in films and became a phenomenal success in live performances. His regular sold-out performances on the stages of Las Vegas in the 1960s and 1970s proved his undying popularity. Among his many songs are "That's All Right Mama" (1954), "Milk Cow Blues Boogie" (1954), "Heartbreak Hotel" (1956), "Hound Dog" (1956), "Don't Be Cruel" (1956), "Viva Las Vegas" (1964), and "Suspicious Minds" (1969).

Record companies recognized, however, that their music was attractive to young audiences and wanted to feature it some way. They solved the problem by hiring European-Americans to "cover" or copy the music.

Elvis Presley's first hit song, "That's All Right Mama" (1954), was written by Arthur Crudup, an African-American blues musician. Elvis was not African American, but he had a feeling for rhythm and blues. He was raised in Mississippi and grew up singing gospel, blues, and country music. He became immensely popular with teenagers and his popularity spread around the world. Elvis's music featured a blend of country-blues-gospel-rock that used electric guitars, bass, drums, piano, saxophone, and back-up singing.

In the mid-1950s, Chuck Berry became the first African-American rock 'n' roll performer to cross over into mainstream popular music. His music had both blues and country elements, which made it popular with both European-American and African-American audiences. His songs were hits, one after the other, and served to influence a whole new generation of rock guitar players, including the Beach Boys, the Beatles, and the Rolling Stones. His song "Johnny B. Goode" has been an "anthem" for rock music ever since.

Chuck Berry (October 18, 1926–). Chuck Berry, singer, guitar player, songwriter, and bandleader, was born in California. His first performance was on a high school stage, where he sang a blues song and received a huge response from the audience. He went on to learn guitar and began to make a career performing in bar bands. He eventually formed his own band and his songs began topping the popular music record charts, as well as the rhythm and blues charts. Over his career he made many records and toured and worked on television and in movies. Chuck Berry's creative guitar style set a standard for rock 'n' roll music that has been imitated by others ever since. He was inducted into the Rock and Roll Hall of Fame in 1986. His songs include "Maybellene" (1955), "Roll Over Beethoven" (1957), "Rock and Roll Music" (1957), "School Days" (1957), and "Johnny B. Goode" (1958).

Chuck Berry

Bo Diddley plays guitar and sings his own songs. He introduced a new kind of **rhythm** with his guitar that was catchy and unusual. The rhythm, which came to be called the Bo Diddley Beat, likely derived from an African rhythm passed down through the generations. This rhythm can be heard in his songs "Mona" and "Hand Jive."

As the civil rights movement of the 1960s helped open doors for more African-American musicians to perform and record, their music became more widespread and popular with European-American audiences. Mainstream radio stations and record companies featured music by them and other ethnic groups. African-Americans Little Richard and Fats Domino and Mexican-American Richie Valens recorded songs that rose to the tops of the *Billboard* charts.

"Rockabilly" music mixed both rock and country music. Buddy Holly and the Crickets had their roots in country music, but they added blues chords played on guitar, bass, and drums to create the "rockabilly" sound.

Bonus Challenge: Bo Diddley Beat The Bo Diddley Beat was most likely handed down from a traditional African rhythm. Bo Diddley made it popular in rock music. Play the following rhythm. Invite someone who can read or play it to lead the group in learning it, or try to figure it out yourself. Play it on drums, books, laps, or tabletops. Play it over and over for at least several minutes until you get it. Developing "a groove"—a smooth steady repetition of the pattern—is the goal.

boom - boom - boom boom-boom | boom - boom - boom boom-boom | (repeat)

Bo Diddley (December 30, 1928–). Born in Mississippi, Bo Diddley is an African-American singer, songwriter, and guitar player. He played his first guitar at ten, and at seventeen he built a cigar box guitar, which became his trademark instrument. He formed a band in high school and eventually moved to Chicago to play in blues clubs. His songs were then discovered and became hits on the radio. Both his guitar playing and songwriting abilities were respected in the mainstream; audiences liked his unusual, African-influenced rhythms. Throughout his life, Bo Diddley has performed in clubs, at concerts, festivals, and on the radio. His songs include "Mona," "Hand Jive," "Who Do You Love," and "Diddy Wah Diddy."

Doo-wop music evolved out of rhythm and blues in the late 1950s. Doo-wop bands were vocal groups singing smooth, **melodic** songs, with **harmony singing,** and strong rhythms. They were known for using **vocables**—like "bop shoo-ah" or "doop-doo-ah"—mixed with the **lyrics.** Doo-wop groups like the Silhouettes, the Coasters, the Shirelles, and the Chantels were popular with both African-American and European-American audiences and helped to spread the music into mainstream America.

Branches of Rock

Throughout the 1960s, rock musicians branched off from the rock 'n' roll styles of the 1950s. These new styles might be called "grandbabies" of the blues.

The influence in the 1960s of the Beatles, from England, cannot go without mentioning when talking about American rock music. The Beatles developed their style by copying the American rock 'n' roll players of the 1950s. But their original blend of harmonies, lyrics, and catchy music created a branch of its own that was copied and expanded on into the present time. Their phenomenal success helped spread rock music around the world.

About the same time, Motown Records from Detroit recorded and promoted music that combined funk and soul with rhythm and blues performed by inner-city musicians. **Motown music** rose to the forefront of mainstream listening audiences with groups like the Temptations, the Supremes, and Gladys Knight and the Pips (see Unit Three, Lesson 15: Soul and Funk).

Buddy Holly (September 7, 1936–1959). Buddy Holly was born in Texas. He was a singer, songwriter, guitar player, and bandleader. His earliest stage experience was winning a talent show with his brothers at age five. He learned to play guitar, violin, mandolin, banjo, and piano, and liked to play in the boogie-woogie style. As a teenager he formed a bluegrass duo and later played country music. As rock 'n' roll was catching on across the country, Buddy was attracted to it and began recording his own songs in the rock style. His music became popular, and with his band the Crickets, he became famous across America and Europe. His songs include "That'll Be the Day" (1957), "Peggy Sue" (1957), "Maybe Baby" (1957), and "Everyday" (1957).

The Beach Boys performed "surf music" from California, which blended rock rhythms and harmony singing with lyrics about surfing, tanned girls, and life on the beach. Songs like "Surfin' USA," "California Girls," and "Good Vibrations" painted a picture of Southern California beach life in the 1960s.

The Byrds played **acoustic guitars** and sang their own songs with rock-style rhythms and harmonies. Their songs made social comments and observations. The music paralleled a movement in the 1960s that focused on developing peaceful solutions to ending the war in Vietnam.

Rock performers Jimi Hendrix and Janis Joplin, and groups like Big Brother and the Holding Company, Quicksilver Messenger Service, Jefferson Airplane, and the Grateful Dead played a "harder" style of rock music. The music featured **electric guitar,** which was often distorted and manipulated to create feedback and strange sounds. Rock music developed another branch at this point. These bands performed in large halls and outdoor arenas with elaborate light shows, big speakers, and huge audiences.

Jimi Hendrix. Photograph by Mark Daughhetee.
Courtesy of Mark Daughhetee.

Did You Know? The screeching sound of electric guitar playing comes from *feedback.* Feedback happens when an electric guitar player stands close to the amplifier, and the sound from the amplifier is loud enough to enter the guitar, where the sound travels back to the amplifier and out of the speakers, causing a feedback loop.

The Science of Music: Electric Guitars Are Electrophones. Instruments that use electronics to create or enhance their sound belong to a family of instruments called electrophones. Some electrophones use electronics to *create* sound—like organs, synthesizers, and digital samplers. Others use electronics to enhance or amplify the natural sound of an acoustic instrument—like electric guitars, electric basses, electric violins, and electric flutes. The electric guitar is shaped like an acoustic guitar, with a body and neck and strings. However, where an acoustic guitar depends on the vibrating air inside its body to make the sound get louder, an electric guitar depends on tiny microphones (called "pickups") attached to the body to make its sound get louder. The pickups send sound signals to an amplifier, which amplifies, or makes the sound louder, through loudspeakers. This technology helps the guitar to be heard over other instruments and create its own unique kind of sound. *Activity: Bring in an electric guitar. Compare it to an acoustic guitar—one that makes sound without electricity.*

Folk rock combines folk music with rock-style rhythms and chords. Although folk music was traditionally passed through the ages by the oral tradition, modern folk musicians began mixing traditional songs with their own songs. Singer Joan Baez (b. 1941 in New York) began singing old English folk songs, and later political songs, which became popular on mainstream radio. Paul Simon (b. 1941 in New Jersey) and Art Garfunkel (b. 1941 in New York) used harmony singing to enhance both traditional songs and songs they composed themselves. When Joni Mitchell (b. 1945 in Saskatchewan, Canada) began singing her own songs in coffeehouses in the 1960s, she was part of a generation of folk-rock musicians who were called "singer-songwriters" performing usually with only a simple guitar or piano as accompaniment. Singer-songwriter Bob Dylan (b. 1941 in Minnesota) sang folk-style lyrics that made strong social comments. He protested the war in Vietnam and expressed detailed observations about society through his music. The song "Hurricane" is a modern folk song about Hurricane Carter, a famous boxer who was wrongly accused of a

Bob Dylan (May 24, 1941–). Bob Dylan was born Robert Allen Zimmerman in Minnesota. He is a singer, songwriter, and guitar and harmonica player. As a teenager, he played piano with local bands, and after graduating from high school, began playing folk and blues in coffeehouses. In 1961, he moved to New York City and became well known in the Greenwich Village folk scene with his powerful and sophisticated lyrics. He was soon discovered by a recording company and began making records, which played on the radio and sold in record stores. He sang narrative ballads, protest songs, and comments on society backed by solo guitar and harmonica. In 1962, he added electric guitar, bass, and organ to his music. Bob Dylan often changed his style over the years, showing that he was experimental and creative. In 1974, he joined a traveling medicine show that performed unannounced in small towns across America. It was called the *Rolling Thunder Revue.* Bob Dylan has continued to tour and make records into the new millennium. Some of his songs are "Blowin' in the Wind" (1962), "Mr. Tambourine Man" (1964), "Like a Rolling Stone" (1965), "Hurricane" (1976), and "Gotta Serve Somebody" (1979).

Unit Four: New American Music

crime he didn't commit. He spent over twenty years in jail for it and was released after his innocence was proved. Bob Dylan's song helped raise public awareness about Hurricane Carter's situation, which influenced his release.

By 2000, many singer-songwriters were taking to the stages across America to perform their own music. Bruce Cockburn (b. 1945 in Ontario, Canada), Greg Brown (b. 1949 in Iowa), Ani DiFranco (b. 1970 in New York), and Jewel (b. 1974 in Alaska) all compose songs in the folk spirit that describe people, events, observations, and circumstances of contemporary life.

Greg Brown. Photograph by Sandy Dyas.
Courtesy of Red House Records.

Country rock music mixes country chords and themes with rock rhythms. In the 1970s, groups like the Eagles brought country-rock music to mainstream audiences and radio stations across North America. Their music became popular on FM radio, which tended to feature an alternative to mainstream popular music. From the southern United States, musicians created another sound that mixed country music with blues, and rock rhythms, and the result was southern rock music, featured by bands like the Allman Brothers, Marshall Tucker Band, and Lynyrd Skynyrd.

Hard rock, or heavy metal, is louder, stronger, more intense rock music with faster rhythms. The performances feature extravagant light shows, huge speakers and smoke, and movement across the stage. Lyrics are often buried under the loud sound. Some hard rock bands from the 1970s into the 2000s are Grand Funk Railroad, Led Zeppelin, Aerosmith, Pearl Jam, and Creed.

Bonus Challenge: Research an Electrophone Pick an electrophone and investigate its origins, how it works, and what kind of sound it makes. Some electrophones are the electric guitar, bass guitar, drum machine, organ, synthesizer, digital sampler, electric violin, electric flute, and electric saxophone. Offer a written or oral report.

Aerosmith. AP/World Wide Photos. Used by permission.

Disco music became a popular form of dance music in the 1970s. Disco is recorded music played by disc jockeys (people who play records) as opposed to live musicians. Disco music has a strong beat for dancing with a backup of electronic guitars, pianos, basses, drums, and synthesizers. During the "disco period" many live musicians were out of work because dance clubs across North America played recorded music instead.

Jazz-rock mixes rock rhythms with jazz chord structures and arrangements. Blood Sweat & Tears and Chicago used horn sections (saxophones and trumpets) with electric guitars, bass, and drums to create this high-energy sound. Steely Dan introduced sophisticated lyrics, chords, and rhythms in this jazz-rock style. The music has a polished flair.

Punk rock musicians played hard with fast-driving rhythms and lyrics. Like many forms of alternative music, punk music expresses themes that are often antisocial and anti-establishment, and also rebellious against disco, popular, and other mainstream music. By the 1980s, a variety of American punk groups were gaining mainstream recognition, including Blondie, the Ramones, and the Clash. Bands like the Talking Heads, Devo, and the B-52s expanded on this style, which later came to be called "new wave" music. New wave emphasized driving rhythms with sophisticated lyrics and musical structures.

Bonus Challenge: Families of Instruments Group the instruments mentioned in this lesson into instrument families: chordophones, membranophones, aerophones, idiophones, and electrophones.

The Ramones

Rap music evolved from the hip-hop culture of New York City, where people gathered at block parties and shared their own raps. "Rapping" is speaking in rhyme to the rhythm of a beat. Rap evolved throughout the 1980s into the new millennium with groups like Run-D.M.C. and Public Enemy, from New York, TuPac Shakur and Cypress Hill, from Los Angeles, and Arrested Development, from Georgia (see Lesson 22: Rap Music).

Grunge music emerged in Seattle, Washington, in the early 1990s, among other musicians reacting against mainstream popular music and culture. They used strong guitar playing, heavy drumming, and lyrics that are often rebellious and strong. Nirvana, Pearl Jam, Alice in Chains, and Soundgarden are some of the most well-known grunge bands.

The influence of rock music has spread all over the world and evolved into a variety of styles influenced by a variety of cultures. Rock music created by Latin Americans, Native Americans, Cajuns, and Asians are just some examples of rock music being performed across America today.

Bonus Challenge: Pick a Rock Style of Music Individually or in groups, pick one of the styles mentioned in this lesson: rock 'n' roll, doo-wop, folk rock, surf rock, country, hard rock, disco, jazz-rock, punk rock, or rap. Read more about its roots, how it developed, and some of the musicians who played in that style. Listen to the music. Offer a written or oral report with illustrations, photos, and CD samples.

Name _____   Date _____

Rock Music Quiz

Instructions: After reading the **Rock Music** student handout, answer these questions (use back of page if necessary).

1. From which American music style did **rock 'n' roll** derive?

2. Why were the first **rock 'n' roll** musicians to be played on the radio European-Americans?

3. Write something about as many of the branches of rock music as you can:

   Motown music

   Folk rock

   Country rock

   Hard rock

   Disco

   Jazz-rock

   Punk rock

   Rap music

   Grunge music

Rock Music Quiz: Answer Key

1. From which American music style did **rock 'n' roll** derive?

    AFRICAN-AMERICAN BLUES, RHYTHM AND BLUES.

2. Why were the first **rock 'n' roll** musicians to be played on the radio European-Americans?

    ALTHOUGH AFRICAN AMERICANS WERE THE FIRST TO PLAY ROCK 'N' ROLL MUSIC, RECORD COMPANIES AND RADIO STATIONS DID NOT PROMOTE THEIR MUSIC IN GREAT NUMBERS BECAUSE THE LAWS AND CUSTOMS OF THE 1950s RESTRICTED THEM. PEOPLE IN THE MUSIC INDUSTRY, HOWEVER, RECOGNIZED THE VALUE OF THEIR MUSIC AND HIRED EUROPEAN-AMERICAN MUSICIANS TO "COVER" OR PERFORM THE MUSIC OF AFRICAN AMERICANS. IN THIS WAY THE MUSIC WAS HEARD BY MAINSTREAM AMERICA.

3. Write something about as many of the branches of rock music as you can:

    Motown music: MOTOWN RECORDS FEATURED SOUL AND FUNK MUSICIANS. THEY BECAME VERY POPULAR ON MAINSTREAM RADIO IN THE 1960s AND 1970s.

    Folk rock: COMBINES FOLK MUSIC WITH ROCK-STYLE RHYTHMS AND CHORDS. INCLUDES TRADITIONAL FOLK SONGS AND NEW SONGS COMPOSED BY MODERN PERFORMERS. HARMONY SINGING. EXAMPLES ARE THE BYRDS, SIMON AND GARFUNKEL, JONI MITCHELL, JOAN BAEZ, BOB DYLAN, BRUCE COCKBURN, ANI DIFRANCO, GREG BROWN, AND JEWEL.

    Country rock: MIXES COUNTRY CHORDS AND THEMES WITH ROCK RHYTHMS AND FASTER TEMPOS. GROUPS INCLUDE THE EAGLES, MARSHALL TUCKER BAND, AND LYNYRD SKYNYRD.

    Hard rock: ALSO CALLED HEAVY METAL. IT'S LOUDER, STRONGER, MORE INTENSE ROCK MUSIC WITH FASTER RHYTHMS. AN EXAMPLE OF A BAND IS GRAND FUNK RAILROAD.

    Disco: POPULAR IN THE 1970s. DISCO IS RECORDED MUSIC PLAYED BY DISC JOCKEYS (PEOPLE WHO PLAY RECORDS) AS OPPOSED TO LIVE MUSICIANS. IT HAS STRONG BEAT FOR DANCING. IS PLAYED ON ELECTRIC GUITARS, PIANOS, BASSES, DRUMS, AND SYNTHESIZERS.

Rock Music Quiz: Answer Key (continued)

Jazz-rock: MIXES ROCK RHYTHMS WITH JAZZ CHORD STRUCTURES AND ARRANGEMENTS. GROUPS INCLUDE BLOOD SWEAT AND TEARS, CHICAGO, AND STEELY DAN.

Punk rock: HARD, FAST-DRIVING RHYTHMS AND LYRICS, OFTEN EXPRESSING THEMES THAT ARE ANTISOCIAL AND ANTI-ESTAB-LISHMENT. PUNK REBELLED AGAINST DISCO MUSIC. AMERICAN MUSICIANS INCLUDE BLONDIE, THE RAMONES, TALKING HEADS, THE CLASH, DEVO, AND THE B-52's.

Rap music: EVOLVED FROM THE HIP-HOP CULTURE IN NEW YORK CITY. RAP IS SPEAKING IN RHYME TO THE RHYTHM OF A BEAT. EVOLVED IN THE 1980s. MAJOR RAPPERS ARE RUN-D.M.C., PUBLIC ENEMY, CYPRESS HILL, AND ARRESTED DEVELOPMENT.

Grunge music: CAME OUT OF SEATTLE, WASHINGTON, IN THE EARLY 1990s. STRONG GUITAR PLAYING, HEAVY DRUMMING, LYRICS THAT WERE OFTEN REBELLIOUS AND HARSH. GROUPS INCLUDE NIRVANA, PEARL JAM, ALICE IN CHAINS, AND SOUNDGARDEN.

♪ Lesson 22. Rap

Lesson Overview

Rap music originated on the streets of New York City. It developed in the 1970s within the inner-city hip-hop culture. It was first played at house parties and block parties in African-American neighborhoods, but then spread into the mainstream through radio and record sales. It has emerged in the 2000s as one of the most widely played musical forms in the world. East Coast "Old School" rap is honest and fun with clever lyrics and play on words. Women rappers speak from a woman's perspective. West Coast "gansta" rap brings out rougher themes. Southern rap has the characteristic of strong bass sounds, with some groups taking on social change as a major theme. *Important: Rap lyrics often contain language and themes with profanity and adult subjects. Some of the rap artists mentioned in this lesson fit into this category. Song titles and rappers' names are offered here as references representing the genre, but carefully screen any rap you plan to play for its school appropriateness.*

Vocabulary. Rap music, deejay (DJ), turntable, scratching, rap, emcee (MC), improvise, compose, turntablism, sample, digital sampler, electrophone.

Purpose. To offer an overview of rap music as it developed in North America.

Preparation. Read the student handout **Rap Music** to familiarize yourself with the material. Preview the CD sample (cue in student handout) and have the CD ready for playing with the students. Consider having additional music samples available to enhance the lesson. *Be sure to preview the examples!* Be prepared to do some or all of the following activities. Also make sure that each student has a music notebook for keeping handouts and activity sheets.

Materials

- **Rap Music** student handout *(following)*
- **Rap Music Quiz** *(following)*
- **Rap Music Quiz Answer Key** *(following)*
- **Music Vocabulary** activity sheet *(Appendix)*
- **My Opinion Page** activity sheet *(Appendix)*
- **Songs as Poetry** activity sheet *(Appendix)*
- **Great American Musicians!** activity sheet *(Appendix)*
- **Music on the Map** activity sheet *(Appendix)*
- **Music notebooks**
- **CD music** example on accompanying CD; cue in student handout
- **Additional music selections**

Activities

- Pass out the **Rap Music** handout for students to read silently or aloud as a group. Afterwards, have students put the handout in their music notebooks. *[Link to language arts, history, geography, social studies.]*

- Give the **Rap Music Quiz** to assess student understanding of the lesson.

- Go over the vocabulary at the top of the student handout before or after reading the text. Refer to the glossary for definitions. *Suggestion:* Include these words in a regular class vocabulary lesson, or pass out flashcards with a vocabulary word on one side and the definition on the other and allow students to drill each other. Use the **Music Vocabulary** activity sheets to write out definitions. *[Link to language arts.]*

- Offer the **Vocabulary Challenge.** Students pick some or all of the words in this lesson's vocabulary list to use in a paragraph, essay, short story, or poem. *[Link to language arts.]*

- **Discuss.** Before reading the student handout, discuss what students already know about the rap music. Read the student handout and discuss it again, letting students add what they've learned. *[Link to language arts, social studies.]*

- **Bonus Challenge: Research a Synthesizer or Digital Sampler.** Have students choose a synthesizer or digital sampler to research. Investigate its origins, how it works, and any other interesting or important information. Have them prepare a written or oral report.

- **The Science of Music: Electronic Instruments Are Electrophones.** Electronic instruments belong to a family of instruments called electrophones—instruments that use electronics to make sound. A section in the student handout describes electrophones. *Activity:* Bring in any electronic instrument (small electronic keyboards are easy to find and inexpensive) and experiment making sounds with it. Some electrophones are the organ, synthesizer, digital sampler, drum machine, electric violin, electric flute, and electric saxophone. Listen to the sounds they make. Compare the electric instrument to an acoustic instrument (an instrument that uses no electricity). For example, compare the sound of an electric guitar to an acoustic guitar, an organ to a piano, electric violin to an acoustic violin, and so on. *Suggestion:* Consider inviting a professional musician, parent, or student who plays electronic instruments to demonstrate; or visit a music class that has keyboards, or go to a live performance featuring electronic music. *[Link to science.]*

- **Bonus Challenge: Research an Electrophone.** Pick an electrophone and investigate its origins, how it works, and what kind of sound it makes. Some electrophones are electric guitar, bass guitar, drum machine, organ, synthesizer, and digital sampler.

- **Bonus Challenge: Families of Instruments.** Group the instruments mentioned in this lesson into instrument families: chordophones, membranophones, aerophones, idiophones, and electrophones. (See Unit Two, Lesson 10: Instruments of the Orchestra.) *[Link to science.]*

Extension Activities

For step-by-step directions and activity sheets, see the appendix.

- **My Opinion Page.** Offer students a chance to freely express their own opinions about the music they hear. *[Link to language arts, critical thinking.]*

- **Illustrate the Music.** Students illustrate a song or piece of music by drawing or painting their ideas of what the music "looks" like visually. *[Link to language arts, visual arts.]*

- **Songs as Poetry.** Students examine rap lyrics for their poetic nature. *[Link to language arts.]*

- **Great American Musicians!** Introduce students to American musicians whose talents have made them notable. *[Link to language arts, history.]*

- **Music on the Map.** Create a map and legend showing musically important places, such as musicians' birthplaces and music hot spots mentioned in the lesson. *[Link to geography.]*

- **Invite a Music Expert.** Invite a rap musician to visit your class and share his or her instrument and musical talent with the students. Plan ahead, because musicians' schedules are often established far in advance. Many professional musicians already work with students and have a planned program to offer—ask about this. Remember that professional musicians might request payment, because this is how they earn their living. Also consider taking students to hear a live performance, or show a video performance. *[Link to social studies.]*

- Because of copyright issues, modern songs are difficult to obtain for the accompanying CD. Consider bringing in **additional selections of music** from other sources to expand the music sample offerings. Read the song selections mentioned in each musician's biography for additional music ideas. Search the Internet, library, or local music store to find them. *Be sure to preview lyrics!*

Name _____ Date _____

Arrested Development.
Courtesy of Arrested Development.

Rap Music

Vocabulary: *rap music, deejay (DJ), turntable, scratching, rap, emcee (MC), improvise, compose, turntablism, sample, digital sampler, electrophone*

Note: Rap lyrics often contain language and themes with profanity and adult subjects. Some of the rap artists mentioned in this lesson perform these kinds of songs. Carefully screen any rap music for its appropriateness.

Rap music came from the hip-hop culture, which emerged in New York's inner city in the 1970s. The culture involved people gathering at house parties and block parties to rap, emcee, deejay, and break-dance. Hip-hop culture is also known for the graffiti art that inner-city artists created with spray paint on subway cars and the sides of buildings.

At a typical hip-hop party, a **deejay** (DJ, or disc jockey) spins records on **turntables**, using his or her hand to stop the record OR play it backwards or forwards so that the sound from the record becomes a rhythm instrument, and other background accompaniment. This method of manipulating the record is called **scratching**.

A **rap** is speaking in rhyme to the rhythm of the beat. An **emcee** (MC, or master of ceremonies) is the person who raps. Emcees rap about their experiences or their surroundings, or express what they're feeling or going through at the moment. There are freestyle raps, where the person both **improvises** (makes it up as they go along) and **composes** raps that are memorized ahead of time.

In the hip-hop culture, rap can be used as an outlet for aggression. Instead of "fighting it out" rappers take their issues to the microphone where they have "rap battles." Rap battles allow people to take turns telling somebody off, or showing each other up somehow. It is the clever use of words and rhyme that determines the winner. Rap battles are nonviolent and let people express anger with words, rather than weapons. Sometimes an entire "rap crew" of emcees from one neighborhood will get together with another rap crew from another neighborhood and take turns trying to "out rap" each other.

East Coast "Old School" Rap

The first rappers recited words that reflected urban street life. There were no rules about what was said. They could rap about a friend, a feeling, or a situation. Rapping gave people an opportunity to express what was important to them and to have an audience for their viewpoints. Old school rap was all about being honest, entertaining, and clever with words.

Old school rap didn't hit the mainstream until 1979, when Sugarhill Gang's song "Rapper's Delight" became a hit single on mainstream radio. Their raps were simple, laid-back, and performed over disco music, funk, and synthesized sounds. Groups like Sugarhill Gang and Grandmaster Flash & the Furious Five from New York became leaders of this style of rap.

In the 1980s, many of the raps became "hardened" and political. Run-D.M.C. used strong drum and digital samples of electric guitar to intensify their sound and create more of a rock beat with their raps. Their music crossed over to rock audiences, which helped spread the music to the mainstream. Public Enemy came on the scene with a heavy, harsher sound. They rapped about social and political issues affecting African-American communities and experimented with unusual sounds—like screaming sirens, famous speeches, strong pulsing beats, and funk music accompaniment.

Turntablism. Turntablism is the craft of spinning records on turntables and manipulating them with your hands to create new sounds, also known as *scratching.* A turntablist can create elaborate music with unusual sounds and rhythms that can be used as background to rappers or as compositions by themselves. Hip-hop turntablists, or deejays, usually use two turntables and go back and forth between them, mixing the music from both records into one sound. Deejays use their own imaginations to come up with the music they create, and they spend a lot of time picking out new rhythms and sounds. "Beat juggling" is when the deejay manipulates the beats from two different records to create a new and different beat. "Digging" is looking for records at garage sales, used stores, or wherever to broaden one's collection. Turntablism is practiced by deejays from many cultures, with many genres of music.

Queen Latifah (March 18, 1970–). Born Dana Owens in New Jersey, Queen Latifah is a rap singer, artist, composer, and actor. She grew up in New Jersey's inner city and recorded her first rap at age eighteen. She immediately showed a strong personality and her songs were sophisticated and energetic with intelligent messages. She is an advocate for African-American people, and offers a positive role model for girls and women. Queen Latifah formed her own record company in 1993 and released her own music on that label. In 1994 she won a Grammy Award for Best Rap Solo. She has acted on television and in movies, and continues to record music in the new millennium. Her CD recordings include *All Hail the Queen* (1989), *Latifah's Had It Up 2 Here* (1991), *U.N.I.T.Y.* (1993), *Order in the Court* (1998), and *Go Ahead: She's a Queen* (2002).

Female rappers often call attention to women's issues. Women rappers like Queen Latifah and the duo Salt-N-Pepa gained respect in the rap world for their powerful lyrics and strong messages for women.

Queen Latifah. Courtesy of Queen Latifah.

Science of Music: Digital Samplers. A **digital sampler** is a computer microprocessor that records, or makes a "sample" of, a live sound, and then plays it back on a keyboard. The process involves recording a natural sound and changing it into a digital impulse called a *sampled sound,* then assigning it to a key on the keyboard where it can be played. Instruments like guitars and drums can be sampled and played back, as well as the human voice, trash can lids, barking dogs, squealing children, and broken glass. Digital samplers allow musicians to play back almost any sound.

The Science of Music: Electronic Instruments Are Electrophones. Electronic instruments belong to a family of instruments called **electrophones**—instruments that use electronics to make sound. Examples are synthesizers, digital samplers, organs, electric keyboards, electric guitars, and other amplified instruments. Synthesizers turn an electric signal into a musical sound. Digital samplers make copies of sounds and play them back on a keyboard. Electric pianos, guitars, violins, flutes, and so on, use small microphones called pickups to pick up the sound from inside the instrument and amplify it.

West Coast "Gansta" Rap

In the 1980s, rappers in California were developing a "West Coast" style of rap, also called "gansta" rap. Performers like Ice-T, NWA, Ice Cube with Dr. Dre, TuPac Shakur, and Cypress Hill were performing a new, more aggressive rap with harsh lyrics about street life and gang-related lifestyle. Dr. Dre's *G-funk* used funk music **samples** and concentrated on slow grooves, synthesized sounds, and booming bass rhythms. The Pharcyde from San Francisco performed raps with humorous lyrics.

Southern Rap

In the late 1980s, rap emerged in the southern United States that featured a strong drum and bass sound—so pulsating, so deep and loud, that it rattled windows and blew out car speakers. 2 Live Crew from Miami stirred up controversy with harsh themes and language that were eventually banned in Florida, and resulted in a national countermovement addressing the issue of free speech. Tag Team from Atlanta had the hit "Whoop! There It Is," but the first southern rap group to become successful based on their music rather than controversy was Arrested Development. This group came on the scene with uplifting lyrics and a positive message. Other Atlanta groups that followed were OutKast and Goodie Mob.

Bonus Challenge: Research an Electrophone Pick an electrophone and investigate its origins, how it works, and what kind of sound it makes. Some electrophones are the electric guitar, bass guitar, drum machine, organ, synthesizer, digital sampler, electric violin, electric flute, and electric saxophone. Offer a written or oral report.

Arrested Development. Arrested Development, from Georgia, performed between 1992 and 1994, with founder Speech (Todd Thomas), DJ Headliner (Timothy Barnwell), singer-dancer-poet Aerle Taree (Taree Jones), dancer Montsho Eshe (Temelca Gaither), singer Dionne Farris, and singer-drummer Rasa Don (Donald Jones). Arrested Development used positive lyrics to rap about African-American history, issues, and political views. Their music was positive and uplifting. One of their songs, "Children Play with the Earth," is a call for children to return their attention to the natural world. The group recorded several albums together, won Grammy Awards, and enjoyed widespread popularity. Their CD recordings are *Three Years, Five Months, and Two Days in the Life Of . . . .* and *Zingalamaduni.*

In the years since its beginnings in hip-hop, many more styles of rap have emerged—Latino rap, alternative rap, jazz rap, pop rap, and Native American rap. Each style expresses something different about the culture and the people rapping it. Rap is storytelling. It paints a picture of a feeling, or experience, or lifestyle. It is music that allows a perspective to be expressed and heard.

Litefoot is a Native American rap artist who raps about the conditions of life for his people and his own personal experiences. His message often encourages youth to grow up to do well with their lives. (See Unit One, Lesson 4: Contemporary Native American Music.)

Litefoot is performing in a genre that is forever expanding, following both the traditions of his heritage and the influences of the cultures around him. He, like all rappers, is a storyteller expressing the conditions of his life and the conditions of his culture.

♫ CD track #35. Listen to "Vision Quest," an example of Native American rap, by Litefoot.

Song and recording: "Vision Quest" written by Litefoot. Copyright © and ℗ 1998 Red Vinyl Records.

Bonus Challenge: Families of Instruments Group the instruments mentioned in this lesson into instrument families: chordophones, membranophones, aerophones, idiophones, and electrophones.

Name _____   Date _____

Rap Music Quiz

Instructions: After reading the **Rap Music** student handout, answer these questions (use back of the page if necessary).

1. What is **rap music?**

2. What is **turntablism?**

3. Write something about as many of these styles of rap music as you can:

    East Coast "Old School" rap

    West Coast "gansta" rap

    Southern rap

Listen to Learn

Rap Music Quiz: Answer Key

1. What is **rap music**?

   RAP EMERGED FROM THE HIP-HOP CULTURE IN NEW YORK CITY IN THE 1970s. RAP IS SPEAKING IN RHYME TO THE RHYTHM OF THE BEAT BY A RAPPER, OR EMCEE (MC). IT INVOLVES A DEEJAY (DJ) WHO "SCRATCHES" OR SPINS RECORDS ON TURNTABLES AS ACCOMPANIMENT.

2. What is **turntablism**?

   TURNTABLISM IS THE CRAFT OF SPINNING RECORDS ON TURNTABLES AND MANIPULATING THEM WITH YOUR HANDS TO CREATE NEW SOUNDS, ALSO KNOWN AS "SCRATCHING." IT IS USED TO ACCOMPANY RAPPERS, OR CAN BE PLAYED BY ITSELF AS ITS OWN COMPOSITION. IT INVOLVES "BEAT JUGGLING" (MANIPULATING THE BEATS FROM TWO DIFFERENT RECORDS TO CREATE A NEW AND DIFFERENT BEAT). TURNTABLISM IS PRACTICED BY DEEJAYS (DJs) IN RAP MUSIC.

3. Write something about as many of the styles of rap music as you can:

   East Coast "Old School" rap: BEGAN AT HOUSE PARTIES AND BLOCK PARTIES IN NEW YORK CITY IN THE 1970s. ITS URBAN THEMES WERE HONEST, ENTERTAINING, AND CLEVER WITH WORDS. PERFORMERS INCLUDE SUGARHILL GANG, GRAND MASTER FLASH & THE FURIOUS FIVE, SALT-N-PEPA, AND QUEEN LATIFAH.

   West Coast "gansta" rap: WEST COAST RAP TENDS TO BE MORE AGGRESSIVE AND HARSH THAN EAST COAST RAP. THE THEMES ARE OFTEN GANG-RELATED. PERFORMERS INCLUDE ICE-T, TUPAC SHAKUR, AND CYPRESS HILL.

   Southern rap: CHARACTERIZED BY DEEP DRUM AND BASS SOUNDS THAT RATTLE WINDOWS. 2 LIVE CREW'S MUSIC WAS BANNED IN FLORIDA FOR ITS HARSH THEMES AND LANGUAGE. ARRESTED DEVELOPMENT OFFERED POSITIVE LYRICS AND MESSAGES.

Extension Activities and Teacher Directions

The lessons in this book include extension activities for further exploration and deeper understanding. Some are designed as ongoing activities that carry from lesson to lesson, like **Great American Musicians!** and **Music on the Map,** which involve gathering information to create an end-of-unit compilation. Other activities can be used to enhance any single lesson. Following are step-by-step directions for the extension activities that appear in the lessons and some new ones.

Additional Music Resources

Throughout this book, consider bringing in additional selections of music from other sources. Read the song selections mentioned in each musician's biography for ideas. Search the Internet, library, or local music store to find selections.

A Musical Story

The goal of this activity is to produce a musical skit or play inspired by information in the student handouts. *Step 1:* Divide students into groups of at least three players. *Step 2:* Each group brainstorms for a story idea related to something from this unit. The story must have a musical plot and include a musical element, such as a song, melody, rhythm, dance, lip-synch, percussion, or instrument accompaniment. Some ideas are a musical experience, a musical person, an event in music history, or the history of an American dance or song. Extra research into the subject may be necessary. *Step 3:* The student teams write the story, beginning to end, as a narrated piece. (By using a narrator, students don't have to memorize lines.) They edit and revise as necessary. *Step 4:* Each group decides on a narrator, actors, singers, and dancers. Those who don't want to perform can work on props or design or build the set. *Step 5:* Groups rehearse their stories with props and instruments. The narrator reads while the actors-singers-dancers play out the story. *Step 6:* Consider performing the stories for parents, other students, or at a hospital or senior center. *(Link to language arts.)*

Call-and-Response Singing

This activity practices call-and-response, or antiphonal, singing. With call-and-response, the singing goes back and forth between two people or groups. This can mean two groups taking turns as two choruses, or a leader singing first and a chorus responding. The leader "calls" and the group "responds." *Step 1:* Form two groups—either with one leader and one chorus or two choruses; the leader must be able to lead a song or recitation (consider having the teacher go first to demonstrate). *Step 2:* Choose a song or spoken recitation to lead. Recitations are a good alternative for shy or inexperienced singers. *Suggestion:* Choose any of the songs mentioned in these handouts, or choose a familiar song. *Step 3:* Follow basic directions offered in **How to Teach a Song** *(following)* for call-and-response singing. *(Link to singing.)*

Dogrib Hand Game

This is a guessing game from the Dogrib First Nations tribe in the Subarctic region. *Step 1:* Divide students into groups of three or four, making sure you have an even number of groups. *Step 2:* Invite each group to choose another group as their opposing team. *Step 3:* One group begins as the "hiders" while the other begins as the "guessers." The hiders put their hands behind their backs and shuffle a rock back and forth between their hands, out of sight from the guessers. *Step 4:* The guessers take turns guessing who has the rock at any one time. If someone picks the correct person, the players switch, and the guessers become the hiders. *Suggestion:* Invite some students to play drums and rattles while the guessers and hiders play the game, which is the Dogrib tradition. Encourage the musicians to keep a steady beat, which may get louder or softer, faster or slower, to accompany the hiding and guessing. *(Link to rhythm.)*

Encyclopedia of Musical Instruments

The ultimate goal of this activity is to create an encyclopedia containing all the instruments mentioned in this unit, and in this book. Consider using **Research an Instrument** *(following)* as a guide for each entry. Illustrate each instrument with a drawing or cutout from the picture pages *(see lesson handouts)*. As students complete their research, compile all the work into an "Encyclopedia of Musical Instruments" notebook. Copy all the research and distribute one compilation to each student. *(Link to visual arts, language arts, science.)*

Families of Instruments

The goal of this activity is to divide the instruments mentioned in the lesson into instrument families grouped according to how they make sound—that is, chordophones, aerophones, idiophones, and membranophones. *Step 1:* Pass out additional copies of the lesson's picture pages (for example, the **Folk Music Instruments Picture Page** in Lesson 6). Give one picture page to each student, or group of students, or allow them to draw the instruments on separate pieces of paper using the picture page as a model. *Step 2:* Students write the instrument name and family group on the lines provided under each picture. *Step 3:* Students cut out each picture (including name and group) and divide the pictures into the family group piles. *Step 4:* As a class, discuss instrument family groups and the characteristics of each. If desired, let students make flashcards with the picture on one side and the name and family group on the other. Allow students to drill each other, or do this as a class. Consider playing **Instrument Shuffle** *(following)* to help in memorizing and understanding the different family groups. *Step 5:* Copy and pass out the **Families of Instruments: Membranophones** (Activity Sheet A), **Families of Instruments: Idiophones** (Activity Sheet B), **Families of Instruments: Aerophones** (Activity Sheet C), and **Families of Instruments: Chordophones** (Activity Sheet D) *(following)* or write these names on the chalkboard, or poster board, for the entire class to see. Invite students to attach the pictures to the correct sheets, board, or poster. *Step 6:* Put finished pages into music notebooks in a section titled "Instrument Families." *Answer key:* Follow these guidelines: *membranophones* are instruments with stretched membranes and include drums; *idiophones* are instruments that are shaken or beaten and include rattles, shakers, and rasps; *aerophones* are blown instruments and include flutes, horns, and whistles; *chordophones* are stringed instruments and include mouth bows, guitars, violins, and cellos. See also the **Science of Music** sections in the Lesson 10 student handouts for a brief overview of each family. *(Link to science, language arts, visual arts.)*

Great American Musicians!

The goal of this activity is to introduce students to American musicians whose talents have made them notable. Consider assembling student work into a class compilation after completing the unit. *Step 1:* Individually or in groups, students pick a musician to learn about—one mentioned in this lesson or one of their own choice from the genre being studied. *Step 2:* Research the musician's life—look at childhood, training, experiences, accomplishments, anecdotes. *Step 3:* Listen to music samples by that musician if possible (search the library or Internet, or get CDs). *Step 4:* Answer questions on the **Great American Musicians!** activity sheet *(following)*. *Step 5:* Put completed sheets in music notebooks. *To extend this activity:* Allow students to prepare one or all of the following: a biography, discography, song lyric compilation, oral report with music samples, poster, props, or any project that investigates the life and music of a great American musician. Make copies of all musician biographies for a class compilation. *(Link to language arts, history, social studies.)*

Illustrate the Music

The goal of this activity is to illustrate a song or piece of music by drawing or painting student ideas of what the music "looks" like visually. *Step 1:* Choose, or allow students to choose, a song or instrumental piece from the lesson. *Step 2:* Read the lyrics, if applicable, and if it is on the CD, listen to it. While they listen, ask students to imagine some images conjured by the song: Is there a story to illustrate? Are there people or animals in the piece? Does the music convey a mood or emotion? Does the title offer any ideas? *Step 3:* Invite students to write, color, draw, or paint their ideas on paper, preferably while the music is playing. *To extend this activity:* Invite students to do this activity at home with their own choices of music and then bring their illustrations to class to put into their music notebooks. Also consider illustrating a song in a short book. *(Link to language arts, visual arts.)*

Illustrate the Music: *Grand Canyon Suite*

The goal of this activity is to illustrate Ferde Grofé's *Grand Canyon Suite*. *Step 1:* Locate a recording of this piece of music. Search the Internet, local music store, a friend's collection. *Step 2:* Note the five movements of the suite: "Sunrise," "Painted Desert," "On the Trail," "Sunset," and "Cloudburst." Note that when the music is playing, the movements are separated by silence, or long pauses. Talk about the desert at sunrise, at sunset, and during a cloudburst. Have students describe the colors, the scenery, the animals, the wind, and the smells. Show pictures of the Grand Canyon. *Step 3:* Pass out paper (five pieces, one for each movement), color pencils, paint, or markers. *Step 4:* Play "Sunrise" (first movement) and allow students to paint or draw a desert sunrise or anything else that the music inspires, while it is playing. Keep working until the movement ends. *Step 5:* Make another illustration for each movement. *Step 6:* The completed group of illustrations will depict the different stages of desert life. *Suggestion:* With younger students, consider fading the music when you notice they are finished or distracted, and move onto the next movement. *(Link to visual arts, geography.)*

Instrument Shuffle

The goal of this activity is to deepen understanding and recognition of the instrument family groups. *Step 1:* With a pile of instrument pictures in front of each student *(see **Families of Instruments**, preceding)*, a leader calls out one of the instrument family names (for example, "Membranophones!") and asks everyone to hold up a picture of an instrument from that family. Correct those who miss. *Step 2:* Repeat this for each family group until students are comfortable and are getting it right consistently. (See the answer key in the directions for **Families of Instruments**, preceding.) *Suggestion:* Consider doing this activity at the end of the unit after compiling a stack of flashcards of all the instruments mentioned in this unit. Invite students to be leaders in calling out the family names and doing the correcting. *(Link to language arts, science.)*

Invite a Music Expert

Invite a musician who plays the type of music described in the unit to visit your class and share his or her instrument and musical talent with the students. Some resources for locating musicians are the Internet, local music and arts organizations, tribal organizations, friends, students, parents. Plan ahead because musicians' schedules are often established far in advance. Tell the musician about the context of your lesson, how much time to plan for, and what you'd like him or her to do. Many professional musicians have a planned school program to offer—ask about this. Also, expect to pay a fee because this is how many earn their living. Also consider taking students to hear a live performance, or show a video. *(Link to social studies.)*

Music on the Map

The goal of this activity is to create a map and legend showing musically important places, such as musicians' birthplaces and music hot spots mentioned in the lesson. This activity works for all lessons that mention place names. *Step 1:* Before each lesson, students pull out their **Music on the Map** activity sheet *(following)*. *Step 2:* Encourage students to notice place names mentioned in the student handout and make a small circle in which to write a number on that spot on the map. Write a number inside each circle. *Step 3:* For example, 2 = New Orleans, birthplace of jazz, or 6 = New York, birthplace of Eddie Cantor, and so on. Use the map for future study of those places and what musical facts happened there. *Step 4:* Place maps and notes in music notebooks. *Suggestion:* Do this for all the place names mentioned in this unit. *(Link to geography.)*

My Opinion Page

The goal of this activity is to offer students a chance to freely express their own opinions about the music they hear. This activity works with all lessons that offer music examples. *Step 1:* Allow students to choose a song from the lesson, or teachers choose a song that everyone will review, or assign a different song to each student or group of students. *Step 2:* Pass out **My Opinion Page** activity sheet *(following)* for writing opinions about the song or piece of music. *Step 3:* Students listen to the song at least one time through and write their answers. *Suggestion:* Have the attitude that there are no right or wrong answers, only interesting ones. *Note:* Some of the questions on the activity sheet assume a basic knowledge of rhythm and melody. If these terms are unfamiliar to you or your students, consider some advance work using the glossary or other resource, or skip these questions entirely. *(Link to language arts, critical thinking.)*

My Musical Traditions

The goal of this activity is to investigate individual family traditions, including musical ones. *Step 1:* Have students reply to questions on the **My Musical Traditions** activity sheet *(following)*. *Step 2:* Discuss student answers. *Step 3:* Put sheets away in music notebook. *(Link to language arts, social studies.)*

Music in the Movies

This activity invites students to listen to the background music in movies to discover the way music creates mood and emotion. *Step 1:* Discuss how music is used in television and movies. Point out that the music during car chases and fights usually becomes loud, fast, and exciting to match the high-paced images on the screen, or how music becomes soft and slow during sad or love scenes. Introduce the idea that mood in movies is created by what we *see* on the screen and what we *hear* in the background. Note that different instruments have different "effects" on mood—for example, the lively sounds of clarinets and bassoons can create a comical mood, brassy trumpets and trombones create a boisterous mood, and violins and flutes can change the mood to soothing and tender. *Step 2:* Choose a movie to show, making sure it has an appropriate rating and descriptive music. *Suggestion:* Any John Williams soundtrack will provide a good example, such as *Star Wars* (1977), *Who Framed Roger Rabbit?* (1988), or *Spy Kids* (2001). *Step 3:* Pass out the **Music in the Movies** activity sheet (see Lesson 17), which asks students to listen to the music as they watch the movie and write their observations about it. *Step 4:* Discuss what students noticed. *Suggestion:* Consider sending an activity sheet to do at home with a movie of their choice. *(Link to language arts, visual arts.)*

Oral Tradition

The oral tradition is the practice of passing words or songs from one person to another by telling or singing—a practice that has kept songs and stories alive for many generations when most people did not have written language. This activity demonstrates the oral tradition by playing the game "Telephone." *Step 1:* Sit in a circle and announce that this activity is like the game "Telephone." In this version, each student in the circle counts as a "generation." For example, the first student is the "child," the next student is the "parent," the next is the "grandparent," the next is the "great-grandparent," and so on, until every student is named (you may have twenty-five generations, but it will clearly illustrate the concept). *Step 2:* The oldest generation (the first grandparent) begins by whispering a short phrase to the person next to him or her. Keep the phrase simple so that it is easy to remember, such as "The children are sleeping quietly," or "Ask little brother to bring the butter." Each student passes the phrase by whispering to the student next to him or her until it reaches the last student (last generation), who says the phrase aloud to everyone. *Step 3:* Discuss what happened to the phrase as it passed from generation to generation. What did it start out to be? What did it end up to be? Why did it change? How does this process happen in real life? *(Link to social studies.)*

Pick an Opera

The goal is to get to know an American opera—its story line, characters, music, and so on. *Step 1:* Individually or in groups, students pick an opera to learn and write about. Use the **Pick an Opera** activity sheet (see Lesson 17). *Suggested operas: Amahl and the Night Visitors,* by Menotti; *The Tender Land* or *The Second Hurricane,* by Aaron Copland; *Porgy and Bess,* by George Gershwin; *Where the Wild Things Are, The Fantastic Mr. Fox,* or *Higglety Pigglety Pop!* by Oliver Knussen. *Step 2:* Students learn the story line from CD liner notes, Internet, library, or music compilations, and write it down in the space provided. For an

Internet search, look for "name of opera" and "synopsis"—for example, "Porgy and Bess synopsis." *Step 3:* Students list the characters. *Step 4:* They list the recitatives and the arias. *Step 5:* They write any interesting information or anecdotes about the opera or characters. *Step 6:* They listen to the music, if possible. *Step 7:* Students write their opinion about the opera. *Step 8:* Consider a class discussion, or oral or written reports. *Step 9:* Put papers away in music notebooks. *Suggestion:* Compile an "American Opera Notebook" with all student opera reviews. *(Link to language arts.)*

Play Along with *Syncopated Clock*

The goal of this activity is to play along with the ticking clock in *Syncopated Clock,* which offers a clear example of a steady beat. *Step 1:* Locate a recording of *Syncopated Clock,* by Leroy Anderson. Look on the Internet or in a music store, or search your personal collection. *Step 2:* Pass out rhythm sticks, or use pencils, pens, hands clapping, or fingertips on a desk. *Step 3:* Play *Syncopated Clock. Step 4:* Tap along with the rhythm of the clock. Stop when it stops. Pay attention to the beat. Try not to go faster or slower than the beat. Note the sound of the clock alarm in the middle of the piece. *Suggestion:* This activity should be something fun to do without worrying about playing along perfectly with the beat. *(Link to rhythm.)*

Research an Instrument

This activity encourages students to become more intimate with an instrument mentioned in a lesson or in this unit. *Step 1:* Individually, or in groups, students pick an instrument mentioned in the student handout. *Step 2:* Using the Internet, library, encyclopedia, or other references, students research the instrument. They discover its history, what it's made of, how it produces sound, and any interesting facts. *Step 3:* Students offer a written or oral report. *Step 4:* Put written reports in a section of the music notebook marked "Encyclopedia of Musical Instruments." *Suggestion:* Invite students to bring in an actual instrument, photographs, illustrations, and sound examples to demonstrate. *(Link to science, history.)*

Sing a Song

The goal of this activity is to learn simple, singable songs from the lessons. Use this activity as an opportunity to learn more about each musical genre. *Step 1:* Choose a song from the student handout or another source. Also see composer biographies for more suggestions. *Step 2:* Read the lyrics and listen to the audio version on the accompanying CD. Read about the composer. *Step 3:* Teach the song line by line *(see **How to Teach a Song**, following)* or sing along with the CD enough to memorize it. Sing as best as you can, but don't worry about perfection. Simply speaking the words is good enough for some. Remind students to "sing out" when their voices get quieter, and encourage them with "You sound great!" when they do. Singing out makes it more fun. *Step 4:* Keep singing the song on a regular basis. The more it is sung, the more familiar it will become. Consider building a repertoire of songs to sing at some regular music time or music event. Singing helps language development, reading, ability to focus, and it is fun! *(Link to singing, language arts.)*

Songs as Poetry

The goal of this activity is to examine the lyrics of songs for their poetic nature. Students should have some knowledge of *some* elements of poetry: meaning, rhyme, imagery, metaphor, personification, allegory, overstatement, understatement, irony, allusion, rhythm and meter, patterns, alliteration, consonation. *Step 1:* Invite students (individually, in groups, or as a whole class) to pick a song from this lesson to investigate, or pick a song from another source in this genre. *Step 2:* Read the lyrics and listen to the song if possible. *Step 3:* Pass out the **Songs as Poetry** activity sheet *(following)* and talk about the elements of poetry. Invite students to write their own answers. Remind them that they don't have to respond to all the elements of poetry listed on the activity sheet, only the ones they recognize, or that apply. *To extend this activity:* Investigate just one of the elements of poetry in depth—for example, how the composer used metaphor in the song—and describe it. *(Link to language arts.)*

Trace an Ancestor

Most people living in North America are descendents of immigrants who came from other cultures and other countries. The goal of this activity is to trace students' ancestors so they can learn about their cultural backgrounds and explore cultural diversity in the classroom. *Step 1:* Pass out the **Trace an Ancestor** activity sheet *(following)* and go over the questions. Ask students to pick an ancestor to learn about: a grandmother, great-grandmother, great-great-grandfather. Ask parents for suggestions. *Step 2:* Try to learn that person's birthday, place of birth, marriage, and children's names. Consider using the Internet to contact the Church of Latter Day Saints, which has developed an extensive genealogical database. *Step 3:* Describe the country, possibly the town or district this ancestor lived in. *Step 4:* Learn about the traditional music of the country. Look for styles of singing, the instruments, dances, costumes, and other cultural aspects that surrounded the ancestor when he or she lived in the old country. Consider bringing photographs, books, CDs, globes, or maps to show. *(Link to language arts, social studies.)*

How to Teach a Song

One easy way to teach a song is line by line, also called *line singing, call-and-response, the Usual Way,* and *learning by ear.* The leader sings a line, and the group sings back, one line at a time. The idea is to allow students to hear the line sung correctly first, then echo it back, which builds a kind of "muscle memory" of the song. Line singing lets listeners hear and memorize only a small part of the song at a time. Here are the steps to follow:

1. Sing the song, or play it on the CD, once through entirely. Let students hear what the song sounds like. Ask them not to sing, even if some know it, to give everyone a chance to hear it clearly without other voices. Don't use the written lyrics; this is a memorization exercise.

2. Let students know you're going to teach them in the call-and-response style. Tell them you'll sing a line first and that they should echo, and you'll do this for each line of the song. Some students will want to sing when you do. Remind them that in the call-and-response style, the leader sings alone.

3. Sing the first line. Consider pointing to your ear to indicate they should be listening. You may need this cue with some students who will forget. (If you feel hopelessly unable to sing or lead the song—that's OK—try playing it line by line on the CD, pausing between each line.)

4. Ask students to sing the line. Use the words "echo" or "repeat." Consider gesturing toward them to indicate it's their turn. Sometimes it gets confusing about whose turn it is, and the gestures help. It's also helpful if you sing with them so that they can be guided by your voice (or the CD) singing it correctly.

5. Sing or play the next line. Repeat the call-and-response pattern. Sing or play the whole song line by line. Repeat for each line of the song. Use the hand gestures if students get confused.

7. If students have trouble memorizing the words, stop singing and just "speak" each line a few times, line by line.

8. If students have trouble singing on pitch, don't worry about it. Some will not be able to do it, and that's the way it is.

9. After you've sung it line by line, sing it all the way through. Do it another time to cement it. It may not sound great the first time. Sing along with the CD if you want. It takes repetition and practice to develop enough familiarity with the song to sing it well. Give it time.

10. Consider having a regular music time to sing songs. Make it a part of your day, or week. Songs need to be sung again and again in order to become familiar and fun. A regular singing time will help that! Remember that singing helps language development and cognitive development, and it is fun!

Name _____   Date _____

Membranophones

Membranophones are instruments that have a stretchy layer of skin or paper (called a *membrane*) stretched over a container. They are played by hitting, or striking. When you hit the membrane, it vibrates. The vibration sets the air around it in motion, which also sets the container and the air inside the container in motion. Vibrating air is what makes sound! The bigger the container, the more air vibrates, the louder and deeper the sound. Big containers make louder and deeper sounds than little ones. A drum is an example of a membranophone. ***Instructions:*** Draw or attach pictures of membranophones from the lesson onto this page.

Appendix: Extension Activities and Teacher Directions   **393**

Name _____   Date _____

Idiophones

Instruments that are shaken, struck, clapped, or rubbed together to make a sound belong to a family of instruments called idiophones. They can be made from gourds, sticks, rocks, shells, bells, or blocks. The sound is created by the objects slapping or clapping together—like seeds slapping against the inside of a container, shells beating against each other, or wooden sticks scraping together. Beating or rubbing causes the objects to vibrate and that causes the air around them to vibrate, and it's the vibrating air that makes the sound! Rattles and rasps are examples of idiophones. *Instructions:* Draw or attach pictures of idiophones from the lesson onto this page.

Name _____   Date _____

Aerophones

Aerophones are wind-blown instruments. *Aero* has to do with air, *phone* has to do with sound. Air-sound! What all aerophones have in common is that you blow them to make a sound. When you blow, you send a stream of wind into a tube or pipe, creating vibrating air inside. It's the vibrating air that makes the sound. A long or fat tube has more air vibrating inside and the sound is low-pitched. A short or skinny tube has less air vibrating inside and the sound is high-pitched. The holes of a flute are there to change the pitch. When all the holes are covered, the column of air will be long and the sound will be low (because more air is vibrating inside). But if you uncover the holes one by one, the tube of air will get shorter and the sound will get higher (there will be less air vibrating inside). Flutes, whistles, and horns are examples of aerophones. ***Instructions:*** Draw or attach pictures of aerophones from the lesson onto this page.

Name _____ Date _____

Chordophones

Instruments with strings that are plucked or rubbed to make a sound belong to the family of instruments called chordophones. *Chord* has to do with string, and *phone* has to do with sound. String-sound! When a string is plucked or rubbed, it vibrates and moves the air around it. When the vibrating string touches the resonator, the resonator starts to vibrate too, and so does the air inside the resonator. It is the vibrating air that makes sound. Mouth bows, violins, guitars, violas, and harps are examples of chordophones. ***Instructions:*** Draw or attach pictures of chordophones from the lesson onto this page.

Name _____   Date _____

Great American Musicians!

Instructions: In this activity, get to know a great American musician by doing the following.

1. Choose a great American musician from this lesson, or from this same genre, to research. Use the library, Internet, or encyclopedia to gather information.

   Musician's name: _____

2. Listen to a music sample of your musician if possible (radio, CD, Internet).

3. Get to know your musician and answer the following questions:

   What is this person's birthday and place of birth?

   _____

   What are some interesting facts about this person's childhood?

   _____

   _____

   What is this person's musical training or experience?

   _____

   _____

   What are some interesting facts about this musician's music career?

   _____

   _____

4. Use the back of this page to write a paragraph about your musician. Add anything you've discovered in addition to what you've already written here.

Name _____   Date _____

Music on the Map

Instructions: Draw small circles on the map where interesting musical events happened, such as places where famous American musicians were born, where there were musical occurrences of great importance, music regions, and so on. Write a number inside the circle. On another sheet of paper, write the number, the place name, and the important fact that goes with it.

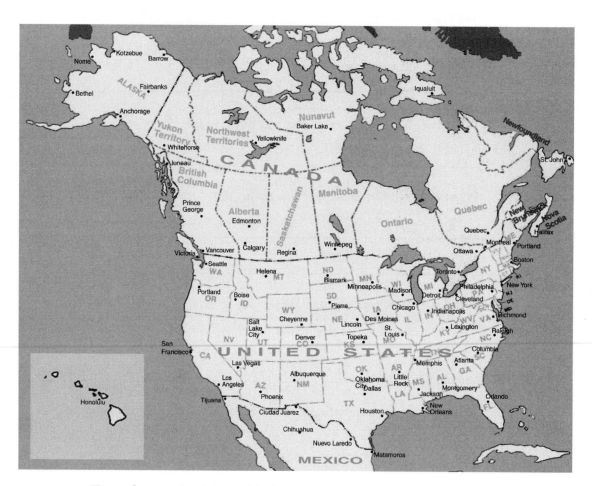

Example: 1 = Louisiana: birthplace of New Orleans jazz.

Name _____   Date _____

Music Vocabulary

Instructions: Use the blank spaces to write the vocabulary words of this lesson and their definitions. Put the completed sheet into your music notebook.

Vocabulary word: **Definition:**

_____   _____

_____   _____

_____   _____

_____   _____

_____   _____

_____   _____

_____   _____

_____   _____

_____   _____

_____   _____

_____   _____

_____   _____

_____   _____

Name _____ Date _____

My Musical Traditions

Traditions are common in all cultures. If you were raised in North America and speak English at home, if you watch American television, play American sports, or watch American movies, then you are influenced by American culture. If you speak more than one language, live in a neighborhood with people from other cultures, or have family members who grew up in other cultures, then you are most likely influenced by their traditions as well. **Instructions:** Answer the following questions to describe some of the traditions in your life. Afterward, put this paper in your music notebook. Use the back of this page if you need to.

1. I was born in (*state or province, country*) _____

    and have spent most of my life living in (*state or province, country*)

    _____ .

2. I speak these languages: _____

3. In my home, these languages are spoken:

    _____

4. I belong to one or more of these ethnic groups (*circle*): Native American, First Nations, European-American, African American, Latin American, Asian-American, Russian-American, Arab-American, other:

    _____

5. Some of my family's traditions are (*examples: family time activities, chores, musical activities, sports, religious or outdoor activities*):

    _____

    _____

6. Some of my family's *musical* traditions are (*examples: the types of music played at home, the music you listen to on CDs or radio, taking music lessons, attending live concerts*):

    _____

    _____

Name_____   Date_____

My Opinion Page

Instructions: Listen to a song or piece of music from the lesson. Listen to the instruments. Listen to the singing style. Listen to the rhythm. Listen to the melody. Listen for what you like and don't like about the music. Then answer these questions (use the back of this page if necessary)

Title of song or piece of music:_____

_____

1. What instruments do you hear? What do you notice about them?

   _____

   _____

2. What do you notice about the singing?

   _____

   _____

3. What do you notice about the rhythm?

   _____

   _____

4. What do you notice about the melody?

   _____

   _____

5. What do you like or dislike about this music?

   _____

   _____

Name _____   Date _____

Songs as Poetry

Instructions: Songs are like poems. They use rhyme, rhythm and meter, and metaphor to create images. In this activity, you will examine a song for its poetic nature. Pick a song from the student handout and then answer the following questions.

Song title: _____

1. Write the lyrics (words) of the song on a separate piece of paper and attach it to this page.
2. What is the song about? Does it describe a feeling? an image? an event? Does it tell a story? Describe what your song is about.
3. Here are terms for some of the elements used in creating poetry. See if you notice any of these elements in the song you've chosen. If you do, write the word (or words) from the song and describe how those words reflect the element. Use the back of this page if necessary.

Rhyme:

_____

_____

Creating imagery:

_____

_____

Metaphor:

_____

_____

Personification:

_____

_____

Songs as Poetry. Activity Sheet continued

Allegory:

_____

_____

Overstatement:

_____

_____

Understatement:

_____

_____

Irony:

_____

_____

Rhythm and meter:

_____

_____

Patterns:

_____

_____

Allusion:

_____

_____

Alliteration:

_____

_____

Consonation:

_____

_____

Name _____   Date _____

Trace an Ancestor

Most people living in North America are the descendents of immigrants from other cultures in other countries. The goal of this activity is to trace one of your ancestors to learn about his or her cultural background. ***Instructions:*** *Step 1:* Pick one of your ancestors to learn about. You might pick a grandmother, great-grandmother, or great-great-grandfather. Ask your parents for suggestions. *Step 2:* See if you can learn that person's birthday, place of birth, marriage, and children's names. *Step 3:* Describe the country, and possibly the town or district, that this ancestor lived in. *Step 4:* Learn about the traditional music of the culture you discover. Look for the style of singing, the instruments, dances, clothing, and other cultural aspects that surrounded your ancestor in his or her place of birth. Consider bringing photographs, books, CDs, globes, or maps to show.

1. Name of ancestor:

   _____

2. From mother's or father's side of the family *(circle one)*:
   mother's side, father's side

3. Birth country of ancestor: _____

4. Ancestor's first language spoken:

   _____

5. Ancestor's birth date: _____

6. Ancestor's marriage date: _____

7. Ancestor's children's names:

   _____

   _____

Trace an Ancestor. Activity Sheet continued

8. What are some of the music styles from your ancestor's place of origin?

_____

_____

_____

_____

9. What are some of the instruments that were played there?

_____

_____

_____

_____

10. What are some of the costumes, dances, and other customs related to the music?

_____

_____

_____

_____

Glossary

a cappella Singing without accompaniment.

accompaniment The music or instruments that play along with the main melody.

accompany To play along with.

accordion A portable instrument that is shaped like a rectangular box and contains a small keyboard; it opens and closes like a bellows; aerophone.

acoustic The natural sound of an instrument or space; no amplification.

acoustic guitar A guitar that is not amplified and features a natural sound; chordophone.

aerophones Instruments that you blow into to make sound, including flutes, whistles, and horns.

anthem A song of praise or devotion, often for one's country or homeland.

antiphonal Singing back and forth between singers or groups; call-and-response.

aria A sophisticated solo song that comments on the story or expresses an emotion; usually accompanied by instruments, performed in opera.

arrangement The written music rearranged for a band or orchestra.

arrhythmic Without a specific rhythm; not rhythmical.

atonal Without a tone center or central key.

bajo sexto A twelve-string, deep-sounding, guitarlike instrument originally from Spain; chordophone.

ballads Songs that tell stories about people, events, history, personal experiences.

banjo A stringed instrument; strings are stretched over a drumlike frame and a neck; chordophone and membranophone.

bar Same as a measure; it contains a group of musical beats.

bass guitar A guitarlike instrument with four strings, same as a double bass but electric; chordophone and electrophone.

beat A unit of music, a tap or strike on a drum, or a note played; what you tap your foot to when you listen to a song.

bebop An up-tempo style of jazz that uses a theme and includes improvised solos by the players.

big band A group of eight to twelve instruments that plays swing-style jazz; these bands were popular in the 1930s and 1940s.

Billboard **charts** *Billboard* is a music industry trade journal that tracks entertainment news, including "charts" of the top-selling records (see *record charts*).

bluegrass music A fast tempo country music performed on acoustic instruments—guitar, banjo, mandolin, fiddle, and bass guitar—that features strong harmony and verse-chorus–style singing. Bluegrass groups also feature "breakdowns," when each instrumentalist takes a turn featuring his or her instrument.

blues A style of music that evolved from African-American spirituals and work songs; uses blue notes (bent notes), certain kinds of chord patterns, call-and-response, and so on.

boogie-woogie A fast tempo, syncopated piano music that evolved from the blues; uses polyrhythms.

brass instruments Horn instruments, including trumpets, trombones, tubas, French horns; aerophones.

Broadway musicals Popular song shows performed on the stages of New York's theater district.

Cajun music A French-based style of music that features singing with accordions and fiddles; developed in Louisiana.

call-and-response When a leader sings and a group or individual responds; two groups singing back and forth.

ceremonial A system of rituals or formal actions connected with an occasion. Native ceremonials usually have singing, instruments, dancing.

chamber music Music written for small groups of classical instruments.

chant A repetitive kind of song sung with vocables or words; may be sung on one pitch or on many.

Chicago blues An evolution of country blues that developed in Chicago.

chord When several pitches are played at once, resulting in harmony.

chord pattern An arrangement of chords into a predictable pattern or structure.

chord structure The arrangement of chords in a predictable structure or pattern.

chordophones Instruments whose sound is made by vibrating strings.

chorus The part of a song that is repeated, usually after each verse; refrain. Also refers to a group of singers.

chromatic scale A set pattern of pitches that moves up by half-steps.

clapper rattle An idiophone that makes a rhythmical sound by slapping or clapping together; may be made from objects such as wood, metal, deer hooves, or bird beaks.

classical music A common term describing European-influenced styles of orchestral music and opera.

comic opera A funny story, or funny stories, acted out and told in song.

compose To create music; it may be written down or remembered in one's head.

composer A person who creates music.

composition A written piece of music.

conceptual Having to do with concepts or ideas rather than visual or physical themes.

concerto A piece of music written for a solo instrument and a full orchestra.

conductor The person who directs, or leads, the orchestra.

contemporary music Music that is played today; modern music.

cool jazz A relaxed style of jazz played on piano, bass, and drums or a solo instrument.

country blues The earliest form of blues to emerge in the South after the Civil War.

country music Music influenced by the traditions of rural America; it has evolved into many modern country styles.

country rock Country rock mixes country themes and chords with rock rhythms and faster tempos; often played with electric guitar, piano, bass, and drums.

country-western music Popular country music; developed in Nashville, Tennessee.

cover song A song that is recorded or sung by someone other than the composer or original performer.

cowboy songs Songs that describe life on the prairie, wagon trains, cattle drives, horses, famous cowboys; sometimes they add cattle calls or are sung to the rhythm of horses' hooves.

deejay (DJ) A person who spins records or otherwise coordinates recorded music for performance; also called a disc jockey.

digital sampler A computer microprocessor that records, or takes a "sample" of, a live sound that can be played back on a keyboard; electrophone.

dissonance When certain pitches played together create a harsh or unpleasant sound.

Dixieland jazz An upbeat style of jazz music originally from New Orleans and revived in the 1940s.

downbeat The first beat in the measure, usually accented for emphasis.

drum An instrument played by striking; usually made from a stretched membrane over a frame or container; membranophone and idiophone.

drumhead The stretched membrane over the frame or container of a drum.

drum machine Electronic device that imitates the sound of live drums; electrophone.

duet A musical composition played or sung by two people.

dulcimer An American stringed instrument usually shaped like an hourglass, played by strumming, striking, or plucking; chordophone.

dynamics The loud and soft parts of a musical composition.

early jazz A style of music that featured wind and rhythm instruments played in an upbeat, syncopated style, with collective improvisation (everyone improvising at the same time) being one of its main characteristics. Later came to be called New Orleans jazz, or Dixieland.

electrophone A musical instrument that uses electricity to make sound.

emcee (MC) In rap music, this is the rapper, the person who talks in rhyme to the rhythm of the beat; also refers to master of ceremonies.

ethnomusicologist A person who studies the music of a culture.

fiddle A stringed instrument, also called a violin or folk violin; chordophone.

field calls Slaves' calls and songs as they worked in the fields.

field holler Another term for field call.

film score Musical compositions performed as background to the action in a film.

finger-picking Using fingers to pluck the strings of an instrument to make sound.

flute A wind-blown instrument that consists of a cylindrical tube with holes; aerophone.

folk music The ethnic music of a culture; the music of ordinary people.

folk opera A story told in song; folk operas are usually about the lives of ordinary people.

folk songs Songs in the folk tradition (see *folk music*).

foot drum A drum played with the feet—for example, stomping on wooden planks placed over a hole; idiophone.

form The structure of a musical composition made of notes, melody, harmony, and rhythm.

frame drum A stretched membrane over a round, bent-wood frame; membranophone.

free jazz A style of jazz that tends to avoid recognizable structure; atonal, arrhythmic.

funk music A mixture of soul music, rock, and jazz; groove-oriented dance music.

fusion A mixture of jazz and rock music that uses electric instruments; groove-oriented; also called jazz-rock.

game songs Songs that accompany games, including skipping songs, jump-rope songs, and so on.

genre A style or type; in music, a style or type of music—rock, jazz, country, blues, for example.

gospel music Sacred music that mixes soulful lyrics with the rhythms and instruments of popular music.

grand opera Opera performed in an elaborate, lavish manner; serious.

guitar A stringed instrument, usually made of wood in the shape of an hourglass; with a neck; played by strumming or plucking; chordophone.

harmonica A wind instrument; a small flat metal instrument with reeds that is played by inhaling and exhaling into different reeds to change the pitch; aerophone.

harmony A combination of pitches sounded together.

harmony singing Many voices singing together on different pitches.

high pitch A high-sounding musical tone; higher frequency of vibration.

honky-tonk music A popular country-style music performed in bars and "honky-tonks" popular in the 1940s and 1950s. The music featured guitar, steel guitar, dobro, fiddle, and bass, with straightforward lyrics about heartbreaks and breakups, good times and bad times, finding love and losing it.

horn A wind instrument with a small opening at one end expanding to a wider opening at the other; may be made from animal horns, tusks, wood, or metal; aerophone.

humorous songs Songs with comical lyrics.

hybrid Of mixed origin; in music, it refers to a mixture of styles—as when country and rock influences combine to make country rock.

hymn A song in praise of God.

hymnal A collection of hymns.

idiophone A musical instrument made from a solid material that is struck or shaken or rubbed to produce sound.

improvise To create music, or make it up, while performing it.

instrumentalist One who plays an instrument.

jazz A style of music born in North America around 1900 in New Orleans; derived from a mixture of blues, ragtime, marching band music, and rural string band music; evolved into many varieties—including New Orleans jazz, Dixieland, swing, bebop, cool jazz, free jazz, and fusion.

jazz-rock Jazz-rock mixes jazz chord structures and arrangements with rock rhythms and instruments such as electric guitar, piano, bass, and drums.

jug A bottle used as a musical instrument to create sound by blowing across the top; aerophone.

jukebox A coin-operated record player or CD player most commonly found in public places.

jump blues A lively, up-tempo dance music punctuated with saxophones, trumpets, and rhythm instruments; popular in the 1930s and 1940s.

klezmer music Jewish dance music with origins in Eastern European traditions.

Latin popular music A form of popular music usually sung in Spanish, played with Latin rhythms. Popular Latin music wins music awards and sweeps mainstream radio, movies, and television.

lead guitar When the guitar is the featured instrument while the other instruments are the support, or backup. Lead guitarists play melody lines called *leads* or *solos*.

light classics Orchestral music that is familiar, popular, light in nature.

light opera A style of opera that is less "serious" than grand opera; fun, comic.

line singing When the singing is call-and-response style—one person or group leads by singing the first line of the song and another person or group follows by echoing.

low pitch A low-sounding musical tone; slower frequency of vibration.

lullaby Song sung to children; it's usually gentle and lulling.

lyrics The text, or words, of a song.

major scale A pattern of eight pitches that when used to make up a song or piece of music is said to create a happy or serene mood. (see *scale*).

mandolin A small, wooden, stringed instrument usually shaped like a pear with eight steel strings (tuned as four pairs); related to the European lute; chordophone.

mariachi music Mexican country music accompanied by violins, guitars, harp, trumpets, and bass guitar *(guitarrón)*.

medley A series of individual melodies or tunes strung together into one musical piece.

melody A sequence of musical tones, or pitches that create a meaningful whole; also called a *tune*.

melody instrument An instrument that plays melodies or tunes; examples are flutes, violins, pianos, horns, and mandolins.

membranophone A musical instrument such as a drum that creates sound through the vibrating of a stretched membrane over a frame or tube.

microphone A device that changes a regular sound wave into an electronic wave, allowing it to be amplified (made louder) or transported through wire (as with the telephone) or airwaves (as with the radio).

minor scale A pattern of eight pitches that when used to make up a song or piece of music is said to create a sad or somber mood (see *scale*).

minstrel shows An American performance style that mimicked the lifestyle, language, and dress of African-American slaves. Shows included songs, dances, jokes, and skits performed in a half-circle on a stage, with performers wearing blackface paint and playing banjo, fiddle, bones, and tambourine; most popular in the mid-1800s.

minstrel song An American style of song popular around the mid-1800s that was sung in the minstrel style, mimicking African-American lifestyle; accompanied with banjo, fiddle, bones, and tambourine.

Motown music A style of music created in the Detroit recording studio, Motown Records; incorporates elements of soul, funk, rhythm and blues.

mountain dulcimer See *dulcimer*.

mountain music Music that developed in the Appalachian Mountains (see *old-time music*).

music notation The written symbols of music.

music publisher A company that owns and manages the business of songs.

musical score The written notes of a musical composition for instruments and voices; the conductor reads the score and directs the performers to play or sing it.

national anthem The official song of a country.

New Orleans jazz An early style of jazz that emerged after the Civil War in and around New Orleans; lively and syncopated and played on brass instruments, banjo, guitar, piano, string bass, and drums.

note-bending When a singer or instrument "slurs" or "bends" the notes go up or down.

old-time music A style of American folk music that developed from European traditions; performed on guitar, dulcimer, banjo, piano, fiddle, and drum.

opera A musical story, or play, told through singing.

oral tradition Passing songs, stories, and legends by word of mouth, from person to person, generation to generation.

orchestra A group of musicians playing together. In the European classical tradition, the orchestra has string, wind, and percussion sections led by one conductor; in other traditions, an orchestra can be made up of any instruments.

orchestral music Music played by an orchestra.

overture The opening piece of a long work, such as the introduction to an opera.

parody A song, poem, or composition that imitates another song, poem, or composition in a humorous way.

patriotic music Music that expresses appreciation and love for a country.

patriotic song A song that expresses appreciation and love for a country.

percussion instruments Instruments that are beaten, shaken, or scraped to make a sound—including drums, gongs, sticks, shakers, xylophones, bells, rasps, cymbals, and triangles.

phonograph record A flat disc with grooves in which vibrations are recorded and converted into sound, played on a record player.

piano A keyboard instrument with white keys and black keys that, when pressed, make hammers strike strings to create sounds; idiophone and chordophone.

pioneer songs These described life on the frontier: Indian battles, the Gold Rush, working on the railroad, and stories of famous people or events.

pitch A musical tone.

pitched instruments Instruments that make high and low sounds (pitches), such as flutes, whistles, violins, harmonicas, and guitars.

player piano A piano that uses a mechanism to "read" the music from special holed paper, resulting in the depression of keys that play the song automatically.

political songs Songs that tell about political subjects—stories, people, or events.

polka A folk style of music and dance, played in a 2/4 meter, originally from Eastern Europe.

polyrhythm Two separate rhythms played at the same time.

polyrhythmic When a piece of music uses polyrhythm.

popular music Music that appeals to the masses, or mainstream.

popular songs Songs that appeal to the masses, or mainstream.

powwow A modern gathering of both native and non-native people to dance, sing, play drums, share native traditions, give gifts, and eat food. Contests are held for the best dances and costumes.

Psalms Songs or compositions that are based on text from the Christian Bible in the Book of Psalms.

Psalters A music book containing Psalms.

quartet A composition for four musicians; a group of four musicians.

radio broadcasting The act of converting sound to signals and sending them through the airwaves to a receiver, which changes the signals back into sounds.

ragtime An American dance music popular in the early 1900s; a lively, syncopated style of piano music.

rallying songs Songs that stir emotions—political rallying songs or sports rallying songs, for example.

rap Speaking in rhyme to the rhythm of the beat.

rap music In rap music the lyrics of songs are spoken instead of sung; often performed over recorded music.

rasps Instruments that are scraped to make a sound; idiophone.

rattles Instruments that make sound from objects beating against each other—like pebbles inside a container or shells strung together; idiophone.

recitative A style of singing that is like speech; tells a story.

record charts One of the ways the music industry observes the public's tastes in music (see *Billboard charts*). Record charts are divided into genres and reflect what is most enjoyed (and purchased) by the general public.

record company A business that records, sells, and promotes music.

refrain The part of a song that is repeated; the chorus.

Regular Singing A term from colonial times referring to the method of using written notation to sing and learn music, as opposed to the Usual Way, which is line singing or memorization.

repertoire A list of songs, musical works, roles, and so on, that a person or group knows and can perform.

resonate To increase the intensity of sound, to make louder.

resonator A device or container that serves to increase the intensity of sound.

rhymes Words that sound the same as another; they are used in the lyrics of a poem or song.

rhyming song A song that rhymes.

rhythm The meter, the beat, the part that moves forward in time in music.

rhythm accompaniment Rhythm instruments that accompany the music.

rhythm and blues Blues music that adds electric guitars, saxophones, drums, and electric bass with up-tempo rhythms. Rhythm and blues was the foundation for rock 'n' roll, and eventually, rap music.

rhythm instrument Instruments that play the rhythm rather than the melody, including drums, percussion, bass guitar, rhythm guitar, and so on.

rock 'n' roll A musical genre that grew from rhythm and blues in the early 1950s; created by African Americans but originally made popular by European-American performers.

roots music Music that originates from the experiences of ordinary people; includes folk songs, country songs, blues, gospel, Cajun, zydeco, Tejano, klezmer, old-time, bluegrass, and some Native American music.

sacred Of a spiritual nature.

Sacred Harp singing Singing in the Sacred Harp tradition involves reading shape notes and singing harmony; it was created by early European-American colonists.

sacred songs Songs that are spiritual in nature; like a prayer; can be requests for guidance, calls for help, expressions of worship, or ways to show thanks.

salsa A lively, rhythmical dance music that mixes the traditions of Spanish, Caribbean, and African cultures. *Salsa* means "sauce" in Spanish, and salsa music is a spicy dance music that became popular in New York in the 1960s.

sample A digital recording of a sound that is processed and assigned to a note on the keyboard.

sampler A computer microprocessor that records, or takes a sample of, a live sound that can be played back on a keyboard (see *digital sampler*).

scale Scales are patterns of notes (or pitches) that are used to make up a song or piece of music. A *major scale* is a pattern of eight notes often said to create a happy mood when it is used. A *minor scale* is a different pattern of eight notes often said to create a sad mood when it is played. A *chromatic scale* is another kind of pattern that uses twelve notes and creates an unusual mood because it is not used very often. When composers create a piece of music, they choose a scale (or key), then pick notes from that scale and put them together in different ways to make up the piece. It is like taking the letters of the alphabet and stringing them together in different ways to make up words and sentences.

scat singing Singing syllables (or vocables) as opposed to lyrics.

scratching In rap music this means stopping, starting, playing forwards and backwards, or otherwise manipulating a record on a turntable to create music or sounds.

sea chanteys Work chants and other songs sung by sailors at sea.

sections Divisions of the orchestra, usually percussion, strings, woodwinds, and brass.

secular songs Nonreligious songs.

sentimental songs These express sentiments, or feelings; they can describe love, beauty, emotions, and more.

shaker rattles Containers with small objects bouncing inside them, such as seeds inside a gourd, pebbles inside a leather container, and so on; idiophone.

shape-note singing A style of singing that developed in colonial times that uses written music in the form of shapes to distinguish different pitches. In the early days of shape-note singing, all singers sang in unison (together on the same pitches), but over time they developed harmony singing (singing on different pitches at the same time). Shape-note singing is the foundation for modern harmony singing.

sheet music Written or published music, both lyrics and notation, sold by music publishers.

signal songs Songs used by slaves that used code to tell of plans for escaping.

singers People who use their voices to make musical tones.

singing Using the voice to make musical tones.

slack key A style of Hawaiian guitar playing that involves finger-picking and loosened strings to create a soothing, soulful music that has come to represent Hawaiian music.

social songs Native American songs performed in public for dances, thanksgiving, memorials, and celebrations.

solo A piece of music performed by one singer or instrumentalist.

song A piece of vocal music that uses a combination of words (or vocables) with a melody.

soul music An American musical style derived from African-American blues and gospel.

spirituals Sacred songs that originated in the African-American slave culture.

state song The official song of a state.

steady beat The regular, consistent, steady ticking away of beats.

steel guitar A stringed instrument made of wood or metal and held on the lap. It is played by gliding a bar on top of the strings with one hand and plucking with the other; chordophone and sometimes electrophone.

string bow A wooden rod strung with gut used in playing a stringed instrument; shaped like a bow.

string quartet A composition for four stringed instruments; in classical music a string quartet includes two violins, a viola, and a cello.

strings Stringed instruments; also, long thin strands of sinew, steel, or nylon material used for plucking or bowing to make sound.

strumming The act of brushing something against strings in order to make a sound; guitar players strum with picks or their fingers; dulcimer players strum with feather quills.

swing music A style of jazz from the early 1930s that used syncopated music and large groups of musicians called *big bands*.

symphonic poem A long movement for orchestra that tells a story or describes a scene through the music rather than lyrics.

symphony A long composition written for an orchestra.

syncopated When the rhythm accents the upbeat (the second and fourth beats in 4/4 meter).

synthesized sound A sound created by electronic impulses.

synthesizer A device that creates sounds using electronic elements; electrophone.

Tejano-conjunto music Folk music that mixes influences from Spanish, Native American, and Czech traditions; popular in Northern Mexico and Texas.

tempo The speed of the music; it may be fast or slow.

throat singing A traditional singing style of the Inuit (Eskimo) of Canada, usually performed by two women standing close to each other, face-to-face, breathing in and out, and repeating low sounds in a fast, pulsing rhythm. It is often a game that ends when the first person laughs.

thumb piano An instrument made of wood with metal tongs that are plucked to make sounds. The tongs are different lengths and make different pitches when plucked; idiophone.

Tin Pan Alley This term has come to represent the popular music publishing industry that came to prominence around the turn of the century (1900); the name comes from a street in New York City where the publishers worked.

traditional Having the quality of being passed down; an established custom.

traditional songs Songs that are passed down through the generations.

traditions Customs or practices that are passed down through the generations.

turntable A device that spins records for playing; electrophone.

turntablism In rap music this is the art of spinning records to create a musical piece on its own.

twelve-bar blues A pattern of chord changes that is repeated every twelve measures (bars); the foundation of many blues songs.

ukulele A guitar-shaped instrument, much smaller than a guitar, with four strings and a higher pitch; chordophone.

unison When people sing or play the same notes together at the same time.

upbeat Lively, fast; also the "weak" beat—for example, in a 4/4 meter, the second and fourth are the upbeats.

Usual Way A term from colonial times that indicated learning music by singing it line by line, or by memorization, as opposed to reading and writing it.

vaudeville A type of variety show popular from the late 1800s to the 1930s. It featured stage acts ranging from singers to actors, dancers, comedians, magicians, puppeteers, acrobats, mimes, clowns, and so on.

verse The words of a song that tell the story and are generally not repeated. In ballads, the first verse begins telling the story, the second verse continues it, and so on until the last verse tells the conclusion.

vibrate To shake really fast.

virtuosic Having the quality of being performed by a virtuoso.

virtuoso A person with outstanding talent.

vocables Syllables that may not have apparent meaning; scat singing uses vocables.

volume In music, the volume is the loudness of sound; high volume is loud, low volume is soft.

washboard A wooden board with ridges that is used for scrubbing clothes; also used as a rhythm instrument that is scraped along the ridges; idiophone.

washtub bass An instrument made from a washtub, long pole, and string, configured to create a homemade standup bass for playing in jug bands; chordophone.

water drum A drum that uses a container filled with water to enhance the sound; membranophone and idiophone.

whistle An instrument without holes that is blown to make sound; aerophone.

wind bands Musical groups whose players consist of wind instrument players.

wind instruments Instruments that are blown to make sound.

woodwinds Instruments that are blown through a mouth hole or reed; they include the piccolo, flute, clarinet, oboe, and bassoon.

work songs In this book, work songs refer to the songs sung in the fields by slaves, but the term may refer to any song sung while working.

xylophone An instrument made of a series of wood or metal bars of different lengths that are beaten with mallets to make sounds; idiophone.

yodel A singing style that involves abrupt changes between falsetto and chest singing.

zydeco music A style of music that evolved in Louisiana from French and African (Creole) traditions; uses syncopated rhythms and upbeat tempos.

Bibliography

Ammer, Christine. *Harper's Dictionary of Music.* New York: HarperCollins, 1972.

Bierhorst, John. *A Cry from the Earth: Music of the North American Indians.* Santa Fe, NM: Ancient City Press, 1979.

Blood, Peter, and Patterson, Annie. *Rise Up Singing.* Bethlehem, PA: A Sing Out Publication, 1992. (Originally published 1988)

Courlander, Harold. *Negro Folk Music, U.S.A.* New York: Dover, 1991. (Originally published 1963)

Curtis, Natalie. *The Indians' Book.* New York: Dover, 1907.

Garbarino, Merwyn S., and Sasso, Robert F. *Native American Heritage.* Prospect Heights, IL: Waveland Press, 1994.

Giglio, Virginia. *Southern Cheyenne Women's Songs.* Norman: University of Oklahoma Press, 1994.

Hamm, Charles. *Music in the New World.* New York: W. W. Norton, 1983.

Herder, Ron. *500 Best-Loved Song Lyrics.* New York: Dover, 1998.

Howard, John Tasker, and Bellows, George Kent. *A Short History of Music in America.* New York: Crowell, 1957.

Leach, MacEdward. *The Ballad Book.* New York: A. S. Barnes, 1955.

McCullough-Brabson, and Help, Marilyn. *We'll Be in Your Mountains, We'll Be in Your Songs.* Albuquerque: University of New Mexico Press, 2001.

Sackheim, Eric. *The Blues Line.* New York: Schirmer Books, 1975. (Originally published 1969)

Scott, John Anthony. *The Ballad of America.* Carbondale: Southern Illinois University Press, 1983. (Originally published 1966)

The author also wishes to acknowledge the liner notes of CDs mentioned in the musician biographies of the student handouts.

CD Song List

Native American Music

♫ **Track #1 (p. 24)** "Gayowajeenayho—Welcome Song," sung by Michele Stock. Recorded by Milt Lee. ℗ 2000 Oyate Productions. Used by permission.

♫ **Track #2 (pp. 24, 36, 56)** "I Had No Ears," sung by Wilmer Mesteth. Recorded by Milt Lee. ℗ 2000 Oyate Productions. Used by permission.

♫ **Track #3 (pp. 25, 36, 57)** "Dance Song of the Night Chant" (Navajo) by Sandoval Begay from the recording entitled *A Cry from the Earth: Music of the North American Indians,* Folkways 37777, provided courtesy of Smithsonian Folkways Recordings. © 1979. Used by permission.

♫ **Track #4 (pp. 25, 63)** "Haagú S'é," from Charles Joseph, Kaal.átk'. Recorded and sung by Roby Littlefield at Dog Fish Camp on the *Tlingit Dléigoox' (Tlingit Lullabies)* CD. ℗ 1998 Roby Littlefield. Used by permission.

♫ **Track #5 (pp. 25, 36, 66)** "The Spider Song," sung by John Pingayak. Recorded by Milt Lee. ℗ 2000 Oyate Productions. Used by permission.

♫ **Track #6 (pp. 25, 36, 67)** "E Komo," sung by Charles Ka'upu. Recorded by Milt Lee. ℗ 2000 Oyate Productions. Used by permission.

♫ **Track #7 (pp. 40, 82)** "She Watches Them Play," written and performed by Mary Youngblood. From *The Offering* CD on Silver Wave Records. ℗ 1998. Courtesy of Mary Youngblood. Used by permission.

European-American Music

♫ **Track #8 (p. 95)** "Amsterdam No. 84," by Robert Seagraves. Copyright © 1991 Sacred Harp Publishing Company. Used by permission. *Recording:* "Amsterdam No. 84," by Robert Seagraves. From 2000 Minnesota Sacred Harp Convention, recorded by Tom Mitchell. ℗ 2000 Tom Mitchell (*www.LoudHymns.com*). Used by permission.

♫ **Track #9 (p. 95)** "The Old Man Who Lived in the Woods." From *The Ballad of America.* Copyright © 1966 by John Anthony Scott. Melody taken from a version by New England folklorist Bill Bonyun. Used by permission. *Recording:* "The Old Man Who Lived in the Woods," performed by Teri Tibbett. ℗ 2001 Migration Music. Used by permission.

♫ **Track #10 (p. 111)** "Haul on the Bowline," performed by Steve Nelson, Greg Pease, and Robert Cohen. ℗ 1988 Migration Music. Used by permission.

♫ **Track #11** (p. 111) "Fendez le Bois," performed by Lynn Noel. ℗ 2000 Lynn Noel. Used by permission.

♫ **Track #12** (p. 111, 335) "Old Joe Clarke," performed by Teri Tibbett. ℗ 2001 Migration Music. Used by permission.

♫ **Track #13** (p. 111) "Jolie Blonde du Bayou," Performed by Dewey Balfa, Marc Savoy, and D.L. Menard. From *Under a Green Oak Tree*. ℗ 1976 Arhoolie Productions. *www.arhoolie.com*. Used by permission.

♫ **Track #14** (p. 111) "Wedding Dance," performed by Robert Cohen. Copyright © 1994 Robert Cohen. *Recording:* ℗ 1994 Zuvuya One Music, Migration Music.

♫ **Track #15** (p. 123) "America, the Beautiful" performed by Teri Tibbett, Alex Nelson, Haley Nelson. ℗ 2001 Migration Music. Used by permission.

♫ **Track #16** (p. 123) "This Land Is Your Land," composed by Woody Guthrie, © TRO Richmond Organization, New York. *Recording:* "This Land Is Your Land" by Woody Guthrie from the recording entitled *Folkways: The Original Version*, SF 40001, provided courtesy of Smithsonian Folkways Recordings. © 1989. Used by permission.

♫ **Track #17** (p. 138) "Goober Peas," performed by Teri Tibbett and Ford James. ℗ 2001 Migration Music. Used by permission.

♫ **Track #18** (p. 138) "Grandfather's Clock," by Henry Clay Work. Performed by Doc Watson on *My Dear Old Southern Home*. ℗ 1991. Courtesy of Sugar Hill Records. Used by permission.

♫ **Track #19** (pp. 150, 160) "Escensas Campetres," composed by Louis Moreau Gottschalk (public domain). *Recording:* From *A Gottschalk Festival* CD. ℗ 1992 Vox Music Group. Used by permission.

African-American Music

♫ **Track #20** (pp. 178, 335) "Hambone," performed by Taj Mahal. From *Shake It to the One You Love the Best*. ℗ 1986 Warren-Mattox Productions.

♫ **Track #21** (p. 193) "He's Got the Whole World in His Hands," performed by Mahalia Jackson, from the recording entitled *I Sing Because I'm Happy*, SF 90002, provided courtesy of Smithsonian Folkways Recordings, © 1992. Used by permission. *Song:* Public Domain.

♫ **Track #22** (p. 208) "Good Mornin' Blues." *Song:* New words and new music arranged by Huddie Leadbetter. Edited and new additional material by Alan Lomax. TRO copyright © 1959 (renewed) Folkways Music Publishers, New York. *Recording:* "Good Mornin' Blues #2" by Lead Belly from the recording entitled *Bourgeois Blues: Lead Belly Legacy*, Vol. 2, SF 40045, provided courtesy of Smithsonian Folkways Recordings. © 1997. Used by permission.

♫ **Track #23** (p. 226) "Maple Leaf Rag," by Scott Joplin. From *Joplin Piano Rags*. Courtesy of The Scott Joplin Foundation. Used by permission.

♪ **Track #24** (pp. 226, 310) **"When the Saints Go Marching In,"** performed by Louis Armstrong. From *Original Jazz Masters Series, Vol. 1.* Courtesy of 1201 Music. ℗ 1201 Music. Used by permission.

♪ **Track #25** (p. 226) **"Boogie-Woogie,"** written and performed by Robert Cohen. ℗ 2001 Zuvuya One Music, Migration Music. Used by permission.

New American Music

♪ **Track #26** (p. 283) **"Old Folks Quintet,"** arranged by Robert Cohen. ℗ 2001 Zuvuya One Music, Migration Music. Used by permission.

♪ **Track #27** (p. 310) **"La Cucaracha,"** arranged by Robert Cohen. ℗ Zuvuya One Music, Migration Music. Used by permission.

♪ **Track #28** (p. 310) **"Take Five,"** by Paul Desmond. © and ℗ 1966, 1988 Desmond Music Company (U.S.) and Derry Music Company (worldwide outside U.S.). Used with permission of the copyright owners.

♪ **Track #29** (p. 335) **"Turkey in the Straw,"** performed by Bob Banghart (fiddle) and Robert Cohen (piano). ℗ 1994 Zuvuya One Music, Migration Music.

♪ **Track #30** (p. 335) **"Whoopie Ti-Yi-Yo, Git Along Little Dogies"** collected, adapted, and arranged by John A. Lomax and Alan Lomax. TRO © 1938 (renewed) Ludlow Music, New York. *Recording:* "Whoopie Ti-Yi-Yo," by Cisco Houston from the recording entitled *Smithsonian Folkways Children's Collection,* SF 45043, provided courtesy of Smithsonian Folkways Recordings. © 1998. Used by permission.

♪ **Track #31** (p. 335) **"Rocky Top,"** composed by Boudleaux and Felice Bryant. Copyright © 1967 House of Bryant Publishers. *Recording:* "Rocky Top" performed by David Sause, Teri Tibbett, Christina Seaborn, Andy Ferguson, and Joe Karson. ℗ 1988 Migration Music. Used by permission.

♪ **Track #32** (p. 353) **"Amor Bonito,"** by Lydia Mendoza. Copyright © 1984 San Antonio Music Publishers. *Recording:* From the CD entitled *Lydia Mendoza: First Queen of Tejano Music.* ℗ 1996 Arhoolie Productions, *www.arhoolie.com.* Used by permission.

♪ **Track #33** (p. 353) **"Allá en el Rancho Grande,"** performed by Adelita Reyes, Angel "El Cuervo," and Valente Pastor. ℗ Produciones Mexicanas Discograficas. Used by permission.

♪ **Track #34** (pp. 82, 310) **"Witchi-Tai-To."** *Song:* © 1968 Floy Pepper. *Recording:* "Witchi-Tai-To," performed by Jim Pepper. ℗ Tutu Records. Used by permission.

♪ **Track #35** (p. 82, 379) **"Vision Quest"** written and performed by Litefoot. Copyright © and ℗ 1998 Red Vinyl Records.

Index

Broadway musicals, 249–250
Brooks, Garth, 334
Brown, Greg, 366
Brown, James, 235–236
Brubeck, Dave, 307–308
Bruce, Ed, 332
"Brush Dance Light Song" (Hupa), 23
Buddy Holly and the Crickets, 362
Buffalo Bill's Wild West Show, 250
Buffalo songs/buffalo dances, 55
Burke, Johnny, 252
Burleigh, Harry Thacker, 278
"Bury My Heart at Wounded Knee," 78
Byrds, The, 364

C

Cage, John, 273–274
Cajun music, 108–109; accordion, 108;
    "Jolie Blonde du Bayou," 109
Call-and-response singing, 6, 173, 384; activity:
    Native American music regions, 51; gospel
    music, 189; soul music, 233; spirituals,
    188; traditional Native American singing,
    23–24
Calloway, Cab, 300
Camai Festival (Alaska), 77
Campanas de América, 348–349
"Camptown Races" (Stephen Foster), 133
Canterbury Pilgrims, The (Reginald de Koven),
    284
Cantor, Eddie, 137–138
Cárdenas, Lázaro, 347
Carson, Fiddlin' John, 323
Carter Family, 323
Cartoons: musical accompaniment, 272
Caruso, Enrico, 284
Carved wood rattle, 35
"Casey Jones," 318
Cash, Johnny, 332
Castenets, 176–177
CBS, 252
CDs, 4, 255
"Centennial Hymn" (John Knowles Paine), 147
Ceremonials, 18, 53
Chadwick, George Whitefield, 147
Chamber music, 145
Changes for Piano (John Cage), 273
Chants, 24
Charles, Ray, 233

Charting the Charts activity, 7, 245, 256,
    261–262
Chávez, Carlos, 282
Chicago, 367
Chicago blues, 222–226; King, B. B., 223–224;
    Taylor, Koko, 225; Waters, Muddy,
    222–223
"Chickasaw Train Blues" (Memphis Minnie),
    201
Chief Joseph, 73
Child, Francis James, 93–94
"Chisholm Trail, The," 319
Chordophones, 40, 157, 169, 396
Chorus, 23, 132, 148, 286–287
Chromatic scales, 267
City blues, 205–208; Smith, Bessie, 208; "St.
    Louis Blues" (W. C. Handy), 206–207
Civil War songs, 133–135; "Bereaved Slave
    Mother, The" (Judd Hutchinson), 133–134;
    "Goober Peas" (A. Pindar & P. Nutt),
    134–135; Howe, Julia Ward, 134
Clapper rattles, 34
Clara Ward Singers, 191
Clarinet, 158
Clarinet Candy (Leroy Anderson, 271
Clarke, Stanley, 310
Clash, The, 367
Classical music, 141. See also Early classical
    music; contemporary, 263–294; defined,
    143; early, 141–152
Claves, 351
Cleopatra's Night (Henry Kimball Hadley),
    284
Cline, Patsy, 330, 331
Cockburn, Bruce, 366
Coe, Nat "King," 302
Cohan, George M., 137, 249–250
Coleman, Ornette, 309
Colonial music, 87–97; activities, 88; Colonial
    Music Quiz, 88, 96–97; Colonial Music:
    Sacred and Secular handout, 88; discus-
    sions, 88; extension activities, 88–89; lesson
    preparation, 87; lesson purpose, 87; mate-
    rials, 87–88; Regular Singing Versus Usual
    Way Singing, 88; sacred songs, 90–91;
    secular songs, 93–95; shape-note singing,
    91–92; vocabulary, 87; Vocabulary
    Challenge, 88
Colonial Music Quiz, 88, 96–97; answer key,
    97

Early popular music, 126–140; activities, 127; ballads, 130; Civil War songs, 133–135; comic operas, 130; discussions, 127; "Dixie Land" (Daniel Emmett), 130–132; Early Popular Music handout, 126–127; Early Popular Music Quiz, 127, 139–140; Emmett, Daniel Decatur, 130–131; extension activities, 127–128; Foster, Stephen, 132–133; "Grandfather's Clock" (Henry Clay Work), 135–136; lesson preparation, 126; lesson purpose, 126; materials, 126; minstrel songs, 130–132; Music Vocabulary activity sheet, 127; "Oh Susanna" (Stephen Foster), 132; patriotic songs, 130; turn of the century, 135–136; vaudeville, 128, 137–138; vocabulary, 126, 129; Vocabulary Challenge, 127; Work, Henry Clay, 135–136

Early Popular Music Quiz, 139–140; answer key, 140

Early radio, 251–253

Earth, Wind, and Fire, 236

East Coast "Old School" rap, 376–378

Easy Instructor (Smith/Little), 91

"Easy Rider Blues" (Blind Lemon Jefferson), 201

"Eat It" (Weird Al Yankovich), 246, 258

Edison, Thomas, 253–254

Edwin Hawkins Singers, 191

Einstein on the Beach (Philip Glass), 290

El Gran Combo, 351

El Niño (John Adams), 290

Electric guitar, 329, 364–365

Electronic orchestral music, 274–276

Electrophones, 223, 274

Ellington, Duke, 220, 252, 300–301

Emmett, Daniel Decatur, 130–131, 317

Emulator sampler, 237

Encyclopedia of Musical Instruments, 6, 385; traditional Native American instruments, 30

Enemyway ceremonials, 57

English and Scottish Popular Ballads, The, 93

Ensembles for Synthesizer (Milton Babbitt), 274

"Entertainer, The" (Scott Joplin), 218

Estefan, Gloria, 351–352

Ethnomusicologists, 53, 104

Ethnomusicology, 52, 104

European-American music, 85–164; colonial music, 87–97; early American composers/ musicians, 86; folk music, 86, 98–115;

minstrel music, 86; mountain music, 86; overview, 86; patriotic music, 116–125; popular music, 86; *Psalters*, 86; stage music, 86

Evans, Dale, 325

Explorer songs, 103–104

F

Families of Instruments, 6, 385–387; music of the slaves, 170; orchestral instruments, 155; traditional Native American instruments, 30

Fania Records, 351

Fantasia/Fantasia 2000: musical accompaniment, 272

Farmer, Art, 307

Farris, Dionne, 379

Farwell, Arthur, 148

Feast of the Animals' Souls ceremony, 64

Federal Music Project, 269

Feliciano, Jose, 351

"Feliz Navidad," 351

"Fendez le Bois—Chop Some More Wood," 103–104

Fiddles, 40, 203–204, 323, 328, 329

Field calls, 172

Field holler, 189

Fields, Dorothy, 248

Film scores, 272–273

Finger-picking, 203

Fisk Jubilee Singers, 189

Fitzgerald, Ella, 306

Flatt, Lester, 328

Flute Dance ceremony, 38

Flutes, 37–38, 158, 172

Foggy Mountain Boys, 328

Folk Instruments Picture Page, 99, 114, 385; answer key, 115

Folk music, 98–115; activities, 99; Bonus Challenge: Compose a Folk Song, 99, 111; brief history of, 101; cajun music, 108–109; discussions, 99; explorer songs, 103–104; extension activities, 99; "Fendez le Bois— Chop Some More Wood," 103–104; Folk Instruments Picture Page, 99, 114–115; Folk Music handout, 99; Folk Music Quiz, 99, 112–113; "Haul on the Bowline," 102–103; klezmer music, 110–111; lesson preparation, 98; lesson purpose, 98; materials, 98–99; mountain music, 98, 104–107; oral tradition, 102; sea chanteys, 102–103;

Talking Heads, 367

Talking machines, 254

Tanana potlatch, 65

Tarras, Dave, 110

Taylor, Cecil, 309

Taylor, Koko, 225

Taylor, Samuel Coleridge, 278

Teaching a song, steps in, 392

Tejano, 3

Tejano-conjunto, 342–346

Tempo, 144, 173, 191

Temptations, The, 233, 363

Tender Land, The (Aaron Copland), 268

Theremin (synthesizer), 274

They Lynched Him on a Tree (William Grant Still), 278–279

Thomas, Theodore, 146

Thomas, Todd, 379

Thompson, Hank, 330

Thompson, Uncle Jimmy, 324

Thornton, Big Mama, 225

Throat singing, 66

Thumb piano, 176–177

Timbales, 351

Tin Pan Alley, 247–249, 302, 325

Top 40 *Billboard* Chart, 245, 256

Tower, Joan, 276–277

Trace an Ancestor activity, 5, 391, 404–405; Native American music regions, 51

Tracker bar, 218

Traditional Native American instruments, 28–48; activities, 29–30; Bonus Challenge: Which Family of Instruments Does a Box Drum Belong In?, 30; discussions, 29; extension activities, 30; lesson preparation, 28; lesson purpose, 28; materials, 28–29; Music Vocabulary activity sheet, 29; pitched instruments, 37–40; rhythm instruments, 31–36; Science of Music sections, 30, 32, 34, 39, 40; Traditional Native American Instruments handout, 29; Traditional Native American Instruments Quiz, 29, 41–42; Traditional Pitched Instruments Picture Page, 29, 47–48; Traditional Pitched Instruments Quiz, 45–46; Traditional Rhythm Instruments Picture Page, 29, 43–44; vocabulary, 28; Vocabulary Challenge, 29

Traditional Native American Instruments Quiz, 29, 41–42; answer key, 42

Traditional Native American singing, 12–27; "Aa Narvaga—Song of the Loon and the Muskrat" (Jennie Jackson), 19–20; activities, 13–14; brief history of, 15–16; call-and-response style of singing, 23–24; chants, 24; "Coyote Warrior Song," 18–19; extension activities, 14; "Gayowa-jeenayho—Welcome Song," 16; "Gomda Daagya—Wind Song," 19; "Haagú S'é—A Boy's Lullaby," 20; heroes and heroines, 16–17; lesson preparation, 12; lesson purpose, 12; lullabies, 20–21; lyrics and vocables, 24; materials, 12; nature and animal songs, 19–20; oral tradition, 13–14; sacred songs, 16; singing styles, 23–24; "Song for a Woman Who Was Brave in War," 17; Talking Circle activity, 13; Traditional Native American Singing handout, 13; Traditional Native American Singing Quiz, 13, 26–27; vocabulary, 12, 15; Vocabulary Challenge, 13; warrior songs, 18–19; women's songs, 22–23

Traditional Native American Singing Quiz, 13, 26–27; answer key, 27

Traditional Pitched Instruments Picture Page, 47–48; answer key, 48

Traditional Pitched Instruments Quiz, 45–46; answer key, 46

Traditional Rhythm Instruments Picture Page, 43–44; answer key, 44

Traditions, 53

Tragedy of the Opera (P. Q. Phan), 281

Tree on the Planes, The (Ernst Bacon), 287

Triangle, 159

Trios, 144, 148

Trombone, 158

Tropical Overture (Dai-Keong Lee), 279

Trudell, John, 80

Trumpet, 158

Tsimbl, 110

Tuba, 158

Tubb, Ernest, 330

Tucker, Sophie, 137

"Turkey in the Straw" (Daniel Emmett), 131, 317

Turntables, 375

Turntablism, 376

Turtle shell rattle, 34–35

Twain, Shania, 331

2 Live Crew, 378

Other Books of Interest

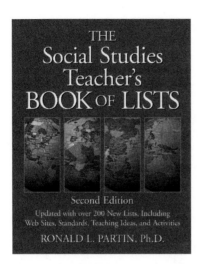

The Social Studies Teacher's Book of Lists, Second Edition

Robert L. Partin

Paperback / 448 pages / 2003
ISBN: 0-7879-6590-1

Enhance your social studies courses with this fun, practical, and intellectually stimulating social studies collection for students in grades 4–12. This unique information source and time-saver for social studies teachers provides more than 550 useful lists for developing instructional materials and lesson planning. In this updated and expanded edition you'll find 200 new lists!

The contents offer a broad range of interesting and challenging information organized for use in teaching United States history, world history, American government, sociology, consumer economics, psychology, and geography. The second edition has been updated to include Web sites, new standards, and a wide range of teaching ideas and additional activities. From alcohol and driving statistics to sites of modern Olympic games, from immigration trends to state Web sites for social studies standards, you'll find a wealth of illuminating facts, startling statistics, practical checklists, and relevant research findings. A special thematic index sorts these activities according to ten standards set by The National Council for Social Studies.

For quick access and easy use, all of the lists are printed in a format that folds flat for photocopying as often as needed for individual or group instruction.

Ronald L. Partin, Ph.D., is a professor emeritus from the College of Education at Bowling Green State University. He lives, writes, and consults in the mountains of Western North Carolina.

Other Books of Interest

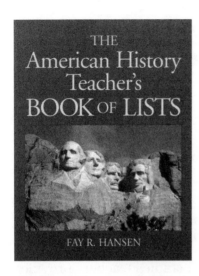

American History Teacher's Book of Lists

Fay R. Hansen

Paperback / 528 pages / 2002
ISBN: 0-13-092572-1

This practical information source is packed with over 325 reproducible lists to help U.S. history and social studies teachers develop instructional material and lesson plans for students in grades 5–12. For quick access and easy use, the lists are organized into six parts, grouped by topic and sequenced chronologically within each section, and printed in a big lay-flat format that can be photocopied as often as needed for individual or group instruction.

Here are the six parts, with an example from each, illustrating the interesting and challenging information you'll find to enrich and enhance your American history and social studies classes: I. Beginnings ("Chronology of the 1600s and 1700s"), II. Political History ("Important Supreme Court Cases"), III. Diplomacy and Military History ("American Nobel Peace Prize Winners"), IV. Economic History ("Women in the Work Force"), V. Social History ("Major Events in the Civil Rights Movement"), and VI. Intellectual and Cultural History ("Best Sellers in the 1960s").

In short, *American History Teacher's Book of Lists* provides an unparalleled source of good ideas, teachable content, teaching ideas and activities that might otherwise take many years and much effort to collect.

Fay R. Hansen (B.A., political science; American history, Florida State University; M.A., European history, Cornell University) is a former teacher and currently a writer and editor of books, articles, and research reports on political and economic trends as well as research analysis for state legislative reforms. Her most recent resource, *Ready-to-Use Citizenship Activities for Grades 5–12*, was published by The Center for Applied Research in Education in 1998.